REVOLUTION

PETER ACKROYD is an award-winning novelist, as well as a broadcaster, biographer, poet and historian. He is the author of the acclaimed non-fiction bestsellers *Thames: Sacred River* and *London: The Biography*. He holds a CBE for services to literature and lives in London.

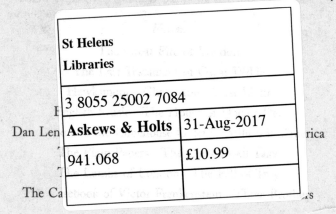

Peter Ackroyd

THE HISTORY OF ENGLAND

Volume IV

REVOLUTION

PAN BOOKS

First published 2016 by Macmillan

First published in paperback 2017 by Pan Books
an imprint of Pan Macmillan
20 New Wharf Road, London N1 9RR
Associated companies throughout the world
www.panmacmillan.com

ISBN 978-1-5098-1147-2

1 3 5 7 9 8 6 4 2

A CIP catalogue record for this book is available from the British Library.

Typeset in Adobe Caslon by Palimpsest Book Production Ltd, Falkirk, Stirlingshire
Printed and bound by CPI Group (UK) Ltd, Croydon, CR0 4YY

Visit **www.panmacmillan.com** to read more about all our books
and to buy them. You will also find features, author interviews and
news of any author events, and you can sign up for e-newsletters
so that you're always first to hear about our new releases.

Contents

List of illustrations

1

What do you think of predestination now?

The king had fled, in the face of an invading army. Even though James II had reached the safety of France and William, prince of Orange, was ensconced in Whitehall, it was not at all clear who was the true sovereign of Britain. So a 'Convention', half way between an assembly of notables and a parliament, was called at the beginning of 1689.* Since no recognized king was readily available to call an election it was a somewhat hasty and improvised affair; but it was not without the most important consequences. It marked a revolution in the affairs of state.

The Convention met towards the end of January 1689 to consider the respective positions of James and William; there was at once a conference on the meanings of a throne 'deserted' or 'vacant', a learned debate but one driven by the need to exclude for ever the absent king. The Commons finally declared that James II had

---

* A new and an old style of dating, the Gregorian and the Julian, were in use independently on the continent and in England, with a difference of ten days in their computations. The Julian style in England was not superseded until 1751, and I have therefore used it up to this date. In the seventeenth century the new year was celebrated on 25 March but I have followed the more familiar precedent of 1 January.

'abdicated', but there was no such term in law so this was essentially
a legislative fiction. Yet there was no plausible alternative to the
usurper's rule. As an authoritarian Catholic, James had been the
worst possible monarch for a strongly Protestant nation. The fact
that a group of notables had asked William of Orange to intervene
in an increasingly fraught situation had granted a measure of legit-
imacy to the prince's easy conquest. Yet he could not be seen as a
king by conquest; that would bring back horrid memories of William I, whom good republicans loved to hate. So he had somehow
to be proclaimed as king by right, a conveniently loose description
that might cover almost any set of circumstances.

By the beginning of February a 'declaration of rights' had been
composed by the members of the Convention. One of its clauses
forbade the establishment of a standing army in times of peace,
regarded as one of the most obvious tokens of arbitrary royal power.
Other clauses tended in the same direction. Laws could not be executed
or suspended without the consent of parliament; taxes could not be
raised for the benefit of the Crown without parliamentary agreement;
freedom of speech in parliament was paramount and, in the final
clause of the declaration, 'parliaments ought to be held frequently'.

The Declaration, later the Bill, of Rights was formally recited
to William and to his consort, Mary, daughter of the deposed king;
they sat in state in the Banqueting House and, after William had
affirmed that 'we thankfully accept what you have offered us', they
were proclaimed to be conjoint sovereigns. It was a delicate juggle.
It could only be assumed that William had understood and accepted
the Declaration as a prelude to his crowning, as William III, but
he had not been pressed to any formal oath of assent. Many now
believed, however, that he had been granted sovereignty by way of
parliament. The divine right of kings had come to an end. Daniel
Defoe declared later that parliament had 'an Unbounded Unlimited
Reach, a kind of Infinite attends their Power'.

William's reticence on the substance of the declaration did not
necessarily imply consent. He was by no means enamoured of its
principles; it was a very English production, being almost entirely
non-theoretical, but he knew well enough that it circumscribed his
power. He said that he had no wish to confirm some of its clauses
but that 'the condition of his affairs overruled his inclinations'; later

he complained that 'the worst of all governments was that of a king without treasure and without power'. On the day after the marquis of Halifax tendered the crown to him in the Banqueting House he told the marquis that 'he fancied, he was like a king in a play'. But he had to maintain his part at all costs.

A combination of gentry and aristocracy had in effect formulated a settlement that eliminated the threat of royal absolutism and protected property from arbitrary seizure. They were not interested in the idea of remedial legislation by parliament for the sake of social good or some benign notion of order. They wanted the rewards for themselves only. So was crafted what became known as the 'glorious revolution' promoted in theory by divine providence but supervised in effect by an organized elite, an aristocracy and oligarchy bolstered by the support of the landed gentry; the members of this elite would retain their power for the next 200 years.

The new order was bitterly opposed by those who believed that former oaths of loyalty to the deposed king could not and should not be broken; if the most solemn pact could be overturned, where could proper order and authority be found? The objectors, who refused to swear a new oath of allegiance to William and Mary, became known as 'non-jurors'. Some of the most senior clerics in the country were of their number, among them William Sancroft, archbishop of Canterbury. Eight bishops, and 400 clergy, adopted his stance. At the coronation of William and his consort in Westminster Abbey on 11 April, the archbishop was absent; the bishop of London raised the crown. Sancroft himself was forced into retirement in the following year.

The non-jurors were the measure of a divided kingdom; many of them became Jacobites, or supporters of the exiled James, in spirit if not in practice. It cannot be doubted that loyalty to William was distinctly muted in many parts of the country, and that he was conceived by some to be a foreign king imposed in the first place by force. Yet what could be done? The crown was on his head. Indifference, or resignation, was the inevitable response.

The Convention was converted into a parliament by the new king, with the simple expedient of delivering a speech from the throne to both houses. In his coronation oath he had consented to govern according to 'the statutes in parliament agreed on, and the laws and customs of the same'; it was a sign of the new balance in the constitution. Yet the relationship between Crown and parliament was not necessarily happy; in a further indication of their new power the members refused to grant William a revenue for life, and failed fully to fund his approaching campaign against France. They had learnt the unhappy lesson of the former king who had been able to support himself without their aid. William was as a result wholly reliant upon frequent parliaments to service his debts. Parliament now met every year, with sessions lasting for several months; general elections were held, on average, every two years. This quickened activity of course raised the temperature of the political atmosphere, encouraging what came to be known as 'the rage of party'.

This was not to the liking of the new king who detested fractious politicians. He did not speak good English, and was in any case reserved in nature to the point of being sullen or morose. He always longed to be back in his native land, away from the hypocrisy and importunity of the English court. He hated pomp. His manner and appearance did not necessarily recommend themselves to his new subjects. He spoke slowly and briefly. He was by nature calculating, cool and methodical. Though he was of slight frame he managed to carry himself with authority; he was an asthmatic, however, and his conversation was interrupted by a continual deep cough. He soon removed himself from the fog and damp air of Westminster to the relatively healthy ambience of Kensington. He was generally severe, or even solemn, and was rarely cheerful; only with his inner circle of Dutch advisers did he relax.

It was rumoured at the time that members of his court were homosexual and that, in particular, two of William's 'favourites', the first earl of Portland and the earl of Albemarle, had been granted half a million acres of land. The wife of Philippe, duke of Orléans and the French king's younger brother, Princess Palatine Elisabeth Charlotte, asked if the court of William had become a 'château de derrière'. Her husband, known as 'Monsieur', was a notorious homosexual; so she may have acquired her information at first hand. A verse was circulated that included the lines:

> Let's pray for the good of our State and his soul
> That he's put his Roger in the right Hole.

Gilbert Burnet, bishop of Salisbury and a firm supporter of the new dispensation, remarked somewhat mysteriously that the king 'had no vice, but of one sort, in which he was very cautious and secret'. This might have been alcohol, but it is unlikely. It is also true that intimations of homosexuality can be found in any male-dominated militaristic court, like that of William III. As in most stories of royal homosexuality, however, there is no actual evidence to support the claim.

William was, in any case, a sincere Calvinist who upheld the strictest possible interpretation of preordination. That is why he possessed a sense of destiny. He had said to Burnet, after he had landed at Torbay ready to confront James II, 'Well, doctor, what do you think of predestination now?' He believed himself to be fated, in particular, to lead a war against the Catholic French king. It was the great cause of his life. His faith may also have provided the context for his bravery and fearlessness in battle. Certainly it influenced his explicit toleration for those dissenters outside the Anglican fold.

One of the first measures of the new parliament was a bill to introduce and to encourage religious moderation. The Toleration Act granted freedom of public worship, and legal protection, to dissenters. Over the next twenty years more than 2,500 chapels or conventicles were licensed for worship. It seemed just and right that William should indulge the inclinations of those believers who were, after all, fellow Protestants if not fellow Calvinists. This is the setting for the Methodist revival of the 1740s, but many in the larger body of Anglicans believed that the rights of the national faith were being overlooked; certainly, by the mid-eighteenth century, the orthodox Church was beset by apathy or indifference in the face of more enthusiastic creeds.

William had declared war on France in the spring of 1689. The principal reasons for the invasion of the previous year had been his intention and desire to recruit the wealth and resources of England in his long campaign against French domination of Europe and, in particular, against French threats to the independence of the Dutch republic of which he was 'stadtholder' or head of state. This had been his guiding purpose for the last sixteen years. In 1672, in the face of French invasion, he had stated that he would die defending his country 'in the last ditch'; in turn Louis XIV had described William as 'my mortal enemy'. The French king wished to create a grandiose Bourbon empire, with himself at its head. He wanted to rule from Versailles. The sun king, or *le Roi-Soleil*, might rise all over Europe. If he conquered Holland, too, he would have defeated the strongest Protestant power on the continent. English ambitions were more simple. They agreed to William's war in order to preserve themselves from the return of James II under French auspices; they did not wish to become, as it was said, 'papists or slaves'. It was hoped that the war would be a brief one.

That hope was not fulfilled. William in effect now guided what became known as the 'Nine Years War' against the traditional foe; he became his own foreign minister and put together a coalition of other powers, including Spain and the Holy Roman Empire, for the attack. That 'empire' was in large part a loose confederation of independent princes who ruled the states of central Europe and who also feared French domination. Yet William's war was only the prelude to a much larger and longer conflict. The war of England against France lasted for fifty-eight years and the long hostility only found its quietus at Waterloo in 1815. This prolonged culture of war changed the social, fiscal and political aspects of English life. Larger and larger armies were brought into operation. Taxes increased exponentially. This will be one of the stories of the volume.

William had already become disenchanted with his English parliament. In the spring and summer of 1689 he complained variously that 'the Commons used him like a dog' and that 'he could not bear them'. The lines between the two largest parties, Whigs and Tories, had been carved in stone during the reign of James II. The Whigs were the enemies of popery and arbitrary government, and thus had attempted to limit royal power; the Tories had determined to defend the monarchy against the onslaught of those whom they considered to be republicans or rebels. Yet with the advent of William III, all had changed.

Of the 'immortal seven' who had invited William to land with his army in England and supplant James, five were Whigs and two were Tories. The Whigs, then, felt that they had the advantage over their opponents. In the first months of William's rule they demanded vengeance for the indignities imposed upon them during the last king's reign; they were also determined to guide William's counsels. But the new king knew well enough that he could not rule with the support of only one party; he had to strive for parity and balance in national affairs, favouring neither Whigs nor Tories but governing with the assistance of both. He wished to construct a 'court party' from the two sides.

The Whigs were not interested. They were particularly incensed against those Tory parliamentarians who had expressed their allegiance to the court of James II. Certain noblemen were accused of treason for joining the Church of Rome. The mayors and aldermen of all the towns and cities who had surrendered their charters to the previous king were to be deprived of any office for seven years. It was even proposed that a retrospective penal law should be applied to the entire Tory party. William, however, expressed his desire for an amnesty, a bill of 'general pardon and oblivion' for any who had engaged in arbitrary or illegal acts in the previous reign; in the summer of 1689 an 'Indemnity Bill' was presented to the Commons but it got no further than a second reading and was left on the table of the house. It was effectively dead.

So as far as William was concerned, parliament had failed. It had achieved nothing to his purpose and, in addition, had not granted him the easy supplies of revenue that he desired. One further imposition antagonized him even more. He proposed to sail with an army to Ireland in order to subdue the Catholics, and the remaining followers of James II, who posed a serious threat to the security of England. But the Whigs did not want him to go. They feared for his health in a land of rain and fog. They disliked the idea of a large army of recruits and mercenaries, many of them from northern Europe, standing on British soil. Before they could act with any decision, however, William dissolved the parliament and called for fresh elections.

The campaign of March 1690 was fiercely fought. 'Never', Diana Paget wrote to her relative, Lord Paget, 'was greater animosities and divisions than there is at this day, Whig and Tory more than ever.' It was, according to Macaulay, a struggle for life or death. Sermons and pamphlets and street ballads raised the temperature; lists of parliamentary divisions were published for the first time, with the purpose of 'informing' the constituents about the competing members. The result in fact favoured the Tories with 'the Church of England men', as they were sometimes called, winning the majority. In this more amenable climate the king returned the compliment by issuing 'an act of grace', for the pardon of all offences committed by the followers of James II; it required only one courteous reading by Lords and Commons in May to pass into law. In the following month William sailed for Ireland with his army.

The case against Ireland was similar to that against France. In both countries the pretensions of the Stuart monarchy were upheld. In the spring of 1689 James II had landed at Kinsale, on the south-west coast of Ireland, with a body of French troops. The parliament at Dublin proclaimed him to be the lawful king and passed a bill of attainder against his rebellious enemies. So in June 1690, William was poised to strike back with artillery and a larger army. The English regiments, from Cheshire, Cumberland and elsewhere, were strengthened with German and Scandinavian mercenaries.

The state of Ireland was for the new English king vexatious. He had already sent an army, under the command of the duke of Schomberg, to subdue the hostile population and its leaders; the duke had remained on the defensive and did not risk open battle, on the good grounds that his troops were untrained and that the opposing troops of James II were at that stage the stronger. William himself was obliged to take command. He sailed from Chester with a further 16,000, carried over the Irish Sea in 280 transports.

When he landed at Carrickfergus on the north-eastern coast of Ireland, he joined with Schomberg's forces and began the march south to Dublin; when he reached Drogheda, 35 miles north of the capital, he received the news that the enemy army was close by on the south side of the River Boyne. The Jacobite force, consisting largely of Irish Catholics, was the first line of defence for Dublin. William had feared that his Irish campaign might be hindered by a wet autumn and a frozen winter, but the opportunity for a decisive victory had come. 'I am glad to see you, gentlemen,' he is supposed to have remarked as he surveyed the Irish forces. 'If you escape me now, the fault will be mine.'

On the day before the battle, 30 June, he was fired upon by two field guns, and the second ball grazed his shoulder. He bent forward over his horse's neck for a moment, and the Irish gave out a great shout of exaltation. But he steadied himself. 'There is no harm done,' he said, 'but the bullet came quite near enough.' His wound was dressed and he prepared himself for the coming battle.

It was important quickly to force the passage over the Boyne. William led his left wing, consisting of the cavalry, while Schomberg was entrusted with the command of those on foot. The watchword was 'Westminster'. Every soldier wore a small green bough in his hat while, on the Irish side, the men wore slivers of white paper. It was hard work for Schomberg's men to cross the river but they pressed forward; they were resolute but they were repeatedly forced back by James's cavalry. They resisted and regrouped, however, and the Jacobite forces were ordered to retreat. James himself had watched the battle from a distance, and at its inglorious close galloped off to the fishing village of Duncannon where he would set sail for the safety of France. He would never return to Ireland and his last, best, hope of regaining his throne had gone. The Irish, effectively abandoned by their king, called him '*Seamus a' chaca*' or James the Shit.

The battle of the Boyne effectively ended any chance of Catholic ascendancy in Ireland. The treaty of Limerick, signed in the following year, promised relatively generous terms to the Irish forces and to the Catholic population. But the Irish Protestants were not ready to concede so much to the religious enemy and, in the Dublin parliament, they set out their own conditions for the end of the Anglo-Irish war. These became known as 'the penal laws'. Those who had fought for James II lost all their property. No Catholic landowner could pass on his estates intact to a single heir. Catholics could not hold office, bear arms, or openly practise their religion. They were also debarred from any legal or military profession. This became known as 'the Protestant ascendancy' but was called by the Irish Catholics the '*long briseadh*' or the 'long breaking'.

Yet English triumph in Ireland was not matched by success in the campaign against the French. The war had suffered a disastrous beginning when, in the summer of 1690, a combined Dutch and English fleet was defeated by the French navy off Beachy Head with the loss of eleven ships. The news created panic fear in London and elsewhere, since it seemed possible and even likely that the enemy might now mount a full invasion of English soil. The local militias were called up, and men armed with swords or pitchforks descended onto the Devonshire coast ready to fight any Frenchman. The silver sea, serving 'as a moat defensive to a house', was in the command of an ancient enemy. What if its fleet sailed up the Thames?

In the event there was no French invasion or, at least, not a serious one. A thousand Frenchmen landed at Teignmouth, where they proceeded to ransack and burn down the fishing village; but then they went back to their ships and sailed away. It was a signal warning, however, of their policy of spoliation. The lord admiral of the fleet, Arthur Herbert, first earl of Torrington, was arrested and taken to the Tower for failures of duty; at a later court martial he was acquitted, but he was shunned at William's court and never taken into service again.

William sailed across the Irish Sea to Bristol in early September 1690, having asked John Churchill, earl of Marlborough, to share command of the continuing Irish campaign with two foreign generals; the king began a slow journey, in part a march of triumph, to his palace at Kensington. In the following month parliament voted him more than £4 million for the army and the navy in their continuing conflict with France; the money itself was to be raised by means of a newly conceived land tax and by the doubling of customs and excise, an increase in revenues that heralded the emergence of what has become known as a financial or 'fiscal' state. It was a gesture born out of fear as well as gratitude; the members of parliament were still alarmed at the prospect of invasion.

The king now travelled to The Hague for a congress in which he would try to organize the military strategies of his allies. With the exception of the Dutch, naturally, they proved to be fractious and unwilling. Denmark and Sweden, for example, considered themselves to be so distant from the scene of conflict that they held back; William suspected them of conniving at a peace with France which would be tantamount to surrender. The elector of Brandenburg would not go to the aid of the Spanish Netherlands. The elector of Saxony recalled his troops from what he considered to be unsatisfactory winter quarters. The Holy Roman Emperor, Leopold I, was more concerned with Turkey than with France. Yet William's great strength lay in the arts of diplomacy; by means of bribes, promises and entreaties he managed to preserve the coalition.

These resources were never more necessary than in April 1691, when the city of Mons in the southern Netherlands, close to the border with France, fell to Louis XIV. The rejoicing at William's discomfiture was not confined to Versailles; the Jacobites in London celebrated his defeat in the taverns and coffee-houses which they openly frequented. He had also another, and more secret, enemy. The first earl of Marlborough was not happy with his position; he had scored a notable victory in Ireland, with a campaign of five weeks in which he had taken Cork and Kinsale, thus blocking the seaways to France. Yet he resented the fact that foreign generals were preferred by the king, and that the dukes and counts of the various principalities of Europe could claim precedence over him.

Marlborough had all the makings of a modern patriot; he was handsome, clever and resourceful, an excellent general, and a politician of persuasive manner. He had distinguished himself twenty years before in the service of the duke of York, and had never since been out of favour. He had deserted his first patron, who had become James II, and had gone over to William's party at the time of the invasion, doing so on the grounds of Protestant piety. But he seemed quite happy to reverse his allegiance once again, if the circumstances were propitious. He was inclined to support whatever and whoever indulged his interests, whether for power, money, or further honours, while all the time remaining tactful, modest and obliging.

Soon after his return from Ireland he seems to have organized or joined a plot to restore James II to the throne. He believed that he had the English army behind him. The evidence also suggests that other English grandees had made their own approaches to James, living as an exile in the Château de Saint-Germain-en-Laye, in the hope of insuring themselves for any possible future. Marlborough's plot was discovered, however, and at the beginning of 1692 he was stripped of his offices and dismissed from the court. Then, in May, he was arrested for high treason and dispatched to the Tower. It was alleged, falsely, that he had been part of a conspiracy to assassinate William. The affair became known as 'the flower pot plot'; a forged document, implicating Marlborough, had been placed under a flower pot in the house of the bishop of Rochester.

He was released from confinement after six weeks and, in a state of partial rehabilitation, eventually returned to the court. William seems to have taken a relatively forgiving view of those grandees who still dabbled in the intrigues of the Stuart dynasty. He had a low opinion of human nature.

The king's principal concern was with the course of the continental war which in this period manifested neither great victories nor stunning defeats. But in May 1692, a French invasion fleet of forty-four ships was sighted off the coast of north-western France in the vicinity of Barfleur and La Hougue; its purpose was to restore James II to the throne of England. After a fierce encounter the French force scattered but the English and Dutch navies, in the course of their pursuit, managed to destroy fifteen enemy vessels. The threat of French attack was lifted.

The Dutch and English were now the masters of the sea while the French were obliged to concentrate upon the strategies of a land war. In the summer of the year, for example, the French army won a victory at Steenkerque in the southern Netherlands, when in the course of vicious fighting five English regiments were wholly destroyed. It is easy enough to list these events in simple chronology but it would need a pen of fire to draw a true portrait of the carnage. In 'A Voyage to the Country of the Houyhnhnms' (1723), the fourth part of *Gulliver's Travels*, Jonathan Swift notes laconically the state of contemporary warfare with 'twenty thousand killed on each side; dying groans, limbs flying in the air: smoke, noise, confusion, trampling to death under horses' feet: flight, pursuit, victory; fields strewed with carcasses left for food to dogs, and wolves, and birds of prey; plundering, stripping, ravishing, burning and destroying'. Another sea of red then covered the field. At a much later date Macaulay reports in his *History of England* (1848) that, after the battle of Steenkerque, 'the next summer the soil, fertilised by twenty thousand corpses, broke forth into millions of poppies'.

The war was no longer popular, if indeed it had ever been. It was simply 'William's war' and on the king's return, after his spring and summer campaigns on the continent, he found unrest and opposition. He had turned variously to the Whigs and to the Tories in the effort to establish a 'court party' wholly committed to the prosecution of the conflict; yet he began to favour the Whigs in the evident belief that the Tories were not necessarily reliable. He was right. The Tories made up a large portion of the 'country party' that turned its face against court and administration. It was distrustful of government, ever suspicious of a standing army and of those members of parliament who were dependent upon court favours.

Recognizable parties in a modern sense, however, did not exist. The permutations of individual members were endless. The Tories were in principle wholly in favour of the royal prerogative, now enjoyed by William III, but among them were many Jacobites who waited for the return of James II; the Whigs were supportive of William, but in theory they were always willing and eager to limit royal power. Where did the balance lie? The king preferred 'mixed' ministries, composed of various political elements, but in practice he was slowly drawn towards the Whigs because of their willingness to maintain the war against France; they were much more firmly opposed to the Catholicism and to the arbitrary despotism, as they saw it, of Louis XIV. Their contacts with the financiers of the City also gave them the ability to raise funds for the prosecution of the conflict, with the attendant promise of profit and interest repayments. They were William's friends. They were led by a group of five peers who by 1695 were being called 'the Junto', after the Spanish word, *junta*, for council.

The exiled king, ensconced in his court at Saint-Germain, was still busily scheming for his restoration; he watched eagerly for any mis-step by William, and acquired supporters or spies wherever he could. The secret Jacobites of England had adopted a key sentence: 'Box it about: it will come to my father.' By which was meant that it was necessary to throw the country into confusion so that James might return. The partisans also adopted a limp when they entered their taverns. 'Limp' was made up from the initials of four names – Louis, James, Mary of Modena, and the young Prince. James, in the spring of 1693, issued a 'declaration' offering a free pardon to those who would not oppose his return and promising that he would abide by parliamentary government.

The position of James's younger daughter, Anne, was a very difficult one; her problems were compounded after the death of her sister, Mary II, in 1694, when she became the only direct Stuart heir who was a staunch Protestant. It was noted that she had a better claim to the throne than her brother-in-law, William, who now made attempts to be conciliatory. In previous years William and Mary had ignored or rebuffed Anne, for a while excluding her from court altogether. In turn Anne, encouraged by Marlborough's wife, the formidable Sarah, had ridiculed the king; in their correspondence they called him 'Mr Caliban' or the 'Dutch abortion'.

Anne was suspected of Jacobite principles on the reasonable ground that she still supported the claims of her father. It was said that, on the death of her brother-in-law, she would invite James to return to his kingdom. This was not very likely; she was wholly averse to Roman Catholicism, and remembered how much damage James had wreaked upon the body politic by his insistence on Catholic emancipation. It is more probable that she herself wished to ascend the throne in order to maintain the order and stability of the Anglican cause, to which she was utterly devoted.

William had more immediate matters to consider. By the sixth year of the war he was again in urgent need of new funds, and he turned once more to the Whigs for assistance. One of the younger members of 'the Junto', Charles Montagu, had the requisite skills. It was he who, more than any other, changed the nature of English finance.

2

A bull or a bear?

How would it be possible to fund the hugely expensive continental war against Louis without impoverishing the country? A solution could be found. Charles Montagu, one of the lords of the treasury, still only in his early thirties, came upon a proposal advanced three years before but never implemented. It was for the establishment of a central bank, the Bank of England, that would lend money to the government on the condition that the repayment of the annual interest would be guaranteed by parliament from funds supplied by new duties on beer and other alcoholic drinks. The subscribers to the bank would thereby have the guarantee of repayment, even if this meant that the government would raise money by making further demands upon the people. This, in essence, was the beginning of what became known as 'the national debt'.

Montagu piloted the Bank of England Act through parliament in 1694, on the understanding that he would become chancellor of the exchequer. He even pledged the considerable sum of £2,000 as his own subscription to the bank. The money for the new venture came in quickly enough. It was proposed to raise £1.2 million from wealthy subscribers, at an annual interest of 8 per cent. Such terms were tempting enough to fill the list within ten days. The king and queen were among the investors who included merchants, financiers and businessmen. It was seen to be a largely Whig enterprise, therefore, with that party closely associated with the City of London. The Tories, who represented the landed classes, considered it to be nothing more than a 'front' to maintain the war. Certainly it had military and political consequences. France had no such financial scheme in operation, and so was placed at a disadvantage in funding hostilities.

This has been considered to represent a financial revolution that laid the ground for steady, if not always competent, government. Parliament, in the first place, was now in supreme command of the nation's funding; it raised the taxes that paid for the interest on the large loans. Within twenty years an annual 'budget' would be presented to its members. In the late seventeenth, and early eighteenth, centuries emerged a number of smaller banks, London 'private' banks and 'country' banks, which specialized in short-term credit and the forwarding of remittances. Their advances to business and public authorities helped to ease the passage of finance and of trade.

The City had been the home of credit ever since the time of the Roman occupation, but the extraordinary growth of business in the latter years of the seventeenth century convinced many contemporaries that it was a wholly new phenomenon. A Fellow of the Royal Society, John Houghton, wrote in 1694 that 'a great many stocks have arisen since this war with France'; he added that 'few that had money were willing it should lie idle', and suggested that greater profits were to be recovered from sources other than those of 'lands, houses or commodities'. The new methods became known very quickly as stock-jobbing; money might be made in the buying and selling of shares like those, for example, in the Bank of England itself. It was described by Defoe in 1724 as 'a trade, which once bewitched the nation almost to its ruin'.

Exchange Alley, near the Royal Exchange, became the centre for these transactions. Two coffee-houses in particular, Jonathan's and Garraway's, were the principal resorts of financial business. An advertisement of 1695 informed the public that at Jonathan's 'may be bought and sold . . . all stocks and shares'. A broker, John Castaing, published lists of stock prices and exchange rates together with the state of the markets in Genoa, Dublin, Rotterdam and elsewhere. It was also the place where wagers were taken, on matters public or private. What will you pay me if I do not drink wine, ale or brandy before Michaelmas 1696? What are the bets that war will be declared against France before Christmas Day? A contemporary print shows several bewigged gentlemen, with tricorne hats, standing and conversing in a large room; they are wearing formal waistcoats and coats. They invested, or represented investors, in government contracts, industrial enterprises, and the stocks of the great companies even then being formed. On the wall behind them are images of a bull and a bear, and one of a lame duck. A bull was supposed to be a financial optimist, and a bear was the opposite; they no doubt represented a mixture of both parties.

Their conversations are reproduced in a play of the period. Susanna Centlivre's *A Bold Stroke for a Wife* (1717) sets a scene in Jonathan's:

> *First broker:* Who does any thing in the civil list lottery? Or caco [coffee beans]? Zounds, where are all the Jews this afternoon? Are you a bull or a bear today, Abraham?
> *Second broker:* A bull, faith – but I have a good putt for next week.

The call goes out from the waiter for 'Fresh coffee, gentlemen, fresh coffee?' or for 'Bohea-tea, gentlemen?'

This was a new, and for some an alarming, practice. The Tories in particular disliked the idea of a rising 'moneyed interest'; they believed that wealth lay in the land of England, and not in financial manipulation. It was argued that those who possessed the soil were the best judges of the country's strengths. The moneyed men were also largely established in London, a Whig stronghold, and the assorted ranks of merchants, financiers, office holders and professionals contained a large number of dissenters and nonconformists. As a rule of thumb, it was said that dissent went with money and Anglicanism with land. As long as the war lasted, and the government was in need of funds, the new rich were assured of large profits from the institutions of public credit. The land suffered in contrast, and there were fears that the market was about to collapse. In *The Conduct of the Allies* (1711) Jonathan Swift returned to the attack upon the Whigs by declaring that the war was being continued unnecessarily 'to enrich usurers and stock-jobbers, and to cultivate the pernicious designs of a faction by destroying the landed interest'.

A further, but related, division arose between Whigs and Tories. Some of the latter group favoured the return of the exiled king or of his son; but if the Stuarts came back they might easily repudiate the national debt worked out by William III and his Whig supporters. The consequence would be financial chaos and ruin for the rich subscribers. It could not be allowed to happen.

The intimations of doom, on both sides, were of course misplaced. In a short period of time, beyond the hot circles of war, the common interests between the moneyed and the landed became obvious to all concerned. As Joseph Addison wrote in the *Spectator*, in the autumn of 1711, 'the trader is fed by the product of the land, and the landed man cannot be clothed but by the skill of the trader'. The representatives of the landed and financial interests came soon enough to entertain certain common ideals of 'the gentleman' and of 'gentle society' that animated social conventions for the next 150 years; the presence of an aristocratic elite, tantalizingly within grasp, wonderfully concentrated the minds of those who aspired to it.

The stability of the financial state was enhanced by a further measure introduced by Charles Montagu. In the year after the establishment of the Bank of England he decided to restore the true worth of the silver shilling, the value of which had been undermined by clipping and adulteration. Something like 95 per cent of the currency was counterfeit or underweight. Silver had never been more base.

Montagu had enlisted the assistance of Isaac Newton; they had both been Fellows of Trinity College, Cambridge, but Newton had subsequently astounded the world with his explanation of the force of gravity in *Principia Mathematica*. In the spring of 1696 Montagu had appointed his celebrated colleague as warden of the Mint, on Tower Hill, since in the previous year Newton had composed a short treatise 'On the Amendment of English Coins'. The new warden was in the doubly fortunate position of being both a superb theorist and a determined experimenter.

A total recoinage was to be effected, and the old impure coins were to be removed from circulation. Montagu had initiated the proposal but had left Newton to administer and organize its implementation. The exercise was in large measure a success, and within months of Newton's appointment the Mint was issuing some

£150,000 worth of silver coinage each week. The monetary standard of the country was assured. The pillars of the state were in place.

The essential nature of that state, as a result of the 'glorious revolution' of 1688, was now clearly recognizable. At its apex remained the monarch, of course. William III was on the throne by the agency of 'the divine right of Providence', however that phrase might be interpreted. It was an ambiguous formulation for an ambiguous position. Was he king by right of conquest or by consent of parliament? And what form of 'divine right' could he possibly claim? He never touched for the king's evil, for example, although his successor Anne would do so, exercising her supposedly supernatural power.

His somewhat indefinite or at least unformulated authority was maintained by the patrician class, which is to say the aristocrats who had steered the new state ever since its foundation. The upper ranks of the aristocracy numbered perhaps 200, among them the dukes, earls and other lords; they had always represented a small but confident and coherent landed elite. Wealth was essential but was not necessarily enough. Blood lineage was equally, if not more, important. A landed estate, which conferred the right to hunt, was a prerequisite. The striving members of the upper gentry would rather join them than beat them and in truth the aristocratic code, and the aristocratic ideal, would pervade the social and political life of the century. Continuity, rather than change, was the key. It was established by habitual patterns of perception and by traditional patterns of activity, as self-evident as they were unexceptionable.

This does not represent some antiquated vision of 'old England' but the living reality of politics and of power. Much has been written about the supposed permeability of the upper class, open to the rich and even to *arrivistes*, but the reality was less promising. It was a fixed principle, even as late as the reign of George III (1760–1820), that no individual engaged in trade could become a peer of the realm.

The lords were also an effective power in the Commons. The head of the family would sit in the upper chamber, while his relations and dependants would sit in the lower; Pitt the elder once described the Commons as 'a parcel of younger brothers'. The various families in turn set up marriage alliances, thus strengthening the power of the few. They stood above perhaps 15,000 of the lower gentry who were not of noble status but who did not have to till their own soil.

For most of the members of the gentry their Church was the state Church, their Anglicanism part of their birthright. Others of course were dissenters, and a few were atheistical, but the preponderance followed the familiar path to the village church or the town church. The Anglican authorities were in the early part of the eighteenth century wholly at the service of the administration. The archbishop of Canterbury had an official seat at the privy council, while of course the bishops were an intrinsic part of the House of Lords. When Bishop Hare once mildly threatened Lord Carteret, a Whig grandee, with the possible retraction of his vote, Carteret replied, 'If I want you, I know how to have you.' The bishops themselves were often of noble blood, and it was considered to be a matter of congratulation that after the rule of Cromwell the grandees were back in their palaces. The Church was viewed as one of the three great professions, alongside law and the emerging science or art of medicine, so it remained an integral part of the social hierarchy.

Orthodox Anglicanism, and it is hard to envisage any other, was primarily a religion of responsibilities and duties. It was reasonable, and not dogmatic. Morality, rather than Christ the Saviour, was the guiding presence. Its liturgy and canons had remained largely unchanged since their inception in the mid-sixteenth century. Habit and indifference completed the picture. Where the parson and the landowner are in agreement, the religious and secular state reflect one another. We may perhaps agree with that enemy of all things English, Napoleon Buonaparte, who remarked that 'I don't see in religion the mystery of the incarnation but the mystery of the social order. It ties up to heaven an idea of equality which prevents the rich from being massacred by the poor.' If this perhaps sounds too cynical then we may turn to that most English of observers, William Hogarth, who in *The Sleeping Congregation* shows the effect of a universal dullness covering all. In his etching the service is dominated by royal, rather than divine, images. Spirituality has been converted into sleep.

Others were more busy. The opportunities of wealth made possible by the 'financial revolution' helped to augment the number and power of what were known as 'the middling orders' comfortably ensconced between the landed gentry and the great army of manual workers and shopkeepers. They would include tenant farmers and factory-owners, government officers and city merchants, small businessmen and clergymen, doctors and lawyers; the rise of the salaried professions was one of the striking features of the early years of the century. If the manuals of conduct are anything to go by, the principal themes of this variously constituted class were those of enterprise, respectability, sobriety and hard work.

Daniel Defoe, himself an exceptional if sometimes erring exponent of the 'middling' virtues, reminded himself in the first chapter of *Robinson Crusoe* (1719) that 'the middle state . . . was the best state in the world, the most suited to human happiness, not exposed to the miseries and hardships, the labour and sufferings of the mechanic part of mankind, and not embarrassed with the pride, luxury, ambition, and envy of the upper part of mankind'.

The numbers of these fortunate citizens were necessarily increased as the economy improved. In the early eighteenth century one in seven was deemed to be of the middle state; a hundred years later, the proportion had become one in four or five. Some of them, however, were uneasily aware of their middle status and tried to insulate themselves from the abyss below them by striving to imitate the manners and customs of their immediate superiors. Appearances must be kept up; it was important to seem, and to be, credit-worthy so as not to 'break'. The ultimate aim was the acquisition of gentility in one or two generations.

The middling ranks included many Anglicans but, proportionately, they contained more dissenters or nonconformists. Theirs was the faith of hard work and enterprise, after all, of ambition and of striving. But already religious dissent had become in part a matter of state compliance. The Presbyterians, the Congregationalists and the General Baptists, for example, had achieved a measure of acceptance with the Toleration Act of 1689 even if they were still excluded from public office. Their chapels and meeting houses were part of the urban and rural landscape. The Quakers who had once stripped naked 'for a sign', in accordance with the twentieth chapter of Isaiah, did, according to an antiquary, Abraham de la Pryme, 'modestly and devoutly behave themselves'. This is the trajectory of all radical faiths. Its adherents become more complacent and more respectable; in particular they become older. It would take the Methodist revival of a later generation to excite the original fire in a bout of evangelical fervour that had not been seen in England since the middle of the seventeenth century.

Of course many of the population were without any religion at all, except for the residue of paganism and natural spirituality that had been inherited from previous centuries. The lower 'classes' of the early eighteenth century could be defined, as was done at the time, as 'the mechanic part of mankind'. They lived by manual labour of a variety of kinds. They were in a literal sense the 'hands' of the country; those who served meals, those who drew water, those who hewed wood, those who stitched and those who spun. They comprised by far the greatest part of the working population, from colliers to mantua-makers, from watchmakers to shopkeepers, from footmen to cooks. Defoe described them as 'the working trades, who labour hard, but feel no want' and 'the country people, farmers etcetera, who fare indifferently'. Some of those who worked on the land could not enjoy its fruits for themselves. If their sows bred piglets, or their hens chicks, these were taken to the market rather than to the table. The workers sold their apples and pears, and lived on skimmed milk and whey curds while their customers purchased milk and cheese. Their perpetual and useful toil reached its quietus in an obscure destiny.

Social historians, as historical fashions change, have concentrated upon those in even more difficult circumstances. It has been estimated that, at any time before the Industrial Revolution, approximately one quarter of the population was in a state of abject poverty. These are the people who in Defoe's phrase 'fare hard'. They can also be called the 'labouring poor'. One such was Jeremy in William Congreve's *Love for Love* (1695) who states that 'my mother sold oysters in winter and cucumbers in summer, and I came upstairs into the world, for I was born in a cellar'. He had since come up even higher in the world, since he was now a gentleman's servant. And that was the worth of the labouring poor. They could be made useful; their very plenitude was God's blessing to the affluent. These were the ranks that helped to make up the industrial population of the factories and the humble skivvies of the kitchen. Discipline, deprivation and hard labour were supposed to be the sovereign curatives for idleness even if, as Sir William Petty put it, they only dragged the stones from Stonehenge to Tower Hill.

Lying beneath all were the miserable, the abject, the worthless. They would include the beggars, the vagrants, the severely crippled, the mad as well as the mass of ragged outcasts who lived in holes in the walls, in subterranean pits, in outhouses, and in bulkheads. One anonymous pamphlet of 1701, *Reflexions Upon the Moral State of the Nation*, reported that 'they live more like rats and weasels and such like noxious vermin, than creatures of human race'. The helpless and incurable poor were generally disregarded except as elements in riot, dissipation or epidemic disease. They were objects of fear and loathing on the streets, and even the most charitable impulses of the reformers could scarcely make room for them. The poor were unavoidable, elemental, but not to be touched.

The death of his wife, Mary, in Kensington Palace at the end of 1694 had provoked in William a grief that was as deep as it was unexpected. The smallpox had taken her during a bitterly cold winter. When her husband had been absent with his army on the continent, she had always been something of a reluctant replacement. She felt herself to be 'deprived of all that was dear to me in the person of my husband, left among those that were perfect strangers to me: my sister of a humour so reserved that I could have little comfort from her'. Mary and her sister, Anne, were in fact hardly on speaking terms. When her husband was by her side, Mary deferred without thinking to the king's wishes but her compliant temper was accompanied by a cheerfulness and vivacity not readily apparent in her husband. When she ruled in his absence, however, she was resolute and not without dignity. She was widely, and perhaps sincerely, mourned.

Her death of course left her sister Anne in a singularly difficult position; she was now heir apparent who had in fact a better claim to the throne than its present occupant. It was incumbent upon William to pay his respects to her after a decade of neglect. Anne herself had come wholly to rely upon her principal lady-in-waiting,

Sarah, countess of Marlborough, and upon Sarah's husband, the first earl of Marlborough. Here were the makings of a court in waiting and, soon enough, the fortunate pair became duke and duchess.

Even while the abbey was covered in drapes of black for the late queen parliament acted, or rather failed to act, on a measure that would have incalculable consequences for the future state of the nation. In the spring of 1695 a resolution for 'regulations of printing and printing presses' was allowed to lapse, almost by oversight, and that chance led ineluctably to the emergence of what became known as 'the fourth estate'. It was, in retrospect at least, a momentous change that emancipated English letters for ever from government control.

The public had previously been forced to be content with the official *London Gazette*. It was established in February 1665, and continues to this day as the official newspaper of record, although Captain Bluffe in Congreve's *The Old Bachelor* (1693) claims, 'Why, sir, there are not three words of truth, the year round, put into the *Gazette*.' But, as a result of the lifting of prohibitions, the public prints were quickly in demand in a party-dominated and war-oppressed age.

Within a fortnight of the end of censorship, a paper entitled *Intelligence, Domestic and Foreign* began to circulate; this was followed by *The English Courant*, *The Post Man*, *The Post Boy*, *The Weekly News-Letter* and others. Some of them left blank spaces so that the reader might fill in more current news before passing on the publication to friends or neighbours; many of the printed items were accompanied by the phrase 'this wants confirmation' or 'this occasions many speculations' or 'time will discover the event'. The affairs of the world were very uncertain.

In the succeeding reign of Queen Anne more than forty newssheets were distributed on the streets and in the coffee-houses of London, many of them also finding their way to the provincial towns and cities. It took a full day to read only the most important of them. We may speak for the first time, therefore, of a politically aware nation, with the concomitant rise of the 'journalist' and the 'essayist'. The power of the new press quickly became apparent and, in a letter from Lemuel Gulliver that opens his *Travels*, the celebrated if fictional surgeon recalls the remark of his cousin that 'people in power were very watchful over the press'.

The first daily newspaper, the *Daily Courant*, was issued on Wednesday 11 March 1702; it is printed on one side of a single sheet with news from Naples, Rome, Vienna, Frankfurt and elsewhere; the majority of its news paragraphs concerned the progress of the war and, in a postscript, its editor disparaged 'the impertinences of ordinary news-papers'. It opened in a characteristically dry style with a report from Naples that 'on Wednesday last, our new viceroy, the duke of Escalona, arrived here with a squadron of the galleys of Sicily'. The sheet was sold next door to the King's Arms tavern at Fleet Bridge, and in the vicinity, very close to the neighbourhood that had already earned the soubriquet of 'Grub Street'.

From the beginning these newspapers were largely business ventures, although some of them were in part subsidized by the political managers of the time who wished to create a discernible volume of 'public opinion' on any particular matter. The public prints relied largely upon advertisements and upon circulation, and so became part of that commercial society that was even then taking shape.

A few weeks after the death of his wife the king wrote to a colleague in 1695 that 'I feel myself to be no longer fit for military command'; yet he added characteristically that 'I will try to do my duty'. His duty compelled him to attempt the recapture of Namur, the most important fortress in the Spanish Netherlands; the citadel looked over a fruitful plain and two rivers, the Sambre and the Meuse, and it had never before opened its gates to an enemy. Three years earlier, however, the French besiegers under the command of Louis himself had broken the spirit of the town after eight days; it was the lowest point for England and its allies in the campaign against the French.

William knew well enough that it would be a signal victory to retrieve Namur after its occupation. After a series of feints and skirmishes he marched straight upon the town at the beginning of July 1695, and there began a series of bloody assaults and battles that endured until the total surrender of the citadel two months later. This is the conflict in which Uncle Toby, of Laurence Sterne's *The Life and Opinions of Tristram Shandy, Gentleman* (1759–67), injured his groin; he modelled the outworks of the citadel in his garden. The excitement and anxiety aroused by the campaign animated the London crowds, who flocked for news to the booksellers and coffee-houses. The king's success was one of the most important victories of the Nine Years War, all the more significant because it had been conducted on land; it was the first major victory of that kind since Cromwell's 'battle of the dunes' in 1658. On his return William engaged in a summer tour, ostensibly in triumph, but his reserved and suspicious nature was in evidence. He did not frequent the well-travelled roads and, in Oxford, refused a dinner for fear that it had been poisoned.

3

The idol of the age

The jubilation of victory was in any case short-lived. Despite the success in the Spanish Netherlands the war itself was becoming too lengthy and too costly to be easily endured. It had procured very little benefit for England itself. At the end of 1695 the exiled king, James II, issued a proclamation from his French court that did 'fully authorize, strictly require and expressly command our loving subjects to rise in arms and make war upon the prince of Orange, the usurper of our throne . . .'. He did have supporters in England who were ready to obey the command, but they could not or would not move without the aid of a French invasion. Such an invasion, however, was a step too far for Louis XIV who already had continental entanglements to deter him.

Some conspirators were willing to act alone. Anne, a proper Stuart, would of course reign in the event of the king's death; this prospect seems to have been the spur for a plot engineered at the beginning of 1696. As the king drove home to Kensington Palace after his weekly hunt in Richmond Park, he was obliged to pass through a narrow lane by the river at Turnham Green. Here he was to be surrounded by armed men and killed. Like most such plots it foundered on whispers and betrayals; William cancelled the hunt, but not before making use of it as an instrument of state. His disclosure of the conspiracy to parliament, in February 1696, caused a sensation and prompted members to form an association in the king's defence not unlike that established to protect Elizabeth I against Spanish plotters.

The general mood, however, was still one of war-weariness. After the victory at Namur, the land war continued with no great victories and no signal defeats. It had become a war of attrition in which both parties were in danger of fighting one another to an expensive impasse. Yet a detached observer, if such existed, might have arrived at certain conclusions. William III had proved to be more than a match for Louis XIV; the energy and perseverance of England's king, together with the support of his allies, had been able to check the progress of the Bourbon empire. The new-found financial strength of England could also prove formidable in future conflicts.

A treaty between the parties was drawn up and signed after five months of negotiation. The Peace of Ryswick, concluded in the autumn of 1697, seems to have favoured William; Louis surrendered much of the territory he had gained and, perhaps more importantly, recognized William III as the rightful king of England. This might seem to have been a significant blow to James II and the Stuart cause, but the promises of a king were not always to be trusted.

After nine years of a bloody and costly war, however, the bells of London rang in celebration on news of the treaty. William himself declared that 'it is impossible to conceive what joy the peace causes here'. The seas would once more be safe, and the merchants might trade with impunity. The burden of taxation, or so it was hoped, would be immeasurably lightened; 75 per cent of the revenue had, after all, been devoted to the costs of war.

As soon as parliament opened, at the beginning of December, a debate commenced on the necessity of preserving a standing army. The king favoured the measure as a way of keeping check upon the French, but the preponderant opinion of the members was for an unarmed government. That was part of the old polity of England. It was now agreed that all the land forces enrolled since September 1680 should be forthwith disbanded and that there should be no bigger force on English soil than that which had obtained in the reign of Charles II. This would amount to some 7,000 men. The country gentlemen were not willing to pay taxes for an imposed army and, in particular, for foreign recruits. It was agreed, therefore, that the army of 7,000 should be comprised only of the king's English subjects; as a result his Dutch bodyguards and his regiments of French Protestants were disbanded. William, hardly dissembling his anger, remarked that parliament had achieved a feat that the French had failed to accomplish in nine years. A victorious monarch could scarcely be more ignobly treated. It is no wonder, perhaps, that he was always pining for his homeland.

Parliament pressed home its supremacy when, at the beginning of 1701, an Act of Settlement was passed utterly debarring the Stuart dynasty from the throne. In the summer of the previous year Prince William, the last surviving son of the seventeen pregnancies of Princess Anne and her husband Prince George of Denmark, had died from fluid on the brain. When Anne assumed the throne, she would have no heir absolute. Although William had died at the age of eleven, he had already been hailed as the new Protestant champion. The king wrote to Marlborough that 'it is so great a loss to me as well as to all England that it pierces my heart'.

The Jacobites had naturally been delighted at the news, hoping that James or his son would be rightfully reinstalled as rulers of the kingdom. But parliament had other ideas. It turned to Germany and, in particular, the only surviving granddaughter of James I. Sophia electress of Hanover was the daughter of the ill-starred 'Winter Queen', Elizabeth, whose rule as queen of Bohemia had lasted for a year before she and her husband were ousted by the forces of the Holy Roman Emperor. So by the strange serendipity of dynasty and fortune Sophia was set to become the next queen of England; if she was unwilling or unable to take the throne, she had a healthy Protestant son by the name of George Ludwig (George Louis) of Hanover.

The clauses of the Act of Settlement, dictated by parliament, made other demands. Every sovereign must be part of the communion of the Church of England. If a king was born beyond the shores of England, no English force would be obliged to defend his native soil. No king was to leave England, or Scotland, or Ireland, without the consent of parliament. These were all measures designed to obstruct any pretensions that the house of Hanover might claim. They might be German, but they would be obliged to rule as English sovereigns.

William knew that the Peace of Ryswick was by no means the end of hostilities, and that the French king's overweening appetite for glory would encourage him in fresh fields of action. Spain proved to be the spur. The Spanish emperor, Charles II, better known as Charles the Sufferer, had endured a life of long disease. He was incapacitated and mentally incapable; his tongue was too large for his mouth, and he drooled continually. He had a huge and misshapen jaw, so that the rest of his face seemed to be in a kind of pit. His body was crooked and his mind more or less unhinged; he believed himself to have been bewitched since childhood, in which opinion most of his court and country concurred. He even allowed himself to be exorcized. He was the last of the Habsburg rulers of Spain, and the overwhelming evidence of inbreeding may have been the occasion for his manifold mental and physical weaknesses. He was an embarrassment in life, yet in death he would become a problem. He ruled Spain and the Spanish Netherlands, now largely consisting of Belgium, and he controlled the empire from the Americas to the Spanish East Indies. It looked more powerful on paper than it did in reality, but still it was grand enough to lure rivals.

In the spring of 1700, when he was months from death, there had been attempts to divide his legacy between the principal claimants. The greed of men, and the mischance of events, left any proposed arrangement in disarray. The Holy Roman Emperor, Leopold I of Austria, claimed the inheritance on behalf of his son in a series of elaborate genealogical calculations; they depended upon the particular clause of a particular marriage contract. No box that Pandora ever opened could contain so much dissension. Louis XIV looked with horror upon an alliance between Madrid and Vienna; it would mark an arrow through French domains. Charles the Sufferer had in fact named as his successor Philip, duke of Anjou, who happened to be the grandson of Louis XIV. William III could not contemplate a union between Paris and Madrid: this could not be allowed. So great a Bourbon empire had never yet been seen.

Yet Louis was not to be diverted. Towards the end of November 1700, three weeks after the death of Charles, the French king proclaimed his grandson to be Philip V of Spain and true successor to the throne; he also took the precaution of interdicting trade between England and the Spanish Netherlands. Such a commercial and political offensive was followed by what might be considered a more private insult. In the middle of September 1701, James II died in the odour of sanctity, having been seized with paralysis while attending Mass in his chapel at Saint-Germain. His perpetual companions had been the austere monks of La Trappe, and he pleaded with his son and heir to follow the precepts and practices of the Roman Church. The French king, who had made vows at the deathbed of the dying king, now kept his promise to his cousin by recognizing the 'Old Pretender', the 'King over the Water', the 'Old Chevalier' – as he was variously known in England – to be James III.

This was a provocation too far. It violated the Peace of Ryswick, when Louis had solemnly agreed to recognize William III as the rightful king of England. It threw into doubt all the French king's promises and avowals, and aroused all the old fears that Louis was about to impose by force popery, tyranny and universal monarchy.

At the beginning of June 1701 William had appointed Marlborough to be commander-in-chief and plenipotentiary in all negotiations concerning the security of England and its allies. The king recognized that Marlborough, already the ensconced favourite of Anne, would be by far the single most important figure and commander of the new regime; he wished above all else for continuity in his struggle against the French. By the end of the year a 'treaty of grand alliance' had been sealed between Holland, England and Austria. So began 'the War of the Spanish Succession'.

William made his decision only just in time. He had for some months been afflicted by shiverings, headaches and nausea, but his quietus was delivered by a humble mole. In February 1702 he was riding through the park of Hampton Court when his horse stumbled on a mole-hill; the king fell and broke his collar bone, the complications leading to his death. For many years afterwards the Jacobites toasted 'the little gentleman dressed in velvet' who had supplied the *coup de grâce* in the park.

William was not greatly mourned, for he had not been greatly loved. He had been, for many, the least bad alternative. He had kept out the Stuart monarchs and their papist pretensions. Yet his legacy was in fact far more substantial than might at first appear. He had defied French power and limited its continental ambitions; he had successfully removed all the memories of the weakness and pusillanimity of the Stuart kings in thrall to money from Versailles. He and his advisers had also been able to place England on a far more advantageous financial footing, with the prospect of public credit stretching onwards. A new dynasty, a new foreign policy and a new economic dispensation, were not negligible achievements.

On 8 March Anne, at the moment of William's death, became queen of England, Scotland and Ireland. She was perhaps not the most prepossessing of monarchs, but she had endured many calamities. She was thirty-seven years of age, and in the last sixteen of them she had suffered twelve miscarriages; of her five other children, four died in very early life. The oldest survivor, as we have seen, expired at the age of eleven. The years of mourning and frustrated pregnancy had affected both her appearance and her character. Her gout was so extreme that she was often to be found swathed in bandages. One Scottish commissioner, Sir John Clerk of Penicuik, came to Kensington Palace in order to pay his respects and was alarmed to discover her 'laboring under a fit of the gout, and in extreme pain and agony'; he added that her face was 'red and spotty', her dress 'negligent' and her foot 'tied up with a poultice and some nasty bandages'. This was not an image of majesty.

Her discomfort, and the disorder about her, were not helped by her evident reticence and shyness in company. At court receptions the foreign ministers and ambassadors would often sit around her in total silence. Her principal lady-in-waiting, Sarah, duchess of Marlborough, recorded that she never really cared for visitors; she was reluctant to ask questions, and even more unwilling to answer them. She confined her conversation to pleasantries of the lightest sort. How long have you been in town? How do you find our weather? She was neither clever nor witty, and upon matters of state 'she never spoke but in a road' or in a leaden, laborious and carefully rehearsed way.

There were reasons for her reticence. She was cautious by temperament, never wholly trusting her own judgement or that of others. Jonathan Swift, who observed her at court, remarked that 'there was not, perhaps in all England, a person who understood more artificially to disguise her passions'. But there were matters for which no disguise was necessary. She was a fervent supporter of the high Anglican Church and, as one devoted to ritual, she was also addicted to protocol. She would remonstrate with a courtier or lady who wore a ruffle or a periwig or a coat out of place.

She began her day with prayers in the royal chapel before immersing herself in public business; on two days of each week she attended long sessions of the inner cabinet (known at the time as the 'secret council'), a practice that had generally exhausted the patience of her predecessors, and attended to the steady business of receiving ambassadors, replying to petitions, signing warrants and letters, giving counsel to, and soliciting advice from, various peers and notables. She told the archbishop of York that she scarcely found time for her prayers. It may be that she felt at a disadvantage as a woman, and a woman without an heir. All the time she heard the steps of the Hanoverians behind her, and indeed refused to allow the heiress elect, Sophia of Hanover, to travel to England. She did not wish to seem expendable.

Her first address to the House of Lords, therefore, three days after the death of the king, may have been something of an ordeal for a woman as shy as she was cautious. From the throne in the Lords she declared that 'as I know my own heart to be entirely English, I can very sincerely assure you, that there is not anything you can expect or desire from me which I shall not be ready to do for the happiness and prosperity of England'.

Her reference to her Englishness was no doubt a hit against William, whom she always despised, and his predilection for Holland. It was feared that she would be too lame from the gout to walk into the Lords but she processed with crown and heavy gown of red velvet with the order of the Garter emblazoned upon it. An eyewitness of the ceremony, Sir Robert Southwell, wrote that 'never any woman spoke more audibly or with better grace'. She blushed, and seemed at times uneasy, but she had demonstrated her regality.

The election of that year had favoured the Tories with a large majority and, within a few weeks of their victory, they introduced 'the Occasional Conformity Bill' which was designed to penalize dissenters and nonconformists in the practice of their religion and in their pursuit of civic office. Ever since the Act of Toleration of

1689 it had been perfectly proper for dissenters to take Anglican communion two or three times a year in order to qualify for public employment; the eucharist became their certificate of health. One of the most famous cases was that of the lord mayor of London, Sir Humphrey Edwin, a Presbyterian, who on one occasion worshipped at the Anglican service in the morning and in the evening attended his meeting house or conventicle at Pinners' Hall on Old Broad Street. This double standard, known as 'playing bo-peep with the Almighty', was in the bill to be prohibited by use of fines or imprisonment.

Anne was herself temperamentally of the 'high church' party, and favoured the measure as proof of Anglican piety, but the Whig majority in the Lords seem to have realized that a nation separated on religious matters might well divide on other issues. Marlborough himself did not see the point of antagonizing a large part of the population at time of war. So, despite the enthusiasm of the Tories in the newly elected Commons, the bill was allowed to drop. The queen herself sweetened the pill by establishing a fund known as 'Queen Anne's Bounty', by which she agreed to surrender her additional revenues from tax on clerical incomes in order to supplement the salaries of those clerks who served in the poorest parishes.

The most significant problem in these early days of her reign, however, was that of war with France. Marlborough was confirmed in office as captain general of the armed forces, although in theory he was inferior in rank to the queen's husband, Prince George of Denmark. George himself was a royal nonentity of whom Charles II had remarked that 'I have tried him drunk and I have tried him sober, but there is nothing in him.' He died in 1708, so for the latter years of her reign Anne was a widow. Marlborough was of course in practical charge of the allied forces. He was the only possible candidate for the post. In fact the first year of the campaign was very much like the final year of the last, with precious little movement on either side; Marlborough, in addition, felt himself hampered by the caution or indecision of his Dutch field deputies. His consolation came in the dukedom awarded to him by the queen in 1702.

Over the next months, despite the dilatoriness of the allies, the new duke was able to capture a number of significant towns along the Meuse, the great river that runs from north-east France into the northern sea beside ports such as Liège, Maastricht and Namur; the victories prompted John Evelyn to write that 'such an concurrence of blessings and hope of God's future favour has not been known in a hundred years'. This may have been something of an overstatement, but a great victory was indeed at hand.

Marlborough's line of fire along the Meuse had prevented Holland from falling wholly to Louis XIV but, together with his ally, Prince Eugene of Savoy, the duke now prepared a greater strategy. In a move as hazardous as it was unpredictable he marched his army away from the Low Countries and across the various German principalities towards Bavaria, the elector of which state was a close ally of the French, and through which a strategically important stretch of the River Danube flowed. His main purpose was to save the Habsburg capital, Vienna, from the enemy. In a feat that has sometimes been compared with those of Napoleon, Marlborough marched 20,000 men across 250 miles of Europe in six weeks while absorbing 20,000 more troops along his route. He had to move in conditions of speed and secrecy in order to camouflage his intentions not only from the French but also from his more pusillanimous Dutch colleagues, who believed that any forces taken from the Spanish Netherlands were thereby wasted.

Marlborough prevailed. At the beginning of August 1704, the two forces faced each other close to the village of Blindheim or Blenheim, which lay in a plain of stubble close to the Danube itself. The French and Bavarians were in defensive position, with the river and woods behind them, but Marlborough's keen and continual attacks eventually broke them. The English cavalry, fighting in lines three deep, moved forward at a brisk trot with their swords ready; the infantry, three or four deep, were armed with muskets and ring bayonets. Towards the close of the fighting the French were compelled to retreat into the village of Blenheim itself, where in the face of overwhelming casualties the remnant was forced to lay down its arms.

The victory was complete; the French lost some 34,000 men, with 14,000 injured or taken prisoner, while the English and their allies lost about 14,000. On the following day the duke wrote to his wife that 'I can't end my letter without being so vain as to tell my dearest soul that within the memory of man there had been no victory so great as this'. The greater the carnage, perhaps, the greater the victory.

Bavaria was knocked from the war, and Vienna was saved. The German principalities were spared the danger of French invasion, and the hopes of Louis for a quick and decisive war were thoroughly overturned. It was perhaps the most decisive battle of the entire War of the Spanish Succession, whereby the military power of England was affirmed and the spectre of Louis XIV was seen to be nothing but a shadow. It took eight days for the news of the victory to reach England, where it was met with jubilation. When Anne was given the news by a courier, she told him: 'You have given me more joy than ever I have received in my life.' But the joy was not unconfined, and it was noticeably lacking among those Tories who were opposed to Marlborough's war policies as an expensive extravagance. What, in their judgement, did such European conflicts actually achieve?

Party rivalry was characteristically intense and bitter during the reign of Queen Anne. She was herself an interim figure, neither Hanoverian nor Jacobite, so the rival ideologies of the realm had an open arena for their fury and resentment. The queen herself was determined to stand above parties, and it was her instinctive and pragmatic inclination to maintain a balance between them so that none should rule her; she wrote that 'if I should be so unfortunate as to fall into the hands of either, I shall look upon myself, though I have the name of queen, to be in reality but their slave'. She disliked and distrusted the violent partisans on both sides; they were 'merciless men' whom she regarded with dread. But would it prove possible to steer an even course between them? The Tories were her church party of redoubtable Anglicans but they opposed Marlborough's wars; the Whigs supported Marlborough and all his works, but they were eager to diminish the royal prerogative in favour of parliamentary rule. To whom could she flee?

The political parties were not yet formally constituted, but they were becoming so. They were, in other words, in the process of turning into caricatures of themselves. In Swift's *Gulliver's Travels* (1726) the two factions of Lilliput, known as 'Tramecksan' and 'Slamecksan', are divided over the respective heights of the heels of their shoes; the former wear their heels high, as 'high Tories', and the latter low. The animosities between them are so great that, as Swift puts it, 'they will neither eat nor drink, nor talk with each other'.

In the real world of early eighteenth-century London the Whigs and Tories frequented their own clubs, coffee-houses and taverns. The Whigs of aristocratic temper met at the Kit-Kat Club, while their Tory counterparts assembled at the Society of Brothers. The Tories patronized Ozinda's Chocolate House in St James's or progressed round the corner to the Smyrna or the Cocoa Tree in Pall Mall. The Whigs collected at St James's Coffee House, perilously close to Ozinda's, or drove further east to Buttons by Covent Garden. Pontack's in Lombard Street, and the Old Man's in the Tilt Yard, were also Whig favourites.

Addison once described London as 'an aggregate of nations', with the customs and manners of St James's as different from those of Cheapside as those of Tunisia or Moscow. Yet each region was united by means of its principal coffee-house that 'has some particular statesman belonging to it, who is the mouth of the street where he lives'. It was a city of coffee-houses. They had begun life in the 1660s, when the burgeoning social intercourse after the godly rule of Cromwell demanded some comfortable venue. They could not have come at a better time for London society, and before long they were considered to be the most essential component of city life. A roaring fire guaranteed warmth and hot water; a penny on the counter brought you a dish of coffee or chocolate; the newspapers, hanging on the wall, were all that were needed for entertainment and conversation. It was a world of news.

The illustrations of the time show that the coffee-houses were simple enough, with a few stools, chairs and plain deal tables. Smoking was the rule, and pipes were in almost every hand. Anderton's in Fleet Street was the meeting place of Freemasons; Child's, in St Paul's Churchyard, was for book-worms and scholars; the Grecian was similarly the venue for learned men; Jonathan's in Exchange Alley was the haunt of stock-jobbers; Batson's in Cornhill was the place of physicians. If an invalid needed an immediate diagnosis, he or she would send a boy to Batson's.

Even the medical profession, however, was not free from the

rage of party. When Doctor Oliphant began to associate himself with the Tories, his Whig patients deserted him. When a prominent Tory, Lord Oxford, found the coach of an equally prominent Whig waiting beside a house door, he refused to enter the premises. London also had its own Whig and Tory hospitals – St Thomas's for the former and Bart's for the latter. Who would wish to be treated by a member of the wrong party? Eton College was divided between the two factions, which resulted in frequent fights and quarrels. When Swift passed through Leicester in 1707 he observed that 'there is not a chambermaid, prentice or schoolboy in this whole town but what is warmly engaged on one side or the other'. The *Spectator* of 3 January 1712 noticed that 'the Whig and Tory ladies begin already to hang out different colours, and to show their principles in their head-dress'. Four years later the *Freeholder* observed that 'Whig and Tory are the words first learned by children'.

So there was more to it than the difference between low heels and high heels. Even Swift, who made the analogy, became a life-long Tory. The animus was such that the dominance of one faction over the other was enough to lead to imprisonment, exile, proscription, confiscation of estates, loss of office and even loss of life. The points of principle were manifold, concerning the role of monarchy itself, the structure of the Church of England, the basis of the Hanoverian succession, the nature of religious toleration, and the conduct of the war. When the conflict between money and land is thrown into the argument, the antagonisms could become fierce indeed. With the fundamental values and beliefs of the nation diverging so strongly, the queen and her ministers had to tread softly. This was by no means an 'age of stability', as it is sometimes described; in some respects it resembled the previous century without the imminent threat of armed conflict.

In the early years of the queen's reign the Whigs tended to be in the ascendant largely because they more eagerly supported Marlborough's war against the French; but there was no basic equipoise, since the parties moved incrementally up or down according to the atmosphere or debate of the day. One of these periodic changes occurred in the general election of the spring of 1705; neither side secured an outright victory, but the Whigs seemed to have overcome the more virulent Tories; as a result the Whigs and more moderate

Tories held the balance, with the latter under the leadership of Robert Harley.

Harley may now have been consigned to the dust of history but he can be exhumed as representative of the eighteenth-century politician, the politician *tout court*, the naked politician. He began his climb as a member of the Commons in 1689 and soon acquainted himself so thoroughly with all the ploys of parliament that he became known as 'Robin the Trickster'. Such was his success that he was elected Speaker in 1701, and soon became the inevitable candidate for higher office. As an orator he was neither fluent nor enlightening, but he made up for the lack of a wide view with a propensity for detail. He was a lover of intrigue and secrecy, relying for the most part on camouflage and dissimulation. He said nothing simple and nothing true. It was observed that he spoke so closely and unintelligibly that even he did not understand what he meant. Alexander Pope remarked that he 'talked of business in so confused a manner that you did not know what he was about; and every thing he went to tell you was in the epic way; for he always began in the middle'. This was an allusion to Horace's advice to the epic poet always to begin '*in medias res*' – in the middle of things.

Yet Harley's design was to obfuscate and confuse his hearers. He was secretive to the point of being mysterious, dilatory to the point of immobility. Lord Cowper, the lord chancellor, remarked that 'if any man was ever born under a necessity of being a knave, he was'. He was odd and awkward in appearance, always ready to bow and smile, but with what the duchess of Marlborough described as 'a constant awkward motion or other agitation of his head and body'.

Yet he was also a politician of apparent good humour, treating every colleague as a potential ally and friend; he was fond of good company, but he had no friends. He was convivial with a purpose; his bonhomie was such that he had a reputation as a conciliator who was able to make the most diverse men and ambitions meet. He knew the secret spring of any man, and was so keen a judge of character that he knew the surest means of touching it. He had no principles beyond those of self-advertisement and self-advancement, although loyalty to the throne may be counted as one of his virtues even if it might be construed as loyalty to his own prospects. He was made for the politics of conspiracy: a perennial contriver and intriguer who tied himself in knots with his specious promises. One year he was a Whig, and the next a Tory. As long as he supported Queen Anne, it made little practical difference. Behold the politician of the age in all his infirmity, and the long line that followed him. We may repeat William Blake's perception that 'nothing new occurs in identical existence; Accident ever varies, Substance can never suffer change nor decay'.

4

Hay day

The early years of Queen Anne's reign were blessed, like some miracle of the gods, by bountiful harvests. Between 1702 and 1708 the price of wheat was below the crucial figure of 30 shillings a quarter that generally provoked distress or riot. This naturally lowered the political and social pressures in the regions, as well as in London, where the market cost of bread was the single most important factor in public content. In the autumn of 1708 Squire Molesworth of Yorkshire wrote that 'we buy nothing but sugar and spice in the market, having all eatables and drinkables at home'. The superfluity of money, among the middling classes, accounts for the increasing purchase of clocks and mirrors, porcelain, carpets and curtains.

Yet not all was of the gods' making. Much can be attributed to aspirations reported in *Gulliver's Travels* that 'whoever could make two ears of corn, or two blades of grass to grow upon a spot of ground where only one grew before, would deserve better of mankind, and do more essential service to his country, than the whole race of politicians put together'. The names of these indispensable experimenters – Jethro Tull, Charles 'Turnip' Townshend, Arthur Young and his *Annals of Agriculture*, Robert Bakewell and his New Leicester sheep – are well enough known in the annals of agricultural progress.

But the specific innovations of a few highly intelligent and observant men could not in themselves have created the 'agricultural revolution' that has been dated from the mid-seventeenth century. If 'revolution' is too strong in its implications, we may at least refer to a long age of improvement. The obstacles were very real. The forces of conservatism ruled the countryside, with the tillage of land and the raising of animals changing little over many thousands of years; the old habits and prejudices of the farmers were as deep as the soil, and anyone who questioned their efficacy was doubting the very nature of providence. Until the middle of the seventeenth century, according to John Aubrey, 'even to attempt an improvement in husbandry, though it succeeded with profit, was looked upon with an ill eye'.

It would be hazardous to identify any specific reason for what became a period of significant innovation, in the later years of the seventeenth century, but some of the impetus may have been the result of the efforts of the Royal Society to investigate questions of drainage and crop rotation. When the level of prices fell in the early years of the eighteenth century there was even more reason to gather profit wherever it could be found.

The extent of further 'enclosure' was also one of the key agents of change. The 'enclosure' of land, making larger estates out of open fields and communal pasture, had been characteristic of English agriculture since the fourteenth century; it helped to arouse the Peasants' Revolt of 1381 and Jack Cade's rebellion of 1450. It became a matter of prominent public debate as a result of Thomas More's *Utopia*, published in 1516, in which More had condemned the conversion of arable land into pastoral. It was a case, he said, of the sheep eating the people.

The rise of population, the finite nature of resources, and the price of foodstuffs combined to make land the most desirable of all goods. When feudal ties were broken, when the laws and customs of manorial society ceased to operate, the demand from the prosperous was for land and more land. In the sixteenth and seventeenth centuries it was an instinctive law of being. The more land you owned, the greater you became. The more powerful you were, the easier it was to take away the customary but unwritten rights of the peasantry to gather the gleanings of the crop or to collect fire-wood; control of land was thereby extended.

A new race of landowners sprang up, and soon enough the landed gentry were a large component of parliament. They were protected, therefore, but the small freeholders and the cottagers were not. Those with the benefit of property purchased small parcels of further land in various locations, planning one day to join them together; they gained the manorial rights of parliamentary boroughs; they bought up 'advowsons' or land granted to the parson. The landowners wished to see their own territory from horizon to horizon, where the fruits of the field would be plentiful. To him who possessed much, more would surely follow.

Until the middle of the eighteenth century these enclosure agreements were organized by private treaty, in which no doubt bribery and blackmail played their part but in which common sense and mutual benefit played the larger role. The owners of the greatest number of strips in the old communal system might decide to join together and exchange land, for example, in order to provide soil for crops and pasture for husbandry. Another method was that organized by private Acts of Parliament. The first of these Acts was introduced in 1604 but the golden age of parliamentary enclosure, if that is the appropriate phrase, took place after the middle of the eighteenth century. It is more than likely that the parliamentary commissioners, employed to survey or to mediate land under dispute, tacitly supported the cause of agricultural reform; that was the spirit of the age. As a result, however, the balance was tipped against the independent voices of rural protest or the grievances of the 'little people'. It required the owners of approximately 75 per cent of the land to initiate proceedings, ignoring the large majority of smaller owners.

Once the farmer owned the land, however he had acquired it, he could do what he liked and had no need to consult his neigh-bours. The advent of better drainage, and the introduction of rotating crops, increased the yield; the hedging and fencing of private land, and the new building necessary for storage, helped to create a wholly new agricultural landscape. The larger farmers were in addition much more open to new methods that encouraged efficiency and productivity. This has been called the economy of scale, or the birth of an agricultural industry based upon market forces.

So the land of England was slowly changed. The distinctive 'checker-board' aspect of the domestic countryside, with hedges or dry-stone walls enclosing the fields, is a direct consequence of the developments of the mid-eighteenth century. At the beginning of the following century Thomas Batchelor, in 'The Progress of Agriculture' (1804), remarks upon the new landscape:

> And hawthorn fences, stretch'd from side to side,
> Contiguous pastures, meadows, fields divide.

The mellifluous balance of Batchelor's verse can be contrasted with the enclosure riots, the counter-petitions against proposed enclosure, and the anger against the withdrawal of common rights in the immediate countryside. Many of the small farmers, and the cottagers, were relegated to the status of labourers hired for money according to seasonal rates. The landed gentry, the richer owner-occupiers, and the larger tenants were in effective control. The peasants and the yeomen (best understood as smaller owner-occupiers), once the staple of the agricultural hierarchy, were diminished and ultimately disappeared. It represented a social revolution in the countryside.

When parliamentary commissioners were sent to a district in order to judge the merits of enclosure they were often met with threats, absence of cooperation, procrastination and wild rumours of local devastation; these hostile and often embittered responses embodied the last stand of custom, habit and tradition under threat from the forces of commerce and efficiency.

Yet the process of enclosure did materially affect the fertility and profitability of the land. It is unlikely, for example, that the farmers could have fed an ever-growing – and indeed rapidly accelerating – population without the benefits of large-scale production. The advantage of newly introduced crops – from sainfoin (or 'healthy hay') to lucerne (or alfalfa), from clover to the ubiquitous turnip – was evident in the fertility of the land that enriched the farmers and fattened the cattle. It soon became obvious and practicable to engage in regional specialization. The hops came from Kent, and the honey from Hampshire; Aylesbury ducks became as well known as Norfolk turkeys. In 1770 Arthur Young remarked that in the previous ten years there had been 'more experiments, more discoveries, and more general good sense displayed in the walks of agriculture than in an hundred preceding ones'.

It has been estimated that by the middle of the eighteenth century the labours of one-third of the population in the field were now able to furnish sustenance for the remaining two-thirds. This was in a period when the economy was still primarily one of agriculture, where the abundance of foodstuff was the most accurate measurement of health, vitality and standard of living. So it was that in 1797 the *Encyclopaedia Britannica* could claim that 'without any improper partiality to our own country, we are fully justified in asserting that Britain alone exceeds all modern nations in husbandry', even though no mention is made of the poverty, distress, dispossession and injustice that accompanied the change in agricultural conditions.

In this age of improvement, however, myriad societies grew up for the betterment of agriculture. It became one of the great preoccupations of the period. Tenants' dinners and farming clubs became the venue for discussions on agronomy; local societies fulfilled a similar purpose and shows, such as the Bath and West, encouraged experiment and innovation among their participants. There was nothing more potent than competition from a neighbour. At a later date periodicals such as the *Farmer's Magazine* and the *Farmers' Journal*, were issued and, in 1754, the Royal Society of Arts instituted a prize for agricultural improvement. As a crowning glory, a voluntary society was established in 1793 known as the Board of Agriculture, which was in a later century transmogrified into the Ministry of Agriculture, Fisheries and Food. The same board went on to distribute many packages of Swedish turnips to all the regions of the country, and to organize Humphry Davy's lectures on 'vegetable chemistry'. The changes in agriculture were all part of the inventive and experimental spirit that had been evident since the middle years of the seventeenth century.

Talk of 'improvement', therefore, was in the air. The new discoveries in metals, mines and minerals were considered to be the harbinger of larger progress while the contemporary dispute between 'Ancients' and 'Moderns' was in part designed to correct the prevalence of ancient errors. Improvement trusts were soon to be established for roads, rivers and canals.

The spirit of enquiry was not always manifest in the higher echelons of the land. When a national census of population was proposed in 1753 it was condemned in parliament by the member for York as 'subversive of the last remains of English liberty' and 'the most effective engine of rapacity and oppression'. When at last the population of Newcastle upon Tyne was counted, the result excited 'universal surprise' at the smallness of the total. The surprise derived from the belief that the population of the nation was fast outstripping its supply. The panic, like so many others, was without foundation.

Yet it is true that the trend of population was, from the early eighteenth century, only in one direction. It can be surmised that a population of some 6 million in 1714 rose to more than 6.5 million fifty years later; by 1781 it had reached 7.5 million and, by the beginning of the nineteenth century, 9 million. It was a history of continual, almost inexorable, development. It may be of some ancillary interest that by the middle of the eighteenth century the rapidly rising population was in the process of moving towards the north as well as to magnetic London.

The reasons for the rise in population have been variously stated. A decline in mortality, and an increase in fertility, are generally adduced as the principal causes; the absence of famine and the dearth of epidemic disease, the prevailing trends towards cleanliness, the increasing demand for labour, the abundance of food, the inclination towards early marriage and the growing success in the battle against sickness have all been cited. With such a wealth of circumstance the great work of fertilizing the soil, and feeding the population, could only go forward.

It was not a question of claiming domination over nature. This would have been considered blasphemous. But the results were clear. If you put the fleecy and fatty 'New Leicester' sheep of Robert Bakewell before the scrawny and ragged specimens of other farmers, the differences were obvious. Within the course of the eighteenth century the average weight of a sheep at Smithfield rose from 28 lb to 80 lb.

That power of change was not exclusively reserved for the beasts of the field. Beneath the soil lay the potential for transformations just as great. The first stage of industrial growth was marked by the transition from wood to coal, from organic to mineral, from a local and perishable source to a substance that seemed to be as old and as imperishable as time. Coal was the foundation. Yet first it had to be reached from the bowels of the earth.

The old fashion of excavating coal had been laborious and dangerous. The miners were lowered by rope many fathoms beneath the surface, where they took their place at the end of the track that they had already worked. They knelt, stooped or lay on one side in order to hack the coal from the main seam by means of pick, wedge or hammer; illustrations show them lying beneath immense layers of coal, as if they were likely at any moment to be crushed and obliterated. Their coal was taken away by pit ponies or by women and children who dragged large baskets from chains fastened to their waists. The hazards were everywhere, from gushing water to falling rocks and escaping steam, from asphyxiation by 'choke-damp' to suffocation in thick clouds of smoke and dust. Miners have always been associated with the dark and with subterranean depths; that is why they have generally been regarded with superstitious awe or irrational fear. They lived in darkness.

The inevitable cost to life was believed to be an economic, rather than a social, calamity. The loss of time, and men, meant loss of money. When the interests of the landowners and the mine-owners were at risk, of course, there was at least an incentive for remedial action. One of the most persistent and damaging problems was that of water gathering in the bases and hollows of the mines. 'Horse-gins', by which a wooden gear mechanism was driven by a horse trudging in a circle, bringing up buckets of water, was a first and not particularly efficient response; the contraption was also used to bring up coal.

The credit for the first 'steam engine', momentous though it may seem, is not certainly known. The palm is generally given to Thomas Savery who in 1698 patented his version of an atmospheric pump. An advertisement in the *Postman* of March 1702 recommended 'Captain Savery's Engines which raise Water by the force of Fire in any reasonable quantities and to any height . . . these are to give notice to all proprietors of mines and collieries which are encumbered with water, that they may be furnished with engines to drain the same'. The 'fire' was a furnace and boiler that provided the steam; the steam created the atmospheric pressure that moved the piston; the piston itself set in motion a pump. The menacing water was thus drawn off.

Savery's engine was refined by a Dartmouth ironmonger, Thomas Newcomen, who by the first decade of the eighteenth century had devised an engine that could reach much greater depths. The first Newcomen engine was in use by 1712 and, at the time of Savery's death in 1715, seven or eight were already in operation. Fifty more were erected over the succeeding twenty years; by the end of the century more than 350 had been installed. The success of the engine is testimony to its efficacy as well as its necessity, only eventually outperformed by the inventive works of James Watt.

It was not necessarily elegant, however, and Samuel Smiles records that

> the working of a Newcomen engine is a clumsy and apparently a very painful process, accompanied by an extraordinary amount of wheezing, sighing, creaking and bumping. When the pump descends there is heard a plunge, a heavy sigh, and a loud bump; then as it rises, and the sucker begins to act, there is heard a creak, a wheeze, another bump, and then a strong rush of water as it is lifted and poured out.

The bulk and complexity of the first engines may have surprised contemporaries in the same manner as the early computers of the 1950s baffled the public. As with the computer, too, the most radical developments were not properly recognized or understood. The steam engine, for the first time, was able to convert thermal energy into kinetic energy. It turned heat into work. This was the source of power that would completely outstrip all previous resources, human or hydraulic, and would lead ineluctably to the enormous increase in industrial productivity that would one day earn the name of revolution. The wheezing and sighing engine changed the world.

5

The prose of gold

The late king had always nourished hopes of a union between Scotland and England, largely for defensive and military reasons; he did not want a Jacobite enemy at his back door, and over the centuries the Scots had notoriously been seen to favour the French. There had already been attempts at dynastic union between the two nations, but they had come to nothing. As dual monarch James VI of Scotland, who in 1603 also became James I of England, joined two crowns but not two realms; still, it was a precedent. Cromwell gathered Scotland in his embrace during the short-lived Commonwealth, but again the union fell apart.

Soon after the accession of Anne, however, a commission was established in 1702 to examine the long-standing dilemma. There was at first a signal lack of enthusiasm on both sides for the proposed arrangement. The leader of the Tories in the Commons suggested that union with Scotland was akin to marrying a vagrant 'and whoever married a beggar could only expect a louse for her portion'. Yet reasons of state, and of defence, were more powerful than petty insults. In 1703 the Scottish parliament passed two Acts, of Security and of Peace and War, that threatened the governance of England. The Scots refused to confer their crown on the Protestant house of Hanover. They still yearned after the Scottish Stuart succession. The second Act declared that, on the death of the queen, the Scots would reserve to themselves any right of peace or war with both France and her allies. They might even withdraw their troops from Marlborough's armies.

The prospect of an unfriendly power on the northern border concentrated the minds of the English politicians. The Whigs needed no persuasion of the need for union; their unequivocal support of the war, and their undeviating loyalty to the Hanoverians, made the choice inevitable. The Tories may in turn not have wished to seem openly disloyal to the queen or the administration, but in any case Anne took the precaution of nominating only one of them to the English commission. So the negotiations took place in an atmosphere of relative good grace amply mollified by bribes and other less overt forms of chicanery.

The commissioners convened at the Cockpit, a suite of offices in Whitehall, during the spring and summer of 1706. The two sides did not meet but instead preferred to exchange written suggestions and proposals, liberally larded with cash and promises to sweeten the Scottish lairds. The Scots contingent also hoped for a large portion of what was known as 'The Equivalent', the sum paid by England to satisfy the creditors of the previous Scottish administration. The 'treaty of Union' can be considered as a deal brokered under the table, therefore, but many of the Scottish commissioners were already in favour of a union with England.

The Scottish economy had been severely damaged by the continuing and apparently endless war with France. With foreign ports closed to its exports, the country more than ever required free trade with England in such commodities as cattle and linen. There seemed to be no doubt that the economic consequences of union would be beneficial. Adam Smith, the high priest of the Scottish economy, later wrote that

> The union opened the market of England to the Highland cattle ... Of all the commercial advantages, however, which Scotland has derived from the union with England, this rise in the price of cattle is, perhaps, the greatest. It has not only raised the value of all highland estates, but it has, perhaps, been the principal cause of the improvement of the low country.

In fact the treaty of Union was able to establish the largest free trade area in the world, and the manifest disadvantages of Scottish industry and agriculture were gradually removed.

Many of the Scottish people, however, were not so happy at the prospect of this arranged marriage. They had no wish to tie themselves to a richer and more powerful state, with all the dangers of being swallowed alive and becoming a Celtic appanage of the English Crown like Cornwall. Why should they turn their backs upon the old Stuart dynasty?

Nevertheless the various Acts of the 'treaty of Union' were passed by the beginning of May 1707, thus incorporating two nations or what Jonathan Swift called 'our crazy double-bottomed realm'. In effect the treaty created a single sovereignty between the two nations and a single parliament, including Scottish representatives, but it also preserved the Kirk, Scottish law and Scottish local administration. From this time forward England, Scotland and Wales were united under the title of Great Britain.

The new flag, incorporating the red cross of St George and the white saltire of St Andrew, was popularly known as 'The Union' but it would of course make little difference to the war now being fought under its auspices. The success of Blenheim had been succeeded by little but disappointment and division among the allies, with neither Italy nor the Netherlands rescued from the French. The duke of Marlborough wished to invade France, and thus cut off the bull at the neck, but his fellow combatants gave him little, if any, support. They were too faint-hearted, and in any case too eager to defend their own territories.

Marlborough returned to the grim warfare in the Spanish Netherlands and, with the assistance of his Dutch and Danish allies, did manage to command a great victory at Ramillies in the spring of 1706. The French commander, Marshal Villars, described it as 'the most shameful, humiliating and disastrous of routs'. As a result of the total defeat of their army the French withdrew from the Spanish Netherlands and abandoned a number of key towns; they retreated from Antwerp and Ostend, Bruges and Ghent and Lille.

The Bourbons were now in general disarray throughout their European possessions; an exception, perhaps, could be made for the Bourbon dynasty in Madrid that still held power through Louis's grandson, Philip V, who remained the king of Spain for virtually forty years after a brief abdication in favour of his son. But now all seemed to be going well for the English and their allies. The capture of Lille in particular promised the key to Paris, and as a result Louis sent an envoy to The Hague for clandestine negotiations.

But the atmosphere in the English camp was not conducive to a treaty. Marlborough wrote to a Dutch general that 'I am one of those who believe that France is not yet reduced to her just bounds, and that nothing can be more hurtful to us on this occasion than seeming overforward to clap up a hasty peace'. So the terms of any treaty were to be formidable. The least of them included the formal recognition of Queen Anne as legitimate sovereign in contrast to the spurious authority of the 'Old Pretender' who in the spring of 1708 added disaster to misfortune with a botched landing at the Firth of Forth; the proposed terms also included the demolition of the port at Dunkirk and the recall of Philip V from Madrid.

Louis XIV seemed prepared to yield all, or almost all. France and England had just suffered the coldest winters in living memory; the Thames became a Frost Fair and Lady Wentworth wrote to her brother of 'post-boys being brought in by their horses to their stages froze to their horses stone dead'. Yet the bitter cold had more severely affected France, already afflicted as it was by famine, shortages and a general sense of failure.

Louis would go so far and no further. He could never sign the thirty-seventh article of the proposed peace which demanded that he remove his grandson from Madrid, by force if necessary, and replace him with the Habsburg Charles. It was an insult. To eject a member of his Bourbon house by arms, in favour of a Habsburg? It could never be. It is possible, even plausible, that Marlborough and his English negotiators made these demands precisely in order that Louis would refuse them and thus continue the conflict. The spoils of war were still very great, especially for a noble leader such as Marlborough. The duke had even asked the queen to confer upon him the title of captain-general for life, but Anne wisely rejected this as unconstitutional. Still, he had done sufficiently well. Blenheim Palace and Marlborough House were only two of the stone baubles he had collected.

The wealth and eminence of Marlborough were of course

resented by those who opposed both him and the war itself; anger and frustration were also directed at the dominant Whig administration that held the purse-strings of the revenue. The Whig financiers were in any case growing rich on the loans they made to the administration, while the Tory squires were paying for government borrowing with heavy land taxes. The equation was not as simple as this, but this was how it appeared at the time. Nothing could be more onerous or more unfair. The Tories opposed the war on grounds of strategy as well as expense. Why fight on behalf of the Dutch who had for centuries been the great trade rivals of England? Why fight obscure battles on the continental mainland when nothing seemed to be gained from them?

The crisis in fact came with the battle of Malplaquet, south-west of Mons, in the early autumn of 1709. The English army and its allies won a paper victory at enormous cost, suffering double the enemy's number of fatalities. The French withdrew in good order, while the English left more than 20,000 corpses on a battlefield that quickly became known as 'the bloodiest in Europe'. Queen Anne sent no letter of congratulation to the duke. If the French could still fight in so spirited and determined a fashion, despite imminent projections of their collapse, who could foresee the end of war? The Tories called out against the carnage incurred, if not devised, by the Whig administration. Marshal de Villars, the commander of the French forces, wrote to the king that 'if it please God to give your majesty's enemies another such victory, they are ruined'. The original quote came from Pyrrhus, who was of course the father of the Pyrrhic victory.

The Whigs had now another enemy of quite a different type. Dr Henry Sacheverell, Fellow of Magdalen College, Oxford, had already alienated the Whigs by his fervent high church tendencies. With the assistance of a high Tory lord mayor, however, and some fellow travellers he was chosen to preach before the City corporation at St Paul's Cathedral on the signal occasion of 5 November 1709. He was known to be an orator with few rivals on the religious stage. 'He came into the pulpit,' William Bissett wrote in *The Modern Fanatic* (1710), 'like a Sybil to the mouth of her cave, or a pythoness upon her tripod, with such an air of fierceness and rage, as is not possible to express.' With pursed lips and keen ferocious glare, he had all the appearance of a martinet. He was not learned but he was authoritative; he was not clever but he was persuasive. He was one of those clerics who can repeat the clichés of the age as if they were written in letters of fire.

His sermon was entitled 'The Perils of False Brethren, in Church and State'. The 'false brethren' were not difficult to identify; in fact they were displayed by Sacheverell like so many puppets on poles. His attack was upon religious nonconformists, in particular the dissenting brethren whom the Whigs sought to protect and who had been granted freedom of worship by the Act of Toleration twenty years before. They had been chosen, according to the preacher, to rule a land of ungodliness and licence. In a previous sermon, delivered in 1702, he had declared that 'presbytery and republicanism go hand in hand', by which he meant that the levelling principle of nonconformity could be applied to politics as well as to religion. It was the old argument, adumbrated by James I in his remark of 'no bishop, no king'.

But Sacheverell now proclaimed it with unparalleled ferocity. He launched into a tirade against religious toleration. He practically accused the dissenters of being regicides. He advocated to the utmost the principle of 'passive obedience' by which the sovereign must be implicitly obeyed; any dissent should be treated as sinful and as unlawful. This could of course be considered to be an implied criticism of the Glorious Revolution that had removed James II from the throne, but more immediately it could be construed by some as a momentous attack upon the Whig cause and its advocates.

The Whigs were at this moment in an unenviable position, beset by the enemies of the continental war and by their opponents whispering in the queen's ear that all was not well in the state. In these circumstances, the best mode of defence was considered to be attack. It was decided, against the advice of Anne herself, that the doctor should be brought before the Commons to explain himself. In the middle of December the Commons condemned his statements as 'malicious, scandalous and seditious libels'; he was placed in custody and impeached for 'high crimes and misdemeanours', for which he could be sentenced to life imprisonment.

The threat of the sledgehammer, raised against a relatively small nut, confirmed all the public suspicions concerning an over-mighty

Whig administration intent upon preserving its own interests. What had Henry Sacheverell done but proclaim his loyalty to the established Church and to cry out that its privileges were being violated? What was the high crime in being a staunch Anglican? Those who attacked him, indeed, might themselves fall under the suspicion of subversion.

It is a matter of some interest that the 'mob', or the 'rabble', or whatever other word covered the ordinarily unremarked inhabitants of London, was traditionalist; the people were by instinct loyal to the established authorities of monarchy and religion, and any cry of 'the Church in danger' could bring them out onto the streets. They might never have attended an Anglican service in their lives but the threat against the Church was enough to rouse them.

As the time for the trial of Sacheverell approached, the London crowds gathered with the aim of sacking the meeting houses of dissenters; the dwelling houses of certain nonconformist ministers were also ransacked, the books and furniture destroyed. The pulpits and pews, even the wainscot, of several conventicles were brought to Lincoln's Inn Fields where they were burned on a pile to the shouts of 'High Church and Sacheverell!' The carriage of the queen herself was stopped while the people cried out 'God save your Majesty and the Church! We hope your Majesty is for Doctor Sacheverell!' Daniel Defoe wrote that 'the women lay aside their tea and chocolate, leave off visiting after dinner, and forming themselves into cabals, turn privy councillors and settle the affairs of state . . . mobs, rabbles and tumults possess the streets . . . even the little boys and girls talk politics'.

The trial before the House of Lords began in Westminster Hall towards the end of February, to the excitement of a packed audience of spectators who had paid heavily for the privilege; a box had been constructed so that the queen might view the proceedings without being seen. Sacheverell himself arrived every morning in a glass coach, surrounded by a multitude of people with weapons and drawn swords. The defence rose to plead that the doctor had done nothing more than to defend the Church in a sermon that had been 'made criminal by a laboured construction of doubtful words'.

Four days later Henry Sacheverell rose to defend himself, in a speech that had been written for him by the much more learned and eloquent bishop of Rochester, Francis Atterbury; Sacheverell claimed that he was only an ordinary priest who had dared to speak out of love for his country and for his religion against blasphemers and infidels. He had won the argument even before he began to speak, and the Whig leaders had cause to regret their ill-timed attack upon a popular favourite. He was deemed to be guilty by a narrow majority, and the sentence was a light one; instead of being consigned to the Tower for life, as he was threatened, his sermons were to be burned and he was suspended from preaching for three years.

In the eyes of the country this was tantamount to acquittal and a severe reprimand for the Whig authorities who had prosecuted him. The crowds of London became wild with excitement; bonfires were lit in the streets and windows illuminated by candles or torches in the old fashion for celebrating a great foreign victory. When Sacheverell read prayers at St Saviour's, Southwark, the press of worshippers was almost too great. The country towns also rang with the bells of victory, and it seemed to many that the national mood was the harbinger of a new Tory era of Church and State.

The election of the following autumn seemed to burnish those hopes ever brighter. The Tories took the lead over the Whigs by a majority of two to one. The newly established government was led by a statesman who has been mentioned before, the political con-volvulus Robert Harley, whose genuine fidelity to the queen was matched by a desire to create a 'moderate' ministry. Yet he had not anticipated the extreme Tory members who were deposited in the Commons by the high tide of their party's success in the election; they formed an association, the October Club, in memory of their famous victory. They may have discharged more spittle than sense, and were described by Defoe as 'moon-blind high-flyers'. Some opponents explicitly attacked them for an attachment to the Stuart cause but this was only barely justifiable; it might more fairly be said that they were Jacobean when drunk and Hanoverian when sober. In that, they embodied a large number of Tories who may have dreamed of a return to the old order but knew well enough that their welfare, their finances and their safety depended upon the house of Hanover.

The October Club, however, represented a powerful combination of those who were weary of war, even more weary of Whigs, and suspicious of the financial cabal that controlled military expenditure and domestic taxation. They were suspicious of Harley, too, who seemed to be willing to admit some of the Whigs into the new administration. Some believed that the spoils of the electoral war should go to the victors rather than to the defeated.

The political debates and divisions have to a certain extent been preserved in aspic by an age that includes the names of Joseph Addison and Richard Steele as well as Defoe, Swift, Congreve and Pope. It can fairly be claimed, in fact, that the reign of Anne represented the golden age of political journalism. By the time the election of autumn 1710 was called, the war between the pamphlets and the periodicals had begun in earnest. Harley in particular had a keen eye for what at a different date might be called 'public relations'. He scooped Defoe out of prison, where the writer had been banished for a contentious pamphlet, and placed him on the payroll both as a tame journalist and as a travelling spy. Defoe had already begun the publication of the *Review*, more formally known as *A Review of the Affairs of France*, in which he employed the events of the day as a force for moral and political satire; it came out in quarto form on three days a week, with digests of domestic and foreign politics, art, commerce, science and trade. It lasted for nine years, and Defoe wrote almost every word of it, steering English journalism in an opinionated direction from which it has never since veered.

Yet Harley also employed Swift. He had a good eye for argument and invective in the most promising of his contemporaries. Harley may have paid Defoe, but he flattered Swift whose status as a gentleman and a scholar was a little higher than that of Defoe as hack and a quondam tile-maker. Harley took Swift with him to Windsor, and the writer was one of the first to attend Harley's Saturday Club dinners in York Buildings. So Swift's *Examiner* was conducted on very different lines from those of Defoe's *Review*; it had more style and scholarship, but less power and pugnacity. Defoe's readership was largely made up of urban merchants and shopkeepers or, as one contemporary unkindly put it, the periodical was 'read by cobblers and porters'; it was essentially appealing to urban loyalists. Swift addressed himself in principle to the rural gentry and the landed gentlemen. Harley needed both constituencies; so he had Swift in one pocket and Defoe in the other.

Swift was, however, in an ambiguous position. The earl of Orrery wrote that Swift 'was elated with the appearance of enjoying ministerial confidence. He enjoyed the shadow; the substance was detained from him. He was employed, not trusted.' Swift believed himself to be a deep-sea diver in politics but Orrery claimed that 'he was suffered only to sound the shallows nearest the shore . . . perhaps the deeper bottoms were too muddy for his inspection'.

His boredom, hurt and disgust at the lies and false promises made to him by the prominent English politicians may have materially added to the weight of his misanthropy in his later and more celebrated writings. In *Gulliver's Travels*, in particular, he seems to be one thoroughly disabused by human deception and disguise; his principal responses are those of mockery and disdain at all the claptrap of the world; he feels disgust but not pity, a disgust combined with the horror of life.

In the spring of 1709 a small folio half-sheet of four columns began to appear three days a week at the price of a penny; it contained an essay on the manners or morals of the day, together with notes and sketches from the various coffee-houses of the City. It was of a moderate Whiggish persuasion, but preserved its chaste and neutral demeanour. The *Tatler* was a London periodical, and in the capital the Whigs were the voice of refinement and discrimination. It professed to teach 'public persons what to think' but promised to contain material 'which may be of entertainment to the fair sex'. It would also provide 'accounts of gallantry, pleasure, and entertainments' under the names of the various coffee-houses and chocolate-houses where its reporters took their refreshment.

Its editor, Richard Steele, assumed the name of Isaac Bickerstaff and adopted the persona of a man of sense and tolerance, not at all willing to subject other parties to superlative praise or to excessive blame. He was a Whig who knew how to keep his temper, especially when the climate grew colder. He supported Marlborough while professing impartiality, and conveyed the essential values of Whig policy as somehow identical with common sense and good taste.

Within two years the *Tatler* had transmogrified into the *Spectator* under the editorship of Steele himself and Joseph Addison. It maintained the Whiggish tone of its predecessor even as the Tory administration of Robert Harley took over the machinery of government, and thus preserved its neutral urbanity. It covered disparate subjects deemed to be of interest to its audience, from the nature of whoredom to the metrics of *Paradise Lost*; it described a night at the theatre and chronicled immediate fashions, like a sudden efflorescence of coloured hoods at the beginning of 1712, everything pushed forward by the stream of forgetfulness that is human life.

The *Spectator* had disavowed any partisan affiliations, with Addison declaring that 'my paper has not in it a single word of news, a reflection in politics nor a stroke of party'. His purpose was to teach manners and not measures, and he added that 'I shall be ambitious to have it said of me that I have brought philosophy out of closets and libraries, schools and colleges, to dwell in clubs and assemblies, at tea-tables and in coffee houses.'

This represents the refining tendency of the eighteenth century. The *Spectator* would civilize the Jacobites, the enthusiasts, the high church Tories and the ferocious partisans, out of existence. The great medium of truth would be sociable discourse and, of all the humours in the casebook of Hippocrates, only good sense would remain. The moral did not need to be emblazoned on the masthead of the periodical since it represented the temperate and tolerant society, the virtuous commonwealth, that was considered to be the proper and appropriate consequence of the revolution of 1688.

Of course the absence of enthusiasm, and the decline in earnestness of all kinds, might in turn arouse cynicism and fatalism. The plays of Congreve, written just before the accession of Queen Anne, are populated by characters who are naturally and instinctively deceitful; the world is a great theatre of folly, in which truth and virtue are nowhere to be found. It is a sphere of wit and foolery, animated only by sexual greed and the pursuit of money; the men lie, wheedle and betray; the women are lustful, silly and untrustworthy. The plays of Richard Brinsley Sheridan, at a slightly later date, are preoccupied with hypocrisy and fraudulence in the service of money; metaphors of banking and finance, so central to the period, hold together the dramatic narratives in bands of gold. Sheridan had nothing but contempt for the vogue of sentiment that came to be so fashionable in the mid-eighteenth century, regarded by many as a trite and naïve refusal to countenance the real truths of the age. 'If you have any regard for me,' Sir Peter Teazle says in *The School for Scandal* (1777), 'never let me hear you utter anything like a sentiment.'

We also have two more voices, from Congreve's *The Double Dealer* (1693), to add to the cacophony of the period after the Glorious Revolution.

> *Brisk:* I have a violent passion for your ladyship, seriously.
> *Lady Froth:* Seriously? Ha ha ha!
> *Brisk:* Seriously, ha ha ha. Gad I have, for all I laugh.
> *Lady Froth:* Ha ha ha! What d'ye think I laugh at? Ha ha ha.

6

Waiting for the day

The desire now was for peace. After ten years of war against the French the nation was weary. The new Tory government, elected overwhelmingly in the autumn of 1710, was all too willing to bow to the public demand. When the new parliament assembled, and the duke of Marlborough had taken his accustomed seat in the House of Lords, the queen commenced her speech by announcing: 'I am glad that I can now tell you that notwithstanding the arts of those who delight in war, both place and time are appointed for opening the treaty of a general peace.' This was a Tory kick against the previous Whig administration but in the subsequent debate Marlborough took exception to the insinuation that he had prolonged the war artificially for reasons of private convenience or profit. When he made his appearance at court in the last week of the year Swift noted in a letter to his close friend, Esther Johnson, that 'nobody hardly took notice of him'.

The duke's principal political opponent had meanwhile become the hero of the hour when, in the spring of 1711, he had been the victim of an unsuccessful assassination by a French spy. Robert Harley had been stabbed twice in the chest but an elaborately ornate and padded waistcoat saved him from serious injury. His wonderful escape was a cause of much triumphalism, and in honour of his safe recovery the queen ennobled him as the earl of Oxford and earl Mortimer as well as promoting him to be lord high treasurer. In this superior capacity he lost no time in prosecuting his opponents still further and, the evening after the queen had denounced 'those who delight in war', he instigated proceedings against Marlborough for bribery and corruption.

The terms for a peace between France and England, so long looked for, were already being discussed in the course of secret negotiations at the beginning of 1711. The principal tenet, if it can be so called, was that the two countries would enter a secret understanding even at the expense of their allies. A Franco-British treaty would be enough to cow them into agreement. The second article would allow Philip V to remain on the throne of Spain in exchange for certain commercial concessions to the British in Europe and on the American continent. There was even some discussion of the 'Old Pretender' returning to England if he espoused the cause of Anglicanism but, in the unlikely event of James Edward becoming an apostate, it remained mere talk. It is a measure, however, of the crucial significance that the Stuart succession still held in English politics.

In November 1711 Jonathan Swift issued one of his most incendiary and effective pamphlets, 'The Conduct of the Allies', in which he declared that 'no reasonable man . . . can be of the opinion for continuing the war'. He accused the Whig oligarchs of placing 'a sort of artificial wealth of funds and stocks in the hands of those who for ten years before had been plundering the public'; he believed that 'we are thus become the dupes and bubbles of Europe'. He accused Marlborough of 'that unmeasurable love of wealth, which his best friends allow to be his predominant passion'. Towards the conclusion of his polemic he states that 'we have been fighting for the ruin of the public interest, and the advancement of a private. We have been fighting to raise the wealth and grandeur of a particular family; to enrich usurers and stock-jobbers; and to cultivate the pernicious designs of a faction, by destroying the landed interest.' It was a comprehensive catalogue of ills.

In the following month the duke of Marlborough was dismissed by the queen from all offices of state. His carriage was chased by angry members of the populace, crying out 'Stop thief!' The victor of Blenheim, and the saviour of Europe from Louis, had good reason to contemplate the turning of Fortune's wheel. 'Ah,' Boethius had written in *The Consolation of Philosophy*, 'dull-witted mortal. If Fortune begin to stay still, she is no longer Fortune.' Marlborough and his wife soon decamped to the continent where they hoped to find more enduring allies. Many of the Whig lords were still supporting the duke, and the further prosecution of the war, but Queen Anne managed to dilute their partisanship by creating twelve new peers on the first day of 1712. Now the House of Lords was in agreement with the Commons.

Sarah, duchess of Marlborough, had already fallen far out of favour. She was an earnest and argumentative Whig who had eventually exasperated and alienated the queen. Her supplanter in the position of royal confidante was Abigail Masham, who became 'keeper of the queen's purse'; Masham was also cousin to Robert Harley and was believed to have maintained the interests of that sinuous survivor. There were further rumours of over-familiarity between Masham and the queen, with what a ballad called 'some dark deeds at night' between the elderly sovereign and her servant. The queen's gout and general ill-health would not have encouraged physical passion, but she may have needed familiar female companionship to withstand the ills of a predominantly male world. The more extreme sexual gossip seems on the face of it unfounded, therefore, but it was still assiduously promoted by the duchess of Marlborough in revenge for her usurpation.

When the eventual peace conference between France and England opened in Utrecht at the end of January 1712, much had already been agreed in clandestine negotiations. When the treaty was eventually signed in the spring of 1713, it had become clear that Great Britain was a world power fit to challenge France, and that in addition it was now the dominant naval power with bases at Gibraltar and Minorca in the Mediterranean. The British took firmer control of North America, with the possession of Newfoundland and Hudson's Bay. And they had been granted the additional bonus of the *asiento*, a treaty that allowed English vessels to ship African slaves to the Spanish colonies of the Americas. The cup of maritime supremacy flowed over, and the articles signed at Utrecht were able to keep the peace between France and England for the next fifteen years.

The rejoicing was by no means universal. The war had continued during the course of the negotiations, and the duke of Ormonde had been sent out to replace Marlborough in command of the English forces. But it was not intended that he should compromise any quiet diplomacy with rough action; he was sent what was called a 'restraining order' that prevented him from taking part in any battle or participating in any siege. All was to be quiet on the various fronts. It did not take long for the allies to become acquainted with the position of their erstwhile colleagues who had suddenly become non-combatants; they reacted as much with disbelief as with fury. They had effectively been deserted on the field of battle.

One of those allies was George, prince-elector of Hanover, who like the other princes and commanders felt that he had been betrayed by the Tory administration desperate for peace. His interests had been sold behind his back. It was clear enough that England would get rid of her supposed friends as soon as they were unnecessary to her. So grew the myth of 'perfidious Albion'. Unhappily for the Tories, however, George, heir to the house of Hanover, was more than likely to become the next king of England. How were Harley and others to shield themselves from his wrath?

In the last year of the queen's reign, party loyalties, therefore, were screwed to the highest pitch. To vote with the Tories for peace was tantamount to disowning the coming prince. To vote with the Whigs for war was to ignore the fervent wishes of the nation. The volatile state of the nation's politics was compounded by the problem of the 'Old Pretender'. It was widely assumed that the queen secretly favoured her half-brother, James Francis Edward Stuart, in the place of the Hanoverians; this may have been true of some of her ministers, but there is no reason to believe that she harboured any such desire. She was fervently Protestant, and could not in conscience have endured the return of a committed Catholic. Since James soon publicly refused to renounce the old faith, the possibility of his succeeding Anne became ever more remote.

Some ministers and councilors still faced both ways, sending messages of assurance to the Stuart court while continuing to deal with the house of Hanover. The duke of Marlborough, now on enforced leave on the continent, was actively preparing his committed forces at Bruges, Ghent and elsewhere for action on behalf of the house of Hanover if it were threatened; yet at the same time he was maintaining contact with the Pretender. This vertiginous ambiguity, performed on a tightrope between two eminences, is an extreme form of the ambivalence felt by the nation between the candidates for the throne.

It is difficult to know, amongst all the bitterness and controversy, where the balance lay. It was said that the first claimant who arrived in England after the death of the queen, James or George, would be welcomed as sovereign. This was silly. The matter of succession had become a poisoned well of suspicion, rumour and intrigue. In a pamphlet of 1713, 'Reasons against the Succession of the House of Hanover', Daniel Defoe records that 'the poor despicable scullions learn to cry "High Church; no Dutch kings; no Hanover!" that they may do it dexterously when they come into the next mob' while their Whig antagonists 'clamour "No French peace, no Pretender, no Popery!"' In the spring of the following year Richard Steele wrote that 'according to the situation of affairs, nothing but divine providence can prevent a civil war within a few years'. These were the gloomy prognostications of those who understood public affairs best. The age of Anne was not an age of stability.

The Tories themselves were at odds one with another. Some of them even crossed the Channel to attend the court of the Pretender while others remained quiet and in a phrase of the era 'waited for the day'. Still others were more moderate or more realistic in their expectations, calmly awaiting the arrival of a Hanoverian king, while others actively supported the Hanoverian cause; they were known as the 'Whimsicals'. The Whigs also remained in a state of confusion, indecision and alarm. Some of them, fearing a *coup d'état* arranged by the 'Old Pretender' and his allies, seem to have arranged themselves in military associations with arms and troops at the ready; but these may have been paper brigades born out of fear and rumour.

The confusion and anxiety of course grew worse as the queen's health began to fail. She had said herself earlier in the year that she had suffered from 'an aguish disposition, succeeded by a fit of the gout', which could mean anything or nothing. Yet her perilous condition did not affect her frantic councillors who, in her own words, 'neither regarded her health, her life, nor her peace'. The future of the country was for them too important to wait for an old woman. Their arguments continued over her deathbed, with the voices of the warring parties echoing through the corridors of state.

It was all too much. She was becoming feverish and bewildered. Her lord chancellor, Lord Harcourt, whispered to her the name of the duke of Shrewsbury; the duke had recently seen service in France and Ireland and, more importantly, he had never professed himself to be wholly Whig or wholly Tory. The white staff of the lord high treasurer would be in safe hands. It was the last appointment she ever made. On the following morning she was dead, with the doctor recording that 'the immediate occasion of the queen's death proved to be the transition of the gouty humour' from knees and feet to nerves and brain. It had flown upwards and taken the sovereign with it.

7

The great Scriblerus

The *Memoirs of the Extraordinary Life, Works and Discoveries of Martinus Scriblerus* was composed privately in 1714 by the Scriblerus Club. The society itself was a parody of the multifarious clubs, literary and artistic and philosophical, that became most prominent at the beginning of the eighteenth century. It was itself composed of two clubs or groups of men with shared affinities. One was a Tory assembly that included Swift and Bolingbroke. The other comprised younger and more facetious men, among them Pope and Gay. They were joined together as the Society of Brothers which began to meet in 1711. Their principal opponents were the Whig authors, such as Addison and Steele, who circulated about the *Spectator*.

It was Pope who in the autumn of 1713 helped to form the Scriblerus Club out of the 'Brothers' with the proposal for a monthly satire that would parody the age. They met on Saturdays in the rooms of John Arbuthnot at St James's Palace; Arbuthnot was personal physician to Queen Anne as well as an author. He is still the least well known of the company. He was born in north-east Scotland but he migrated to London in his twenties, when his first book was published. It was entitled *Of the Laws of Chance* and was addressed to the prevalent taste for gambling, including back-gammon, dice and the lottery. Gamblers, after all, were at the political forefront of the age. Arbuthnot discovered, or his colleagues discovered for him, a vein of wit and satire that made him the perfect companion and co-worker.

Swift said that the Scriblerus Club represented 'a friendship among men of genius', and Pope returned the compliment by remarking that it comprised 'some of the greatest wits of the age'. In the early summer of 1714 Pope wrote to Swift that 'Dr Arbuthnot is singular in his opinion, and imagines your only design is to attend at full leisure to the life and adventures of Scriblerus . . . The top of my own ambition is to contribute to that great work, and I shall translate Homer by the by.' Swift himself remarked, some years after, that 'I have often endeavoured to establish a friendship among all men of genius, and would fain have it done. There are seldom above three or four contemporaries, and if they could be united would drive the world before them.' One of its members, Robert Harley, had of course been first lord of the treasury, and the queen's principal minister, since 1711, and so its significance became ever greater.

The *Memoirs* was at first designed to become part of the satirical periodical that Pope had proposed. Instead it became a single treatise, a mock biography of a foolish and gullible hero who has all the makings of a learned simpleton. The text was revised and enlarged from time to time, culminating in its publication in the second volume of Pope's prose works in 1741.

Satire had become the single most important response to public events in an age that eschewed polemic and serious argument. You were not a gentleman if you took life too seriously. It was also a question of common sense; a word that, with its meaning of 'good sound practical sense', is first noted by the *Oxford English Dictionary* in a text of 1726. But that common sense must be combined with moderation or, as Pope had put it in *An Essay on Criticism* (1711), 'not dully prepossest, nor blindly right'. Amiability was also a key term of the time, but it had its limits. Balance was the key. It was part of the movement of the time with the disquisitions of the Royal Society on the one side and the essays of the *Spectator* on the other; it represented an easy plainness, a modest and sensible attempt at truth. The historian of the Royal Society, William Sprat, characterized the prose of scientific discourse as 'a close, naked, natural way of speaking; positive expressions; clear senses; a native easiness: bringing all things as near the mathematical plainness, as they can'. The men of letters, poets and dramatists as well as essayists, were intent upon using to best advantage the language that men do use. It was said by a contemporary critic, Colley Cibber, that the plays of John Vanbrugh seemed 'no more than his common conversation committed to paper'.

The rhetoric of speculation, and of enthusiasm, was now being displaced by the prose of fact and opinion; satire was taking the place of dogmatism and, although the age of theological disquisition was by no means dead, there was an emphasis now upon 'characters' and 'observations' in the public prints. This helped to reanimate the discourse of the political news-writers and pamphleteers. The essay was the true sermon of the period and, as the *Spectator* noted in a dramatic context, 'the town has an opportunity of doing itself justice in supporting the representations of passion, sorrow, indignation, even despair itself, within the rules of decency, honour and good breeding'.

The growing class of readers, or what soon became known as 'the reading public', fastened upon what was contemporary and what was immediate; it took an unusual and even perhaps unprecedented interest in the affairs and interests of polite society. It was the immediate bed from which rose the novel in all of its forms, and of which the journalists Swift and Defoe were two of the most accomplished practitioners. And what might else explain the rise of what could be called the conversational, rather than rhetorical, drama at the command of Congreve, Vanbrugh and John Gay?

If we are to hear, or overhear, the voice of the age of Anne, therefore, it is perhaps in the pages of its literature. The tone is at once learned and comic, inspired and facetious; it is quite unpretentious and is designed in fact to deflate pomposity of every description. It represents a reaction against revolutions, glorious or otherwise, against warfare that seemed both endless and unproductive, against political and religious animosities that were now regarded as outdated and unnecessary.

Satire of course had existed as long as fools or hypocrites could be found but, after the bitter controversies and proclaimed certainties of the seventeenth century, its themes became enlarged with irony and condescension. It was not enough to defeat an opponent in argument. It was necessary to ridicule him. Pope and Swift, in particular, were masters of acerbic derision. It was the temper of the time. All the members of the Scriblerus Club had already constructed several satirical personae.

Pope himself had much to be acerbic about. As a Catholic he was debarred from university or government employment; he suffered from tuberculosis of the spine that rendered him a cripple of low and bent stature. It was he who complained about 'this long disease, my life'. His poetry, composed largely in heroic couplets, became first the fashion and then the expression of the period. His couplets evinced the formal and artificial style, at a time when formality and artificiality were in any case the marks of good breeding.

Yet the safety of the clipped couplet did not, in the case of Pope, preclude eloquence and genuine feeling. The early decades of the eighteenth century are depicted as those of restraint, but there was much wild feeling and enthusiasm to be restrained. It was no longer considered proper to wear your heart upon your sleeve. All was to be achieved by allusion and indirection. If it were indeed an 'age of reason', as the older textbooks allege, it was reason that gave the point to passionate analysis. What could be a more passionate pursuit than to reason oneself out of the darkness of the recent past?

The *Memoirs* was from the start a collaborative enterprise designed, in the words of Pope, 'to have ridiculed all the false tastes in learning, under the character of a man of capacity enough that he had dipped in every art and science, but injudiciously in each'. So the little book became an assault against fashionable taste and the purveyors of contemporary wisdom, conceived in the spirit of what Swift described on his funerary monument as '*saeva Indignatio*' or savage indignation. In particular the Scriblerians, if the term may be allowed, were the absolute opponents of contemporary science – known as 'mechanical philosophy' or 'corpuscular philosophy' – that reduced everything to its material constituents; they abhorred the technical language of the experimentalists as so much nonsense, as well as the assumption that there was no spiritual component to be discovered in the world.

There was no shortage of other targets. One of the intellectual controversies of the time was that between the 'Ancients' and the 'Moderns', those who revered classical learning against those who followed the new philosophy of science and experiment. Both schools, or tendencies, are satirized in the *Memoirs* for their avowal of fixed positions and of unfruitful speculation. The book ridicules the coffee-house bores, the clubbable bores and the pedantic bores who took advantage of what was a relatively new social freedom. Everyone seemed entitled to his or her own opinion.

Martin Scriblerus is born in the neighbourhood of Seven Dials, well known for its astrologers and doctors who, in the absence of proper medical attention, were the resort of both rich and poor. The allusion here is to the credulity and superstition that swept through the eighteenth century, led from the front by those who put their faith in book learning rather than experience. Martin's father, Cornelius Scriblerus, had previously consulted the works of Aristotle to discover the best moment for conception.

Martin himself is first seen frequenting 'the outside of the palace of St James's' in the reign of Queen Anne 'which, notwithstanding those happy times which succeeded, every Englishman has not forgotten'. He was later to be glimpsed 'under the piazza by the dancing room in St James's', and it is not wholly impossible that this neighbourhood contained his simple lodging 'in a small chamber up four pairs of stairs'. It may even have resembled Arbuthnot's own lodgings in the palace.

The author is wary of astonishing the reader with too much low detail, however, since 'I dare promise the reader that, whenever he thinks any one chapter dull, the style will be immediately changed in the next'. The remark is in the same tone as that of a later passage in which it is revealed that 'the style of this chapter in the original memoirs is so singularly different from the rest that it is hard to conceive by whom it was penned'. It is impossible to think of a seventeenth-century author who would write in such a manner. It is, however, very close to the style of *Tristram Shandy*, the first two volumes of which were published in 1759. The combination of cleverness and facetiousness can be considered as a true token of eighteenth-century sensibility.

One habit of the time was 'the recovery of manuscripts, the effossion [digging up] of coins, the procuring of mummies'. In this

period, too, much attention was paid to physiognomists, phrenol-
ogists and chirographists who analysed the faces, heads and palms
of their clients in the belief that inward qualities could be deciphered
from outward signs. The Scriblerus Club satirizes all of these
pseudo-sciences that, together with quack remedies like hartshorn
and Hungary water, dominated the world of eighteenth-century
medicine. 'What makes the English phlegmatic and melancholy
but beef? What renders the Welsh so hot and choleric but cheese
and leeks? The French derive their levity from their soups, frogs
and mushrooms.'

Medical practice, as well as theory, was investigated. Martin
Scriblerus, in search of enlightenment, 'purchased the body of a
malefactor', freshly hanged, and 'hired a room for its dissection, near
the Pest-fields in St Giles's, at a little distance from the Tyburn
Road'. The 'pest-fields' were those open spaces where the victims
of the plague had been buried in the previous century. His manservant carried the corpse back in a hackney coach at midnight, for
fear of provoking attention, but when the corpse farts (a very
eighteenth-century touch) the household is plunged into confusion.
In the ensuing commotion the manservant is brought before a local
justice, but his plea in his own defence is composed entirely of puns.
This was another hit against the tastes of contemporaries. In 1719
was published *The Art of Punning; or, The Flower of Languages*; it
was composed by Tom Hood, one of the notable 'punsters' of the
time.

The narrators also satirize the modern practices of logic and
philosophy that turn antique syllogisms and propositions into
absurdity. This was the prolonged curse of scholasticism that had
dominated the medieval period. How do angels pass from one
extreme to another without going through the middle? Much of
this was aimed at the universities where the philosophies of Aristotle
and Aquinas were still considered to be holy writ. Classicism was
the only curriculum.

The young Scriblerus also evinces an interest in the literatures
of Persia and Araby. He takes pleasure in the exhibitions of wild
animals and other 'wonders' that delighted the people. They included
a dwarf and conjoined twins, the horn of a unicorn, the foot of an
elk and the thigh bone of a giant. The curious came to the freak

shows, like that 'at Mr John Pratt's, at the Angel in Cornhill' or that 'over against the Mews Gate at Charing Cross', and had to pay sixpence for entrance. Foreign lands were also the object of wonder and enquiry rather than of possession and domination. This was still the world of Samuel Johnson's *The History of Rasselas, Prince of Abissinia* and other exotic fantasies.

The Scriblerus Club itself seems to have dissolved, or gone into a decline, soon after the death of Queen Anne in the summer of 1714. Yet the close connection of wit and satire anticipated the greatest works of its members, among them *Gulliver's Travels*, *The Dunciad* and *The Beggar's Opera*. It was part of a unique period in English literature as well as English history.

8

The Germans are coming!

Queen Anne died on the morning of 1 August 1714, and on the same day the high officers of state congregated at the gateway of St James's Palace where they proclaimed 'that the high and mighty Prince George, Elector of Brunswick-Lüneburg, is now, by the death of our late Sovereign, of happy memory, become our only lawful and rightful liege Lord, George, by the Grace of God, King of Great Britain, France and Ireland, Defender of the Faith etcetera . . . '. George had won the race over James Edward. It has been estimated that fifty-seven other people had a better hereditary claim; nevertheless the elector of Hanover, as he was also informally called, was the only Protestant among them and had therefore been acclaimed as monarch.

The cry went up after the proclamation that the Germans were coming in droves, eager to adorn themselves with the treasures of England, but in the event only ninety staff or entourage made the journey with the new king. Among them were the usual courtiers and officials, together with apothecaries and tailors as well as a complete kitchen staff (the culinary expertise of the new and unknown country could not be taken for granted); on the ship also were George's two Turkish body servants, Mehmet and Mustafa, and two court mistresses who caused almost equal astonishment.

Fräulein von Schulenberg was a lover of long standing, and one of her two 'nieces' betrayed a close resemblance to the new king; she had first refused to travel to England with George, according to Lady Mary Wortley Montagu, 'fearing that the people of England who, she thought, were accustomed to use their kings barbarously, might chop off his head in the first fortnight'. She changed her mind only when she learned that her rival was also on the way. At a later date Horace Walpole, the man of letters and connoisseur, recalled Frau von Kielmannsegge sporting 'two fierce black eyes, large and rolling . . . two acres of cheek spread with crimson, an ocean of neck that overflowed'.

The London mob was highly delighted by the fact that one was very thin, and the other very fat. It was like a nursery rhyme. The new sovereign's unhappy wife, Sophia, was not to be seen. She had been imprisoned for almost twenty years in the castle of Ahlden after being found in an illicit liaison with a German count; the count himself disappeared in mysterious circumstances, thus giving the Hanoverian court something of the atmosphere of the castle of Otranto. George's wife never left confinement, but her son did eventually become king of England.

'George Ludwig' landed at Greenwich on 18 September and in the following month was crowned in Westminster Hall. He was not exactly a golden prince. Sophia, before their doomed marriage, had shouted that 'I will not marry the pig snout' and thrown his miniature against a wall. She was perhaps a little unfair. He was rather short but his physiognomy was not out of the ordinary; he had a somewhat heavy countenance, with a high broad forehead, which showed little sign of liveliness or animation. He had a large nose and what were described as 'vacant' eyes. He was reserved to the point of woodenness, a natural hesitation that made him slow in speech and in thought. As a result he was considered to be stiff and cold in manner, but this may only have been a defensive stance in an alien environment. As Lord Chesterfield said, England was too big for him.

It is not clear whether or not he could speak English, but surviving documents suggest that he understood a lot and wrote a little. In any case he had French, the international language of diplomacy, to support him. He had certain characteristics that he shared with the preceding Stuart dynasty, among them ruthlessness and stubbornness. Perhaps these are the traits of any successful monarchy. He had embarked on his first military campaign at the age of fifteen so he could not be accused of faint-heartedness, and he had ruled Hanover for sixteen years. He was no neophyte. Thackeray wrote of him that 'he was more than fifty years of age when he came among us; we took him because we wanted him, because he served our turn; we laughed at his uncouth German ways, and sneered at him. He took our loyalty for what it was; laid hands on what money he could; kept us assuredly from Popery and wooden shoes. I, for one, would have been on his side in those days.' Wooden shoes were a token of French servitude.

Since he was by nature reserved and informal he did not keep a majestic court. He maintained an inner German retinue that carried out the necessary duties, and as a result he seemed to his subjects to be essentially remote. He rose early but did not emerge from his chamber until noon to consult his ministers; after these meetings and conferences, which could last as long as three hours, he retired once more to his bedchamber. He walked in the gardens of St James's in the late afternoon, and spent the evening playing cards with one of his mistresses. Visits to the opera or theatre were occasional, and they were not accompanied by any ritual or fanfare; the king avoided the royal box. The courtiers themselves were not vainglorious; they did not dazzle; there was no attempt to maintain the cult of monarchy. With the exception of Mustafa and Mehmet, and of course the thin and the fat mistresses, there was nothing exceptional about them.

The new king came to England with an instinctive dislike of Tories. He believed, rightly or wrongly, that many of them still supported the Stuart cause. And he could not forgive the Tory politicians who engineered the treaty of Utrecht by leaving their allies deserted on the field, of whose number he was of course one. Nevertheless it was widely believed that, like Anne, he would attempt a moderate administration combined of both parties; but in practice this even-handedness lasted for a moment only.

On his accession, for example, the new king stripped the duke of Ormonde of his military command; Ormonde had succeeded Marlborough, and had given the order for his troops to stand down. In the following year the duke was impeached for high treason on suspicion of supporting the Jacobite cause. The Tories in general were cast into outer darkness accompanied by menaces of impeachment, dismissal or permanent exclusion from office. The great earl of Oxford, once mere Robert Harley until the dagger went through his waistcoat, was sent to the Tower where he remained for two years. Others, like Ormonde himself, fled to France and to the embrace of the 'Old Pretender'. These self-imposed exiles flocking to the court of Saint-Germain did more harm to the Tory Party than a thousand vicious pamphlets. To be a Tory was now reckoned, in some quarters, to be a Jacobite. The established Anglicans, who were associated with the Tories, also lost some of their lustre; the king conformed to the national liturgy, but at heart he remained a fervent Lutheran.

The new Whig administration, now sheltering under the aegis of the king, was no longer a radical force in politics; it had quite naturally lost the anti-monarchical fervour, for example, it had adopted during the 'exclusion crisis' of 1679 when James II was the target. It had now become the ruling party; it represented the merchants, the tradesmen, the professional classes and the urban gentry who controlled the financial institutions of the country. Yet any ruling class, faced with no coherent opposition, will become an arena for ambition, envy and private antagonism; there is always someone who wishes to be pre-eminent.

There were indeed many splits and schisms between the dominant Whigs, leading the French ambassador to remark that the English would crucify Christ again if he returned to govern England. Young Whigs fought against old Whigs, the 'court' Whigs were opposed to the 'country' Whigs, the parliamentary Whigs were hostile to the royalist Whigs. Without an interesting or interested Tory party, parliament seemed to be of no earthly use. One Tory member, Sir Charles Sedley, was rebuked for walking along the Mall during a particularly important debate. He replied that he knew exactly what was going to happen, 'and an honest man signifies no more in that house to rectify it, than a drop of essence to perfume a pail full of stale piss'.

Yet the Whigs themselves were not entirely approved or accepted. The majority of the population, most of whom did not have a vote, were equally indifferent to the German dynasty; it was estimated in 1715 by the Austrian Resident in England, Johann Philipp Hoffmann, that two-thirds of the nation were in fact actively hostile to the Hanoverians. This was an exaggeration. Riots in the streets of London were commonplace, however, and attacks upon the meeting places of dissenters continued as if the Sacheverell 'High Church' riots had never ceased. On the anniversary of the Restoration of 1660 a crowd assembled before the statue of Queen Anne, in front of St Paul's Cathedral, and called out 'Down with the house of Hanover!' and 'God bless King James III!' The health of the 'Old Pretender' was drunk in inns and taverns all over the country. On the evening of King George's birthday, May 28, a mob gathered at the Stock Exchange, armed with sticks and clubs, calling out for 'High Church and Ormonde!' At Cheapside the people cried out 'No Hanoverian! No Presbyterian Government!' The London Record Office reported the arrest of one citizen who laid 'fifty guineas that the king did not reign twelve months'.

The protests were not on a revolutionary scale but they shook the new Whig ministry and questioned its administration of the rule of law. This was the burning context for the drawing-up of a statute known as the 'Riot Act' by means of which a crowd of twelve or more was guilty of a capital felony if it failed to disperse within a hour of a proclamation ordering it so to do. Any officers, under the instructions of the magistrates, were granted indemnity for their actions in dispersing the new breed of rioters. The Act was of great benefit to the authorities in periods of civil unrest, such as disruption in time of famine or unemployment, and was in fact so useful that it remained on the statute book until 1967.

Some of the native frenzy was dispelled, however, when the real Jacobites gathered upon British soil. The incident became known as 'the Fifteen'. At the beginning of September 1715, the earl of Mar set up the Jacobite banner at Braemar in Aberdeenshire; it was reported that 10,000 men had taken their place about it. The Jacobite court had heard of the disaffection among the populace, and hoped to take advantage of it. But the population was never so warm as the active, and probably drunken, minority who had acclaimed James Edward Stuart.

The report of the insurgency created something like panic in London where the Hanoverian king was not wholly secure upon his new throne. The newly created Riot Act was deployed with full force; Tory hawkers selling ballads or pamphlets were dispatched to the nearest house of correction, and anyone suspected of uttering treasonable sentiments was likely to be scourged or pilloried.

Small forces from Lancashire and Northumberland, still Catholic in sympathy, joined the rebellion but these luckless few were defeated in a battle at Preston in November. Some were executed for treason while others were transported as convicts to America. When the bulk of them were marched to London, according to the diary of Countess Cowper, 'the mob insulted them terribly, carrying a warming pan before them, and saying a thousand barbarous things, which some of the prisoners returned with spirit'. The warming pan was a symbol of the supposed illegitimacy of the 'Old Pretender' who was said to have been smuggled into the royal bedchamber in just such a vessel. The earl of Mar, at the head of the larger Jacobite army in Scotland, had also been defeated at Sheriffmuir in the same month; he waited anxiously for his Stuart master to arrive and take command of the perilous situation.

The coronation of James Francis Edward, James III of England and James VIII of Scotland, had been supposed to take place on 23 January 1716, at the palace of Scone but, unfortunately, none of the participants arrived in time. James landed at Peterhead towards the end of December and started to make his way to the palace. Yet his steps were of course being followed by spies, and his army shadowed; aware of his dangerous position he took ship at Montrose on 5 February, together with the earl of Mar, and arrived in northern France five days later.

In truth the rebellion had had little chance of success. The French, under the leadership of a regent after the death of Louis XIV only a month before, was in no position to raise an army for the 'Old Pretender'; more importantly, they had no will to do so. Without foreign assistance any domestic rebellion was unlikely to succeed. Those Tories who supported the Jacobite cause (which may be confidently considered to be a minority) had no plan, no leader and no arms. They might as well have supported the king of Brobdingnag. The dislike of the Whig government did not translate into active opposition, and the fear of a Catholic king was enough to dispel any affectionate loyalty to the old cause.

The Whig administration, however, was taking no chances with the volatile electorate. As a direct result of the Jacobite scare, parliament passed a Septennial Bill that extended its life from three years to seven years. What might have been a dangerous election in 1718, therefore, was postponed until 1722. It made it much harder for Tories to exploit Whig divisions if there was no possibility of an imminent election. It lent an air of security and authority to the administration and, as an additional advantage, it granted a further element of constitutional power to parliament itself.

In the summer of 1716, two months after the Septennial Bill had been enacted, the king returned to Hanover. It was always where he longed to be. The territory had been granted to George's family by the Holy Roman Emperor, Leopold I, after some timely assistance against the Turks; it was small, comfortable, peaceable, and in all respects unlike England. It was the king's intention to return there frequently, to hunt and to take the waters, but the problems of England restricted him to only five visits in thirteen years. Even these were too many for his English ministers who did not relish the administration of the kingdom at one remove. Wind and weather sometimes delayed his return, on which occasions parliament itself had to be prorogued. A minister of state always travelled with him, and any determined minister could create trouble for his colleagues a few hundred miles distant. It did not help matters that on this visit the king decided to remain in Hanover for six months; six months, even then, was a long time in politics both foreign and domestic.

It was possible, after all, that the king might favour the interests of Hanover over those of England. He was intimately associated with the affairs of the Baltic region, with which England had very little to do, and the ministers in London were not eager to be drawn into what were for them provincial quarrels.

Splits of a more personal nature soon became evident within the royal family. The truth was that the father, George Ludwig, hated the son, George Augustus, prince of Wales, and the son repaid that hostility in equal measure. It was in part the old problem of a living heir, waiting impatiently behind the arras for the fall of his predecessor; it has been a conundrum as old as monarchy itself. There were also certain ministers and courtiers who, feeling deprived of what they considered to be a proper measure of respect or reward, waited in expectation for the light of the rising son to restore them to health. In the fractious climate of early eighteenth-century politics, these factions became all the more vicious.

When the king left for Hanover, for example, he appointed his son as 'guardian of the realm and lieutenant', an office not exercised since the time of the Black Prince in the fourteenth century. It was considered by the prince and his cohorts to be an insult, rendered more odious by the restraints that the king imposed upon his son's supposed regency. The prince was to take no decisions on foreign policy without the approval of the king; he could not fill any of the more important positions of state, and should postpone any royal assent to parliamentary bills. Foreign dispatches were to be kept from him. Yet certain other dispatches, concerning his own behaviour, were to be sent onward to Hanover.

The prince was of course flattered by the king's adversaries; now that he considered himself free of political responsibility, having been allowed none of his own, he came to realize that he might become an independent force in the formulation of policy. He might be able to create a faction or party in parliament itself that worked against the king.

An unfortunate quarrel at the baptism of the prince's first son, when the king's choice of godfather was angrily opposed, led to a further division in November 1717. The king ordered his son to leave St James's Palace, whereupon the wife of the heir, Caroline of Ansbach, decided to follow him. It was decreed that anyone who visited the renegade couple would be formally barred from any converse with the king. This would be war. Nothing like it had been seen since the days of the struggle between Mary I and Elizabeth I. Lord Hervey wrote of the prince that 'he always spoke of his father as a weak man rather than a bad or dishonest one; and said . . . his father had always hated him and used him ill'.

The prince of Wales and his consort removed themselves to Leicester House, north of Leicester Square, where they established what was to all intents and purposes a rival court. The prince no longer attended cabinet meetings as a sign of his status as an internal exile. When any minister fell out with the king, he had a natural welcome from his son. In Leicester House congregated disaffected

Whigs and disgruntled Tories, disappointed place-seekers and divisive troublemakers entertained by music, dancing, feasting and fashionable conversation. The king, thoroughly discomfited by his son's social success, broke the habit of a lifetime and also began to hold assemblies and public dinners. The drawing room at St James's Palace was open three days a week; music, dancing and fireworks were enjoyed at Kensington Palace.

Father and son were not reconciled for three years, and even then it was a half-hearted affair. The prince told his wife that when he entered the royal closet, formal but contrite, the king could only mutter 'Votre conduite . . . votre conduite', meaning 'Your behaviour . . . your behaviour'. When they were seen in public on the following day they did not speak.

In the interim a shadow, no thicker than a bubble, had passed over the court, the city and the country.

9

Bubbles in the air

The bubble first arose from an attempt by the Tories to set up an institution that might rival the Bank of England in providing public credit. In the spring of 1711 the South Sea Company was established. It comprised in the first instance all those who were owed money by the government for war loans approaching £10 million; they were persuaded to give up their annuities for stock in this new and enterprising company. They were guaranteed 4 per cent interest, funded by indirect taxes, but they were also to be partners in the projected profit from all trade with the Americas in a period when the proceeds of Spanish commerce were conceived to be enormous. It was a convenient way for the administration to handle existing debts, at a relatively low rate of interest, while shareholders might dream of another Eldorado. During the years of the War of the Spanish Succession, trade and industry were naturally subdued. But when Philip V of Spain entered a quadruple alliance with Great Britain, France and the Dutch republic early in 1720, in the treaty of The Hague, it was believed that the mineral wealth of the Americas would come to London as Zeus had come to Danaë in the form of golden rain.

The fever hit when at the beginning of 1720 the *St James's Weekly Journal* reported that 'we hear that the South-Sea Company have in a manner agreed with the Treasury for taking into their capital the annuities of ninety-nine years'. The company had become so formidable and so confident that it had swallowed up a large part of the national debt. Its power and profit now depended upon the rise of the price of its stock. And what could stop an irresistible force? The value of its stock kept on increasing in the early months of the year, and by 24 June £100 of government stock was worth £1,050 of South Sea stock. The more shares were sought and prized, the higher their value rose; the higher their value, the more desirable they seemed.

The first subscription was immediately filled. Sir John Evelyn sold some of his land to gain a share. Everyone pursued a quick profit, and everyone was chasing everyone else. You could buy the stock at one rate, selling at another rate for an enormous profit a few days later. It was reported that shares were purchased on the Stock Exchange 'ten per cent higher at one end of the alley than at the other'. The men went to find their brokers in the taverns and coffee-shops; the women flocked for the same purpose to the milliners and haberdashers. Ministers and members of parliament were bribed by the company with free distributions of stock that could then be resold at the going rate. It quickly became known as 'the bubble age'. 'Bubble' became the synonym for any kind of deception or deceit. Schemes and contrivances and projects were all 'bubbles'.

Tobias Smollett in his history of the period wrote that 'Exchange Alley was filled with a strange concourse of statesmen and clergymen, churchmen and dissenters, whigs and tories, physicians, lawyers, tradesmen, and even with multitudes of females.' Various other schemes for quick rewards were advertised at the time, taking advantage of the fatuity and gullibility of the moment. A scheme was proposed for making quicksilver malleable. A plan was suggested for importing jackasses from Spain. Projects were advanced for making salt water fresh. In this period eighty-six different schemes were advertised to potential investors, among them 'for improving of gardens', 'for insuring and increasing children's fortunes', 'for furnishing funerals to any part of Great Britain' and for 'a wheel of perpetual motion'. Projection was gambling under another name. Projection was speculation. Projection was a lottery.

When Robinson Crusoe profited from his merchandise, before setting off on his famous voyage, 'my head began to be full of projects and undertakings beyond my reach'. Defoe knew of what he wrote. His first published volume was entitled *An Essay upon Projects* (1697), in which presciently he lamented 'the general projecting humour of the nation'; every day arose 'new contrivances, engines and projects to get money, never before thought of', and from these devices we may 'trace the original of banks, stocks, stock-jobbing, assurances, friendly societies, lotteries, and the like', not forgetting 'those Exchange mountebanks we very properly call brokers'.

It was part of a culture in which the gambler was king. Sometimes the habit was confined to the card tables that could be found in palace and tavern, whorehouse and drawing room. A character in Richard Steele's *The Tender Husband*, composed in 1705, laments the fact that 'women can imagine all household care, regard to posterity and fear of poverty, must be sacrificed to a game at cards'. Gaming houses for men were everywhere. This mania for speculation and quick profit was materially responsible for the new interest in fire, marine and life insurance; insurances were made out for marriages and births, as well as deaths. Private gambling therefore became an intrinsic part of the public economy. It also had a more arcane consequence when the complex calculations encouraged Pascal and Fermat to devise mathematical probability theory.

Gaming affected all classes. Horace Walpole reported that at Brooks's club 'a thousand meadows and cornfields are staked at every throw'. Politicians would win or lose thousands at Almack's before returning to the debates at parliament; the more accomplished the politician, the more imperturbable his countenance. A particular costume was worn at Almack's, consisting of a great-coat, pieces of leather to protect the ruffles, and a high-crowned hat with a broad brim to keep out the light; the hats were festooned with flowers and ribbons. On one occasion a Whig politician, Charles James Fox, sat for twenty-two hours playing at Hazard. Gentlemen bet on the life expectations of their fathers. Thomas Whaley, an Irish gambler and parliamentarian, bet that 'he could jump from his drawing room window into the first barouche that passed and kiss the occupant'. When a man fell to the ground in a stupor opposite Brooks's, the members of that club laid bets whether he was alive or dead. Others with fewer resources would bet on skittles or on dominoes in the local taverns, on the result of an election or the sex of an unborn child; the throwing of dice was not unusual during church services.

Lotteries were instituted by the government in 1709, and for every year until 1824 a lottery bill was passed. The popularity of these gigantic confidence tricks was manifest from the very beginning. On 21 January 1710, it was reported that 'yesterday books were opened at Mercers' Chapel for receiving subscriptions for the lottery and, 'tis said, above a million is already subscribed'. Lotteries were sometimes known as 'sales' to lend them an air of respectability. If you bought a ticket for twopence, and thereby won a set of 'new fashionable plate', it could be regarded as a bargain. It was announced that six houses in Limehouse 'are to be disposed of by tickets, and the numbers are to be drawn by two parish boys out of two wheels, at the Three Sun tavern in Wood Street'.

Gambling and lotteries were considered by many to be the natural manifestation of a city based largely upon fraud and avarice, and of a society established upon wanton violence and corruption, where the vast disparities of wealth encouraged wicked or unscrupulous behaviour. The *London Journal* of 1720 excoriated the avarice and love of luxury of the age, while a few months later the *Weekly Journal* believed that the South Sea Bubble was 'but the natural effect of those vices which have reigned for so many years'. In truth there have always been bubbles, and the measure of fraud and corruption in the city has not noticeably grown or diminished over the centuries. The regularity of panics became a matter of observation; they were often called 'convulsions', as if the financial body had succumbed to a fever. There does come a time, however, when one of the bubbles bursts with a more than usually resounding pop.

This particular crisis came, as most financial crises do, suddenly and unexpectedly. A ballad was quickly doing the rounds of the fairs and markets:

> A bubble is blown up in air;
> In which fine prospects do appear;
> The Bubble breaks, the prospect's lost,
> Yet must some Bubble pay the cost.
> Hubble Bubble; all is smoke,
> Hubble Bubble; all is broke,

Farewell your Houses, Lands and Flocks
For all you have is now in Stocks.

It was discovered that the South Sea Company did not have the cash available to pay for any stocks being returned. The projected profits on the Eldorado of Spanish trade were a mirage. When confidence disappeared, the mist of gain and of fortune evaporated. The value of the stock, which had originally been used to replace the annuities on government debt, plunged. By September 1720, it seemed that all was gone. The stockholders had lost their investments.

Tobias Smollett wrote that 'such an era as this is the most unfavourable for an historian; that no reader of sentiment and imagination can be entertained or interested by a detail of transactions such as these which admit of no warmth, no colouring, no embellishment; a detail of which only serves to exhibit an inanimate picture of tasteless vulgarity and mean degeneracy'. Yet the business of the bubble does much to elucidate, as one book's title has it, *Extraordinary Popular Delusions and the Madness of Crowds*. The craving for riches and the experience of failure, the giddy descent from wealth into poverty, the mania which gripped many thousands of people without good cause, the suicides, the dissolution of family ties, say more about the period than a thousand battles.

It soon became apparent that certain ministers and directors of the company had sold out before the reckoning, and the anger of the public against them was boundless. There were calls for the principal among them to be broken on the wheel. The only stay against civil strife was the feeling that the ruin was so general that 'something' would be done; the whole financial order could not be undermined.

At this juncture the rotund and rubicund figure of Robert Walpole may be introduced; for it was he, more than any other politician, who calmed the panic and restored the South Sea Company to something like solvency. He was a Norfolk man who never lost his accent and who seemed to represent the frank and candid image of the born countryman; he chewed his home-grown apples on the front bench and kept his temper. He was said to read the reports from his farm manager before he turned to the news-papers.

He was thick-set, short and plump with a noticeable double chin; in the many portraits he looks genial enough, if a little blasé, and in life he was known to be good-humoured and convivial. He was always the first to welcome new members of parliament in what soon became his domain. He dressed well, in particular for the sessions of parliament when he was outfitted like a groom for a bride. He knew how the Commons worked; he knew how its members felt. He believed that the only safety for a minister lies, as he said, 'in having the approbation of this House'.

He understood people all too well. He was reported as saying that there were 'few minds which would not be injured by the constant spectacle of meanness and depravity' and he told a future first minister, Henry Pelham, that 'when you have the same ex-perience of mankind as myself you will go near to hate the human species'. Yet this black and misanthropic pessimism never affected his apparent affability. He made the most of all human weakness. He liked others to drink in his company so that he could take advantage of their indiscretions. He knew the price of every man, and he did not hesitate to rid himself of those who owed him only dubious loyalty. He was in charge of all appointments, both local and national; he superintended the offices of the Church no less than those of the army or the navy. He created what at a later date might be called an 'establishment'. No office was too unimportant, no sinecure too small, to escape his attention.

If he had a fault, in society, it was his excessive coarseness. Even for the eighteenth century his ribaldry was considered a little too much. Princess Caroline once had to chide him for lewd language in front of her ladies. The fourth earl of Chesterfield, albeit a doyen of excessive respectability, described him as 'inelegant in his manners, loose in his morals, he had a coarse strong wit, which he was too free of for a man of his station'. Walpole could laugh off criticism of this kind, however, since for twenty years he held the state in his hands.

He was one of those English politicians who survive on their reputation of bluff common sense. He would stand no nonsense. He professed to believe in common sense and, so he said, in fair play. He wanted moderation at all costs. He wanted balance. He wanted peace at home and abroad so that trade might flourish. Flatter the time-servers. Meet emergencies with expedients. Pay bribes when they were necessary. Give way in the face of public clamour, however misconceived. One of his favourite proverbs was '*Quieta non movere*', 'Don't disturb things that are quiet'. It might be the motto of his legislative career, and that of many subsequent politicians.

He was a pragmatist in the very literal sense that he really had no policy except that of survival. A man of business and an administrator, he was marked by energy and capacity for work. At a later date Chesterfield wrote that George II said of him that he was 'by so great a superiority the most able man in the kingdom, that he understood the revenue, and knew how to manage that formidable and refractory body, the House of Commons, so much better than any other man, that it was impossible for the business of the crown to be well done without him'. This of course implies that he was nothing of a thinker and, as he said himself, that he was 'no saint, no Spartan, no reformer'.

He always was a thoroughbred Whig, however, who for a short time had even been imprisoned in the Tower by the Tories during their ascendancy. 'I heartily despise', he wrote to his sister, Dolly, 'what I shall one day revenge.' Incarceration in fact did him no harm at all. He had accepted various offices of state, and in 1717 became for a period first lord of the treasury and chancellor of the exchequer; he made a great deal of money in a mysterious and still unknown fashion before resigning 'because I could not connive at some things that were carrying on'. It was not a matter of principle, however, but of internal politics. Nevertheless in June 1720, at the height of the Bubble, he became paymaster general of the forces and was thus in a position to help direct the affairs of the treasury.

The Bubble was indeed his opportunity; he had been associated with financial matters for almost as long as he had been in parliament and, as a Whig, he was on the best of terms with the directors of the Bank of England. He had been suspicious of the South Sea Company, as a direct rival to the bank, but nonetheless had invested some of his funds with it. He was not one of those who made a quick or sensational profit, however, and it seems more than likely that he lost a large sum of money on his transactions. This also lent him further credibility in his scheme to salvage the situation. He had shown his acumen in the past, but it was now necessary to demonstrate his equanimity.

By the summer of 1720 he was effectively the chief minister in his attempt to restore confidence in the finances of the country. In this undertaking he was supremely equipped by nature. Chesterfield noted in his *Characters* that Walpole 'was so clear in stating the most intricate matters, especially in the finances, that while he was speaking, the most ignorant thought they understood what they really did not'. He had to give the impression that financial stability had been restored and that the national debt was under control. He persuaded the directors of the Bank of England to buy up some of the South Sea Company's holding of government stock, thus reducing the company's debt and placing it on a more stable foundation. He confiscated the ill-gained wealth of the company's directors and distributed it as liberally as he might. He also maintained a 'sinking fund', which he had in fact devised three years earlier, revenue set apart for future projects and financed by special or specific taxes; this was also a measure to ensure future confidence in the financial system. For this relief he was given much thanks by king and government. It is difficult to overestimate the calming effect that the right politician can induce. Walpole stilled the storm to a whisper, and the waves of the sea were hushed.

He had performed another service also, for which he earned the further nickname of 'the Screen' or 'the Screen-Master General'. Certain ministers had colluded with the directors of the South Sea Company in the illicit making of profit; the king himself, together with his mistresses, had also been involved in what might be considered to be illegal profiteering. Walpole was concerned above all else to maintain the balance and the apparent integrity of the state. A parliamentary committee was established and the directors of the company were forbidden to leave the country. One or two still fled abroad to general execration and one noble peer, Lord Stanhope, died of apoplexy after being charged with corruption. A death or two might be convenient, since the dead cannot speak or confess, and Walpole was not particularly concerned with the directors of the company; they could be sacrificed to public anger.

But he was concerned to shield his ministerial colleagues from attack, even though some of them had been his personal enemies; by dint of intimidation and the suborning of witnesses, therefore, the principal suspects were cleared of all charges. He had indeed been the screen behind which the great could conceal themselves, and his power was vastly increased. In the spring of 1721 Robert Walpole became once again first lord of the treasury, with immense powers of patronage. All strings led to him. The subsequent period has been variously known as 'the age of Walpole' and 'the age of stability'. He was for twenty-one years the dominant minister in the country, who was able to combine political mastery with economic supremacy in a manner previously unparalleled. He had no party. He had only the support of the king, and was obliged to rely upon the independent members of parliament as well as the natural supporters of the court. That is why he always moved so carefully. He was required to balance the various forces within the nation to sustain his mastery; he had to satisfy the financiers as well as the aristocrats, the dissenting merchants as well as the Anglican gentry.

To call his period one of 'stability' is perhaps the merest truism. That, after all, was what mattered to him. But he did not single-handedly create that stability. The durability of the house of Hanover, with the threat of the Stuarts removed, had something to do with it. The happy employment of making money, and the ingenious promotion of trade, also had a large part to play in the quiescence of financiers and merchants. Anglicanism was accepted and acceptable, if not entirely loved. The Septennial Act, which restricted general elections to every seven years, maintained a period of calm. Party fervour and religious enthusiasm were therefore contained; an improving standard of living, together with more employment, worked their own spell upon the body politic.

Yet Walpole had his own fair share of luck, an indispensable requirement for a successful politician. The chaos of the Bubble had revealed a record of government weakness and financial incompetence of which its Stuart enemies could have taken advantage. The Speaker, Arthur Onslow, recalled that, at the time the Bubble was pricked, 'could the Pretender then have landed at the Tower, he might have rode to St James with very few hands held up against him'. Others also considered the possibility of James Edward Stuart taking advantage of this opportunity and regaining the throne. One of the principal Jacobites, Francis Atterbury, bishop of Rochester, had concealed himself in lamb's clothing as an unexceptionable Tory. In the spring of 1721, however, he wrote to James that 'with a very little assistance from your friends abroad, your way to your friends at home is become easy and safe'. Yet Walpole's quiet was not disturbed.

The first minister was on the watch. It has been said that he saw Jacobites everywhere, even under his bed, but he knew well enough that any Jacobite plot would taint the Tories still further and attach the king more closely to his loyal government. It had been arranged by James's supporters, for example, that the duke of Ormonde would invade England with a body of Irish troops. It was not perhaps the most sensible plan, and was in any case immediately bedevilled by divisions among the English rebels and by a plethora of spies who were ready to reveal anything and everything for money. All of course came to nothing. The bishop of Rochester was himself arrested and sent into exile.

Walpole was aware that the conspiracy had never really amounted to much, but he would not let the opportunity pass. Onslow remarked that the discovery of the Jacobite plot, 'was the most fortunate and greatest circumstance of Walpole's life'. The king was with his first minister forever. The Tories were discomfited, because of their implicit association with the Jacobites, and many of them withdrew from public life; the recovery of their party was, for the foreseeable future, impossible. In the summer of 1723 the ministers of the king ordered that 'all and every person whatsoever' over the age of eighteen should submit to an oath of allegiance to the present sovereign.

In the same period Robert Walpole gracefully and gratefully declined a peerage, knowing full well that his real power lay in his command of the Commons. His decision, which seemed surprising to some, was an indication of the fact that parliament had indeed become the sovereign body of the nation with responsibilities and duties far beyond those of the monarch. It was now the final arbiter of English liberties, which could be no longer left to the mercies of even the most benevolent Hanoverian sovereign. Parliament had become the arena in which conflicting political views, or political factions, could be heard with the minimum of controversy. It was the great forum for the address of grievances. That is why only thirty years later, in 1757, a Lincolnshire crowd protesting against the plan for a reserve of professional soldiers agreed that 'if parliament was not to be trusted there would be an end of all things'.

Yet no sooner had Walpole mastered all the tricks and balances of administration than a major player in the game of power was suddenly taken away from him. At the beginning of June 1727 George I began a journey to Germany in order to be greeted by all his favourite relatives. Seven days into his travels, he complained of stomach pains arising from too many strawberries and oranges. Many sovereigns suffered from surfeits of food. He grew pale and faint, revived only by a liberal dose of smelling salts. Then he fell into an uneasy and noisy sleep that deteriorated into lethargy and unconsciousness. He had the strength to raise his hand in greeting to his old childhood palace at Osnabrück, but died the following night.

This was a grave and possibly fatal blow to Robert Walpole. He had been close to and influential with the old king. His relations with the son and heir were hardly marked by the same sympathy and understanding; indeed the heir treated the politician with a great deal of suspicion. But the new king had the inconceivable good fortune of a wife, Caroline of Ansbach, who understood the leading players of the nation much more acutely than her husband. When Walpole managed to provide a civil list granting George II far more funds than his father, his happy and influential position was retained.

It is hard to estimate the legacy of George I, on the presumption that you cannot prove a negative. He had maintained the stability of the Hanoverian dynasty, and his own familial ties and alliances had managed to reconcile Britain to the varying leaders and factions of Europe. In this endeavour he was assisted by Wapole who above all else hated war. It was bad for business and wrecked the economy.

A Dutch diplomat at George I's court reported that 'he is much concerned with his reputation but is not excessively ambitious; he has a special aptitude for affairs of state, a well-ordered economy, very sound brain and judgement . . . he bears justice in mind at all times and, withal, he is goodhearted'. These are the familiar marmoreal words used to embalm mediocrity, or at least those sovereigns who avoided catastrophe.

It should be added that the life and energy and progress of the nation were taking place without the first George knowing or caring anything about it.

10

The invisible hand

Between 1724 and 1726, in the last decade of his life, Daniel Defoe published an encomium to his native country in three volumes entitled *A Tour through the Whole Island of Great Britain*. It is not at all clear whether he made this tour contemporaneously in person or nostalgically in spirit; it is also uncertain whether he used observers on the spot or relied upon a capacious inventory of recollected details. He was blessed with a powerful memory and a gift of almost perfect observation, and so we can forgive the touches of imagination that give the book its life and energy. It has survived because it captures the very spirit of the time.

The spirit was one of energy and of progress, in a constant rehearsal of 'the improvement in manufactures, in merchandises, in navigation'. The 'present time' was his ideal. When the polite world and the not so polite world were in a fever of gambling, the industrious and trading classes were taking advantage of unprecedented conditions for growth in what Defoe describes as 'the most flourishing and opulent country in the world', with its improvements in 'culture' as well as in 'commerce', with its increase in 'people' as well as in 'buildings'. He notes of Devonshire, for example, that 'the people are all busy, and in full employ upon their manufactures'.

At a time when 'manufactures' were not associated with the coming revolution in industry, their improvement and ubiquity were already a matter of astonishment. In the solid houses of the more prosperous citizens were displayed the cloth from Malmesbury, the knives from Sheffield and the glass-ware from Nottingham. What drove all was trade, the great engine of growth. For Defoe trade is 'an inexhausted current which not only fills the pond, and keeps it full, but is continually running over and fills all the lower ponds and places about it'.

The temples of trade were the towns. The indigenous trade of a town or city 'is a kind of nostrum to them, inseparable to the place' such as the clothing trade of Leeds, the coal trade of Newcastle upon Tyne, the herring trade of Yarmouth and the butter trade of Hull. Defoe rejoices in Norwich, 'the inhabitants being all busy at their manufactures, dwell in their garrets at their looms, and in their combing shops, so they call them'. Work was available for everyone. Defoe was pleased that in Taunton 'there was not a child in the town, or in the villages round it, of above five years old, but, if it was not neglected by its parents, and untaught, could earn its own bread'.

The antiquarians of the previous century, such as Elias Ashmole and William Camden, snuffled out the traces of antiquity as if they comprised the perfume of England; but for Defoe the medieval town of Worcester 'is close and old, the houses standing too thick'. Instead he praises the village of Stratford outside London for the fact that 'every vacancy [is] filled with new houses' with 'the increase of the value and rent of the houses formerly standing'.

This was the century in which trade came to be regarded as the most important activity of the nation, quite opposed to religious and political considerations. New kinds of book multiplied, published in the late seventeenth and eighteenth centuries, among them Charles Davenant's *Two Discourses on the Public Revenues and Trade of England*, Adam Anderson's *An Historical and Chronological Deduction of the Origin of Commerce*, David Macpherson's *Annals of Commerce*, Charles King's *The British Merchant* and William Wood's *Survey of Trade*. And of course it would be remiss to ignore Daniel Defoe's own *The Complete English Tradesman*.

'Our trade is our chief support,' Lord Carteret explained in the Lords, 'and therefore we must sacrifice every other view to the preservation of our trade.' Where once the English had congratulated themselves on the purity of their religion or the balance of their unwritten constitution they now prided themselves on the extent of their commerce; it was widely believed, and reported, that it was the most considerable in the world. Which nation, effectively, could rival it? Which country had the navy to do so? In one of the *Letters Concerning the English Nation*, 'On Trade', Voltaire, the French philosopher and historian, noticed opportunely that England had become 'so powerful by its commerce, as to be able to send in 1723 three fleets at the same time to three different and far distanc'd parts of the Globe'.

Commerce was, essentially, power gained without war. John Gay conveniently expressed it in verse :

> Be commerce, then, thy sole design;
> Keep that, and all the world is thine.

And of course all this implied great social changes, in which the merchant and the trader were no longer considered to be in the lower half of the social spectrum some way down from clergymen or barristers. In the same letter Voltaire noted that the brother of Lord Townshend, a minister of state, was a merchant in the City and that the son of the earl of Oxford was a tradesman in Aleppo. Robert Walpole married the daughter of a timber merchant. Commerce possessed not only freedom but also prestige. That is why the Whigs, the patrons and masters of commerce, had the advantage over the Tories. Trade now created gentlemen, even if they had not yet permeated the upper ranks of the aristocracy.

The merchants were now accepted as potentially the most useful members of the commonwealth. Thomas Turner, a local shopkeeper from East Hoathly, near Lewes, kept a diary between 1754 and 1765 in one entry of which he notes 'how pleasant is trade when it runs in its proper channels, and flows with a plentiful stream. It does, as it were, give life and spirit to one's actions.' It was as necessary as the blood running through the veins. It had become the national metaphor.

The two great topographical facts of the century, related in necessarily intimate ways, are the growth of London and the growth of the towns. The union of England and Scotland had created the largest free trade area in the world, and therefore within the bounds of this island state the finance of London was combined with the commerce of Liverpool, the coal of the midlands and the industries of the textile north. So everything grew together as if they were under the silent guidance of a fundamental law of being.

The figures tell their own story. In the course of the eighteenth century imports, as well as exports, increased five times; in the same period re-exports increased by a factor of nine. In the years between 1726 and 1728 imports rose 22 per cent, exports rose 27 per cent, and re-exports increased by 57 per cent. Re-exports is the neutral name for colonial produce that by law had to be shipped to Britain before being taken in turn to continental Europe. The English then got the best of the bargains by buying cheap and selling dear. It was also the most effective manner of acquiring, in return, much-needed European goods.

The cloth from the East India Company, the sugar from the West Indies, the tobacco from Virginia and Maryland as well as all the tea and the rum and the spices from various parts of the world transformed the appurtenances of English life; this transformation amounted to great cultural and social as well as commercial change. When the commodities and fashions and luxuries were poured into the country, trade and customs naturally expanded.

In his *Tour* Defoe notes the sudden and unexpected growth of English towns. Frome, in north-east Somerset, 'is so prodigiously increased within these last twenty or thirty years that they have built a new church, and so many new streets of houses, and these houses are so full of inhabitants'. The population of Halifax has 'increased one fourth, at least, within the last forty years, that is to say since the late Revolution'. Of Liverpool he writes that 'I think I may safely say at this my third seeing it, for I was surprised at the view, it was more than double what it was at the second; and, I am told, that it still visibly increases both in wealth, people, business and buildings: what it may grow to in time, I know not.'

In 1700 Norwich was the only provincial town with more than 25,000 inhabitants; by 1820 fourteen more could be found. The inhabitants of towns such as Hull and Nottingham, Leeds and Leicester, had increased five times in the same period. The populations of Liverpool, Birmingham and Manchester had expanded twenty times. In 1700 less than one quarter of the people lived in towns; a century later that figure had risen to an average between one-third and two-fifths. England was slowly but ineluctably becoming a cohesive urban society, quite unlike Germany, France, or Italy.

There was hardly a town, large or small, that had not been in part rebuilt. They arrived as wattle-and-daub, or as oak and other timber, but they were revived in brick. The marble for the assembly rooms and the baths would soon arrive. Brick, however, was the material of choice for the emerging middle class. The prosperous enjoyed the comfort of brick with the additional advantage of large windows; the houses were considered to be 'classical', meaning of regular proportions, and they were built into a variety of well-tempered shapes. The square, the circus, the arcade and the crescent were all in the height of architectural taste.

The paradigm for this extensive renovation and refurbishment was London itself. On one of her journeys Celia Fiennes observed of Nottingham that it was 'the neatest town I have seen, built of stone and delicate, large and long streets, much like London and the houses lofty and well-built. The marketplace is very broad – out of which runs a very large street, much like Holborn, but the buildings fine.' The emphasis here is upon space and spaciousness; the new town was to be carefully distinguished from the cramped and noisome quarters of the Jacobean and Stuart city. These were increasingly reserved for the poor or for the industrial workers. As population increased throughout the century, and as the need for space grew ever more pressing, the more prosperous citizens tried to create enclaves for themselves like Old Square in Birmingham that has now in its turn been razed.

And so we can date the rise and rise of the country town. It was no longer the small town, no longer the market town, but the prosperous hub of what was quickly becoming a provincial society with its services, its shopkeepers, its entertainments and its meeting places. There was an increasing need for domestic and professional services; lighting and clean streets would soon become required in this newly constructed environment. By the 1730s sixteen provincial towns had introduced oil-burning lamps onto the thoroughfares. Coffee-houses and concerts, balls and literary societies, were also no longer the prerogative of the capital.

The architecture of the period was one characterized by harmony and restraint; Gothic excesses or mannerist convolutions were no longer required. As in the social conduct of the gentlemen and ladies, all was to be governed by restraint and decorum. The proportions of the edifice were to be exact and harmonious, following the golden rule of symmetry in the placing of windows and the subdued use of ornament. This in turn encouraged a balance and proportion of streets, crescents and squares with the stated ambition of promoting social harmony in the newly built or newly extended towns and cities of the country. Nothing should be singular, excessively individual, or idiosyncratic. There was a new lightness in the air, eschewing the heaviness and ponderousness of the recent past. White was the colour of modernity. But were the houses and public buildings, with their Doric columns and pilasters, like unto whited sepulchres? Propriety can itself act as an enervating force, as became obvious in the regimented and restrictive life of Bath or Tunbridge Wells. For turbulent or eccentric spirits, if any by chance happened to find themselves there, these spas might have been the equivalent of open prisons.

In the domestic interiors of the middling sort, in the 1740s or 1750s, the fashion for propriety and harmony also prevailed. To drink tea out of a blue-and-white china cup was the *beau idéal*. The cup could then be placed upon a tea table, made of walnut or mahogany, highly polished and lacquered. Oak was no longer fashionable, too redolent of the Stuart times. Silver tea sets and linen napkins were part of the setting. The windows would have curtains, if they were to be wholly respectable, and the walls themselves were furnished with a clock, a mirror, a print and an engraving. The floors were no longer made up of plain boards but were covered with deal and ornamented with carpets. The old stone fireplaces had given way to marble. Writing tables and card tables were expected. There might even be a bookcase. The plain and thick-set furniture of a previous age was supplanted by chairs and sofas of a greater lightness and curvilinear elegance. The line of beauty was, according to Hogarth, serpentine. In advertisements for the new domestic comforts, praise was lavished upon the 'neat' and the 'neatly done'.

Of the poorer dwellings we know very little. The hovels of the labourers, the rooming houses of the clerks, the small houses of the shopkeepers, the lodgings of the artisans, all have been swept away or so changed as to have become unrecognizable. The small cottages and shacks have been torn down, sometimes by human agency and sometimes by the wind and the rain. They did not contain Wedgwood china or patterned wallpaper; at most they included a bed, a table, and two or three chairs that were so badly made that they would not even now find their way into a provincial museum.

The more affluent dwellings possessed between three and seven rooms, designed for a family of approximately five members with two or three servants. Two female servants and a boy were the standard repertoire of domestic service. The rooms themselves were arranged on a different pattern. In earlier periods an observer would be forgiven for thinking that the whole range of human activity could take place in one or two rooms; but by the eighteenth century, in the wealthier households, there was a noticeable separation of functions. The [with]drawing room came to be used for conversation, the dressing room for female intimacies; the bedrooms and nurseries were always upstairs, and the servants were relegated to the back of the house. In poorer families the parlour took the place of the drawing room, but in even more pinched quarters the life of the household still revolved about the kitchen. These domestic conditions survived well into the twentieth century.

There is no better evidence for the growing wealth of the country than the rising status of the provincial town as a focus for social life. Just as the population began a steady migration towards the towns and other urban centres, so the national culture in turn acquired an urban tone that had previously been confined to London and the largest cities. Much of it derived from the pressure of emulation, the greatest solvent of social change. The weekly stage-coach brought down the newest London goods, and it was the ambition of every relatively prosperous householder to make the annual journey to the capital. London actors trod the boards of the New Theatre in Norwich or the Leeds Theatre in Hunslet Lane; London books made their way onto the shelves of the circulating libraries, by means of which books were rented for a period rather than purchased. The *Annual Register* of 1761 noted that 'the same wines are drunk, the same gaming practiced, the same hours kept and the same course of life pursued in the country and in the town . . . Every male and female wishes to think and speak, to eat and drink, and dress and live after the manner of people of quality in London.' And so by a miracle of metamorphosis emerged the gardens, the walks, the pleasure gardens, the theatres, the concert venues, the libraries and the booksellers.

The 'walk' might be a gravelled path, or a promenade, or a tree-lined avenue, or a terrace, where ladies and gentlemen might perambulate without being accosted by the lower sort or polluted by unnecessary noises or smells. These walks also outlined a form of social discipline and observation where the fashionable or the notable could be greeted with a bow. It was customary for the upper and middling classes to go on parade when the lower classes were still at work, thus avoiding any untoward encounters. It is perhaps worth noting, in this increasingly commercialized culture, that these rural walks were the direct begetters of the shopping parades or 'window-shopping'.

Those who now considered themselves to be part of what became known as 'polite society' patronized these places as much to be seen as to see; there was nothing so snobbish as a country town, even in its new incarnation. There were now certain ways to dress, to greet acquaintances, to sip coffee, to converse, or to dance. The local theatres were schools of manners that replaced the 'courtesy books' of an earlier civilization. The concern for 'improvement' that played so large a part in the mercantile and mechanical aspects of life could now be applied closer to home. Throughout human history the city has always been the symbol of political and aesthetic life; it is possible to speculate that, in the eighteenth century, Britain began that urban experiment on a national scale.

The professions flourished, creating an entirely new class of middling society. The town gentry made space to accommodate the clergymen, the attorneys of common law courts and the solicitors of Equity and Chancery; the physicians and even the surgeon-apothecaries were also acquiring new status with the emergence of the charity hospitals which provided treatment for the poor at no charge. The number of professional government servants rose, creating a career bureaucracy which became well versed in business of every sort pertaining to the administration of the country. By the beginning of 1714, 113 commissioners were at the head of eighteen different offices, each of them well staffed. By the 1720s some 12,000 public servants had become permanent employees. The eighteenth century marked the emergence of government as we have come to know it.

The public buildings – the town hall, the corn exchange, the guildhall, the court house, the mansion house, the financial exchange – began to be dressed in a new and more imposing fabric in which civility and sociability were the guiding principles. Fashions were followed even in charity: the schools were the first to be granted more imposing premises, succeeded in turn by hospitals and then by prisons. The polite person was also the sociable person that, by definition, meant the charitable person. The great increase in charitable funding happened at precisely the time when polite society found its name and calling. Twenty-four hospitals were established between 1735 and 1783, nine of which were raised in the 1740s and 1750s. The public institutions of the time, from prisons to schools, were the project of voluntary organizations and had nothing whatever to do with any central administration. So we read of the Marine Society, the Philanthropic Society, the Royal Humane Society and many others, all of them memorialized in stone buildings that largely survive. Politeness also meant morality.

If the public institutions of the provincial town represented its spirit of improvement, one other new arrival epitomized the recent fashion for sociability. 'Assembly rooms' were precisely that, large rooms in which people might congregate for a variety of functions. They were quite a modern thing, infinitely preferable to the old gatherings at assizes or at horse-fairs; in his *Tour* Defoe in fact criticized 'the new mode of forming assemblies, so much, and so fatally now in vogue'. He was possibly commenting upon what might be considered the indiscriminate mingling of the sexes on such occasions, although the codes of conduct were very severe.

The Assembly Rooms at York looked like nothing so much as the gallery of a great palace with individuals, couples, or groups sauntering idly through. A tearoom and a card-room were among the more polite amenities; but the great venue was the ballroom, in which three tiers of seating around the room allowed the spectators to see the dancing, the dresses and the jewels.

Balls, and dances, were often held on a weekly basis; an annual subscription or ticket allowed you access to a supposedly glittering world of wax candles, chandeliers, branched candlesticks and lighted sconces. To the sound of a score of musicians in the gallery the couples would dance the minuet or, later, the more robust country dances of the period. Everyone would be watching everyone else; strangers would be observed and criticized; sudden meetings and pairings would be noticed at once. This was still the country, and not the city.

It was all very artificial and very tiring, the exhaustion of the male participants no doubt alleviated by frequent resort to the bottle. Balls might be described in somewhat impersonal terms as mating displays in which either sex looked for and, if fortunate, found a prospective partner. There was an element of make-believe in it, with a veneer of classical order and harmony coating some more traditional activities, but no more so than in many eighteenth-century social pursuits.

The other great innovation of the age was the 'pleasure garden', a direct descendant of the 'tea garden' of the seventeenth century which had generally been the rural adjunct to an inn. Yet the pleasure garden was planned on an altogether more brilliant and ambitious scale, with musical performances, balls and promenades along tree-lined walks; even plays were sometimes performed. Statues and ornaments and paintings and frescoes and architectural conceits completed the panoramas of pleasure.

The two most celebrated of these gardens, Vauxhall Gardens south of the River Thames and Ranelagh Gardens in Chelsea, were soon attracting thousands of visitors who were regaled with tea, liquor and ham sandwiches so exiguous that they became the butt of theatrical jokes. It was claimed that a competent waiter could cover the 11 acres of Vauxhall with the slices from one ham.

The gardens were lit at night by a thousand lamps, thus giving the illusion of Scheherazade and the nights of Arabia, but in a relatively short time they became the venue for more impolite colloquies and engagements in which darkness was favoured. It was almost inevitable, perhaps, that the more high-minded aspirations towards culture should be turned into what were essentially entertainments of a not very inspiring kind. It is said that there were more prostitutes in the gardens than there were waiters. This may also provide an insight into the eighteenth-century city.

Another eighteenth-century attraction, the 'spa', was the epitome of healthful and rational pleasure; it was closely followed in popularity by the regimen of exercise and social intercourse to be found in the seaside towns. It was considered good, and even necessary, to escape from the 'great wen' of London with its clouds of disease and corruption. The spas were descended from the healthful wells, or holy wells, that had emerged over many hundreds, and even thousands, of years of religious celebration. But the religion was now wholly forgotten. The Roman goddess of the Bath waters, Sulis Minerva, was silent. The Virgin Mary, patron of many medieval establishments, was no longer heard. St Chad, the patron saint of medicinal springs, was entirely forgotten. Instead we encounter the figure of Beau Nash, the presiding master of ceremonies at Bath, complete with slender cane and white beaver hat. He conducted a regime of what might be described as pleasurable or curative servitude, with the attendant delights of plays, concerts, gaming, horse-racing, card-playing, bookshops and all the other paraphernalia of Georgian cultural life.

There were competitors in the great game of health but Bath held the palm. This was the place where ageing or ailing politicians, sick of the pressures of Westminster, would go for what generally turned out to be a temporary or wholly ineffective remedy. Any visitors of distinction would be greeted by a peal of bells from Bath Abbey and a musical serenade at the door of their lodgings. There was no question of anonymity in this world; the whole point was to be recognized as an eminent social being. One of the many rules at Bath prohibited the use of screens in public places lest 'they divide the company into secluded sets, which is against the fundamental institution of these places'. The pre-eminent concern was for society itself.

The baths were the first engagement of the day, followed by the coffee-shops for the male and shops of dainties for the female; there was time for concerts, lectures, or more spiritual pastimes before noon. The two or three hours before dinner could be filled with outings, promenades and card-playing before another official visit to the pump room in the evening. Large spaces were provided for all these communal activities, once more emphasizing the vitalizing and benevolent flow of social life.

The life of the seaside towns was perhaps a little more boisterous, with the uncertain impact of the wind and the waves on the polite society assembled there. There was as yet no settled view of nature other than as something vaguely picturesque and, in the right hands, ripe for 'improvement'. Gardens could be manicured or tempted into sinuous rills but the sea was altogether ungovernable except by those sailors who despite their recent triumphs still had a somewhat unsavoury reputation. For those of an iron constitution there were manuals such as Richard Russell's *Dissertation upon the Use of Sea-Bathing*, published in 1749, but even by this decade only the most hardy visitors could be lured into the water. It was much better to promenade along a safely covered walk.

Civilization meant civility; this comprised, in the spas and seaside towns, order and sociability. It meant all the gestures of recognition and of greeting, all the gradations of talk, the conventions of formal introduction, the manner of advancing into a room or of a male opening the door for a member of the opposite sex. The sociable man was the man par excellence. It was he who, literate and polite and urbane, embodied the spirit of the age. The flow of social life, as it has been described, softened and modulated the person. As the earl of Shaftesbury put it in *Characteristics* (1737), 'we polish one another and rub off our corners and rough sides by a sort of amicable collision'. Thus both men and women could be described as 'genteel' or 'complaisant' if they observed the fashions and conventions of the day. It was not done to be jaunty, or enthusiastic, or even in a hurry. We may be tempted to recall the remark of Tacitus upon the manners of the native English under Roman rule: they called it civilization, when in fact it was part of their servitude. These eighteenth-century worldlings were slaves to the false gods of the aspiring middle classes – the minor gentry, the professional classes, the wealthy merchants – who followed the theatrical posturings of the elite.

The unruly man, the impolite man, was one who according to Samuel Johnson in the *Adventurer* of February 1754 manifested 'a rejection of the common opinion, a defiance of common censure, and an appeal from general laws to private judgement'; he was, in other words, anti-social. The other extreme, from which all polite men also fled, was the effeminate creature of nods and bows and grimaces. The attendance at Italian opera and the drinking of tea were both signs of male effeminacy, and they signalled a very real fear that the new taste of the age was destroying the older masculine culture of the Stuart and Elizabethan worlds. The new fashion of men kissing, on greeting, was particularly deplored. In Colley Cibber's *Love Makes a Man; or, The Fop's Fortune* (1700), one actor congratulates another. 'Sir, you kiss pleasingly. I love to kiss a man. In Paris we kiss nothing else.'

The great medium of sociable life was of course the conversation in which public judgement and private taste were finely mingled; it was widely assumed that civilized values and public truth were best acquired through social intercourse and dialogue. Samuel Johnson could not have existed without the conversation with kindred spirits that calmed the over-heated excitements of his brain; it made him aware of the larger world in which he had his being, so different from the silence of terror or torpor that he feared. As he said in the *Rambler* of January 1752, 'none of the desires dictated by vanity is more general, or less blamable, than that of being distinguished for the arts of conversation'. This may not have been recognized by Isaac Newton or by William Blake, but it was readily apparent to those who lived in the middle years of the eighteenth century. A man was made for conversation.

Certainly it accounts for the notable emergence of clubs as the medium of male exchange, not least the 'Conversation Societies' which met weekly in well-regulated venues. 'Whether the study of natural philosophy, or that of profane history, is more useful to mankind?' 'Is it a duty incumbent upon parents to inoculate their children, as a means to preserve life?' The clubs were intended to foster cheerfulness and conviviality, friendship and mutual understanding, perhaps in unconscious aversion to the political and religious divisions of the last century.

Clubs were now to be found everywhere. Some clubs made their

homes in taverns, among them the Essex Head Club, the Ivy Lane
Club, the Turk's Head Club; all of these had some connection with
Samuel Johnson. John Macky, in *Remarks on the Characters of the
Court of Queen Anne* (1732), observed that 'almost every [London]
parish hath its separate club where the citizens, after the fatigue of
the day is over in their shops, and on the Exchange, unbend their
thoughts before they go to bed'. Joseph Addison, one of the high
priests of eighteenth-century civilization, remarked that 'man is a
sociable animal' but perhaps he did not include women within this
truism, since none of the clubs noted at the time catered for female
members.

Every male industry, trade, interest, tradition, activity, art, or
ambition now had its club. London numbered 3,000, while Bristol
had approximately 250. There could scarcely have been a time when
an Englishman needed to be alone. It is perhaps no wonder that
the pleasures of solitude were among those adumbrated by the
coming 'romantic' movement of the early nineteenth century. Yet it
was also a time of seclusion for those who wished it; partitioned
churches and partitioned taverns were as common as more open
settings. There is the story of the man who had eaten at the same
tavern for twenty-five years. Over those years he and his neighbour
in the next cubicle had never spoken. Eventually the man plucked
up the courage to call out:

'Sir, for twenty-five years we have been neighbours at dinner,
and yet we have never spoken. May I enquire your name, sir?'

'Sir, you are impertinent.'

It is a very English exchange.

To 'club' was to come together for mutual benefit, to create a
common stock or pursue a common end, to become partners or to
make up a specified sum. Some clubs were therefore akin to trading
organizations and there were clubs for coal-heavers and clubs for
silk-weavers, clubs for hackney-cab men and clubs for shoemakers,
clubs for clock-makers and clubs for wig-makers, clubs for farriers
and clubs for gingerbread-makers.

There were Art Clubs and Music Clubs, Philosophical Clubs
and Literary Clubs, Mug House Clubs and Fox Hunters Clubs; at
the Terrible Club, which met in the Tower at midnight on the first
Monday of the month, its members had to cut their beef with a

bayonet and drink a concoction of brandy and gunpowder. Some other clubs sound too arcane to be taken seriously. At the Lazy Club members were supposed to arrive in their nightshirts, and at the Silent Club not a word was allowed to be spoken. The Club of Ugly Faces specialized in just that. The Tall Club, the Surly Club and the Farters' Club had a similarly specialized membership. Some of the members of the Kit-Kat Club, painted by Godfrey Kneller, still adorn the walls of the National Portrait Gallery. With Addison, Vanbrugh, Congreve, Walpole and Steele among them, the visitor will become acquainted with the faces of early eighteenth-century English society, culture and now history.

11

Consuming passions

It is often suggested that the fairs and markets of medieval or Elizabethan England diminished and died a natural death. That was not strictly true; wherever there was a chance of making money a stall could be put up or a trestle table placed against a house door. Fairs and markets survived to serve the needs of their local area, as markets do still. But they were to be 'improved'. The old open marketplaces were swept away and the market crosses taken down as nuisances to traffic; in the newly designed markets the various goods were grouped together and given a ration of space.

Yet something else had arrived that would eventually change the nature of retailing all over the country. By the mid-eighteenth century every village had a shop. A shop came to differentiate the village from the hamlet. The impetus had come from London, the source and spring of marketing. There had since Roman times been emporia of many goods and many nations in the capital. So it was at this later date. The Royal Exchange in the City, built in 1567, was, for example, rivalled by the New Exchange on the Strand constructed forty-two years later. They were two quintessentially London institutions. In the earlier years of the seventeenth century shops were usually no more than sheds or stalls or basements, but the Great Fire of 1666 in particular gave them room to expand and to breathe.

Certain houses, or the ground floors of houses, were designed for retailing; it was not long before the virtues of display became paramount. Glass windows were still too expensive for the poorer retailers, but they could open up their fronts and sell there before boarding them again at night. And in a gawking, loitering age of display it was inevitable that the larger shops should take on the characteristics of a theatre of taste. They had assumed the functions of the Royal Exchange and the New Exchange by being at the same time both warehouses and galleries, auction rooms and bazaars; soon enough sash windows gave way to bow windows for the display of even more goods and delicacies.

'The shops are perfect gilded theatres,' the *Female Tatler* observed in 1709, 'the variety of wrought silks so many changes of fine scenes, and the mercers are the performers in the opera . . . "This, Madam, is wonderfully charming. This, Madam, is so diverting a silk. This, Madam, my stars! How cool it looks".' It was a perpetual puppet play, in which commerce is transformed into an art or into a game. Sophie von la Roche noted in her diary for 1786 that 'behind the great glass windows absolutely everything one can think of is neatly, attractively displayed, in such abundance of choice as almost to make one greedy'. It was the beginning of what has been described as leisure shopping. She passes 'a watch-making, then a silk or fan store, now a silver-smith's, a china or glass shop'. These are the harbingers of Heal's, Swan & Edgar, and Fortnum & Mason, all of which arrived in the eighteenth or early nineteenth centuries.

It has been described as a 'commercial revolution' but of what, precisely, did this revolution consist? The contents of the more prosperous households may provide a clue to the prevailing or fashionable taste. The inventory of a rich City merchant, Mr Crowley, taken in 1728, revealed 'two pairs of India blue damask window curtains . . . damask hangings lined with canvas, six carved and silvered bark stools shifted and covered with silver and gold brocade . . . a settee and two square stools . . . a Persian carpet, a carved and silvered frame for a tea-table and one ditto for a tea water kettle . . . a small ebony cabinet inlaid . . .'. The list goes on to include other goods of relatively high worth. By the standards of the day this was not necessarily an opulent household although, in earlier periods of English life, it would have been considered lavish in the extreme. A rich grocer's widow, Mrs Forth, seemed to luxuriate in mahogany with a dressing table, a bed, a chest of drawers, an easy chair and fourteen other chairs of the same wood. The number of households that possessed cups for hot drinks rose 55 per cent in the thirty years before 1725, demonstrating the speed and specificity of fashion.

An inventory of a great manufacturer, Boulton & Fothergill, gives another impression of the time with 'snuff boxes, instrument cases, toothpick cases – gilt, glass and steel trinkets, silver filigree boxes, needle books etcetera – all manner of plated goods, as tea urns, tankards, cups, coffee pots, cream jugs, candlesticks, sauce boats, terrines . . .'. By 1702 wallpaper was coming in and, according to an advertisement of the period, 'at the blue paper warehouse in Aldermanbury (and nowhere else) are sold the true sorts of figured paper hangings, some in pieces of twelve yards long, others after the manner of real tapestry'; in the following year hangings were offered 'in imitation of gilded leather'. Clocks, pictures, prints, mirrors, all of them could now be seen behind the bay windows of the most select shops.

But if you turned the corner from the Strand into Catherine Street, or from High Holborn into the passages beside Drury Lane, the characteristics of a consumer society would have been much more difficult to recognize. There were no luxuries here, only the necessary aids for survival. There were no names above the shops, only rudimentary signs. There were no windows, only open doors into dimly lit interiors. In Hogarth's 'Noon' a small girl snatches eagerly from the gutter a piece of broken and discarded pie.

It has been estimated that there were 3,000 shops in the neighbourhood of Holborn and more than 2,500 in the area of Southwark. In the City approximately 6,500 shops had a ratio of twenty-two customers to each shop; the proportion of people to shops in Clerkenwell was thirty to one.

The majority of these would be small backstreet shops or 'petty shops'. Like the village shops which they most closely resembled, they would have a range of essential goods on their shelves including tea, sugar, cheese, salt and butter. Other items were bought occasionally and measured in small quantities, among them yellow soap, spices, dried fruits, nuts, treacle, candles and flour. The customers would buy only on a daily basis, purchasing precisely what they required to survive until the following day. They might often rely on credit. The shopkeepers were frequently as poor as the customers themselves, all of them living off the same plain diet.

In the more prosperous neighbourhoods, however, the nature and quality of demand were hard to foresee with any accuracy; in an age in which taste and fashion had suddenly become important considerations, the patterns of consumption became of absorbing importance. China-ware was unknown in 1675 but had become so familiar as to be the object of satire by 1715. Cabinet-making became a major trade by the turn of the century, and cane chairs had a brief but spectacular reign in the drawing room. The purchase of books and of clocks, too, suggested a more sensitive awareness among the newly prosperous of what was 'expected'. Defoe, in his *Weekly Review* of January 1708, wrote of printed cotton fabrics that they first 'crept into our houses, our closets and bedchambers; curtains, cushions, chairs and, at last, beds themselves were nothing but calicoes or Indian stuffs'.

Emulation was the key. As the *British Magazine* put it in 1763, 'the present rage of imitating the manners of high-life hath spread itself so far among the gentlefolks of lower-life that in a few years we shall probably have no common people at all'. A more considered analysis of English society, given four years later by Nathaniel Forster in *An Enquiry into the Causes of the Present High Price of Provisions*, noted that

in England the several ranks of men slide into each other almost imperceptibly, and a spirit of equality runs through every part of their constitution. Hence arises a strong emulation in all the several situations and conditions to vie with each other; and the perpetual restless ambition in each of the inferior ranks to raise themselves to the level of those immediately above them. In such a state as this fashion must have uncontrolled sway. And a fashionable luxury must spread through it like a contagion.

There were no social 'classes' in perpetual enmity – the idea had never occurred to anyone except the Diggers and Levellers of the previous century – but rather a multiplicity of different ranks each eager to outdo one another in the race for prosperity.

The confirmation that this new dispensation also affected the labouring poor can be found in the many surveys that demonstrate the rise of real wages in the first half of the century. In the first book of *The Wealth of Nations* Adam Smith observed that the increase in wages ensured that 'the real quantity of the necessaries and conveniences of life which it can procure to the labourer has, during the course of the present century, increased perhaps in a still greater proportion than its money price'. Grain was cheaper. Potatoes were half the price. Turnips and cabbages could be had for a song. Some of this may be explained by wishful thinking, or by faulty observation and calculation, but the general restlessness and busyness of the age suggest that there was a general resurgence in economic activity.

You have only to look at the printed advertisements, almost a new thing in the culture of England. Sixty different advertisements were placed in the public prints for George Packwoods's razor cleaners and shaving paste; Dr James Graham advertised his 'celestial, or medico, magnetico, musico, electrical bed'; he added that 'in the celestial bed no feather is employed . . . springy hair mattresses are used . . . in order that I might have for the important purposes, the strongest and most springy hair, I procured at vast expense the tails of English stallions'. Hawkin and Dunn offered 'COFFEE MADE IN ONE MINUTE', while Jasper Taylor advertised a range of ready-prepared sauces such as 'SAUCE EPICUR-IENNE'. Adverts appeared for 'POMMADE DIVINE' or 'PEARS TRANSPARENT SOAP'. Smaller notices promoted Dixon's antibilious pills, Butler's restorative tooth powder, Godbold's vegetable balsam for asthma and Hackman's pills for the gravel and the stone. The 'puffs', as they were often called, were placarded over walls and windows as well as journals and periodicals. It was truly a society of the spectacle, far removed from the sixteenth century when only playbills were plastered on the posts.

It was perhaps the hyperbole that caused Dr Johnson to confess that 'the trade of advertising is now so near perfection that it is not easy to propose any improvement'. Illustrations of jugs, and shoes, and hats, and plates, and tureens, and capes, and glasses, were everywhere. William Blake, the poet of eternity, designed some advertisements for crockery from Josiah Wedgwood with perhaps one of his great phrases on his lips: Eternity is in love with the productions of time.

The notion of the 'consumer' in the marketing sense emerged first in the 1720s as the belated recognition of the growing phenomenon. Belinda, in William Congreve's *The Old Bachelor*, produced in 1693, explains that 'the father bought a powder-horn, and an almanac, and a comb-case; the mother, a great fruz-tour [false headpiece], and a fat amber necklace; the daughters only tore two pairs of kid-leather gloves with trying 'em on . . .'. Belinda is describing the appearance of a country squire and his family in a fashionable London shop.

It was no doubt their first visit. These were the newly prosperous who had enough leisure on their hands to travel up to the city in an equipage or at least a coach. No doubt they went back to houses already furnished with carpets, screens and window curtains. The original meaning of 'consumer', in the *Oxford English Dictionary*, is of one who 'devours, wastes, or destroys'.

All was done in the name of fashion, the god of the metropolis. Samuel Oldknow, the cotton manufacturer from Lancashire, declared that 'nothing but new things will please fashionable women'. One of the correspondents of the *Spectator*, at the beginning of 1712, heard a woman in an adjacent pew of the neighbourhood church whispering to her companion that 'at the Seven Stars, in King Street, Covent Garden, there was a mademoiselle completely dressed just come from Paris'. A 'mademoiselle' was a 'moppet' or puppet dressed with the newest fashions in the latest style. A month later another correspondent in the *Spectator* was complaining that his wife had changed all the goods and furniture in the house three times in seven years. Between 1770 and 1800 some thirty almanacs or annuals were issued for the fashionable woman, with all the panoply of advertisements and prints. No lady in society could afford to be 'out of the fashion'. The men, too, were encouraged by their tailors 'to strike a bold stroke' with their latest attire.

Henry Fielding, the novelist and London magistrate, noticed

in one of his many somewhat acidulous asides that the growth of commerce had quite changed the face of the nation, and particularly of the 'lower sort'; as far as he was concerned, they had become greedy, crafty and vain. Trade also encouraged equality between buyers and sellers; ready money was the only mark of distinction. The old attitudes of deference to authority, orthodoxy and tradition had no place in the thriving market. There was no question of any religious duty to avoid excess profit. There was no sense of a 'just price' to be set by the community at large. In matters of vital sustenance, such as bread, the old tradition of prices was maintained for a little longer. But in the larger world the obligations had been sundered. This was becoming a secular and individualistic, no longer a corporate, world. Trade restrictions, and labour controls, gradually gave way. The power of the old guilds in dictating the terms and the nature of employment was severely curtailed.

The new commercial world affected other pursuits. Sir John Hawkins, friend of Samuel Johnson and historian of music, wrote that 'the spirit of luxury rages here with greater violence than ever . . . the great articles of trade in the metropolis are superfluities, mock-plate, toys, perfumery, millinery, prints and music'. Johnson himself might not have agreed with his friend's judgement since, like many other observers in the eighteenth century, he believed that luxuries gave employment and income to the industrious poor. 'Now the truth is', he said, 'that luxury produces much good.' Unnecessary and superfluous commodities, such as Venetian looking glasses, Turkey carpets, Japan screens, Flanders lace, vases from China and statues from Italy, were the lifeblood of high commerce.

The more humble cup or saucer of tea was considered, on its first arrival in England in the middle of the seventeenth century, to be an intolerable luxury that spread depression and lassitude among its consumers. It was conceived by many to be a dangerous, insidious and powerful concoction. It was not nutritious. It weakened the nerves. It prevented healthy sleep.

By 1717, however, green tea had become the drink of choice; and its use was now common among all classes and any attempt at prohibition, suggested by some, was sure to fail. The average annual import during the 1690s was some 20,000 pounds in weight; by 1760 it had reached 5 million pounds. The amount of sugar consumed, to sweeten the bitter herb, increased fifteen times over the century. The human cost of what was essentially colonial exploitation will be discussed in a later chapter. Behind the spoon of sugar lay the back-breaking labour of the slave. An abolitionist of the late eighteenth century, Elizabeth Heyrick, wrote that 'the laws of our country may hold the sugar cane to our lips, steeped in the blood of our fellow creatures; but they cannot compel us to accept the loathsome potion'. It is ironic perhaps that the daily diet of sweetened tea helped to sustain the wage-earning slaves of the English cities.

All the roads of luxury and fashion have the signpost 'To Etruria' standing beside them. The master of that destination was of course Josiah Wedgwood, the tradesman who more than any other epitomizes the Georgian culture of commerce. He was born in the summer of 1730 at Burslem in Staffordshire, the heart of the pottery country, and the spirit of place animated him soon enough; he was truly a native genius. Little is known about his early years but it is clear that he soon embarked upon an ambitious programme of research and improvement. He began a life of labour and experiment on glazes and colours while at the same time becoming a pioneer of industrial design; he was determined to fashion the best cream-ware in the world. 'I saw the field was spacious,' he wrote, 'and the soil so good, as to promise an ample recompense to anyone who should labour diligently in its cultivation.'

He realized from the beginning that his trade should be concentrated upon the rising ranks of 'middling people', 'which class', he wrote in a letter of 1772, to his business partner, Thomas Bentley, 'we know are vastly, I had almost said, infinitely superior in numbers to the Great'. This might be described as the manifesto of the new consumer society. He realized, too, the vast importance of fashion in such an enterprise. 'Fashion', he wrote, 'is infinitely superior to *merit* in many respects.' He was reflecting in part on the enormous success of his creamware in the replacement of porcelain. He wrote to Bentley again that 'it is really amazing how rapidly the use has spread almost over the whole globe, and how universally it is liked'. But then he asked, '[H]ow much of this

general use, and estimation, is owing to the mode of its introduction – and how much to its real utility and beauty?' It was a
most pertinent question but one that did not and does not readily
afford an answer.

The 'mode of its introduction', however, was of paramount
concern to Wedgwood and his associates. His methods included
those of elegant display and of widespread advertisement; he
pioneered the use of catalogues and of trademarks to distinguish
his products. If the name of a patron could be attached to a certain
range of ware, so much the better. He opened a London warehouse
and other showrooms where the merchandise was treated as if it
were part of a gallery or museum; when he opened a new showroom
on the corner of St Martin's Lane and Great Newport Street, he
made sure that its address was published in the *St James Chronicle*
perused by 'people of fashion, and which I suppose is that wherein
the plays are advertised'.

He employed travelling salesmen, and took pains to export his
ware to the royal and noble families of Europe. He had the ambition of being 'Vase Maker General to the Universe' which, in a
manner of speaking, he became. If we can name him one of the
founders of a commercial society, he can also be called one of
the pioneers of a new industrial society. Many visitors made their
way to his factory, where his employees were regimented and distributed with the same precision and order as the cups and tureens that
came off the production line. The factory was in effect three large
blocks running 150 yards alongside the Grand Trunk Canal with
several courtyards and towers containing kilns and ovens. It was
described by a foreign rival, Louis Victor Gerverot, as 'an enormous
building, practically a small town . . . a marvel of organisation'.
We shall come across similar descriptions of English factories when
we descend further into the bowels of the Industrial Revolution.
The enterprise was designed for mass production along an assembly
line, the first of its kind in the pottery industry.

Wedgwood divided the manufacture of pottery into components
such as slip-casting and transfer-printing, each with its own experts
working in unison. His purpose was 'to make such *machines* of
the *Men* as cannot err'; continued and uninterrupted production
could thereby be achieved. It could have been Orwell's *Nineteen*

Eighty-Four rather than 1769. He did not tolerate faulty goods. He had an artificial leg, as a result of a childhood illness, and it is said that he would smash inferior items of crockery with a blow from his wooden limb. He rang the bell for work at 5.45 a.m., and devised a form of 'clocking in' that became the standard practice of the factory system.

In the world of English commerce everything, from the time of 'clocking in' to the time of leaving, breathes and has its being through the agency of the market; if we may paraphrase Hermes Trismegistus on the nature of the divine, it had its centre everywhere and its circumference nowhere. The concept of the market, in anything like a contemporary sense, was in fact even then being devised. Two of the earliest references are to be found in Adam Smith's *An Inquiry into the Nature and Causes of the Wealth of Nations* (1776), the book that can be said to be the founding text of the modern economy; when Smith alludes to the trade in a particular commodity or product, he calls it 'the market'.

He believed that trade should be free, altogether liberated from the restrictions that had their origin in the medieval system; there should be no control over wages, hours, rates of interest, or prices of good; the mobility of labour and the flow of capital should not be regulated by any external authority. 'Protection', in all its forms, should come to an end. The sphere of traditional and paternalistic values should be destroyed and in its place a system of supply and demand should be instituted.

This of course had wider ramifications. Richard Price, writing on civil liberty in 1776, the same year that Smith completed *The Wealth of Nations*, wrote that 'all government even within a State, becomes tyrannical as far as it is a needless and wanton exercise of power, or is carried further than is absolutely necessary to preserve the peace or to secure the safety of the State'. The duty of government was to promote internal justice and to defend against external aggression. That was all. The natural operation of supply and demand, therefore, would be to the advantage of all parties; and the best possible market was one allowed to regulate itself.

Just as trade was considered pre-eminently good in itself, so the basic principles of trade – to buy cheap and to sell dear – became paramount. What might be called the market nexus covered a whole range of social activities, from marriage to a hackney-carriage licence. Moll Flanders, in Defoe's novel of that name, remarks that 'the market is against our sex just now'. The result might be construed as 'laissez-faire', a phrase that became popular in the 1750s.

It was believed, for example, that businessmen and private investors should finance the building of bridges and roads, without involving the central administration, while the promotion of technology and science was to be left to aristocratic patrons and learned societies. Surely this would apply with redoubled force in financial and economic matters? The conviction slowly percolated through to the Commons and in 1796 William Pitt lamented the occasions 'when interference has shackled industry' and declared that 'trade, industry and barter will always find their own level and be impeded by regulations which violate their natural operation and derange their proper effect'.

This was the permanent consequence of *The Wealth of Nations*. Smith himself was an unlikely prophet; at a young age he had been kidnapped for a short time by tinkers from his native Kirkcaldy, and it may be that some of his oddities were a result of that unplanned expedition. He had a habit of smiling and talking to himself, proceeding along the streets of Edinburgh in what was described as a 'vermicular' – worm-like – manner; he had a harsh voice and teeth like tombstones. He was once discoursing on the division of labour to certain colleagues, when he fell into a tannery pit of fat and lime; he had to be taken home in a sedan chair, complaining all the while.

He believed that an individual should take his own course in the belief that 'the natural effort of every individual to better his own condition, when suffered to exert itself with freedom and security', has enough intrinsic power to carry any society towards 'wealth and prosperity'. When an individual attends to his own gains he is led 'by an invisible hand' to promote an end that was far from his intention, which may be described as the general good. It was he rather than Napoleon who described England as 'a nation of shopkeepers', thus justifiably defining the nation as uniquely dependent upon trade. In the second chapter of *The Wealth of Nations* he proposes that 'it is not from the benevolence of the butcher, the brewer, or the baker, that we expect our dinner but from their regard to their own interest'. From this sentence sprang an insight that controlled social and economic theory for more than a century. It is in fact one of the enduring legacies of the eighteenth century.

12

The What D'Ye Call It?

The old king had died, after waving farewell to his favourite German palace, but the information did not reach the royal apartments at Richmond Lodge until three days later. It was the duty of the pre-eminent minister, Robert Walpole, to broach the report to his new sovereign, George II, who promptly asked the minister to inform Spencer Compton; Compton was the treasurer of the new king's household, and seemed likely to secure effective power. Yet it was not to be. Those who gleefully anticipated Walpole's demise had underestimated his effectiveness.

His equable relations with George's wife, Queen Caroline, have been noticed; it also became clear that Walpole had unrivalled command of the Commons. Walpole was in any case by far the most competent and authoritative man in the country, a fact which even a new king could not easily ignore. The king himself spoke English but with a strong guttural German accent, so he might sometimes need the aid of an emollient translator.

Yet he had lived in England long enough to be acquainted with the most powerful men and women in the country, and seems from the beginning to have decided to rule in a way different from that of his father. This bias obviously gave hope to the Tories who had been systematically excluded from power by George I. They flocked to court, but the best of intentions can sometimes be thwarted by events; as it was, the powerful forces ranged against them effectively barred them as possible Jacobites. The Tories had also been averse to the continental wars, of which Hanover had been a part, and were therefore still suspected.

The king himself was by no means a majestic spectacle. He was very short, and relied upon the effect of wigs and high shoes to accentuate the positive. The flatterers noted that he had bright blue eyes and a noble Roman nose; his enemies saw only feebleness of intellect and of character. He was somewhat stiff in his bearing, with the attendant characteristics of obstinacy and bad temper. It was reported that his ministers were forced 'to bear . . . even with such foul language that no one gentleman could take from another'. The pattern of his conversation was one of boastfulness, bullying and bluster. Some of his words to his wife have been recorded by Lord Hervey, vice-chamberlain in the royal household. 'Before she had uttered half of what she had a mind to say the King interrupted her, and told her she always loved talking of such nonsense and things she knew nothing of . . . she was always asking some fool or other what she was to do; and that none but a fool would ask another fool's advice.'

Understandably for a monarch he had a great sense of his own importance, but he did not necessarily impress his peers. A caricature shows him with his leg lifted to kick out; he was well known for kicking his servants, and also for being brusque or even rude to casual visitors. He was more obdurate in appearance than in reality, however, and a courtier, George Bubb Dodington, recorded in his *Diary* that the king 'would sputter and make a bustle but when they told him that it must be done from the necessity of his service' he went ahead and did it. He was by obligation, if not by nature, a pragmatist.

He was aware that a Hanoverian king was not necessarily adored or admired by the English, and took care to manifest his status. He dressed strictly, according to the codes of etiquette, and carried himself with more hauteur than was perhaps necessary; he adored the regal world of pageantry and spectacle. Yet he was also aware of the sensitivities of his subjects; he did not claim any semi-divine status by touching for the king's evil, and he discouraged any attempt at a cult of majesty with portraits or statues.

In fact he loved his subjects no more than they loved him. Lord Hervey records the king's running commentary upon the faults and follies of the English. 'No English or even French cook could dress a dinner; no English confectioner could set out a dessert; no English player could act; no English coachman could drive, or English jockey ride, nor were any English horses fit to be drove or fit to be ridden; no Englishman knew how to come into a room, nor any English-woman how to dress herself . . .' The palm in all these activities went of course to his German compatriots. This plain favouritism brought problems in a larger sphere, and it was feared by his ministers that he might try to steer England's foreign policy in a Hanoverian direction without consulting the nation's best interests. What had Westminster to do with Russia or with Sweden except as a way of obtaining wood? He had never been allowed to visit Hanover during the reign of his father but, after his own accession, he made many and prolonged visits to his electorate. He was a Guelph, one of the most ancient dynasties of all Europe, and it can be claimed with some confidence that he took a wider view of the continent than did his ministers.

Certainly he was meticulous in his duties; he was not one of those sovereigns who lose all cares of state on the hunting field. He read everything that was put before him, and every day was divided into its separate duties. Even the affairs of the heart were regulated. He visited his mistress, Henrietta Howard, at seven in the evening; if he was a little early he paced up and down outside her door with his watch in his hand until the tremendous moment came.

Walpole seems quickly to have got the measure of him, and confided to Hervey that 'his majesty imagines frequently he shall do many things, which, because he is not at first contradicted, he fancies he shall be let do at last. He thinks he is devilish stout, and never gives up his will or opinion; but never acts in anything material according to either of them but when I have a mind he should.' He concluded that 'he is, with all his personal bravery, as great a political coward as ever wore a crown, and as much afraid to lose it'. He advised that 'the more you can appear to make anything to be his own, the better you will be heard'.

So Walpole had to be an artist of stage management as well as of decorum. The weights and balances of power were still somewhat ambiguous and he had to tread very carefully. In Westminster itself, of course, and in what were later to be called the corridors of power, Walpole was still pre-eminent. Robin ruled the roost. His command of men and management in parliament was paramount; the front bench was composed almost entirely of his nominees, and he knew how to touch the 'secret springs' of others' loyalty by promotion or by the discreet distribution of secret service money. He promised the king a quiet life, than which nothing suited George II better. 'Consider, Sir Robert,' he is supposed to have said, 'what makes me easy in this matter makes for your ease too.' They were friends for life.

Since the king was not called upon to do very much his reputation seemed to rise, and a French envoy noted in 1728 that 'the king is much more popular than George I. As much as he can, he tries to make himself popular.' This was in part the result of the efforts of Queen Caroline, who added a much-needed tone of levity and entertainment to what might otherwise have been a rather stiff court. Clearly his private animadversions against the English did not reach the public ear. The growth in wages and commerce, as outlined in a previous chapter, could have done nothing but increase his status.

Of course Walpole had many and various opponents; anyone with a dislike of the country's administration could find a ready target in the rotund figure of the first minister. A large number of dissident Whigs regarded him as their enemy; he had not only kept them out of power but he was in the process of creating a despotism in the halls of Westminster. The Hanoverian Tories were by nature and instinct opposed to any Whig autocrat, especially when he held the strings of commerce and of patronage in his hands. And then there were the Jacobites, waiting hopefully for the day when the monarch over the water would return to claim his proper kingdom. These multifarious opponents might agree on ousting Walpole but they could not really concur in a coherent and positive alternative policy.

Many of the public prints were opposed to Walpole, most notably the *Craftsman* which as its name might imply was dedicated to exposing the men of craft or subterfuge. The first issue, published at the end of 1726, declared that 'the mystery of *State-Craft* abounds with such innumerable frauds, prostitutions, and enormities, in all shapes, and under all disguises, that it is an inexhaustible fund, an eternal resource for satire and reprehension'. Thus was launched a sustained invective against Walpole and his allies.

A month later in the *Craftsman* came a character assassination of the first minister as a 'man, dressed in a plain habit, with a purse of gold in his hand. He threw himself into the room, in a bluff ruffianly manner. A smile, or rather a sneer sat on his countenance. His face was bronzed over with a glare of confidence. An' arch malignity leered in his eye.' A later number issued a more general denunciation. 'Corruption is a poison, which will soon spread itself thro' all ranks and orders of men; especially when it begins at the fountain-head. A spirit of baseness, prostitution and venality will universally prevail.'

There was even a serial publication of a ballad, 'History of the Norfolk Steward':

> A story concerning one Robin
> Who, from not worth one groat
> A vast fortune has got
> By politics, Bubbles and Jobbing . . .

Other periodicals and pamphlets joined the hunt, assisted by notable combatants such as Swift and Pope, but nothing was more successful than a London musical.

In a letter of summer 1716, Swift suggested that his friend and fellow Scriblerian, John Gay, should write 'a Newgate pastoral, among the whores and thieves there'. This was the cue, taken up eleven years later, for the most famous and successful musical comedy of the eighteenth century. *The Beggar's Opera* was described by many names – comic opera, ballad opera, burlesque, satire, musical – just as victory in war still had many fathers. But no one knew quite what it was. In the course of the century, some of the theatres played it as low farce and others as sentimental tragedy. It was both, and neither. It goes from pathos to pantomime in the space of a line, and from cynicism to lyricism in a moment; there are passages in which the heterogeneous tones and styles cannot be distinguished, leading to bewilderment or exhilaration according to taste.

When we consider Pope's *Dunciad*, Sterne's *Tristram Shandy*, Swift's *Gulliver's Travels*, we note the resemblances. This was a doubting and ambiguous age that found its quietus in satire and ridicule. To that end *The Beggar's Opera* adopted all the popular modes and forms of the time, from street ballad to farce and folk song. All the life of the streets was somewhere within it, in implicit protest against the phalanx which ruled the state.

The eighteenth century is not supposed to have been a felicitous age of drama, with its 'serious' tragedies filled with sententious moralizing and sentimental pieties that sank John Dryden, for example, below the waterline. But *The Beggar's Opera* did provide surprise and delight to the London stage, written as it was according to the *Daily Journal* 'in a Manner wholly new'. It was still new when Bertolt Brecht purloined it for *The Threepenny Opera* of 1928.

The Beggar's Opera was first presented on 29 January 1729, at the Theatre Royal in Lincoln's Inn Fields (not to be confused with the Theatre Royal in Drury Lane) where it ran for sixty-two nights. This marked an overwhelming public response, when most other new plays lasted for only six or seven. It concerns two young women who are in love with, and believe themselves married to, a resourceful highwayman named Macheath ('son of the heath'). Polly Peachum, the daughter of a receiver of stolen goods, and Lucy Lockit, the daughter of the keeper of Newgate Prison, vie for his love in a setting of taverns and Newgate apartments filled with pimps, thieves, whores and all the other inhabitants of contemporary low life. Nothing but rough words and rough sentiments can be heard, while the lovers' complaints are ringed with ambiguity and satire. It was unforgettable and was for the period a breath of fresh air (if the term can be allowed for such insalubrious elements) after a period of achingly boring acting on moral stilts.

The fact that Newgate Prison is the setting for much of the plot confirms its central place in the consciousness of the eighteenth century. Everybody knew it, by reputation if not by sight and smell. It had become the common name for any prison, and a 'Newgate bird' for any prisoner. It had stood on the same site in various incarnations for 600 years and was once more rebuilt in 1770, by which time it had inspired more poems and plays than any other building in England. All the characters of *The Beggar's Opera* revolve around it, as if it were a dark sun, just as some of the most famous personalities of eighteenth-century London were associated with it.

The role of Polly's father, Peachum, for example, was loosely based upon Jonathan Wild; Wild was a receiver of stolen goods and a notorious 'thief-taker' who would impeach the unnecessary, incompetent, or injured members of his own gang in return for a payment of £40. He devised the robberies and then advertised the stolen goods in the columns of a newspaper, thus gaining the rewards for his own crimes. It was a common trade of the time, but Wild was its supreme exponent. He was hanged in 1725 but such was his continuing fame that Henry Fielding wrote his supposed biography, *The Life of Mr Jonathan Wild the Great*, eighteen years later. Wild was a cunning and violent man in a profane and ruthless age. His surname was his character. Fielding himself described eighteenth-century London as a wilderness, 'a vast wood or forest in which the thief may harbour with as great security as wild beasts do in the deserts of Arabia and Africa'.

The hero or anti-hero of the opera, Macheath, is a highwayman, one of the great professions of the eighteenth century. Although Gay portrays him as a poor piece of work, entirely dependent upon the bottle, the highwayman himself was often seen as a cavalier adventurer, a gentleman of the road, a man of honour. His victims were recommended to him by landlords or tapsters of the various inns, where they were called 'worth seeing' or 'worth speaking with'.

In his diary Horace Walpole recalled that 'a black figure on horseback' stopped the chaise in which he was riding with a Lady Browne. The highwayman asked for the lady's purse, saying, 'Don't be frightened. I will not hurt you.' He added, 'I give you my word that I will do you no hurt.' When she gave him the item he told her, before riding away, 'I am much obliged to you. I wish you good night.' This was perhaps the acceptable face of eighteenth-century crime, although it did not of course prevent the perpetrators from being hanged. Gay may even have helped to burnish the reputation of thieves and prostitutes. One contemporary remarked that 'highwaymen and women of the town are not romantic figures, but our poet had made highwaymen handsome and lively, and women of the town beautiful and attractive. Over all he has cast such a glamour of romance and sentimentalism that even Newgate comes to resemble a select pleasure resort.' But the real pleasure came in coins and notes.

This was a world of money, of stocks, of bubbles, of bullion and new paper notes of 1695 from the Bank of England. The language of trade and finance occurred naturally to Gay. He did not have to introduce it, or comment upon it; it came to him effortlessly because it reflected the temper of the time. Such terms as 'business', 'account', 'interest', 'profit', 'debt' and 'credit' are of many applications but they float up into the play with the bubble of money. This is a world of greed and gain. It is a culture in which someone could be bought or sold as easily as a piece of plate. Self-interest is the key as large as that which opened the great doors of Newgate itself. 'Honour' itself is false, when even pickpockets can call themselves 'men of honour'.

Who was, then, the gentleman? Lockit was known as 'the prime minister of Newgate', and Fielding wrote that 'Jonathan Wild had every qualification necessary to form a great man'. These were representative of the men who effectively ruled London and its surrounding countryside much more successfully than the men of Westminster who were nominally the masters.

When Peachum recites the names of the members of his gang, he mentions 'Robin of Bagshot, alias Gorgon, alias Bob Bluff, alias Carbuncle, alias Bob Booty'. From that time forward Walpole was often disparaged as 'Bob Booty' or 'Bluff Bob'. He had actually attended the first night and with characteristic sang-froid had applauded the references to himself, even asking for an encore. Yet the allusions to him may be of a more general application. As Lockit puts it,

> Lest the Courtiers offended should be:
> If you mention Vice or Bribe,
> 'Tis so pat to all the Tribe;
> Each crys – That was levell'd at me.

The Italian opera was a relatively new fashion, introduced to the London stage in 1705. There had always been musical dramas and ballad operas ever since the Mysteries and Miracle Plays of the medieval period. Shakespeare's characters break into song at every conceivable opportunity, and *The Tempest* might be described as an English opera. But the Italian style, with its use of recitativo and aria, its masque-like scenery and improbable plots, its castrato and its prima donna, captured the imagination of the early eighteenth century. In *The Beggar's Opera* Gay satirized its happy endings, as well as its more melodramatic moments, but seems to have loved its deliberate excess. Contemporary moralists and critics (there was sometimes little difference between them) condemned the Italian opera for being depraved, enervating and effeminate; Gay shows no signs of agreeing with them, while stealing from the operas themselves the constant strain of excitement and exhilaration.

When two rival sopranos came to blows on the stage of the Opera House, in Haymarket, the admirers of either lady pitched in with what one report described as 'cat-calls, howlings, hissings and other offensive manifestations' so that 'the evening concluded in one general and alarming riot'. It was the scene Gay revisited in the jealous rages between Lucy Lockit and Polly Peachum.

He adapted his music from the airs and ballads sung all around him; some were anonymous folk ballads while others were taken from fashionable operas and popular songs. A washerwoman could have sung them, or a porter whistled them. Tunes and melodies were always in the air.

Gay himself was a Devon boy, born and raised in Barnstaple where he attended the local grammar school. At some point in his seventeenth year he made the familiar journey to London where he was apprenticed as a draper's assistant; drapers' assistants were in this period often unfairly characterized as effeminate but Gay himself seems to have been diffident, uncertain, almost invisible. He once wrote that 'the world, I believe, will take so little notice of me, that I need not take much of it'. He ascended from apprentice to literary hack by producing small prose items for a twice-weekly periodical entitled the *British Apollo OR Curious Amusements for the INGENIOUS*. He emerged as a public writer, rather than a private hack, with a number of poems and pamphlets which were well received.

Then began the long, cruel search for patrons. Patrons were more invidious and inconstant than Grub Street. Yet impoverished authors still needed them. This was not an age when publication alone brought many rewards. Swift characterized the aspiring authors good-naturedly in *A Tale of a Tub*. 'They writ, and rallied, and rhymed, and sung, and said, and said nothing; they drank, and fought, and whored, and slept, and swore, and took snuff; they went to new plays on the first night, haunted the chocolate-houses.'

Gay turned his hand to everything in the fashionable mode – farces, satires, heroic tragedy, mock heroic and the strange mingling of moods and modes that are enshrined in the titles he chose such as *Trivia*, *The Toilette* and *The What D'Ye Call It?* He may justifiably have despaired of literary immortality, but he had been able to secure his immediate future with an appointment as a commissioner of the state lottery with rent-free lodgings in Whitehall. It was not a great deal, but it was something. He still complained of 'disappointments' but he remained on the treadmill of the court, kept revolving by gossip and malevolence. He may have consoled himself with the fact that the true poets of the age were the bankers and jobbers who conjured gold out of thin air and raised glittering palaces without any foundations at all. His career, like that of so many others at the time, was one of ambition and dependency, of fawning and favouritism, always in hope of further advancement but frequently overlooked.

All this changed with the first performance on that late January evening of 1729. No one had seen anything quite like it before and, soon enough, fire-screens, fans and playing cards were adorned with scenes from *The Beggar's Opera*. The manager of the theatre, John Rich, packed the theatre to bursting. On the evening of 23 March, for example, ninety-eight spectators were accommodated on the stage itself. William Hogarth painted six versions of the climactic prison scene. Pope wrote to Swift that 'John Gay is at present so employed in the elevated airs of the opera . . . that I can scarce obtain a categorical answer – to anything.'

The actress who played Polly Peachum, Lavinia Fenton, was surrounded by admirers wherever she went, and had to be escorted home after each performance. One observer remarked that 'the audience catches her fire and enthusiasm. The curtain drops. A wild burst of applause – "Polly!" "Polly!" – from every side of the house. A pretty bow, a kiss, then off the stage she runs . . . past the scenery, out of the stage door, into a waiting coach-and-four – and away,

away, away over the muddy roads of London.' The poet Edward Young remarked that she 'has raised her price from one guinea to 100, tho' she cannot be a greater whore than she was before, nor, I suppose, a younger'. But she did manage to catch a duke, and became the duchess of Bolton. Thus did the social, theatrical and financial worlds mingle.

The *Opera* was literally the talk of the town, including endless speculation over the presumed or suggested targets of its satire. In truth it had many and various victims, among them courtiers, tradesmen, thief-takers, politicians and those strange creatures who were hysterically in love with opera and opera divas. But its general complaint was against human corruption. Lockit remarks that 'Of all Animals of Prey, Man is the only sociable one. Every one of us preys upon his Neighbour, and yet we herd together.' In the 'condemned hold' Macheath sings a lament to the tune of 'Green Sleeves':

> Since Laws were made for ev'ry Degree
> To curb Vice in others, as well as me,
> I wonder we han't better Company
> Upon Tyburn Tree!

The Beggar's Opera was, all in all, very funny – not the elaborate and artificial comedy of Sheridan or Oliver Goldsmith, but the uproarious fun of the 'low' theatres. It outshone the sentimental comedies and heroic tragedies that were the staple of the age with its own particular mixture of burlesque and carnival, smut and innuendo. A male actor dressed in drag to play Polly Peachum, in a performance of 1782, whereupon one member of the audience 'was thrown into hysterics which continued without intermission until Friday morning when she expired'. The episode consorts well with the epitaph John Gay composed for himself.

> Life is a jest; and all things show it,
> I thought so once; but now I know it.

13

The dead ear

Sir Robert Walpole's revenge upon Gay came rather late in the day when, in 1737, he introduced a bill to curtail the liberty of the stage. All plays had to be submitted to the lord chamberlain fourteen days before performance, and of course the vicious insinuations on the stage against Bob Booty ceased at once. The Licensing Act was in fact not fully revoked until 1968, and so Walpole's retribution affected generations of playwrights.

But were the insinuations against Walpole in fact justified? He was always robust in his own defence, accusing his opponents of being 'mock patriots, who never had either virtue or honour, but in the whole course of their opposition are actuated only by motives of envy and of resentment'. It is true that he kept so tight a grasp on government policy and government patronage that there were some who felt unjustly excluded. Yet of course there was more to it than that. Venality was as intrinsic to the House of Commons as points of order; it is often the case that men and women who make the law also believe themselves to be above the law.

In the time of Walpole direct bribes were not uncommon but corruption might take a more subtle guise. The granting of pensions, the distribution of honours, the placement of offices, the giving of sinecures, were accepted and acceptable means of gaining the support of any particular member. In a period when parliamentarians were not paid, a fine line divided justifiable patronage and bribery. It was not through his public salary alone that Walpole himself could have built the magnificent stately home of Houghton Hall. A reading of Anthony Trollope, however, might persuade detractors that the same tricks and devices were still at work in the 1860s. In more indirect forms they continue to this day. One of the principal rewards of power is money.

Yet Robert Walpole, despite his power and prestige, could not buy the House of Commons. Not every man had his price. A large number of parliamentarians still voted according to their consciences or to their principles. There was no more striking instance of this independence than in 1733, when Walpole wholly misjudged the mood of the members. He had wanted to free the Port of London from its entanglements with customs regulations and customs officers which actively served to deter trade. He proposed that all tobacco be placed in a bonded warehouse for a small fee. The goods destined for re-export could recoup the fee while tobacco destined for the domestic market had to pay the conventional excise of 4 pence per pound. The same methods would be applied to the import of wine. It was a way of expediting the export trade, curtailing the prevailing vice of smuggling and simplifying the customs' work at the Port of London.

Unfortunately it was not seen in this benevolent light. Excise was believed to be an unnecessary and intrusive tax on the necessities of life. The subtleties of the scheme were ignored or misunderstood, and replaced by a vision of an army of excisemen combing the land in searches for offenders who had not paid the tax. Walpole's opponents were quick to spread the rumour that he intended to apply excise to food and other necessaries, and that British liberties would be sacrificed; the model would then become the heavily administered and heavily taxed nations of Europe. True-born Englishmen would soon be reduced to the state of French peasants.

A pamphlet, 'A Letter from a Member of Parliament for a Borough in the West', noted that 'little handbills were dispersed by thousands all over the City and country, put into people's hands in the streets and highways, dropped at their doors and thrown in at their windows; all asserting that excise men were (like a foreign enemy) going to invade and devour them . . .'. Like most panics it

1. An inset from the ceiling of the painted hall of the royal naval college at Greenwich, with William III and Mary II in majesty.

2. Queen Anne. A singularly unhappy and gouty queen.

3. John Churchill, 1st Duke of Marlborough. A great general and a great spendthrift – Blenheim was his shining star.

4. A scene from the Battle of Blenheim. 'I am very sensible that I take a great deal upon me,' he wrote before the battle, 'but should I act otherwise the Empire would be undone . . .'

5. George I of England, who had a
very fat mistress, and a very thin mistress.
It is almost a limerick.

6. George II was full
of bullying, boastfulness
and bluster.

7. An animated table at a London coffee house, *circa* 1700.

8. Robert Walpole. Plump, genial and a master of intrigue. All political strings led to him.

9. William Pitt 'the Elder', prime minister twice, with the badly misquoted line 'unlimited power corrupts the possessor'.

10. The Old Pretender, James Francis Edward Stuart, son of the deposed James II who quite improperly considered himself to be James III.

11. The Young Pretender, Charles Edward Stuart (*circa* 1740), otherwise known as Bonnie Prince Charlie.

12. Illustration from *Hogarth Restored: The Whole Works of the Celebrated William Hogarth.* The artist was the Rowlandson and Rembrandt of the age.

13. The spinning jenny, the latest example of industrial torture.

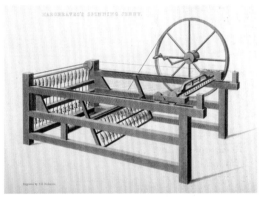

14. The horrors of gin and, at the time, spirituous frenzy.

15. John Dryden, poet, playwright and the first official Poet Laureate.

16. Jonathan Swift, satirist, pamphleteer and progenitor of the famous Gulliver.

17. Alexander Pope, perhaps contemplating 'this long disease, my life'.

18. Scrofulous and scruffy, Samuel Johnson was the giant of the age.

19. George III: He lost his reason and the American colonies.

20. The Prince Regent, later George IV, was fat, dissolute and entangled with wives. He was the model of a Hanoverian monarch.

was unjustified; but, like most panics, it was effective in the short term.

Walpole realized soon enough that the cause was hopeless. His effigy was burnt in the public markets, to a fanfare of rockets and bonfires, while cockades were worn with the motto 'Liberty, property, and no excise'. The Whigs were still associated in the public mind with war taxes and the machinations of the Whig financiers who ruled the City; the people were understandably suspicious of what seemed to be new ways of raising money. After a supper at Downing Street, when the servants had left the room, he declared to his colleagues that 'this dance it will no farther go, and tomorrow I intend to sound a retreat'. He had not altered his position but 'the clamour and the spirit' that had emerged over the excise had persuaded him to retire from the combat 'for prudential reasons'. After the bill was abandoned he had to face a mob outside parliament; protected by a bodyguard he was obliged to flee in and out of a coffee-house before making his escape.

Walpole had miscalculated. His native optimism had triumphed over his natural caution. The earl of Egmont noted in his diary that 'it may be foretold that Sir Robert's influence in the House will never again be so great as it has been'. Even though the king held fast to him, for fear of something worse, the opposition against him was growing ever greater. A general election in the spring of 1734 lengthened the odds against his eventual survival; his party, or what might be called the ministerial Whigs, acquired 347 supporters while the combined opposition of Tories and recalcitrant Whigs numbered 232. It would require great care and management to keep things in order, especially since the opposition Whigs, among them a group known by Walpole as the 'boy patriots' or 'cubs', were eager for power at any cost. They were sick of the 'old gang' or 'the old corps' or whatever opprobrious name was thrown at Walpole and his closest colleagues. What George II thought of the situation is unclear; he preferred conversation in the royal closet to correspondence, but his sympathy for Walpole remained.

If there was one constant principle and motive in Walpole's policies it was the wish to avoid war. He had an aversion to conflict. It was wasteful of men and money. It was uncertain, and provoked divisions within the nation. As early as 1726, the year before the old king's death, there had been rumours of a war with Spain as retribution for attacks on British ships, but a somewhat half-hearted blockade of Porto Bello, the Spanish fort and naval base off the coast of Panama, came to nothing. Negotiations ensued which were, for Walpole, the next best thing to peace.

Walpole also managed to stay out of the 'War of the Polish Succession' which began in 1733, one of those continental imbroglios involving many nations vying for mastery over slices of territory, but this was perhaps at the risk of ignoring international obligations and undermining previous alliances. The war lasted for five years until 1738, while Walpole remained on a neutral course. Many now sought an active war, however, largely on the understanding that France and Spain were denying English vessels access to foreign markets. Nothing more infuriated the English than the loss of trade. It was widely believed that Walpole had treated the Spanish with more leniency than they deserved. Petitions were presented to parliament setting out in animated language the continued Spanish attacks on English vessels, despite the 'understanding' Walpole had negotiated. Alderman Wilmot, otherwise unknown to history, lamented that 'seventy of our brave sailors are now in chains in Spain! Our countrymen in chains, and slaves to Spaniards! Is this not enough to fire the coldest? Is this not enough to arouse all the vengeance of a national resentment!'

A previous incident further inflamed the situation. In 1738 Captain Robert Jenkins displayed to the Commons the severed ear that had been struck from his head by a Spanish officer in the course of an embarkation seven years before in 1731. The ear was too old to be confirmed as his, but it served the purpose of provoking public fury. It is possible that the captain lost his ear in some other disciplinary proceeding. The leathery appendage might have been picked up at a London hospital, or found in the street. Who knew, or cared to know, the truth? You could pick a fight over a dead ear.

The Spanish were not eager for conflict, and Walpole still favoured the slow dance of peace, and so a 'Convention' was cobbled together to cover all differences. It was not well received, particularly in the Commons. Walpole spoke for two and half hours in favour of the arrangement, but then a young man rose to speak against the contrived peace. 'Is this any longer a nation?' Shall we 'bear to hear of the expediency of receiving from Spain an insecure, unsatisfactory, dishonourable Convention? It carries fallacy or downright subjection in almost every line.'

William Pitt sat down, having fired one of the first verbal salvoes in what was for a while known as 'the War of Jenkins' Ear'. It would have taken a political seer of genius to realize that this young man of thirty would determine the nature of English politics, after Walpole, for forty years. William Pitt – 'the elder', as he later became known after the exploits of his equally famous son – came from a family that had grown rich on the spoils of India; his grandfather was called 'Diamond' Pitt. The young man followed the familiar course of Eton and Oxford before joining the 1st Dragoon Guards in 1731. He took a parliamentary seat four years later. It was his destiny.

He was known as one of the 'cub Whigs' because of his youthful opposition to Walpole's administration. He had also attached himself to Frederick, prince of Wales, who was implacably opposed to his father, George II, and thus to his father's principal minister. Queen Caroline said of her eldest son that 'my dear first-born is the greatest ass, and the greatest liar, and the greatest *canaille*, and the greatest beast in the whole world; and I most heartily wish he was out of it'. Nevertheless Pitt set himself up in the prince's headquarters at Leicester House and was eventually installed as a 'Groom of the Bedchamber'. From early on, therefore, Walpole marked him down as his enemy. Pitt's speeches against peace were simply another token of their hostility.

Yet his rhetoric could sting. Horace Walpole, the first minister's son, remarked 'how his eloquence, like a torrent long obstructed, burst forth, with more commanding impetuosity! . . . haughty, defiant, conscious of injury and supreme abilities'. It was believed that he did not know what he was going to say until he was on his feet but then, extempore, he drove all before him.

It was sometimes difficult, in fact, for his spellbound auditors to recall exactly what he had said. Another parliamentarian, Henry Grattan, remembered that he voiced 'great subjects, great empires, great characters, effulgent ideas and classical illustrations'. Pitt had a great fondness for Shakespeare and would read out the more tremendous passages to his family; he would quote only from the tragedies, and would pass the comedies to someone else. It is an inkling of his dramatic imagination. When we examine his illustrious contemporaries, in fact, the politicians of the age were on the whole consummate actors. Lord Shelburne, one of his closest allies in later life, described him as a 'completely artificial character'. 'He was always acting,' Shelburne said, 'always made up, and never natural, in a perpetual state of exertion, incapable of friendship, or of any act which tended to it, and constantly upon the watch, and never unbent . . .' This was the man who became known as the great commoner.

Shelburne also described Pitt as 'tall in his person . . . with the eye of a hawk, a little head, thin face, long aquiline nose, and perfectly erect'. Extant portraits reveal a somewhat haunted face with watchful and weary eyes. He began to suffer physical ill-health at Eton which in the medical manner of the time was diagnosed as 'gout'. Over succeeding years the 'gout' attacked various parts of his body so that he had the appearance of an invalid, spare and lean. When he began to suffer from bouts of mania and depression he was diagnosed with 'gout on the brain'.

For a man almost constantly in pain, and weary with the impor-tunities of clients and colleagues, it was almost inevitable that he stayed somewhat aloof. He was cold and reserved, except in the company of his few intimates. He could be directed or swayed, but he would not be dictated to. That is also why he earned the repu-tation for being incorruptible, although in truth he was not without ambition and desire for profit; he also had the gift of changing his principles rapidly when the occasion demanded it. Yet he once spoke of the sense of personal honour 'which makes ambition virtue'. There is not one public man in whom contraries do not collide. We may say in these early years of Pitt's political career, however, that he had two principal ambitions; he aimed for English supremacy at sea and England's supremacy over its neighbours.

Pitt, then, was one of those who hammered Walpole on the necessity for war. He also hailed his political ally, Frederick, the prince of Wales, as the protector of the naval strength of England and the guardian of the trade of the country. Liberty of the Seas!

Liberty and Property! Prosperity of the City of London! These were the catchphrases used by Pitt and his youthful allies. Adam Smith described a war against Spain as a 'colony war' to safeguard the high seas as well as British possessions overseas. Horace Walpole blamed the martial pressure upon 'the disaffected and discontented part' in parliament, and also upon those who belonged to the court of the prince of Wales who wanted to create a warrior prince on the model of a medieval monarch. 'My God,' Queen Caroline said, 'popularity always makes me sick; but Fretz's popularity makes me vomit.'

Yet it was public opinion itself, animated by these belligerent parties, which pushed Walpole into a war that he did not wish for. To compound the insult many of his former allies now blamed the first minister for acquiescing in the fervour for conflict. When he eventually declared war in October 1739, there was an outburst of popular rejoicing. 'They now ring the bells,' he said in one of his more maladroit remarks, 'they will soon wring their hands.'

All seemed to go well with the first victory of the conflict when Admiral Edward Vernon in November 1739 captured the Spanish base of Porto Bello in South America. It was greeted with jubilation and in the following year, when Vernon was preparing a second fleet, 'Rule Britannia' was first sung at the prince of Wales's country retreat at Cliveden. The towns and cities of England organized festivals to the 'Immortal Vernon' and his name was aligned with those of Francis Drake and Walter Raleigh. The stunning success of the 'blue water' policy was also a harsh rebuke to Walpole and those ministers who preferred a less belligerent policy.

But no war goes to plan, as Walpole was uneasily aware. The conquest of Porto Bello lasted for no more than three weeks, and in the following summer Admirals Nicholas Haddock and John Norris failed to stop the Spanish and French fleets from sailing into Caribbean waters. Another truism of war states that one conflict can blend into another without the protagonists being fully aware of the fact. So the war against Spain was changed, as if by a transformation scene at the ballet, into the 'War of the Austrian Succession'.

This is how it happened. The Holy Roman Emperor, Charles VI, had no son, so it had been agreed that he should be permitted to leave intact his Habsburg dominions (including Austria, Hungary,

Bohemia, the Netherlands and parts of Italy) to his eldest daughter, Maria Theresa. No sooner was the emperor in his grave, however, than the various interested parties pounced on his legacy. There was no honour among thieves, even if they were sovereigns; they swarmed about the sight of blood. Frederick II of Prussia invaded the Habsburg province of Silesia since, in his own words, 'ambition, interest, the desire of making people talk about me, carried the day, and I decided for war'. He was, at least, candid. Spain and France were also two of the principal aggressors and, since they were also two of England's most prominent enemies, England itself was in 1740 perforce drawn into the European conflict. There were too many monarchs, and too few thrones, to satisfy every combatant. New dancers came on the stage with reverberating clashes of thunder and bolts of lightning.

In September 1741 George II astonished his ministers, and his people, by declaring the electorate of Hanover neutral. It was understandable. His territory was surrounded by the larger powers which already had their mouths open for more. Yet he had withdrawn from a dispute in which England was still an active participant; he had in effect two foreign policies, one of peace and one of war. A nation at war cannot be led by Janus, and it was widely believed that the foreign interests of the country were subordinated to those of Hanover. Pitt in particular was scathing about what he considered to be the parasitical Hanoverians, a stance that incurred the lasting enmity of the king.

Walpole had endured enough, and in the first month of 1742 he resigned his office. 'This war is yours,' he told a fellow minister, soon to become the duke of Newcastle, 'you have had the conduct of it. I wish you joy of it.' Newcastle himself deserves a reference in this history in his own right since he was quintessentially, inimitably, of the eighteenth century; he could have come from the stage of Congreve or the pages of Smollett. He was a powerful Whig grandee and consummate master of electoral tactics, but he was also something of a buffoon. In an age of tears he was well known for copious weeping; he refused to sleep in beds not previously slept in, had a great aversions to chills and damps, would not travel by sea, and never stopped talking. It was said that he had woken half an hour late in the morning and spent the rest of the day trying to make up for lost time. W. E. H. Lecky, in his *History of England in the Eighteenth Century*, described 'his confused, tangled, unconnected talk, his fulsome flattery, his promises made at the spur of the moment and almost instantly forgotten, his childish exhibitions of timidity, ignorance, fretfulness, perplexity . . .'.

His rapid and garbled speech was accompanied by nervous jerking movements so that he was never for a moment at rest. He loved the hustle and agitation of business rather than the formulation of policy; but he went about his affairs in such a gyratory and sporadic way that his colleagues were often openly scornful of him. He did not seem to mind their derision, but any attempt to curtail his power sent him into paroxysms of paranoia; he lived in perpetual fear. Yet he enjoyed large levees, or grand assemblies, where to general amusement he hugged, kissed and embraced everyone in sight. Nevertheless he had within him the secret of longevity; he held major offices of state for almost forty years.

Robert Walpole left for honourable retirement and was created earl of Orford for his labours; he returned to Houghton Hall where he could gaze upon the fruits of his public office. His departure was greeted with great joy and celebrations, as if all the disappointments of war rested upon his shoulders.

But the fortunes of war were not materially improved by his absence. Its wavering course was not followed with any eagerness, and seems to have been prosecuted mainly by subsidies and mercenaries. No one cared much about its victories or its vicissitudes. Who took Juliers or Berg, Brieg or Wohlan, were matters of indifference. The conflict was marked in its last six years by treachery and criminality, double dealing and division, defections and secret treaties, lies and bloodshed on an enormous scale. When peace was signed at Aix-la-Chapelle in 1748, not a moment too soon, it could record no single important result. Thomas Carlyle, the great Scottish historian with a style of fire, eventually described it as 'an unintelligible, huge English-and-Foreign Delirium'.

Everyone had wanted Wapole to retire, including his closest associates, but in truth his retirement made very little difference; the members of the old team were still there, now looking for support from some of the 'new Whigs' and the 'prince's party'. There was no great millennial change, as some had wanted or suspected.

More Whigs of various tendencies did in fact join the ministry, and in time became known with some of their Tory counterparts as 'broad-bottomed'. They could sit on anything. Whigs now battled against Whigs, Tories against Tories, Tories and Whigs against Whigs and Tories, in a game of internecine struggle that lasted for some sixteen years. Of course everybody became bored in the end. The earl of Stair noted in 1743, a year after Walpole had gone, that 'London seems entirely employed about whist.'

Some excitement was aroused by the landing of Charles Edward Stuart, the son of the 'Old Pretender', in Scotland during the summer of 1745. The Young Pretender, better known to posterity as Bonnie Prince Charlie, was taking advantage of the continental war to cause a little local difficulty. Some troops fighting in Flanders were recalled to home soil but the prince was able to occupy Edinburgh and to score a notable victory over the ancient enemy at Prestonpans to the east of the city. There ensued something like panic in London. The fear rather than the reality of an invasion necessarily caused consternation. To breach the moat defensive to a house was always a momentous event, especially at a time of general war.

The Young Pretender gathered with him some 5,000 men and marched south into England where he reached as far as Derby. Further panic ensued. He was in fact unlikely to have advanced much further. The Scots did not flock to his banner, and the Tories that were inclined to the Jacobite cause went to no great lengths to support him. In a country generally concerned with national prosperity, no social or political revolution is ever likely; the Bank of England effectively destroyed the Stuart cause. Charles demanded from his French allies an invasion, but the French were too engaged in Flanders to oblige. At Derby the Jacobite generals knew that their game was lost and, over the prince's strenuous objections, they eventually retreated into the Highlands. It was not the end of their humiliations.

Charles chose with his advisers to fight the enemy on the open moorland of Culloden and, within an hour, his troops were wholly defeated by the British army under the guidance of the duke of Cumberland. Some of the Scots were ready to fight again in more auspicious circumstances, but their resolve was undermined by the Young Pretender's decision to return to France. So ended the last attempt by Scotland to affirm its independence by violent means. Jacobitism was dead, its exequies marked by the brutal licentiousness of Cumberland's soldiers who went through the highlands in a systematic campaign of rape, slaughter, theft and execution. In the aftermath of the bloody defeat all Highlanders were obliged to surrender their arms, and any man or boy wearing 'the Highland clothes' would be imprisoned for six months without bail. Transportation would follow a second offence. It was a deliberate policy of cultural genocide.

The cheers and applause of the victors may have been enough to drown out the tears and lamentations of the renegade Scots. 'Rule Britannia' had been set to music five years before, and 'God Save the King' was published in the *Gentleman's Magazine* at the time of the Young Pretender's landing before becoming a popular refrain.

The young prince ventured one further journey to England when, in 1750, he travelled to London in disguise. He seems to have stayed with a staunch Jacobite in Theobald's Road, and conformed to the Anglican faith in the empty hope of being eventually accepted as sovereign. He must have worn a mask and costume as he walked through the streets of London; but, in that respect, he was very much part of a city that was often no more than a great stage.

14

Mother Geneva

When an eighteenth-century visitor, Matthew Bramble, arrives at London in Tobias Smollett's novel, *The Expedition of Humphry Clinker* (1771), he is much astonished by the fact that 'the different departments of life are jumbled together – the hod-keeper, the low mechanic, the tapster, the publican, the shop-keeper, the pettifogger, the citizen and courtier *all tread upon the kibes of one another*'. Profligacy and licentiousness 'are seen everywhere, rumbling, riding, rolling, rushing, jostling, mixing, bouncing, cracking, crashing in one vile ferment of stupidity and corruption – all is tumult and hurry; one would imagine they were impelled by some disorder of the brain, that will not suffer them to be at rest'.

Some years earlier another innocent visitor had arrived, fresh from the coach, in the yard of the Bell by Wood Street. In William Hogarth's representation of the scene, Moll Hackabout is immediately surrounded by strange sights. Chamber pots are being aired on some railings, while some ragged underclothes are hanging above a balcony. A well-dressed 'rake' is looking at her and fondling himself in a doorway. But the strangest sight of all is that of an elderly woman, patched and peeling with old beauty spots, who greets her as her cousin from the country. Her name is Mother Needham, a notorious procuress of the 1720s and early 1730s; she was eventually displayed in the pillory, and died of the injuries inflicted on her by the public.

These two images of London are closer to the truth of the eighteenth-century city than anything found in the *Spectator* or the *Gentleman's Magazine*; they are not caricatures, but intensely realistic. The polite literature of the period adverts to the auction houses and the coffee-houses, the reading societies and the debating clubs, the assembly rooms and the dancing masters, the masquerades and the balls, the theatres and the galleries, the lecture halls and concert halls. These were indeed part of the vesture of eighteenth-century London but beyond them was a deeper and darker life that had not changed for the better. No 'improvement' could touch it. The wider streets and the open bridges, the fashionable squares and the shopping arcades, had nothing to do with the shadows that London had always cast. Close by the rooms devoted to this 'age of pleasure' were those devoted to an age of privation, an age of poverty, an age of punishment and an age of pain.

The smell of London was noticeable from several miles away, comprised, according to a tract of 1733, George Cheyne's *The English Malady*, of 'the infinite number of fires . . . the clouds of stinking breaths, and perspiration, not to mention the ordure of so many diseased, both intelligent and unintelligent animals, the crowded churches, church-yards, and burying places . . .'. Above all else mounted the smell of horse-dung.

The smell of the streets was a great leveller for the ranks of artisans, wits, apprentices, publishers, rakes, clerks, men about town, clergymen, stationers, ladies, serving-girls, actors and singers, politicians and vagrants who walked along them. There was a phrase that 'one is not smelt where all stink'. The footpaths were not only thronged with pedestrians but by hackney-chair men and porters, dust-carts and post-chaises, dogs and mud-carts, the boys with trays of meat on their shoulders and the begging soldiers, the flower girls and the chair-menders, the second-hand-clothes merchants and the pastry sellers. There was not one culture, but several, in the space of a single street.

It was no good trying to avoid these inconveniences by hiring a coach; the streets were so narrow and circuitous, the obstacles so many, that all the drays and carriages were often brought to a dead halt or 'lock'. The coachmen would then begin to whip each other's horses and often jump down from their vehicles to engage in a fist-fight, encouraged by a circle of citizens who liked nothing so much as a free brawl. The air of the city was always blue with oaths and maledictions, blasphemies and curses. The noise of the streets was like that of Bedlam; from a distance it resembled a great shout echoing into the firmament. To some it sounded like a volcano.

This was the old violent London, which never went away and will never go away; the eighteenth-century city, until the improvements of its latter decades, was the arena for public hangings and floggings. The mad people of Bedlam were one of the city's sights, as were the gibbets along the Edgware Road and the rotting heads on top of Temple Bar. The mendicants bared their ulcers, while the prostitutes tried to cover their sores.

Moll Hackabout became just such a prostitute, and indeed it was a common fate for those who came up from the country or for those who were simply born and bred in the streets. Sex was plentifully available in the eighteenth century, from the most expensive harlot with lodgings in Covent Garden to the small boy or girl who was easy prey for a penny. Cheap and plentiful sex was the undercurrent of London's energy. The richer citizens or merchants could have more or less whomever they wanted, and it is hard to believe that the religious pieties of the day prevented them. In his *Autobiography* (1771–1854) Francis Place, a radical campaigner, even at the end of this period when metropolitan 'improvements' were meant to be ubiquitous, noted that 'the breasts of many [prostitutes] hung down in a most disgusting manner, their hair among the generality was straight and hung in rats' tails over their eyes, and was filled with lice, at least was inhabited by considerable colonies of these insects . . .'. They would go 'behind the wall' for twopence.

Addison left a more tender picture of the trade in his account of being accosted in St James's Street by a slim and pretty girl of about seventeen. 'She affected to allure me with a forced wantonness in her look and air; but I saw it checked with hunger and cold: Her eyes were wan and eager, her dress thin and tawdry, her mien gentle and childish.' The same figures populated the streets more than a century later, provoking the journalist William Thomas Stead into writing *The Maiden Tribute of Modern Babylon* (1885). Some aspects of London seem to be eternal.

Crime and violence belonged to its streets as much as its flints and stones. There was of course no organized police surveillance except the decrepit system of watch and ward, its elderly members boiling tea or gin in their little watch-houses. The streets were dark and treacherous, the tenements grim and the slums dangerous. The night was filled with crimes to which no one responded. At times of crisis the press-gangs sought out unwilling recruits for the navy. When James Watt came to London in 1754 he hardly dared stir out of his house for fear of being taken up.

'One is forced to travel', Horace Walpole wrote in 1751, 'even at noon as if one were going to battle.' The thieves had their own lodging houses, clubs and taverns where they were divided even as an army might be, into housebreakers, pickpockets, footpads and highwaymen. Yet the detestation of a standing army was so great that even the call for more police was resisted by some citizens who did not wish to live in a military camp.

As the city grew through the eighteenth century, its boiling point was lowered. Matthew Bramble, in *Humphry Clinker*, remarks to an acquaintance that 'in the space of seven years eleven thousand new houses have been built in one quarter of Westminster, exclusive of what is daily added to other parts of this unwieldy metropolis'; so 'unwieldy' that 'the capital has become an overgrown monster; which, like a dropsical head, will in time leave the body and extremities without nourishment and support'. Bricks arrived at the building sites before they were cool enough to be handled, and the bemused traveller might stand amazed at a nasty wilderness of half-finished houses.

There was a driving method behind this madness of speculation. London was power and money. The voracious demand for food in the city helped to revolutionize the agriculture of the country. Tea and hemp and cotton cloth came from all over the earth. Sugar was 'boiled' in the capital. It was the largest industrial city in the world. The densely packed factories lined both banks of the Thames at the eastern end. This was the place of scientific equipment, kitchen ranges, gas meters, furniture and hackney carriages. The coal came down the east coast to stoke the fires.

The divines and moralists, listening to the swearing and indecency rising up from the dens and caves of the city, were not slow in predicting an ultimate judgement. The songs of London were considered enough to arouse divine wrath:

> I'm sure she'll go to Hell,
> For she makes me fuck her in church time . . .

It should be remembered that Londoners as a whole were tremendously superstitious, as if they knew that they lived in a doomed city. Phantoms and witches and apparitions were reported in the city, and the king himself was said to believe in vampires – although that may have been part of his Germanic legacy. You should never listen to a cuckoo without money in your pocket. You should return home if a snake crosses your path. You should look down if a raven flies over your head. A screech owl in the morning presages a day of danger. Crowds flocked to a house in Cock Lane when numerous knockings and scratchings were heard. Samuel Johnson was one of a committee established to investigate the phenomenon, which turned out to be no more than the tricks of an older daughter. The reports of a ghost had nevertheless caused a sensation.

A lady from Godalming, Mary Tofts, began to give birth to rabbits, after she had miscarried when trying to catch one. She was brought to London where at a bagnio in Leicester Fields she was visited by the more prominent doctors of the day. A courtier, Lord Hervey, reported that 'every creature in town, both men and women have been to see and feel her: the perpetual motions, noises and rumblings in her belly, are something prodigious; all the eminent physicians, surgeons and man-midwives in London are there day and night to watch her next production'. This, too, was all an imposture. But it had worked on the superstition and credulity of the London crowd.

On 8 February 1750, the tremor and reverberation of an earthquake were felt beneath London and Westminster; the people ran out of their houses, fearing an apocalypse. On precisely the same day one month later, 8 March, a second and more violent earthquake shivered to dust some of the foundations of the houses and occasioned much damage in the streets. It was now considered certain that a third earthquake, even more terrible and destructive than its two predecessors, would erupt on 8 April. The *Gentleman's Magazine*, perhaps best known for its rational bias, reported that 'earthquakes are placed among those methods by which God punishes a wicked and rebellious people'. The sins of London, mounting ever higher for many years, seemed to have found their apotheosis. The city was too black, too poisonous, too diseased, too venereal, to survive the wrath of the heavens. The bishop of London wrote a pastoral letter in which he denounced 'the abominations of the public stews', the 'histories and romances of the vilest prostitutes' and books by deists and others who scorned 'the great truths of religion'.

A week before the expected tremor those who could leave London did so. A performance of Handel's oratorio, *Judas Maccabaeus*, was cancelled. Horace Walpole counted 750 carriages passing Hyde Park Corner into the relative safety of the country. Many of those who were panic-stricken migrated into the fields of North and South London. The centres, the black centres, the City and Westminster, were to be shunned. In the event all was calm. God rested. But the phenomenon and the panic were enough to turn some, if not all, to thoughts of repentence. Others had already turned to a different source of consolation. The arms of Mother Geneva were open.

William Hogarth's *Gin Lane* was issued in 1751, from the Golden Head in Leicester Fields, in the same year that Henry Fielding warned in a pamphlet, 'An Enquiry into the Causes of the late Increase of Robbers', that 'a new kind of drunkenness, unknown to our ancestors, is lately sprung up amongst us . . . by this Poison called Gin'. In Hogarth's print a pawnbroker is engaged in a thriving trade; he inspects a carpenter's saw while a harassed woman presses upon him a kettle and saucepan. Beneath their feet is to be seen a gin-cellar with the familiar sign of Gin Royal hanging above it. It is no more than a hole in the wall, a dark tunnel leading to the lower depths. Above it are printed the words.

> Drunk for a Penny
> Dead Drunk for twopence
> Clean Straw for Nothing.

It is unlikely that such words were ever inscribed for a gin shop, and Hogarth himself could well have invented them, but nevertheless they have become proverbial.

Gin Lane is unknown to the topographer and gazetteer but Hogarth has situated it in the parish of St Giles, notorious for its beggars, cripples, vagrants and the very poor. The site of the print is now at the northern end of Shaftesbury Avenue. A dazed and drunken woman sits upon some steps. It looks as if time has been suspended around her, except that an infant is falling from her useless arms onto the ground below. An emaciated ballad-singer lies dying on the steps immediately below her. Close by, a man and a dog quarrel over a filthy bone.

But the woman is the centre of this part of the composition. She has the tokens of syphilis upon her legs. She is filthy, and her clothes are in tatters. She must have been on the streets of St Giles to pay for her addiction. A commentary on the print noticed that 'if a woman accustoms herself to dram-drinking, she becomes the most miserable as well as the most contemptible creature on earth'. A recent case pointed the moral better than words. Judith Defour had taken her two-year-old child to a workhouse where it received better care and a set of new clothes. She returned to the workhouse a few days later and claimed the child; she then took the infant to a nearby field where she strangled it and dumped the body in a ditch before pawning the new clothes for a shilling which she then spent on gin. It was an extreme case, but not so extreme as to be implausible.

Beside Kilman Distillery, on the right of Hogarth's print, two young girls are quaffing the gin, while some beggars fight for a dram and a young mother is pouring the drink into her baby's mouth. Signs of death are everywhere, with a suicide hanging in plain sight, a baby accidentally impaled upon a spit, a swinging coffin as a sign of an undertaker's shop, and a makeshift funeral. The pawnbroker's sign hangs like a cross over the street scene while in the distance is the steeple of St George's Bloomsbury with a statue of George I on its pinnacle. He is the only king so to be honoured in London, but on this occasion he seems as cold and remote from his realm as the church itself. Hogarth's print is composed of minute particulars which, taken together, make up one overwhelming statement. The two girls, for example, wear their parish insignia of 'GS' or St Giles. The churchwardens, the vestry and the overseers of the poor are exposed as incompetent or irresponsible.

Hogarth's print sold for a shilling, together with its companion piece, 'Beer Street', and although its cost would have been beyond the reach of the poor, it is reasonable to suppose that it found a place on the walls of the tavern or the alehouse where it might act as a satire or as a corrective. An advertisement in the *London Evening Post* remarked that 'as the Subjects of these Prints are calculated to reform some reigning Vices peculiar to the lower Class of People, in hopes to render them of more extensive use, the Author has publish'd them in the cheapest Manner possible'.

The craze for gin began, approximately, in 1720 but it had been readily available since the time of the Glorious Revolution in 1688. William III brought the drink with him from the purlieux of Rotterdam, and soon enough the Dutch spirit had supplanted the taste for French brandies. Anything French was suspect. The soldiers of William's army were encouraged to imbibe 'Dutch courage' before action. Two years after his successful invasion an Act was passed 'for encouraging the distilling of brandy and spirits from corn'. The farmers and distillers were further rewarded when the duty on their liquor fell from a shilling to a penny a gallon. London had always been a city of hard drinking but in the streets of the capital the current of gin grew stronger and faster. In times of want, and pain, and cold, many ran into it willingly. A nasty steam, or fog, arose from the vats of the distillers.

The gin was sold in the shops of weavers, dyers, barbers, carpenters and shoemakers; the workhouses, prisons and madhouses were awash. There were degrees of nastiness and discomfort. Inns had lodging rooms for guests, while alehouses provided 'houses of call' for the various trades of the city; the brandy shops or dram shops were of the lowest grade, where cellars, back rooms and holes in the wall provided shelter for copious consumption. Gin was sold from wheelbarrows, from temporary stalls, from alleys, from back rooms and from cheap lodging houses. It was consumed greedily by beggars and vagrants, by the inmates of prisons or workhouses, by Londoners young and old. It was a particular favourite of women, who also used liberal quantities of the stuff to silence children and to ward off the privations of cold and hunger. It was a way of staving off the world.

The consequences were dire. Children would congregate in a gin shop, and would drink until they could not move. Men and women died in the gutters after too much consumption. Some drinkers dropped dead on the spot. It was not at all unusual to see people staggering blindly at any time of night and day. Fights, and fires started out of neglect, were common. A foreign observer, César de Saussure, noted that 'the taverns are almost always filled with men and women, and even sometimes children, who drink with so much enjoyment that they find it difficult to walk on going away'. It kept the poor warm and dazed, at least for an hour or two.

William Maitland, whose *The History of London* was published in the mid-eighteenth century, reckoned that 8,659 gin shops were operating in the city, with particular clusters around Southwark and Whitechapel. The sale of spirits had doubled in a decade, with 5.5 million gallons purchased in 1735. Women were not only customers but also vendors. It has been estimated that between one quarter and one third of unlicensed sellers of spirits were female. It was one London trade from which they were not excluded, and the influx of girls and young women into the capital provided a ready source for exploitation. In a pamphlet of 1736, 'Distilled Spirituous Liquors: The Bane of the Nation', it was recorded that the dram shops were filled with 'servant maids and laboring men's wives', emphasizing the belief that gin was in some sense a female drink. It was known as 'the ladies' delight', and the passage of the Gin Act in 1736 was said to have provoked 'widows' tears' and 'shreeks of desponding Matrons'.

Several attempts were made to administer or temper the sale of gin, with diverse consequences. The Gin Act introduced a duty of 20 shillings per gallon on spirituous liquors, and retailers of gin were required to purchase an annual licence of £50. This simply served to encourage the illicit selling of spirits that now expanded out of all proportion. Gin was sold as medicinal draughts or under assumed names such as Sangree, Tow Row, the Makeshift or King Theodore of Corsica. Subtle means of distribution were invented. An enterprising trader in Blue Anchor Alley bought the sign of a cat with an open mouth; he nailed it by his window and then put a small lead pipe under one of its paws. The other end of the pipe held a funnel through which the gin could be poured. It was soon bruited 'that gin would be sold by the cat at my window the next day'. He waited for his first customer, and soon enough he heard 'a comfortable voice say, "Puss, give me twopennyworth of gin"'. The coins were inserted into the mouth of the cat, and the tradesman poured the required amount into the funnel of the pipe. Crowds soon gathered to see 'the enchanted cat' and the liquor itself came to be known as 'Puss'.

The evidence of Westminster interference in the once flourishing gin trade provoked riots in the poorer parts of the city; the turmoil became so violent that it was deemed by some to be a danger to the state. Shoreditch and Spitalfields were practically under siege. Informers, those who swore to the justice that a certain establishment was selling gin unlawfully, were hounded and struck down by the mobs. Some of them were beaten to death, while others were ducked in the Thames, the ponds, or the common sewers. It was a form of street power. A woman in the Strand called out 'Informers!' whereupon 'the Mob secur'd' the man involved 'and us'd him so ill that he is since dead of his Bruises'.

The legislation of 1736 proved impossible to enforce. The Act was modified in the light of public complaint and a new Act was drawn up seven years later; it was known as 'the Tippling Act', and in 1747 the gin distillers won back the right to sell their product retail. Spirit, raw or mixed with cordial, was once more the drink of choice. It was estimated that, in Holborn, one in five dwellings was used as a gin shop.

The effects were predictable and familiar. In 1751 Corbyn Morris, a customs administrator, noted the fall in births as well as 'the sickly state of such infants as are born'. He observed also that the hospitals were crowded with 'increasing multitudes of dropsical and consumptive people arising from spirituous liquors'. The drink was also associated with sexual licence, and it was reported that 'young creatures, girls of twelve and thirteen years of age, drink Geneva like fishes and make themselves unfit to live in sober families . . . there is no passing the streets for 'em, so shameless are they grown'. This was the immediate context for Hogarth's print and Fielding's pamphlet.

Yet, in one of those ultimately unfathomable changes of taste, the craze for gin subsided. This had nothing to do with the attempt at prohibition, which had become a dead failure. Bad harvests rendered gin more expensive. The influence of Methodism was growing even among the urban poor. And, suddenly, there was the new fashion for tea.

It is fitting that William Hogarth should have become the most celebrated observer of this London craze, as he was of other urban phenomena. This was the Hogarthian moment. He was a Londoner by birth, out of Smithfield, and an urban tradesman who started his career as a goldsmith's engraver. His first paintings were of a scene from *The Beggar's Opera*. He is as intrinsic to the eighteenth century as Samuel Johnson or Henry Fielding. He was a model and an inspiration for the new generation of novelists. 'It would take the pencil of Hogarth', Tobias Smollett wrote in *The Adventures of Roderick Random* (1748), 'to express the astonishment and concern of Strap.' Samuel Richardson's *The Apprentice's Vade Mecum* (1733) wishes that 'the ingenious Mr Hogarth would finish the portrait'. In *The History of Tom Jones, a Foundling* (1749), Henry Fielding interrupts his narrative to exclaim, 'O Hogarth! Had I thy pencil!'

Hogarth touches upon so many and so various eighteenth-century concerns that he might be called the presiding deity of the period. He understood the randomness of life from the chance encounter to the unexpected event, from the fall of a building to the overturning of a coach; he also understood the extremes of living, rich beside poor, sick and dying beside the healthy, vice beside virtue. He loved the low life of the streets, and spent much of his life in celebrating it. Melodrama and spectacle, as common on the streets of the city as among the players of Bartholomew Fair, were some of the spirits of the age. 'We will therefore compare subjects for painting', Hogarth wrote, 'with those of the stage.'

He was also an astute man of business. He became the professional above all others. He advertised his prints in the newspapers and sold directly to purchasers without going through the medium of dealers or print-sellers; he hung a shop sign outside the door of his house. He also secured the passage of legislation, known as 'Hogarth's Act', that managed to protect the copyright of engravers. Artists had always exploited the market, and manipulated their patrons, but perhaps in never so overtly a commercial fashion. Whether in his robust moralism, or in his evocation of urban fever, or in his financial acuteness, he caught the temper of the times.

15

The pack of cards

William Pitt would be conceived and fashioned in war; from the beginning he had despised Robert Walpole's policy of peace at any price. He had taken on Walpole and won. Now his time had almost come, when he would be saluted as the war master of the age, the 'great commoner' who had become a great warrior. Eight years after the Peace of Aix-la-Chapelle, negotiated by Britain, France and the other combatants of the War of the Austrian Succession, his first intimations of blood came in the distant colonies across the ocean. It took once again the form of Anglo-French enmity. The policy of France in North America, as far as the English were concerned, was one of expansion and aggression; it was believed that they aimed for 'universal commerce'. They had settled on the St Lawrence to the north, and on the Mississippi to the south, and were thus in a position to control with a line of forts all the territory west of the New England colonies. If the British were confined to that narrow strip along the Atlantic shore, they would have no part in the burgeoning and profitable fur trade. It did not help that the French were in alliance with the confederation of Native Indians known as the 'Six Nations'. In April 1754, a French force from Canada occupied the fort that would one day be the site of Pittsburgh. Offensive expeditions were in turn sent out by the British, but with very little effect. The battlegrounds were not yet important.

America was still a far-off land of which the British knew very little. Snippets of news from 'the colonies' appeared in the public prints, under the headings of 'American Affairs' or 'British Plantations', but there was no genuine bond of sentiment or sympathy between the two communities. America was considered to be a nation of farmers, in a wilderness dotted with small farms and villages. That was far from the case – Harvard and Yale had already been established, Harvard more than a century before. The merchants of England of course also knew better; they traded in fish and lumber products, as well as the great wheat and grain crops that were already pouring out of the 'bread colonies'. And then there was the tobacco of Virginia and Maryland. In the end these commodities would be the root and cause of war.

The relations between France and England, exacerbated by the tensions in America, were becoming more ominous closer to home. In March 1756, an invasion scare prompted the administration to send for Hanoverian mercenaries to defend the shores. The use of German troops was unparalleled and raised a tempest against the presence of Hanoverians and Hessians. Their strength, however, was never tested; it may be that the French never intended to invade but were making a feint in advance of more serious hostilities. Sure enough, on 18 May, a general war was declared which can be seen as the aftermath of the War of the Austrian Succession. War was the familiar bed-fellow of politics and trade.

All the old alliances were give a new twist, however, when England and Prussia were joined against Austria and the Bourbon powers of France and Spain. The struggle had many names, according to the theatres of battle: in North America it was known as 'the French and Indian War', in India 'the Third Carnatic War'. On the European mainland it was called 'the Pomeranian War' or 'the Third Silesian War'. In England it eventually came to be known, more directly, as 'the Seven Years War'. It probably did not occur to any of the participants that the conflict would last so long.

Even before war was declared it was ascertained that a French fleet was being prepared at Toulon for action in the Mediterranean. The French had for a long time threatened Minorca, the island having come under British control in 1708, and so a defence force of ten ships was dispatched from Gibraltar under the command of

Admiral Byng. The battle was confused and uncertain, compounded by Byng's caution and the poor condition of his ships. When it was believed that the English could do no more, Byng sailed back to Gibraltar without assisting the British garrison on Minorca itself. The garrison surrendered in June, just a month after the general war had been declared. It was not a happy beginning.

The Admiralty was eager to shift the blame to an expendable officer, and Admiral Byng was court-martialled before being shot on the deck of HMS *Monarch*; Voltaire had said of the incident that 'it is a good idea to kill an admiral from time to time, simply to encourage the others'. But the sacrificial killing of Byng did not appease the English public who considered their nation to be the acknowledged ruler of the high seas. There was a rise in public suspicion and anger with which Newcastle, still the first minister, was singularly unable to deal. Byng may have been burned in effigy by irate crowds, but the images of others were also held up in derision. A ballad of the day declared 'to the block with Newcastle and the yardarm with Byng'. In the autumn of the year the duke of Newcastle resigned. All eyes were now upon William Pitt who, much to the king's annoyance and even disgust, seemed likely to be the new leader of the administration. It had been Pitt, after all, who scorned the Hanoverian loyalties of the king. But Pitt was certain of himself. He informed the duke of Devonshire that 'I am sure I can save the country and nobody else can.' In the conventional histories of the period one figure exits stage left while another makes a grand entrance. But it was never as simple as that.

All the cards were to be reshuffled. The players crowded around the table and met in corners. The remarks in the political correspondence of the period set the scene.

There are so many wheels within wheels that no eye can see . . . the patriot of Monday is the courtier of Tuesday, and the courtier of Wednesday is the patriot of Thursday . . . if he is a good boy in the meantime . . . the opposition, like schoolboys, don't know how to settle to their books again after the holidays . . . more than one has thrown away a very good game . . . Pitt has lent his paws to draw the chestnuts out of the fire . . . you know here is no such thing as first minister in England, and

therefore you should not seem to be so . . . he treated it as
words and mere amusement . . . patriots we have none, all is
election jobbery.

The discourse concerned demands, deceits, threats, conspiracies,
manoeuvres and intrigues. X wished to be chancellor of the exchequer
but, if Y vetoed the proposal, he could become minister for the
House of Commons with the lucrative post of paymaster. A wanted
B to remain lord lieutenant of Ireland, so that B could relinquish
the office to A in an emergency. It would not surprise an observer
of political life, in any century, to acknowledge that politics took
precedence over policies.

Pitt, however, held all the trumps with the support of the public
and with the confidence of the Commons; so in the face of the
king's opposition he became secretary of the southern department,
the most senior secretary of state, and allowed the duke of Devonshire to become nominal first lord of the treasury. He took office
at a time of unease and failure, marked also by Pitt's dismay at the
convenient execution of Admiral Byng. He hardly had time to
expedite his own war policy when the king's younger son, the duke
of Cumberland, refused to take up his command in Germany while
Pitt remained in charge. It was the opportunity for which George
II had waited, and at the beginning of April 1757 Pitt was dismissed.

All was confused and uncertain. For three months a succession
of ministers attempted to co-ordinate policy against France, but
none of them had the verve or self-confidence of Pitt. In May a
French army invaded Hanover, George's own electorate, and at the
battle of Hastenbeck in July the allies were beaten; the defeated
commander, the duke of Cumberland himself, was forced to concede
a treaty that gave authority to the French. The king was beside
himself with fury, and laid the blame upon his incompetent son.
He greeted him with a frigid silence. 'Here is my son,' he told his
courtiers, 'who has ruined me and disgraced himself.' Since Cumberland never again took up a military office, his animus against Pitt
would no longer be a consideration. It must have occurred even to
the king that a strong hand was required against manifold enemies.

At the end of June, when it was feared that the great wheels of
the machine might stop, Pitt had agreed to enter a coalition with

that veteran of all veterans, the duke of Newcastle. Pitt would take care of the war while Newcastle would administer all domestic business, including the raising of the revenues that Pitt required. Pitt and Newcastle were by no means natural allies; in fact they despised one another. They were united only in their desire to be ministers. 'Fewer words, if you please, my lord,' Pitt told the voluble Newcastle, 'for your words have long lost all weight with me.' The unlikely coalition turned out to be one of the most successful in English history.

The circumstances of Pitt's return were not propitious. The earl of Chesterfield wrote at the time that 'whoever is in, or whoever is out, I am sure we are undone, both at home and abroad; at home by our increasing debt and expenses; abroad by our ill luck and incapacity . . . We are no longer a nation. I never yet saw so dreadful a prospect.' In the autumn of 1757 John Wilkes, soon enough to become a vociferous agitator, wrote that there was 'the most general discontent I ever knew, and every person I converse with, of all parties, seems to be under the dread of something very terrible approaching'.

Pitt was faced with what, in the circumstances of the time, looked very much like a global war. From Quebec to Guadeloupe, from Senegal to East Frisia, from Prague to Louisiana, the two combatants and their allies faced each other in a battle for naval and commercial supremacy. It was the kind of war Pitt was born for. His over-arching policy was to open as many 'fronts' against France as possible, in order to tie down its forces, and to promote and support as many of its enemies on the field of battle. For this he needed ships, men and money, the latter of which Newcastle furnished him by imposing additional taxes. Pitt told the Commons that he needed funds 'for the total stagnation and extirpation of the French trade upon the seas, and the general protection of that of Great Britain'. He demanded sovereignty over the high seas, in other words; he also faced a war of four fronts other than that of the European mainland – against the French on the continent of America, among the islands of the Caribbean, along the African coast, and in India.

Macaulay wrote in an essay in the *Edinburgh Review*, in 1834, that Pitt had serious weaknesses as war minister. He wrote that 'we perhaps from ignorance, cannot discern in his arrangements any appearance of profound or dexterous combination'. Pitt was, perhaps, just lucky. He could not of course have by himself conceived and carried out all the manifest events of the war; much of the praise must be ceded to the officials of the Admiralty. But, if any man held together the various strands of the war effort, it was Pitt. His panache and energy were accompanied by hauteur and by sarcasm to his colleagues; he had very little faith in their abilities, and rarely confided in them. He was egotistical with the proud and domineering with the weak. Yet he had a vision of England and of the nation's destiny, bound not by the narrow frontiers of Europe but by a global trading empire that would ensure the nation's commercial and naval supremacy.

16

What shall I do?

On a May evening in 1738 John Wesley was walking along Aldersgate Street in order to attend a Church of England religious society; in this period the walls of London were scrawled with messages such as 'Christ is God' and 'Murder Jews' while rising above him beyond Aldersgate Street was the recently finished dome of St Paul's Cathedral. He had the proper Anglican credentials for an orthodox religious society; he had been a tutor of Lincoln College, Oxford, where he and his brother Charles set up a small society of fellow believers known as the 'Holy Club'. In the late autumn of 1735 he had travelled across the ocean to the newly established colony of Georgia, a settlement of yeoman farmers that had turned its back on slavery. He returned, after a legal dispute, at the end of 1737.

He had a companion in spirit. George Whitefield had joined the 'Holy Club' with the Wesley brothers and soon became known for his histrionic genius; he could make a congregation swoon in sorrow and David Garrick, the actor, told a friend that he would give £1,000 to utter an 'Oh!!!!' in the manner of Whitefield. But Wesley was temporarily bereft of his spiritual comfort. In 1738 Whitefield had also made the journey to Georgia.

Yet by the time Wesley walked out of the little society in Aldersgate Street he was spiritually changed. One of the members of the society was reading to the assembly Martin Luther's *Preface to the Epistle of the Romans* 'about a quarter before nine'. He was reciting the passage that describes 'the change which God works in the heart through faith in Christ'. As Wesley put it: 'I felt my heart strangely warmed.' This was the first stage in what became known as 'the awakening', that moment when in Wesley's words 'God began His great work in England' and which gathered its fruit in the Methodist movement.

Wesley had found in Luther's preface the belief that 'we are under grace and not under the law'. That grace was the great bounty and blessing he tried to instill in congregations never before touched by the spirit. On his own return from Georgia, in 1739, George Whitefield preached in the open air, itself a rare and almost unknown occurrence, to an assembly of colliers at Kingswood outside Bristol. His words acted as a sword, releasing acts of collective piety and mass emotion. 'Come poor, lost, undone sinner, come just as you are to Christ.' It was this outward call to repentance that galvanized the Methodist cause. Crowds assembled from the local neighbour-hoods to listen to what they considered to be the voice of God, and in March 1739, Whitefield wrote to Wesley that 'you must come and water what God has enabled me to plant'. Four months later he wrote in his journal that 'a great and visible alteration is seen in the behavior of the colliers. Instead of cursing and swearing, they are heard to sing hymns about the woods . . .'

It was an unprecedented event in the history of English spirit-uality. 'Field preaching' had in previous centuries been the preserve of a few unorthodox or marginal figures, and the Dominicans had set up their pulpits in the marketplaces of the towns, but now whole communities who had never before been known to attend a church, gathered in the hills and open spaces.

Whitefield said that 'a preacher, whenever he entered the pulpit, should look upon it as the last time he might preach, and the last time his people might hear'. He cried aloud; he stamped on the wooden platform; he wept. 'Oh my hearers, the wrath is to come! The wrath is to come!' Wesley himself noted of one Methodist congregation that 'the people [were] half-strangled and gasping for life'; 'great numbers wept without any noise; others fell down as dead; some with extreme noise and violent agitation. One man hurled himself upon a wall again and again, calling out "Oh what shall I do? What shall I do? Oh for one drop of the blood of Christ!".' It was said that Methodist preachers were 'paid by the groan'.

In previous centuries the Church would have turned on them with all the guile and fury at its command; the Lutherans of the sixteenth century, the Quakers and Anabaptists of the seventeenth century, felt the fist and the fire. But the Church was now not so strong. Anglicanism was, shall we say, slumbering? Many of its members were easy or indifferent; they attended worship every Sunday as a social duty, but nothing more.

The Toleration Act of 1689 achieved exactly what its critics had prophesied; the religious temper was cool where it was not cold. Voltaire wrote in *Letters Concerning the English Nation* that 'if one religion only were allowed in England, the government would very possibly become arbitrary; if there were but two, the people would cut one another's throats; but as there are such a multitude, they all live happy and in peace'. Various religious sects and groupings came together in public debates where matters of grace and redemption were argued in an atmosphere of civility. There was nothing mean or trivial about that, of course, but it did not provide the best response to the fierce piety of the Methodists and other evangelicals. The established emphasis now rested on a faith that was 'pure' and 'rational', amiable and undogmatic. The philosopher, David Hume, described it as 'the most cool indifference'.

'Old Dissent' was in no better state. It had in its own fashion become orthodox. It contained no surprises and offended no one's sensibilities. Once even the most fervent Church becomes established it surrounds itself with rules and regulations, customs and conventions, that weigh it down. The adherents of Old Dissent were the craftsmen and well-known traders; they had become as much part of English society as the squire and the parson. One of their number, Philip Doddridge, explained that they did not accommodate 'the plain people of low education and vulgar taste'. Concerning the Roman Catholics the same bland latitude obtained. Daniel Defoe, in *A Tour Through the Whole Island of Great Britain*, commented upon Durham that the town is 'old, full of Roman Catholics, who live peaceably and disturb nobody, and nobody them; for we, being there on a holiday, saw them going as publicly to mass as the dissenters did on other days to their meeting houses'. Popular suspicion and resentment of them, however, among the London mobs, would once more emerge in the 1780s.

In 1740 Wesley and Whitefield came to a crossing from which two paths led. Whitefield took the less travelled path and adopted the predestinarianism of the Calvinists, together with the exclusive notion of 'election'; Wesley remained true to the Church of England, and in particular to the doctrine that redemption was available to all who willingly sought their salvation in Christ. He was a man of great talent for administration and organization and was sometimes called 'Pope John'. In the course of his ministry he established 356 Methodist chapels, and organized the faithful into 'classes' and 'bands' with an annual conference at which he would exhort, condemn, praise and rebuke his followers.

Wesley himself was a man whose optimism was matched only by his energy. 'I do not remember', he wrote when he was an old man, 'to have felt lowness of spirit for one quarter of an hour since I was born.' That enthusiasm lasted for all his eighty-seven years. He rose long before dawn, and preached his first sermon at five in the morning. In his eighty-fifth year he preached eighty sermons in eight weeks, and in the last year of his life travelled 70 miles on horseback in a day. He preached 800 sermons a year and in the course of his life travelled one quarter of a million miles. Such is the effect of burning conviction. More orthodox Anglicans (for Wesley insisted all his life that he remained a firm and committed Anglican) were afraid of his fire. He noted in his journal at the beginning of his ministry that 'I was roughly attacked in a large company as an enthusiast, a seducer, and a setter forth of new doctrines'. Yet he always remained calm and self-disciplined, turning away wrath with a soft answer.

One of Wesley's critics denounced his followers as tinkers, barbers, cobblers and chimney sweeps; but in truth his constituency was much wider. It included a large body of artisans as well as those workers who were associated with commerce and manufacture; these might be described as the newly significant trades, among them miners, quarrymen and hand-loom weavers. The association between the Methodist 'awakening' and the onset of industrialism, however, is not easy to discern. It may be that Methodism offered its adherents a tight-knit social community, with its own principles of cohesion, at a time when other social ties were being weakened. It is also instructive that approximately half of the Methodist congregation were women, perhaps alienated from the male preserve of Anglicanism.

The faith spread in the manufacturing districts of the north-east, the north midlands and the Potteries; it flourished in the mining areas and in the fishing villages, areas that had tended to protect themselves from official authority. Cornwall and Wales were, for that reason, centres for those of Methodist persuasion. Methodism, more than Anglicanism, was aligned to native sensibilities; Wesley, for example, was happy for his preachers to speak in Welsh. Methodism also appealed to that sense of rapture dear to the Celts and to many other oppressed peoples. Towns were more susceptible than villages. It was perhaps not surprising that Wesley, who professed himself to be a Tory and a devout Anglican, should gather together a motley congregation of whom many were radical and anti-authoritarian in tendency. The message of individual redemption, beyond the orthodoxies of the established Church, was more important than the messenger. As a result, individual Methodists were denounced as levellers, democrats and even atheists.

Methodism was also the spring and fountain of the evangelical enthusiasm that materially affected the climate of English spirituality in the 1780s. The meetings of the Methodists were well known for weeping and hysterical laughter, cries and shouts and confessions; it was returning in spirit to the 'enthusiasm' of the previous century that had largely been extinguished at the time of the Restoration. The early eighteenth century had not been a time for God's elect, but under the leadership of Wesley the elect returned in armies to the Lord. 'Old Dissent' was in turn partly replaced by 'New Dissent', when the enthusiasm of artisans and other urban workers affected the congregations. The middle decades of the eighteenth century were indeed the time for sects who walked and prayed on wilder and wilder shores. In the streets of mid-eighteenth-century London appeared little clusters of Moravians, Muggletonians, Sandemanians,

Hutchinsonians, Thraskites, Salmonists, Swedenborgians and Behmenists. For the young William Blake it was a 'golden city'.

The evangelical revival seems to have appeared at approximately the same time as the emergence of Methodism; this is not at all unexpected, since they were the roots of the same tree. As the Methodist movement grew in strength and intensity, so did the emphasis on a new awakening infuse Anglicans and dissenters with the same desire for personal spiritual renovation. Yet the evangelicals, as they became known, were averse to open-air meetings and to the wilder manifestations of enthusiasm; some of the more famous of them, like William Wilberforce and Hannah More, worked quietly but actively for social reform and the inculcation of Christian manners. They worked against all the forces of eighteenth-century society that they deemed to be immoral – gambling, drinking and cruelty to animals among them. They were also strict Sabbatarians. They belonged to the world of property and patronage, and can perhaps be best seen as the more established or higher-ranking equivalent of the lowly Methodists. One of Hannah More's great successes was a little book of 1795 entitled *Tales for the Common People*.

It was much more likely, therefore, that their missionary activity would take the form of societies and small groups of like-minded supporters such as the Clapham Sect or Clapham Saints which began to meet in 1790. Societies for the 'reformation of manners' became familiar, among them the Society of Universal Good Will, the Society for Carrying into Effect His Majesty's Proclamation against Vice and Immorality, the Society for Promoting the Religious Instruction of Youth, the Society for the Suppression of Vice. They were complemented by the Society for the Propagation of the Bible in Foreign Parts, the Society for Promoting Christian Knowledge, the London Missionary Society, the Church Missionary Society, the Religious Tract Society and the British and Foreign Bible Society.

One of the principal effects of the evangelical revival, however, was the steady growth of 'Sunday schools' in the later years of the eighteenth century. The Sunday School Society was established in 1785, and within half a century some 17,000 schools had been instituted for the benefit of poor children who might acquire the elements of reading and writing. But the first purpose of these institutions was to promote religious and moral instruction, and in particular to indoctrinate the children with the rules of discipline and obedience. Many of the pupils in fact became part of the child labour force that was a significant aspect of the Industrial Revolution.

17

Do or die

William Pitt's vision, of global supremacy, seemed within reach. The early course of the Seven Years War was wholly changed by the victories of Frederick of Prussia, the ally of England, who soon acquired a reputation as the Protestant hero of Europe. In November 1757, at Rossbach in Saxony, he defeated the combined armies of France and Austria. A month later, at Leuthen in Bavaria, Frederick defeated a much greater Austrian army and seized Silesia. As if emboldened by these victories another allied commander, Prince Ferdinand of Brunswick, chased the French out of Hanover and pushed them back across the Rhine. Chesterfield, so doleful before, conceded that 'the face of affairs is astonishingly mended'.

Pitt was now free to pursue a continental strategy, with his enemy in retreat, but already he had more extensive ambitions. In the spring of 1758 an allied force captured the French fort of St Louis in Senegal; its principal commodity of slaves was now secure for the British Crown. At the end of the year an English force took Gorée, an island off the coast of Dakar, which thirty years later would contain the notorious 'House of Slaves'. So from the boiling and fever-stricken coastlines of West Africa came slaves and ivory, gum and gold dust, that were packed for the Caribbean or for England and then stored in factories with armed guards supplied by the local chieftains.

News came in this year, also, that Robert Clive had emerged victorious from the battle of Plassey and had taken control of Bengal, with its 30 million inhabitants, in a campaign Clive himself described as a medley of 'fighting, tricks, chicanery, intrigues, politics and the Lord knows what'. The victory led directly to British domination of South Asia and to the subsequent extension of imperial power. Yet not all welcomed these developments. There was a sense of unease over this meddling with exotic and alien foreign lands. There seemed to be no sure foundations on which to build. Only in the nineteenth century were these doubts resolved.

Within three years the French had been compelled to leave India. Without effective sea power they were destined for disappointment. The East India Company soon had all the trappings of an oriental state, with its own police force and native army. It was the tiger in the jungle, dripping with blood and jewels. India became the cockpit in which it was shown that trade was war carried on under another name. In the poetry of the period, in fact, allusions to Africa and India became commonplace; they had become part of the imagination. Yet there was still no talk of empire.

The West Indies had become the most profitable possession, even if the prize had to be shared with the French, the Spanish and the Dutch. An expedition sailed in the winter of the year and took Guadeloupe, the home of cotton, sugar and molasses; for Pitt the island of sugar was a greater prize than Canada, so much stronger were commercial than territorial ties. It sent forth each year 10,000 tons of sugar and in return required 5,000 slaves. It was considered to be a fair bargain. In the hundred years after 1680 some 2 million slaves were forcibly removed from their homes to the work camps of the West Indies.

The conditions of the enslaved workers were notorious. Another sugar island of the Indies, Jamaica, was described by Edward Ward in *Five Travel Scripts* (1702) 'as sickly as an hospital, as dangerous as the plague, as hot at hell, and as wicked as the devil'. The slaves could not breed in these torrid conditions, so even more had to be transported. These were the least of the slaves' torments. Many of England's overseas possessions were no more than penal colonies rivalling any of those in Stalinist Russia.

Slaves were simply beasts of burden. They were already suspended on a cross of three points, known as 'triangular' trade: they were purchased on the west coast of Africa with the proceeds of cloth or spirits before being transported across the ocean where they were sold to the plantation owner; the merchant seamen then returned with their holds filled with sugar, rum and tobacco. It was simplicity itself. A few local difficulties sometimes marred the smooth running of the enterprise. The slaves were manacled to the inner decks with no space to move, with women and children forced promiscuously among the male prisoners. When a ship was in danger of foundering, many of them were unchained and thrown into the sea; when some of them hit the water they were heard to cry out 'Freedom! Freedom!' The putrid and malignant diseases from which they suffered, in close proximity to one another, spread all over the vessel. The 'middle passage' across the ocean often created the conditions of a death ship.

Yet the church bells were ringing all over England. Even as the stinking and putrescent slaves were marched onto Jamaican or Bajan soil the new year in England, 1759, was being hailed as an '*annus mirabilis*'. The early capture of Guadeloupe was only the harbinger of overseas victories that guaranteed England's global supremacy. Horace Walpole remarked that the church bells had been worn thin by ringing in victories, and wrote to Pitt 'to congratulate you on the lustre you have thrown on this country . . . Sir, do not take this for flattery: there is nothing in your power to give what I would accept; nay there is nothing I could envy, but what you would scarce offer me – your glory.' That had always been considered the French virtue above all others; *gloire* and *le jour de gloire* were later to be immortalized in the second line of 'La Marseillaise'. But in 1759 they had been snatched away.

After the capture of Guadeloupe, Dominica signed a pact of neutrality with the victors. Canada, or New France as it was then known, was to come. In June General Amherst captured Fort Niagara and, in the following month, Crown Point. These victories were followed by the fall of Quebec in the autumn, when Major-General James Wolfe stole up the Heights of Abraham like a thief in the night. The capital of the French province lay on a precipitous rock at the confluence of the St Lawrence and St Charles rivers. Early assaults had come to nothing against what seemed to be an impregnable position. Wolfe wrote in his dispatches that 'we have almost the whole force of Canada to oppose'.

Do or die. He planned to land his force on the bank of the St Charles, to scale what seemed to be the insuperable heights, and then to attack Quebec from the relatively undefended rear of the town. Recovering from their surprise at the success of the enterprise the French attacked but were beaten back. The French commander, Montcalm, was shot as he stood; Wolfe received a wound in the head, followed by two other bullets in his breast and his body. Yet in death his was the victory. The beaten and demoralized French army evacuated much of Canada and retired to Montreal; a year later the garrison at Montreal also surrendered, and Canada joined the list of England's overseas territorial possessions.

The consequences of human actions are incalculable. With the threat of the French removed from the British settlers over the ocean, they began to resent the presence of English soldiers. Who needed the protection of the redcoats now that the enemy was gone? And so from small events great consequences may arise. An action that Voltaire derided as a conflict 'about a few acres of snow' gave rise in time to the United States of America.

The events in the European theatre were no less promising. The threat of French invasion was diverted. The reports of an invasion force, complete with flat-bottomed boats for landing, provoked Pitt into calling out the militia to guard the shores. At Quiberon Bay in November 1759, off the coast of southern Brittany, the French navy was caught and for all purposes destroyed. There would be no further threat of a French invasion.

And that, it might seem, was that. England had achieved maritime supremacy and gathered up more territorial possessions than ever before. The economic strain at home was beginning to show, however, with multifarious taxes imposed to bolster the revenues for the war. Yet if there was a sense of war weariness, it was not evident to the first minister. Pitt had been successful in Canada, the East Indies and the West Indies but he was determined to guide the destiny of Europe and confirm the strength of his country's global trade. The duke of Newcastle wrote to a colleague that 'Mr Pitt flew into a violent passion at my saying we could not carry on the war another year; [he said] that that was the way to make peace impracticable and to encourage our enemy; that we might have difficulties but he knew we could carry on the war and were one hundred times better able to do it than the French . . . in short, there was no talking to him'. Pitt knew that his colleagues were now in favour of a negotiated peace; negotiation meant, for him, compromise with the French. He would not rest until their most important possessions were in his hands. But the most carefully laid plans do not always come to fruition.

Suddenly all was changed. On 15 October 1760, George II rose early to drink his chocolate; he then felt the need to visit the water closet from which the *valet-de-chambre*, according to Horace Walpole, who seems to have known the most arcane secrets of the royal family, 'heard a noise, louder than royal wind, listened, heard something like a groan, ran in' and found the king on the floor with a gash on his forehead. The king expired shortly afterwards, bequeathing a new king to a not necessarily grateful nation.

18

The violists

In January 1759, the year of victories, the British Museum was formally opened at Montague House; it was largely designed to accommodate the extensive collection of Sir Hans Sloane who, in the manner of an antiquary of the old school, had collected books, manuscripts, works of art and objects of natural history. It represented prize specimens from all over the world, and what better home might it have than London? The collection included a pointed flint hand-axe, one of the first evidences of primordial antiquity; the mirror of Doctor Dee, the conjuror who had held out a vision of the English Empire to Elizabeth I; some birds-of-paradise from Papua New Guinea as a reminder of the exotic world just over the horizon; some ritual wooden artefacts from Jamaica that had now become an island of blood; an ivory figure of Xiwangmu, a Chinese goddess known as 'the queen mother of the west'; and a brass astrolabe from Isfahan for calculating the position of the sun and other stars.

In 1768 the Royal Academy had been established, of which Sir Joshua Reynolds became the first president. It was pre-eminent in a city that had, in the previous decade, harboured no art galleries or exhibitions of any kind. The first public exhibition was held in April 1760, at the Society of Arts in the Strand; the crush was so great that several windows were broken. But it inaugurated, if nothing else, a new relation of art with the public. There was a new market. There was a new commodity. It was perhaps no coincidence that the first recorded reference to the phrase 'fine arts' comes from 1767 when Dr James Fordyce stated of young women that 'they . . . wanted instruction in the principles of the Fine Arts'.

There had been in the earlier part of the century associations for young artists, most notably among them a new academy in St Martin's Lane where William Hogarth was a member. The members were, or had been, apprentices to one of the decorative arts; but now they sought other opportunities based on European models, and were particularly interested in 'life drawing'. The aspiring painters among them would previously have been confined to ceilings, stages and portraits, but their ambitions were also lifted. They had become interested in the style of the light and agitated line, or what Hogarth called 'the serpentine line of beauty'.

Soon enough the novels and plays of the age would be full of a new and interesting figure, the young artist. The young artist who is hired to superintend the lessons in drawing for young ladies. The young artist who is invited to paint a country house and its occupants. The young artist who has recently removed himself to Rome where he might study the classical masters and perhaps act as a cicerone for Englishmen and Englishwomen on the grand tour. The young artist who earned a precarious living in London, loitering around the Royal Academy or the auction houses in the hope of inviting stray custom. The virtuosi of course considered only works in oil by the Italian masters, or canvases that at least resembled them, to be worth examination. But watercolours and line drawings were coming to seem respectable on the walls of the aspiring middle class. It was no longer considered pretentious or laughable to style yourself an 'artist'. This was one of the new professions.

So the Royal Academy became a notable centre for aspiring artists who were bolstered by their membership of what was already a grand national institution. Art had arrived in the public arena. William Blake entered the Royal Academy Schools in 1779; James Gillray had entered in the previous year, and Thomas Rowlandson in 1772. In 1789 James Mallord William Turner made the journey to Somerset House as a student. In the following year the Royal

Academy opened its doors to the public. An entirely new national enterprise had begun under the most favourable circumstances.

A new London concert society, the Concert of Ancient Music, began giving performances in 1776 at what became its regular venue, the Crown & Anchor in the Strand. Its name suggests an association with ale and spirits but in fact it was a 'great assembly room' with staircases and lobbies. This was the meeting place of a respectable and indeed formal group of musicians devoted to the English music of the sixteenth and seventeenth centuries. It soon became common for them to treat as 'ancient' any music composed twenty years before, which is perhaps an indication of how the grip of 'modernity' – what was recent, what was new – imbued the nature of the fine arts in the period.

There was a suggestion of lightness, or what in another era was known as 'pleasaunce', about English fine art. In *Essays on the Nature and Principles of Taste* (1790) Archibald Alison remarked that 'The fine arts are considered as the arts which are addressed to the imagination, and the pleasures they afford . . .' They might include an essay, a print, a watercolour, an epigram, a light air, a Chinese bowl, all of which comprise elegant pleasures that, in the words of the philosopher Lord Kames, furnish 'love of order' and 'delicacy of feeling'.

The members of the Concert of Ancient Music were independent professionals, no longer necessarily tied to a court or a church. The feudal ties had been severed, with sometimes unintended consequences. Haydn was overwhelmed by the liberality of his fees in London after the rigours of the Esterhazy court; he earned extravagant sums for concerts and for individual commissions; after receiving £800 for a concert in 1794 he remarked that 'this one can only make in England'. The sum is equivalent to £45,000. It was the true mark of a new musical culture.

The first professional concert series took place in the 1760s, in the same period as the first public exhibitions of art were also held in London. A concert room was built in Hanover Square in the subsequent decade, together with the Pantheon in Oxford Street whose manager brought Hadyn to London. There came a time when many large towns and cities had their resident orchestras.

Another sign of that new culture could be found in the unlikely purlieux of Clerkenwell where in Jerusalem Passage a 'small coals' man, Thomas Britton, organized a series of weekly concerts where could be heard performances of music, vocal and instrumental, that were acclaimed as 'the best in town'. A 'small coals' man was a coal-merchant, and above his store-room he had created a musical space where some of the most ingenious composers and instrumentalists of the day came to perform in front of an appreciative audience. So the public recognition and reward of music emerged in venues high and low.

Music had of course always been the accompaniment of social life. In the sixteenth century England had been described as a 'nest of singing birds'. But in the eighteenth century it took on a public and more formal structure. This was no longer the private and improvised music in which Samuel Pepys participated. Music was now expected at pleasure gardens and at tea gardens, by chalybeate wells and in theatres, at masques and polite assemblies. Musical evenings were organized with spinet and harpsichord, and chamber music became a fashionable entertainment. Music clubs and music rooms and concert rooms became the arena for professional musicians; the amateur singers around the drawing-room table were no longer the mode. In the eighteenth century music had become the natural and inevitable accompaniment to all public or semi-public gatherings. It invited pleasure rather than duty or contemplation. You could not go to an assembly hall, a theatre, a ballet, or a pantomime without being surrounded by the sound of violins and violas. Sometimes they even invaded the fashionable shops and the coffeehouses. The players were known to Samuel Johnson as 'violists'.

19

A call for liberty

The accession of George III in the autumn of 1760 marked a profound change in the English monarchy. He was the first of the Hanoverian kings to be born and educated in England, and the first to avoid the broad German accent of his predecessors. In his draft for the speech from the throne to parliament he declared that 'I glory in the name of Briton; and the peculiar happiness of my life will ever consist in promoting the welfare of a people whose loyalty and warm affection to me I consider as the greatest and most permanent security of my throne.' These were unexceptionable sentiments, no doubt written by a secretary. But they would soon be tested.

He had come to the throne at the height of Pitt's war that had endured for four years, and had already brought signal advantages to the nation. Yet the new king hated the war, and hated Pitt. He associated them both with his grandfather, George II, with whom he had conducted a family feud ever since he could reason. He believed that his grandfather had been a 'king in chains', in thrall to greedy and mendacious ministers. He believed that Pitt had used him and his father, Frederick, prince of Wales, to leap into the royal closet; he denounced the minister as possessing 'the blackest of hearts' and as having been a 'snake in the grass'. It was inevitable that he would wish to make his own way. His mother had often repeated to him, 'George, be a king!' He did not intend to disappoint her. The image of Duty was always hovering before him.

He seems to have inherited a strain of obstinate self-righteousness from his Hanoverian predecessors; he had the deficiencies of a closed mind, including overweening self-confidence combined with long spells of resentment and sullenness. Lord Waldegrave, his early governor, described him in his *Memoirs* as 'scrupulous, dutiful, ignorant of evil and sincerely pious; but neither generous nor frank'. He was in certain respects something of a zealot, or prude, and sincerely regretted the lack of decency or propriety at court. A week after his accession he issued a proclamation 'for the encouragement of piety and virtue, and for preventing and punishing of vice, profaneness and immorality'. He had a high opinion of the royal prerogative and would no doubt have gone to the death in defending the Anglican Church; fortunately he did not live in a period which demanded such self-sacrifice or indeed such strident leadership from any king.

He demanded order and system as the watchwords of the new reign. It may have come as a warning to the courtiers that he kept a collection of clocks and barometers; rigour and precision would be the accompaniments of proper service. He knew all the little things about the Army List and courtly etiquette; he knew what buttons should be worn and on what occasions; he knew the routine of everyone attending court, from the highest ambassador to the lowliest page. He rose at six in the morning, and then shaved and dressed before attending to the correspondence that had arrived in the night. He rode before breakfast, which was his only meal before dinner at four. The day was given to business, formal or informal, but he met selected guests for supper at ten. He was always a frugal eater and a prudent drinker.

Yet it would be wrong to paint too staid a portrait of a king who, after all, was only following the example of his Elizabethan and Stuart predecessors in insisting upon the prerogatives of a king. Nothing he said or did would have shocked Elizabeth I or Charles II, except perhaps for his protestations of piety. He loved the outdoors, revelled in sports such as riding and hunting; later in his reign he picked up the soubriquet of 'Farmer George' for his love of all aspects of the land.

In the draft of his first formal proclamation to the privy council he had written of 'a bloody and expensive war'. Pitt of course could not allow any such judgement on the conflict that he had guided towards victory, and in the published version the sentiment had been transformed into this 'expensive but just and necessary war'. It was believed, not without reason, that the young king had been bullied or otherwise persuaded by the first minister into changing his declaration; this was a lesson that the king would not forget in all his later dealings with his politicians. He came to believe that he had a right to implicit support, and he refused to make concessions; he was not dismayed by criticism and opposition because he knew that he was right. 'I know I am doing my duty', he once said, 'and therefore can never wish to retract' to which may be added the remark that 'I would rather risk my Crown than do what I think personally disgraceful.' This was the habit of mind that lost America.

At first George III revelled in the name and nature of the 'patriot king', and even earned the praise of the acerbic Horace Walpole as 'handsome, open and honest'. The duchess of Northumberland compounded the praise by describing him as 'fair and fresh coloured' with blue eyes and white teeth. What more could a king enjoy? But who could have known or guessed that during his long reign he would face madness, the French Revolution, the glory of Napoleon and the loss of America?

Yet already he had ideas of his own, and such a monarch might turn out to be dangerous. He had conceived a hatred for Whigs and Tories alike; he despised the cynicism and the back-biting, the profiteering and the posturing, the lies and the hypocrisy. So he decided to rule without the aid of any party at all, bringing in a variety of ministers as and when he thought fit. It was hoped and believed that this would introduce a new period of peace and understanding in which the Tories, in particular, hoped for the dismantling of the Whig juggernaut and a return to royal favour. The king would once more assume a central political position. This was more than a policy; it was a moral duty.

He brought in a close confidant to help him; Lord Bute was in his late forties and had been his cherished councillor since childhood, and the equally intimate companion of his mother, Augusta of Saxe-Gotha. The young king, not trusting any of the councillors and politicians who had clustered around his grandfather, relied upon him for everything. Two days after his accession he told Pitt that 'the king would have no meetings held at which he [Bute] was not present'. This did not of course impress Pitt, who was accustomed to managing matters in his own way. 'I know', he wrote, 'it is impossible for me to act in a responsible ministerial office with Lord Bute . . . I can't bear a touch of command, my sentiments in politics like my religion are my own. I can't change them . . . I cannot be dictated, prescribed to . . .'

The king's trust and dependence upon Bute, however, do suggest that he was still too modest, or too diffident, or too anxious, to exercise his power with proper self-confidence; he always possessed a strain of melancholy and nervous excitement that may have contributed to his later periods of madness.

Bute repaid the trust with loyalty and gratitude, but in other respects he did not seem altogether suitable for the highest offices. He was by no means popular. Scotland was his birthplace and ever since the Act of Union in 1707 the English had had an ambivalent attitude towards the Scots themselves, born out of pride and prejudice. They condemned the majority for their slatternly habits and yet at the same time denounced the most prominent for rapacity and ambition. The fact that his name chimed in the popular ear as Lord Boot was not helpful.

Lord Waldegrave noted that Bute 'has a good person, fine legs, and a theatrical air of the greatest importance . . . for whether the subject be serious or trifling, he is equally pompous, slow and sententious'. The new king's father had once remarked that he would make an excellent ambassador in a court where nothing happened. It seems that he was dry and awkward in company, but he compensated for his social incapacity by endless business. Chesterfield noted that 'he interfered in everything, disposed of everything, and undertook everything'.

The politics of the realm were in confusion, with the principal ministers at loggerheads. The king and Bute wished to discontinue the war as soon as practicable; Pitt and Newcastle were in favour of its full continuance. There was a lack of trust at the highest levels, therefore, and Pitt in particular felt that he was impeded and hindered. The Tories hardly knew who or what they were any more, having found royal favour after almost fifty years in the wilderness, and the Whigs were split and dissipated into so many factions and interests that they scarcely recognized each other. As one member, Henry Conway, put it, 'parties seem not only to have lost their animosities, but the very line that distinguished them is effaced'.

Encouraged by the presence of the king and of Bute, with their known animosity towards Pitt's war policy, there was a general movement towards peace among the political classes. It was well known that the country was tiring of war but, more particularly, it was tiring of taxes to pay for it. The first move came from the French king, Louis XV, who believed or hoped that the financial resources of the enemy were close to exhaustion. At the end of March 1761 he issued a declaration that talks between the parties should be held on the basis of territorial possessions now held. The technical term for this arrangement, *uti possidetis*, was a diplomatic nicety that could be interpreted in any number of fashions.

In this period, perhaps fortuitously, a general election was held that engrossed the attention of political spectators. It was a hard and expensive campaign with Horace Walpole describing 'West Indians, conquerors, nabobs, and admirals' descending on every borough. 'West Indians' were the owners of plantations and 'nabobs' were the English who had picked up the riches of India. Bribery and corruption increased proportionately and one parliamentary borough, Sudbury, even advertised itself for sale. Given the confused and heterogeneous mixture of alliances, groups, loyalties, factions and coteries – all of them floating above the divisions between Whigs and Tories – it was of course difficult to decide who, if anyone, had 'won'. The inevitable result was insecurity, and instability, at a time when the challenges to the king's administration had never been greater.

Pitt, however, was still the dominant minister until the parliament assembled in October 1761. One member, Richard Rigby, described him as 'the Dictator' and the French ambassador, François de Bussy, remarked that 'he has few friends in the Council, but there is no one there strong or bold enough to try to replace him'. He was of course all for continuing the war against the French, on the principle that it is better to knock out your enemy when he is already down.

Pitt also called for a pre-emptive war against Spain so that the two Bourbon powers might not have the time or opportunity to ally against the common foe. He called together his colleagues to reveal to them the information that France and Spain had indeed concluded a family pact. It was doubly important to intercept the annual plate fleet from the Americas that filled its treasury. 'France is Spain,' he told them, 'and Spain is France.' His colleagues were not inclined to draw the same conclusions. The City declared that there was not enough money for further warfare; Admiral Anson complained that the fleet was not ready. A thousand plausible reasons could be given for caution or inaction.

Pitt reacted in the only way he knew. He would, he said, 'be responsible for nothing but what he directed'. He resigned on 5 October, to the great relief of Spain, France, the earl of Bute and the new king. 'I would say,' George wrote, 'let that mad Pitt be dismissed.' But Pitt, to the dismay of his supporters and the incredulity of his opponents, then decided to accept a government pension of £3,000 per year. The cynical response, although brief, was overwhelming. The great patriot could be bought after all, and his selfless direction of his country could now be seen by cynics in a different light. As Horace Walpole put it, 'Alack! Alack! Mr Pitt loves an estate as well as my Lord Bath.' Pitt's resentment was such that his supposed retirement from politics turned out to be temporary. He burned for revenge on his calumniators.

It was now the turn of the earl of Newcastle, the old warhorse of the administration for thirty-eight years, to bow to the force of the 'new men' and resign his office as first lord of the treasury. He had already complained that 'my advice or opinion, are scarce ever asked, but *never* taken. I am kept in, without confidence, and indeed without communication.' His lament emphasizes the extent to which public policy was determined by a small handful of councillors. In the early years of George's reign a group of principal men, generally seven or eight in number but reaching up to thirteen, now took on the name and nature of an inner cabinet as opposed to a larger outer cabinet of assorted worthies. The earl of Bute himself took command of policy with a profound sense of self-importance. Lord Shelburne had remarked that he was 'always on stilts'.

By the new year Pitt's prognostications had in fact proved to be correct. The treasure ships sailed into Spanish harbours and the Spanish authorities, so provided, rejected complaints concerning their provocations against English vessels. A war upon Spain was declared in January 1762, and the superiority of English sea power was manifest in the conquest of Havana and Manila. From the West Indies to the Philippines the Royal Navy seemed to be invincible. Yet even as the smoke cleared Bute was pursuing the path of peace; through various intermediaries he was in contact with the courts of Madrid and Versailles. He was perhaps in concert with the popular mood, since in this year there occurred a sharp economic depression which was the harbinger of a decade of droughts and poor harvests.

The preliminary articles of peace were signed at Fontainebleau at the beginning of November, and in the welter of complex negotiations it became clear that England was the gainer of most spoils. Minorca, Nova Scotia, Canada, Senegal, St Vincent, Grenada and other territories now became her property by conquest. The French also ceded British supremacy in India. But Pitt, the man who had fought the war, was not content. He came to parliament with his legs and feet wrapped in flannel; he suffered so badly from gout that he was allowed occasionally to sit as he spoke. Nevertheless his speech against the preliminaries of peace lasted three and a half hours, in which time he described France as a powerful and dangerous rival who should not be rescued at the last minute. Yet the war was over.

The treaty of Paris, signed in February 1763, set the seal on the general peace that followed. The countries of Europe were exhausted after seven years of conflict, and the majority of them had gained little if anything from the bloodshed and the destruction. Nobody could keep a list of the homes pillaged, the fields devastated and the inhabitants destroyed by invading armies. Nobody kept a list because nobody cared. The mood, in England at least, was sanguine to the point of smugness. Horace Walpole wrote to a friend that 'you would not know your country again. You left it a private little island, living upon its means. You would find it the capital of the world . . . St James's Street crowded with nabobs and American chiefs, and Mr Pitt attended in his Sabine farm by Eastern monarchs and Borealian electors, waiting till the gout has gone out of his foot for an audience.'

It would seem, then, that by the early 1760s England took its place at the centre of what was rapidly becoming a vast trading network from Canada to Bengal. It was still not seen in imperial terms, and the concept of empire was usually reserved for the vast Chinese Empire, the Ottoman Empire, or the Mughal Empire; it was not a European pursuit as Edward Gibbon's *The History of the Decline and Fall of the Roman Empire*, published thirteen years later, helped to demonstrate. Nevertheless the gains acquired during the Seven Years War seemed to some to have political as well as mercantile associations, and allusions to empire became more frequent in the 1770s. But there was no planning, no strategy, no coherent policy for the vast agglomerate of colonies, territories, provinces and states that were now under English rule. The response was one of caution and indecision. The prevailing mood was one of unease and uncertainty, with an upsurge in prophetic dissent and apocalyptic moralism that tried to counter what many contemporaries denounced as laxness and irresponsibility. England had a relatively small population on a small island. It was predicted that within a few years more people would inhabit North America.

Trade was the key. Trade promoted wealth and independence; trade nurtured strength. The standard theory of mercantilism held that there was only a finite amount of bullion in the world, and that England should control the largest share. Commerce could, according to Edmund Burke, be 'united with and made to flourish by war'. Slaves, sugar and tobacco were the principal commodities that expanded in the new climate. The war had repercussions at home, with the gun-smiths, sword-smiths, and dock-workers in eternal demand; the foundries, forges and mills were red-hot. It was not yet clear to contemporaries that this was the prelude to something on an altogether larger scale.

The effort of funding a world war for seven years, of furnishing ships, of paying mercenaries, of collecting taxes and of begging for loans from companies, also ensured that the nation itself would be changed inexorably. It was no longer a private little island that could, theoretically, keep to itself. It had become a giant enterprise with all the demands and appurtenances of state power. It relied upon an expanding treasury and the support of high finance; it depended upon an ever-increasing number of bureaucrats and administrators

– let alone the teeming excise men and customs men – to maintain its authority. By the 1720s it had enrolled 12,000 government servants.

A foreign observer noted that 'the English are taxed in the morning for the soap that washes their hands, at nine for coffee, the tea and the sugar they use at breakfast; at noon for the starch that powders their hair; at dinner for the salt that savours their meat, and for the beer they drink'. The bricks that built their houses, and the coals that kept them warm, the candles and even the windows that gave them light, were also the subject of tax. It is perhaps ironic that the people who complained most loudly about taxation, on the grounds of liberty, were in the end the most willing to pay it. It was part of a generally equivocal attitude towards authority that encouraged revolts but not revolution.

By these means, and others, the English administration consumed the largest proportion of national income of any European state. A substantial 83 per cent of this public money was spent for military purposes. Between the reigns of James II and George IV, at the beginning and end of this volume, taxes had multiplied sixteen times; in the same period England had declared war against foreign enemies on eight separate occasions. The administration had become in effect a war machine directed principally against the Bourbons. It was the most egregious fiscal and military country in the world. Whether many people understood the implications of that fact is another matter. Their awareness is more likely to have expressed itself in the popular patriotic songs that rang out in the halls and tea gardens where it was taken for granted that:

> Rule, Britannia! Britannia, rule the waves!
> Britons never, ever, ever shall be slaves.

Bute had said of the treaty of Paris that 'he wished no other epitaph to be inscribed on his tomb than that he was the adviser of it'. Yet two months later he resigned from office; his pride was of the brittle kind that is shattered by criticism. There were some who complained like Pitt, for example, that Spain and France had been let off too lightly. It was Bute who had defended the peace and his thin skin does not seem to have been capable of withstanding assault. He had already been badly rocked by the imposition of a cider tax that provoked riots in the West Country and elsewhere. And so, on 8 April 1763, he went. He did not disappear altogether. It was believed that he simply slipped 'behind the curtain' to lend the king clandestine advice for the next three years. From that position, therefore, he was about to watch two of the most incendiary events in eighteenth-century English and American history.

20

Here we are again!

He was called 'Dictionary Johnson' and 'the old elephant', the former term both more eloquent and more accurate after the publication of Samuel Johnson's *A Dictionary of the English Language* in the spring of 1755. It was an age of prescription as well as of enquiry; what was loose was confined; what was energetic or exuberant was chastened by rules of good order. The language had been in Johnson's own words characterized by 'perplexity', 'confusion' and 'boundless variety'. He himself was a great shambling devourer of words, a bibliophile and an antiquarian all at once.

The *Dictionary* was not in one sense unique or unusual. Many dictionaries had already been written, the first of them being Robert Cawdrey's *A Table Alphabeticall* published in 1604. The eighteenth century itself was the epoch of dictionaries, with John Kersey's *A New English Dictionary* in 1702 and Nathan Bailey's *An Universal Etymological Dictionary* published nineteen years later.

The first *Encyclopaedia Britannica* was published in 1768. A rage for order permeated public consciousness, with a new interest in sources and beginnings, derivations and definitions.

But Johnson's work was different. He was not an etymologist or a lexicographer, but a writer. He poured all his eloquence, and his learning, into the anatomy of words with abundant examples of their use from a multiplicity of authors. In the definitions of 'brim' and 'brimful' he enlists Bacon and Crashaw, Swift and Dryden, Milton and Sidney, and others, but he is more than a hunter-gatherer of allusions. He called it 'my Book' and it was for him the book of books, a distillation of the language which was a history and an encyclopaedia, a treatise and a moral tract. It was the expressive world of the English.

He spent his youth in his father's bookshop on Breadmarket Street in Lichfield, from which he was dispatched to a dame school and then to the local grammar school where he first encountered the sacred mysteries of Greek and Latin. In the *Dictionary* 'school' is defined as 'a house of discipline and instruction'. He attended Pembroke College, Oxford, for a while until a shortage of funds drove him home to Lichfield. A spell of schoolmastering there did not endear him to the life of a pedagogue and, with David Garrick as his companion, he moved to London where a world of hackery awaited him. This was his proper home, and he embraced it like a lover. The *Dictionary* was his first major work.

He has become a representative eighteenth-century personage and in truth he could not have flourished in any other century. His melancholy was nothing new, but his melancholy madness smacks of the age of Christopher Smart, William Cowper and George III. Like Cowper he believed himself to be in imminent danger of perpetual damnation; he took large quantities of opium and desired to be confined and whipped. One of his diversions was the new taste for travel literature; his first published work in 1735 was a translation of Father Jerome Lobo's *A Voyage to Abyssinia*, and he never lost that contemporaneous taste for the exotic and the unknown.

He is also deemed to characterize the eighteenth century as a result of his enormous eccentricity. The engravings of Hogarth and the fictions of Henry Fielding and Laurence Sterne afford ample evidence of the same preoccupation with extraordinary characters. In the work of artists and novelists London becomes a pantomime and a masquerade populated by grotesques. Johnson's most famous biographer, James Boswell, noted that 'while talking or even musing as he sat in his chair, he commonly held his head to one side towards his right shoulder, and shook it in a tremulous manner moving his body backwards and forwards, and rubbing his left knee in the same direction, with the palm of his hand'. In the intervals between talk 'he made various sounds with his mouth, sometimes as if ruminating, or what is called chewing the cud, sometimes giving a half whistle, sometimes making his tongue play backwards from the roof of his mouth, as if clucking like a hen . . .'.

When he walked 'it was like the struggling gait of one in fetters; when he rode he had no command or direction of his horse, but was carried as if in a balloon'. He wandered in his walk, swerving from one side of the path to the other in a zig-zag, and he had the obsessive habit of touching every post he passed in the London streets; if accidentally he missed one, he hastened back to tap it. He might stop in the middle of a thoroughfare and raise his arms above his head; before he crossed any threshold he would whirl around in order to make the sudden leap. He enjoyed rolling down hills and climbing trees. He was deeply marked by the scars of scrofula, contracted in his childhood; he was slovenly, often dirty and dressed absent-mindedly. He may be seen as the epitome of the way in which the eighteenth century developed an interest in, and relish for, human character.

The century also marked the true beginning of a taste for reading among the newly literate that included a section of the labouring population; a French observer, César de Saussure, noted in the 1750s that 'workmen habitually begin the day by going to the coffee-house in order to read the latest news'. Instruction manuals and even novels were scrutinized to learn the principles of good behaviour, of dress and diction; books of practical education, in trade and in agriculture, were greatly in demand. Two years after he had finished his dictionary Johnson persuaded the managers of the *London Chronicle* to begin reviewing books in its pages. It was an 'age of authors', as Johnson had written. Johnson himself was of course one of the most celebrated. That is a prime reason for his emblematic status.

The style of the *Dictionary*, at once sonorous and peremptory, accounts for some of its power. He himself was sometimes obliged to be 'Johnsonian'. He once said of a drama that 'it has not wit enough to keep it sweet' and then corrected himself with 'it has not vitality enough to preserve it from putrefaction'. When he said of somebody that 'the woman had a bottom of good sense' there was general laughter; he bridled at that and continued, in solemn fashion, 'I say the woman was *fundamentally* sensible.' The registers of eighteenth-century speech could be measured and taught. The purpose of the *Dictionary* was didactic as well as creative, and was very much in the spirit of the age.

He began his preparations by excessive and intuitive reading. He was an omnivore of books, sometimes literally tearing them apart to get at their contents. When he came upon a word he liked or needed, he would underline it and then mark out the extract in which it was embedded. His small and sometimes ragged retinue of assistants, sometimes four and sometimes six, occupied the upper chamber of his house in Gough Square where they sat at tables like clerks in a counting house. Johnson himself sat on an ancient elbow-chair, with three legs and one arm, propped against a wall.

When he had finished with a book it was passed to one of his companions who would then copy the marked passages onto a quarto sheet; when the sheet was filled with a column of references it was cut into single slips which were then deposited into a number of 'bins'. In the first edition of the completed work there were 40,000 words and more than 110,000 quotations. It was a wholly practical method of dealing with recalcitrant material, and must compare favourably with the prolonged discussions among the learned scholars of Paris or Florence about their own dictionaries. But it was also the great business of his life, expelling idleness and there-fore melancholy. He wrote it, as he said, 'amidst inconvenience and distraction, in sickness and in sorrow', but the majesty and impor-tunity of his work sufficiently elevated him.

He wrote a 'Plan', a 'Preface' and a 'History of the English Language' to accompany his work. He believed that the *Dictionary* itself would uncover 'the exuberance of signification' and would in the process comprise 'principles of science', 'remarkable facts', 'complete processes', 'striking exhortations' and 'beautiful descrip-tions'. Yet these were essentially 'the dreams of a poet doomed at last to wake a lexicographer'. He began his quest in the time of Philip Sidney and ended at the Restoration, because the period from the mid-sixteenth to the mid-seventeenth centuries was the one in which 'the wells of English undefiled' were to be found and tasted.

He treated his sources with the bravura of a master; sometimes he quoted them whole but, more often than not, he abbreviated them or condensed them. He refused to quote from Thomas Hobbes because he believed his works to be wicked; he quoted much from Milton's verse but only once from his prose, on the understanding that the prose-writer Milton was a radical and subversive. Johnson considered his *Dictionary* to bear a moral as well as didactic purpose; he furnished even the simplest words with devotional or ethical associations. 'Table' was defined by a sentence from John Locke that 'children at a table never asked for any thing, but contentedly took what was given them'. It was a work of practical morality. He was a devout and orthodox member of the Anglican communion, for whom words were the building blocks of faith. The first illustration of 'teach' comes from the Book of Isaiah with the sentence that the Lord 'will teach us of his ways, and we will walk in his paths'.

In the course of his survey he came upon words that in a later period would seem hard or strange, but were then part of common discourse. So in succession we find 'breedbate', a starter of quarrels, 'brontology', the science of thunder, 'brunion', a fruit somewhere between a plum and a peach, 'bub', strong malt liquor, 'bubbler', a cheat, 'bubby', a woman's breast and 'budget', a bag. A 'bedpresser' was a heavy or lazy man, while 'pension' was 'generally understood to mean pay given to a state hireling for treason to his country'.

He lists 134 uses for 'take', in an account which covers five pages and amounts to 8,000 words. Johnson, however, was not omniscient. He often stated that 'I know not the meaning'. 'Tatterdemalion' is defined as 'tatter and I know not what'. Of 'plication' he merely remarks that it is 'used somewhere in *Clarissa*'. Words fade or disappear while new ones emerge; some glimmer for a while before being extinguished while others thrive to become great roots for new systems of thought. In his Plan for the *Dictionary* Johnson remarked that 'all change is of itself an evil' but in the end he was obliged to realize that words are born and die like mortal beings. In that sense it is both a very personal and a very necessary book. To browse through it is to walk through the eighteenth century rendered more vivid by flashes of lightning.

At dawn on the morning of 6 September 1769, a triple discharge of seventeen cannon and twelve mortars on the shores of the Avon at Stratford announced the opening of the Shakespeare Jubilee. It was to be a national festival lasting three days, designed by David Garrick in honour of the nation's greatest writer; there were to be pageants and plays and processions, attended by all the notables of the time. Dukes, duchesses, actors, politicians, admirals and generals came out in force. Boswell turned up, dressed as a Corsican in order to boost sales of his recent account of that island. He wrote that Garrick 'observed me. We first made an attitude to each other, and then cordially shook hands.'

The first day passed well enough but on the second the rains of autumn intervened; the cobbles of the town were under water and the waters of the Avon were rising dangerously. Many of the public events were cancelled or abandoned, and the audiences for what remained were wet and miserable. It had not been altogether a triumph but it was in its own terms a *succès d'estime*; it was the beginning of the festive commemoration of Shakespeare that at a later date would be termed half-ironically as 'bardolatry'. It also marked the beginning of the national celebration of English drama as an expression of the national spirit. The playwright was a token of growing cultural self-confidence and an emblem of patriotism.

Boswell's sense of occasion was immaculate since, in the period, drama was the form and substance of the age. Everyone, from the politician to the preacher, took his cue from the stage. The dialogue was noted down and copied. The costumes, of the actresses in particular, were observed. When Boswell 'made an attitude' on first seeing Garrick he was copying a gesture from the stage. Snatches of stage dialogue became catchphrases. The most popular performers became the object of burlesque and street theatre. The whole of London was a theatre with even the mendicants 'dressing up' for their roles on the streets of the city; there was a costume for the parlour maid, and a costume for the fishwife. When people began to dress 'above their station', as was often reported, then social chaos beckoned. The names of Congreve, Sheridan and Aphra Behn are familiar; but every hack writer or journalist, every out-of-work actor or Oxbridge scholar down on his luck, turned to the stage as the most likely means of earning a living.

The two principal licensed London theatres were the Theatres Royal at Covent Garden and Drury Lane, to which the usual variegated London crowd thronged. The gentlemen and those who considered themselves gentlemen were happy to pay 3 shillings to sit on benches in the pit, close to the action, while citizens and their wives paid 2 shillings for the first-floor gallery. The lower sort had the higher seats in the upper gallery, where fruit-sellers and prostitutes wielded their various wares. The most celebrated or wealthy patrons had already hired boxes for their private pleasure. These two theatres at Covent Garden and Drury Lane were alone licensed to present spoken drama, but of course this did not prevent other venues from providing theatre of a different kind.

Some old relics, used in Elizabethan and Stuart times, were pressed back into service. In 1728 the 'Old Theatrical Booth' by the Bowling Green in Southwark, for example, presented operas and 'an entertainment of dancing in grotesque characters'. The same theatre promised dramatic entertainments on Jack Sheppard, the notorious criminal and escapee, as well as 'dramatic operas' and 'ballad farces'. Other theatrical booths were set up in the courtyard of the George Inn along Borough High Street and by the hospital gate at Smithfield. We read in the *Daily Advertiser* of 22 October 1776, that 'the beautiful Patagonian Theatre' has reopened in 'the Great Room, over Exeter Change' with a burletta entitled *Midas* and a pantomime called *The Enchanter*. Most of these venues were eventually abandoned, decayed, or burned down. But they are a reminder of London's teeming theatrical life. By the beginning of 1726 some thirty-six theatrical productions were being advertised.

Everything was of the moment; the jokes and remarks were topical, the allusions immediate, the objects of satire were such modern phenomena as Methodists and 'bubble' speculators. People came to hear the latest news or the latest rumours, no doubt from the other members of the audience as much as from the stage. Romances, melodramas and what another age would call variety shows, were also played.

The audience was just as much a matter of attention and speculation as the actors; the chatter of gossip and comment continued through the performance, and there were times when the actors could hardly make themselves heard. The denizens of the pit ate plum cake and blew on tin whistles if they disapproved of any action; the sounds became known as 'cat-calls'. The theatre was an occasion when the town came to regard itself, as well as to look upon its image on the stage. It was truly a communal experience. The auditorium itself was better lit than the light of day, and the audience had some of the characteristics of the London crowd from which they came – violently so on those occasions when riots took place over the price of seats or the presence of foreign performers. There were times when the interiors of the theatres were wrecked, even, and especially, after the manager had come upon the stage and appealed for calm.

In the world of the eighteenth-century theatre the spectator could often take on the role of the actor. Well-known theatre-goers were the talk of the town. One spectator in the upper gallery of the playhouse signalled his approval of the action of the stage by giving loud knocks, with an oaken staff on the benches or on the wainscot, that could be heard all over the house. He was, according to Addison, 'a large black man whom nobody knows' and was known as 'the trunk maker in the upper gallery' after the noises made by those workers. Another 'lusty fellow, but withal a sort of beau', again according to Addison, would leap from one of the side boxes onto the stage before the curtain rose; here he took snuff and made several passes at the curtain with his sword before facing the audience. 'Here he affected to survey the whole house, bowed and smiled at random, showed his teeth which some of them indeed were very white. After this he retired behind the curtain, and obliged us with several views of his person from every opening.'

The paucity of playhouses in the capital meant that several were built without a formal royal licence; demand prompted supply. Two were opened in the Haymarket, for example, one for the opera in 1705 and one for miscellaneous variety in 1766. A third theatre had been established in Ayliffe Street, Whitechapel, in 1727; there had been an earlier theatre in that vicinity in 1703 where yet another playhouse was created in 1732. So Whitechapel was the second home of drama. The unlicensed playhouses were given tacit permission to open on the understanding that, if their plays gave serious offence, they would be immediately closed.

The Licensing Act of 1737, which obliged plays to be corrected by the lord chamberlain, had an immediate effect upon the stage. There would be no oblique passes at obscenity or blasphemy; there were to be no more political satires. From the defenestration of the eighteenth-century theatre emerged a moral and sentimental drama with appeals to right feeling and right thinking. As Dangle says in Sheridan's *The Critic* (1779), 'Now egad, I think the worst alteration is in the nicety of the audience – no double entendre, no smart innuendo admitted, even Vanbrugh and Congreve obliged to undergo a bungling reformation.'

But the restrictions of the Act not only created a theatre of moral sentiments. They also prompted writers in new directions, thus changing the nature of fiction itself. All the inventiveness and energy, all the wit and drama, were transferred from the stage to the page. The Licensing Act heralded the rise of the serious and successful novel in England. Previously fiction had been considered by Defoe and his contemporaries as simply a digression from journalism, but now it took on a wholly independent life.

Fielding and Smollett, for example, had previously turned their attention towards the stage, Fielding being so successful that he was dubbed 'the English Molière'. Now their comedy found a new form of expression. What could no longer be seen on stage could still be described in *Tom Jones* or in *The Adventures of Peregrine Pickle*. The comedy and the innuendo, the dramatic confrontation and the melodramatic reversal, had become the stuff of fiction.

The six volumes of Henry Fielding's *Tom Jones* appeared in the early months of 1749 and the four volumes of Tobias Smollett's *Peregrine Pickle* were published exactly two years later. As a fitting prologue for the immensity of these productions the full seven volumes of Samuel Richardson's *Clarissa, or The History of a Young Lady* appeared in 1748. Three incomparable novels had appeared in four years. The eighteenth-century novel had come of age with the implicit declaration that prose fiction could encompass the whole range of human experience in ways that transcended the limitations of the stage.

It became the age of novelists. In the literary history of the mid- to late eighteenth century we hear little of poets or of dramatists; all the attention is drawn to the innovation and invention of the writers of prose fiction. Fielding himself, in the second book of *Tom Jones*, described prose fiction as 'a new province of writing' and declared 'I am at liberty to make what laws I please therein'. There are no dramatic 'unities' to keep and no orders of scansion to follow. The novels of the eighteenth century have very little command of narrative structure; one chapter is very much like the preceding and succeeding ones, but with intricate variations to maintain the reader's interest.

Smollett, in his preface to *The Adventures of Ferdinand Count Fathom* (1753), describes a novel as 'a large diffused picture, comprehending the characters of life, disposed in different groups and exhibited in various attitudes, for the purposes of a uniform plan, and general occurrence, to which every individual figure is subservient'. Since the presence of 'a uniform plan' was the greatest truth of the age, its use here is not necessarily significant. Smollett was in essence remarking that the subject of the novel was human life in all its various detail. There were no rules. So Fielding described *Tom Jones* as 'this heroic, historical, prosaic poem', which might mean anything or nothing. Smollett's *Peregrine Pickle* is another case in point in its combination of satire, melodrama, bawdry, theatricality, sentiment, pathos, realism, bathos, suspense and comedy. All that had been banned from the stage, even the characters themselves, poured in crowds onto the page crying out 'Here we are again!'

Despite the provenance of some of the novelists – Smollett was born in Dunbartonshire and Fielding in Somerset – theirs was a distinctive London vision. The novel was an urban form. It had its origin in satire and in journalism, not necessarily in romance or in allegory. Fielding himself called the novel 'a newspaper, which consists of just the same number of words, whether there be any news in it or not'. The London roots go very deep. Fielding had a thoroughly urban sensibility which embraced the pantomimic and the scenic, which revelled in energy and adventure, and betrayed little interest in psychological or moral complexity. The outrageous eccentric was his version of the subtle personality. Smollett's characters in *Roderick Random* also had to struggle to be heard among 'the modish diversions of the town, such as plays, operas, masquerades, drums, assemblies and puppet shows'.

Another aspect of the novel's popularity was concerned precisely with the 'middling' classes who now comprised many of its readers. The novel dealt directly with those of 'quality', whether foul or fair; in the country they were squires or landowners, and in the city ladies and gentlemen. For those aspiring to gentility, therefore, the novel could become an instruction manual or 'pattern book'; novels were guides to etiquette and polite society. The characters attain wealth and status through their individual virtue, and Samuel Richardson's *Pamela; or, Virtue Rewarded* (1740) was advertised at the time as written 'in order to cultivate the principles of virtue and religion in the minds of the youth of both sexes'. Richardson no doubt meant it, but the sentiment may have been taken with a grain of salt by Hogarth and Smollett. The general mood of eighteenth-century fiction is one of high-spirited if ironic gaiety, where the dominant tone of voice is at once comic, inspired and facetious. But the best and truest word is irony.

21

The broad bottom

The earl of Bute, stung and surprised by his general unpopularity, had resigned. After the water covered Bute's head, up rose George Grenville eight days later. Grenville was from a distinguished family and had enjoyed an equally distinguished political career, partly in association with William Pitt whose animus against France he shared. He was not, however, a favourite of the king who did not relish the replacement of his Scottish confidant with what might be considered a standard Whig politician. He also detested his long-winded and hectoring manner. 'I had rather see the devil in my closet', the king said, 'than George Grenville.' The king also said of him that 'when he has wearied me for two hours, he looks at his watch, to see if he may not tire me for an hour more'. But the arch-bore became first minister in the spring of 1763.

The new minister's first test of fire came before the month was out. In the king's speech at the opening of parliament on 19 April, he hailed the treaty of Paris signed two months before as 'honourable to my Crown, and beneficial to my people'. This was still open to question. The year before, John Wilkes had established a newspaper under the name of the *North Briton* as an ironic allusion to Scottish Bute. He was now set upon vilifying Grenville and the king. Madame de Pompadour, the principal mistress of Louis XV, had asked Wilkes how far press liberty in England reached. 'That', he replied, 'is what I am trying to find out.'

In the forty-fifth number of the *North Briton*, published on 23 April 1763, he effectively accused the king of lying; there was no peace with honour, but peace born out of corruption and weakness. He wrote that 'every friend of this country must lament that a prince of so many great and amiable qualities, whom England truly reveres, can be brought to give the sanction of his sacred name to the most odious measures, and to the most unjustifiable public declarations, from a throne ever renowned for truth, honour and unsullied virtue'. To accuse a king of lying, even indirectly, was a case of sedition.

The name of Wilkes was in everyone's mouth. The standard portrait of the man as a grinning malevolent was the creation of William Hogarth; so was the wig curiously reminiscent of the horns of the devil. Wilkes, however, was genuinely cross-eyed. He was in fact a London radical of an old-fashioned sort. The son of a malt distiller from St John's Square in Clerkenwell, the home of radical groups and meetings since the time of Wat Tyler, he had a somewhat scandalous early life and two or three lacklustre years in parliament before his pen came vividly to life in the pages of the *North Briton*.

The outcry against his attack on George III was immense. The calls for his arrest were predictable but, perhaps unfortunately, the government issued a 'general warrant' that could be used against anyone whom the authorities deemed to be deserving of it. Wilkes himself was placed in the Tower, but in two appearances in Westminster Hall at the beginning of May he denounced general warrants as illegal; as a member of parliament, also, he claimed freedom from arrest. In his second speech to the judge he declared that 'the liberty of all peers and gentlemen, and what touches me more sensibly, that of the middling and inferior set of people . . . is in my case this day to be finally decided upon'. Whereupon the chief justice set aside any charges of felony or treason, and ordered Wilkes to be freed. Wilkes had applied the usual practice of the political radical, not by identifying with a popular cause but by creating a popular cause out of his own situation. He proclaimed that he was an honest citizen who had become enmeshed in the toils of the Crown and its servants. In his own person he posed the question whether English liberty 'be a reality rather than a shadow'. So arose the slogan that echoed through the streets of London, 'Wilkes and Liberty!' A crowd of thousands escorted Wilkes from Westminster to his house. Soon enough there would be a plethora of handbills, posters and pamphlets proclaiming his cause.

Immediately after his release Wilkes sued the secretary of state, the 2nd earl of Halifax, for signing the general warrant; he was awarded £1,000 in damages by a sympathetic court. Wilkes had effectively taken on the government apparatus and had won. It was a boon for those who felt that something was wrong with the machinery of power.

But power itself could be malicious and devious. Some years before, Wilkes had played a part in the composition of a satiric parody of Alexander Pope's *An Essay on Man* entitled *An Essay on Woman*, an obscene elegy ascribed maliciously to the bishop of Worcester. One of the objects of its insinuations was Fanny Murray, erstwhile mistress to the 4th earl of Sandwich. The poem opened, 'Awake, my Fanny!' which in some texts appeared as 'Awake my C . . .'. She was also compared to the Virgin Mary.

Wilkes had perpetrated a joke but he had also committed a blunder. Parts of the poem were now read aloud in the House of Lords. The noble gentlemen, far from supporting a parliamentarian who had demanded immunity from prosecution, were outraged at one who had the mob and the judges on his side. The leading Whigs held back from expressing their support. In November the Lords condemned *An Essay on Woman* as 'a most scandalous, obscene and impious libel'. In the same period the Commons had concluded the forty-fifth issue of the *North Briton* to be 'a false, scandalous and seditious libel' that should be burnt by the common hangman at the Royal Exchange. A large crowd of Londoners assembled on the site, however, and prevented the sheriffs from consigning the paper to the flames.

The Commons now decided that Wilkes himself was not immune from a charge of seditious libel. Although he was detained by a bullet in the groin as a result of a duel with a political opponent, he recovered in time to slip away to France at the end of 1763, avoiding a certain defeat in the courts at the hands of his powerful opponents. He had not lost his sense of humour, however. When asked to play a game of cards he declined on the grounds that 'I cannot tell a king from a knave'.

In his absence he was tried for seditious libel, found guilty and sentenced to exile. In Paris, according to reports, he was never so happy, preferring the wit and culture of the erstwhile enemy to the more formal and prudish manners of his London contemporaries. Tobias Smollett, in *Peregrine Pickle*, concedes that 'France abounds with men of consummate honour, profound sagacity, and the most liberal education.'

Wilkes might have been equally welcome in North America where his impassioned defence of liberty was universally acknowledged; it was said by some that Wilkes and America would stand or fall together. While he had been incarcerated in the Tower, Virginia sent him tobacco and Boston dispatched a consignment of turtles; South Carolina sent him £1,500 to clear his debts and the newly established American colleagues, Sons of Liberty, addressed to him a formal declaration of amity and sympathy. He was fighting their cause against a corrupt administration.

The situation of the American colonies was in any case precarious. Some of them had already been attacked and harassed by a confederation of Native Indian tribes in what became known as 'Pontiac's War' (1763–6) after the name of one of its leaders. The vicious fighting seems to have been confined to the Great Lakes region, to Illinois country and to Ohio country, but the panic fear spread among all the colonists. It was said that the English troops, in retaliation for native atrocities, spread among them blankets infected with the smallpox virus. This was unlikely. It was agreed in London that a large military force should be permanently stationed in North America, not only to discourage the Native tribes but to deter any French incursions on what had once been their territory. France still held the area around New Orleans, in any case, and so controlled the mouth of the Mississippi. Pontiac's War lasted for a little more than two years.

This conflict of course had to be financed and it seemed to the first minister, George Grenville, only reasonable that the colonists themselves should bear part of the burden of cost. The king had already accused him of having the mind 'of a clerk in a counting house'. It was entirely in character, therefore, that the minister should devise a 'stamp tax' on the grounds that it was not too onerous or too obvious; it was raised on the stamps required to authenticate official documents. He even gave the colonists a year to come up with any proposal of their own to raise the required sums. Yet he failed to anticipate the clamour against what was a wholly new tax imposed without colonial consent. It was worse than a provocation, it was an insult. The Americans were, in a phrase of the time, 'jealous of their liberties' and apt to condemn any intervention from England as a form of tyranny.

George Grenville resigned four months after he had introduced the Stamp Act but not as a result of his ill-starred proposal, even though the Act has some pretension to being the most disastrous piece of legislation in English history. He was obliged to leave because he had angered the king once too often. It was over a matter of place involving the king's mother, but on his dismissal from office the wheels of fortune began to turn. The Butes, the Rockinghams, the Chathams, the Grenvilles, the Shelburnes, the Foxes and the Norths circled around and around on the vast gaming table of state until the golden ball dropped. The marquis of Rockingham was the fortunate recipient of the prize, but he did not last very long; he was in office for a year. When seventeen years later he picked up the golden ball a second time, death mercifully intervened after four months.

This did not encourage steadiness or coherence of policy. Grenville's Stamp Act had already provoked a furious reaction from the Americans. Virginia was the first to protest with a series of resolutions that were described as 'the alarm bells to the disaffected'; the officer chosen to administer the Act in Boston was hanged in effigy from a tree and his office was levelled to the ground. The riots spread and became more violent, with the houses of officials ransacked and the records of the courts burned. The merchants of the various colonies agreed that they would order no more goods from England, and cancel all existing contracts; this would have a significant impact upon trade. It may not have been rebellion, but it looked very much like it.

In October 1765, a Stamp Act Congress was convened in New York, when a number of colonies agreed to petition for relief, and also denied that parliament had any power of taxation in their territories. Yet it seems that the Americans were in many respects as confused and as uncertain as the English. Some were enraged at the apparent intention of the mother country to impose a system of colonial oppression, with a standing army. Others supported the king to whom they still believed that they owed allegiance. It has been estimated, but cannot be proved, that between one-third and one-fifth of the colonists were committed loyalists. The fact that each of the thirteen colonies had a different constitution and different precedents only served further to heighten the confusion.

On 1 November 1765, the date on which the Stamp Act came into law, the bells of the American churches were tolled in funereal style and the flags hung at half-mast. The English response to this unhappy and unlooked-for revolt was divided; some ministers argued for compromise, while others wanted to stand fast on a matter of principle. Rockingham, only recently appointed as first minister, realized that it was better to bend in a gale than snap in a storm; he also recognized that the British administration was effectively powerless to mend matters across the wide Atlantic. In March 1766 ministers and members came to an agreement to repeal the Stamp Act with a decisive majority of more than 100 votes. Edmund Burke, Rockingham's secretary, described it as 'an event that caused more universal joy throughout the British dominions than perhaps any other that can be remembered'. It was of course a concession to force and to the threat of force, but it was accompanied by a 'declaratory Act' that the British legislature had the right 'to make laws and statutes' which would 'bind the colonies and people of America . . . in all cases whatsoever'. It was, in other words, a compromise and a muddle which few people noticed at the time. It was enough that the hated Act had been repealed.

Some saw its significance at a later date. Thomas Paine, the champion of American independence, asserted in a pamphlet of 1782 'that the "declaratory act"' left the colonists 'no rights at all; and contained the full grown seeds of the most despotic government ever exercised in the world'; he added that 'it went to everything. It took with it the whole life of a man . . . It is the nature of law to require obedience, but this demanded servitude.' He sensed that it had been the real cause of war in 1775 and British defeat. Another proximate cause might be in the Stamp Act Congress itself, which brought together various colonies in the face of a common enemy.

Rockingham did not last long enough to savour the consequences of his policy, however, since in the summer of 1766 he was replaced by the ageing Pitt who was still under the impression that he was a man of destiny. He had made what to many had seemed to be the mistake of accepting an earldom; he was no longer the 'great commoner' of political legend. As earl of Chatham, however, he was forced to convey his policies from the Lords where he was neither as authoritative nor as eloquent as he had been in the lower house. A 'squib' or pasquinade exposed his pretensions. 'To be disposed of, considerably under prime cost, the stock in trade of a late eminent patriot, consisting of a large assortment of confident assertions, choice metaphors, flowery similes, bold invectives, pathetic lamentations, specious promises all a little worse for wear.'

He chose to become lord privy seal, and the relatively unknown Augustus FitzRoy, 3rd duke of Grafton, was appointed first lord of the treasury, a recipe for unstable administration. The new earl of Chatham had never been known for his attention to administrative detail, but that incapacity now became fatal in a summer when a failed harvest led to bread riots and mob action. He pieced together a cabinet from diverse sources, which Burke described as a 'tessellated pavement without cement', so unknown to each other that the first question was often 'Sir, your name?' or the first comment 'Sir, you have the advantage of me'. Frederick of Prussia told the British envoy in Berlin that it was impossible to do business with the British government; it was too unstable. Chatham was a dead failure and perhaps knew as much since, within a matter of months, he had descended into illness. He was first laid low again by gout, that universal ailment, and remained in Bath for October 1766; he then spent the first two months of the new year in the same resort. An absent first minister (even though he did not take the name) is not good for business. By the summer of the year he had grown infinitely worse and one contemporary, Lord Lyttelton, a former chancellor of the exchequer, believed that he now suffered from 'insane melancholy'. Pitt the former, as he might be known, refused to deal with any administrative matters and an official letter would send him into a fit of trembling; he would sit in a darkened room in silence and suffering.

Grafton became the effective leader of the government while Chatham was out of commission; Charles Townshend was chancellor of the exchequer who in 1767 seemed entirely to have forgotten the lesson of the Stamp Act. He devised what became known as the 'Townshend Acts' which imposed duties on certain items imported into America, among them tea, glass and paper, with the precise intention of paying for the expenses of the colonial administration. The money would go into the pockets of the governors and the military, giving them a large degree of independence from what were still called the colonists. 'Every man in England', Benjamin Franklin wrote, 'seems to consider himself as a piece of a sovereign over America, seems to jostle himself into the throne with the king and talks of *our* subjects in the colonies.' The American reaction to the new Act was one of thorough rejection. Court records were destroyed, and merchants refused to do business with England.

Yet this reaction was less vociferous than that against the Stamp Act. Economic prosperity, and an instinct for moderation or compromise, guided counsels on both sides of the Atlantic and led to three years of relative inactivity. There was in any case now little interest in London concerning American affairs. A much more interesting, and apparently more dangerous, conundrum had emerged in the shape of John Wilkes.

He had returned from his self-imposed exile in France, in February 1768, and if he hoped to cause a scandal he was disappointed. The authorities were not interested in arresting him. It would cause too much trouble. Yet he was determined to make an impression and decided to stand for the City of London in the forthcoming general elections, to be held between March and May, but came last in the voting list; the support of the craftsmen and City masters had not been enough. Not dismayed or deterred he turned his attention to the more radical neighbourhood of Middlesex which, with its market traders and small businessmen, was in a sense an outcrop of London. He managed the election at Brentford Butts, on 28 March, with a consummate sense of theatre: 250 coaches, filled with Wilkes's supporters sporting blue cockades and brandishing 'Wilkes and Liberty!'

placards, set out for the hustings. He came at the head of the poll, much to the fury of the king and the delight of the populace. The citizens were obliged to light their windows in celebration or watch their glass being shattered, and it was reported that the number '45' was scrawled on every door from Temple Bar to Hyde Park Corner; the seed of the scandal had appeared in the forty-fifth issue of the *North Briton*. It was reported in the *Annual Register* that 'the rabble was very tumultuous'.

Wilkes had an instinctive understanding of London life ever since his adolescence in Clerkenwell; he could connect himself with the innate radicalism of the crowd in a city where dissident opinion was commonplace. Radical clubs and fellowships met in alehouses and taverns, where they loudly proclaimed their fight against the threats to liberty and freedom by an arbitrary executive. The citizens who followed him were small men of property, urban freeholders, tradesmen, shopkeepers, craftsmen and labourers who were all ostensibly at the mercy of the larger powers of the City and the nation.

'45' became a war cry in the streets of the city, therefore, but it was also a symbol of the cause. It was perhaps not coincidence that the last Jacobite rising had occurred in 1745. A candlestick of forty-five branches was manufactured for a publican in Newcastle upon Tyne. The *Newcastle Journal* reported that a Wilkes dinner in April, just after the election, consisted of forty-five diners who 'at 45 minutes past one drank 45 gills of wine with 45 new laid eggs in them'. Five courses were served with nine dishes each, making up the magic number, while in the middle of the dining table rested a sirloin of beef weighing precisely 45 pounds. And so it went on. It became a craze – forty-five toasts, forty-five pipes of tobacco, forty-five sky-rockets, wigs of forty-five curls. On the flags his supporters had carried into Brentford were inscribed the words 'FREEDOM. LIBERTY! BILL OF RIGHTS. MAGNA CHARTA!' It was the ancient discourse of the English.

The king demanded that this seditious and disruptive scandal-monger should be prevented from taking his seat in parliament and there was much debate whether a convicted criminal, albeit one sentenced in his absence, should be able to disport himself in public. Wilkes himself then took the initiative and announced that he would surrender himself to the judiciary, and waited for the verdict in the

King's Bench Prison in Southwark. His partisans crowded the district and the tumult grew so violent in the adjacent St George's Fields that on 10 May 1769, a regiment of Scottish soldiers was sent in to keep the peace. In the subsequent disturbances a group of soldiers shot an innocent passer-by; the Riot Act was read for the second time and as a result some five or six others were killed, among them 'Mr William Redburn, weaver, shot through the thigh, died in the London Hospital' and 'Mary Jeffs, of St Saviour's, who was selling oranges by the Haymarket, died instantly'.

In June Wilkes was fined and imprisoned for twenty-two months on the old charge of seditious libel; his confinement was relatively comfortable, however, bolstered by gifts of food and money from his more wealthy supporters. The Commons tried to compound his disgrace by depriving him of his new seat in Middlesex. His expulsion provoked some sporadic rioting in London, and the 2,000 freeholders of Middlesex determined to nominate him once more for parliament. There then ensued a political comedy in which Wilkes was returned unopposed before once more being disqualified; he stood again, but his victory was annulled. He was once more chosen by the electors of Middlesex, but then promptly expelled on the grounds of his 'incapacity to be elected'. He stood for the fifth time and was again victorious in the ballot, but the Commons proceeded to invite one of his opponents to take the seat.

In the spring of the following year he was duly released from the King's Bench Prison to wild acclaim from the crowd for a popular hero who had shown both bravery and imagination in confronting the forces of authority. He had no political programme as such, and can hardly be claimed as a radical let alone a revolutionary; he appealed to what were considered the traditional liberties of the people, but he did so with an acute awareness of what might be called the power of the press. He orchestrated the political sense of the nation by a mixture of mockery, satire and denunciation. He was a symbol of defiance and independence. When canvassing in Middlesex, in his days of freedom, he was told by one householder that 'I'd rather vote for the devil'. 'Naturally,' Wilkes replied, 'but if your friend is not standing, may I hope for your support?' His statue now stands at the bottom of Fetter Lane, the only cross-eyed effigy in London.

The power of the press was not lost upon others. There had been a growing awareness in the middle decades of the eighteenth century of public opinion 'out of doors' as evinced in the circulation of the newspapers. The *Morning Chronicle* was established in 1770 and the *Morning Post* two years later; by 1777 there were seventeen newspapers published in London, seven of which were printed daily. A year later the *Sunday Monitor* became the first Sunday newspaper in England.

It was in any case a great age for political excitement. The long decay of the earl of Chatham came to its culmination with his withdrawal from office in the autumn of 1768, confirming Grafton's supremacy. It was Grafton who weathered the storms over Wilkes and the American tax revolt, but he was not made for leadership at a time of riots, petitions and the ridicule of the press.

One anonymous contributor to the press created a sensation. A correspondent by the name of 'Junius' suddenly emerged in the public prints. He had a talent for scurrility and vicious abuse, but it was his anonymity that prompted the greatest excitement. As Samuel Johnson wrote, 'while he walks like Jack the Giant-Killer in a coat of darkness, he may do much mischief with little strength'. Was this a minister or ex-minister telling secrets from behind the curtain? His essays were printed in the *Public Advertiser* from 1769 to 1772, at the very height of the Wilkes affair, and he did much to inflame public opinion. The duke of Grafton was 'a black and cowardly tyrant', one 'degraded below the condition of a man', while the king is described by inference as 'the basest and meanest fellow in the kingdom'. The king's mother, the Dowager Princess Augusta, was denominated 'the demon of discord' who 'watches with a kind of providential malignity over the work of her hands'. When the dowager was dying of cancer Junius wrote that 'nothing keeps her alive but the horrible suction of toads. Such an instance of divine justice would convert an atheist.' It was lurid and sensational, morbid and maleficent, and acted as a perfect complement to the fashion for political caricatures by Gillray and others in the 1780s.

Their cartoons revealed a world of political horror and degradation, Westminster was consigned to Sisyphus where monstrous growths and wens disfigured all the bodies politic, where huge and pendulous arses squirted shit and where all the participants were crooked or disfigured. The so-called statesmen slavered over their spoils while spectators pissed themselves with excitement or fear. You can almost smell their foul breath. Political opponents blow each other apart with enormous farts, liberally mixed with excrement, or vomit out their greed or venom in vast waterfalls of sick. One politician is crowned with a chamber pot of piss, while another waits for a flagellation. It was a pictorial world of degradation that had no parallel in other centuries, unless we count the 'babooneries' sketched in the margins of medieval manuscripts. It was the tradition of salacious and scabrous English humour whipped up into delirium. There was also much horror in the real world. The duke of Grafton offered the lord chancellorship to Charles Yorke; Yorke accepted the office but then, overwhelmed by anxiety, cut his own throat.

It was a time of riot, compounded by the agitation over Wilkes and the example of defiance demonstrated by the American rebels. Insurrection was in the air. Benjamin Franklin, writing in 1769, declared that 'I have seen, within a year, riots in the country, about corn; riots about elections; riots about workhouses; riots of colliers, riots of weavers, riots of coal-heavers; riots of sawyers; riots of Wilkesites; riots of government chairmen; riots of smugglers, in which customs house officers and excisemen have been murdered, the king's armed vessels and troops fired at'. In the previous year merchant seamen mutinied at Deptford, Newcastle upon Tyne and other key ports, while the hatmakers of Southwark struck for higher pay. In the year before that, there had been food riots, looting and general disquiet.

Political clubs and fraternal associations emerged in greater numbers, particularly in the larger cities. Yet we may guess that every inn and tavern had its local Cromwell or Hampden inveighing against the squire or the parson or 'them at Westminster'. Between May 1769 and January 1770 petitions were addressed to St James's Palace from thirteen counties and twelve borough towns, all of them asking for or demanding a speedy dissolution of parliament. Public meetings, rather than crowds or riots, became for the first time an aspect of political life. In the summer of 1769, 7,000 people congregated in Westminster Hall to express their grievances against the administration.

The duke of Grafton gave way under the pressure of events, and in his place the king nominated Frederick North, the 2nd earl of Guilford, who had climbed the greasy pole without as yet falling to earth. Lord North, as he was commonly known, has often been viewed by posterity as a dunderhead who managed to lose America in an act of clumsiness; but in fact he was a shrewd political agent not unlike Robert Walpole in his command of parliament. He was of an unfortunate appearance, rather like a caricature of the king himself; his bulging eyes and flabby cheeks gave him, according to Horace Walpole, 'the air of a blind trumpeter'. But he had a broad bottom, as the phrase went, of sense and good humour that gave him balance and composure in times of crisis. When one member castigated him for running or, rather, ruining the country while he was asleep on the treasury bench, he opened one eye and replied, 'I wish to God I were.' He was circumspect, cautious, patient and methodical. 'He fills a chair', Johnson remarked.

In England he was by some act of political magic able to induce a mood of somnolence or lethargy upon what had been a heated populace. 'After a noted fermentation in the nation,' Burke wrote, 'as remarkable a deadness and vapidity has succeeded it.' The violent agitation followed by sullen torpor is not readily explicable, except on some analogy with individual human psychology. Certainly Lord North did not have the same effect on the American colonies, where his efforts to calm the agitation served only to inflame the situation.

On becoming first minister in 1770 he decided to abolish all the taxes Townshend had imposed upon American imports, except that upon tea. The measure was supposed to be a palliative, like the commodity itself, but it acted as a very plausible grievance. The lifting of the duties could be claimed as a moral victory by the Americans but the surviving tax on tea could be used as a call for further action; it was a token of American servitude.

On 5 March 1770, a crowd of Bostonians surrounded the English soldiers who had been ordered to guard the customs house of the port; the Americans insulted, threatened and finally attacked them. The order was given to fire; three Bostonians died immediately and two expired later from their wounds. The English withdrew from the customs house under a persistent hail of stones, but a town meeting demanded that they leave the area altogether; consequently they were ordered to remove to Fort William on an island 3 miles away. The Americans had won another token victory. The event inevitably became known as 'the Boston Massacre' and inspired much magniloquent rhetoric. One oration to commemorate the occasion described 'our houses wrapped in flames, our children subjected to the barbarous caprice of the raging soldiery; our beauteous virgins exposed to all the insolence of unbridled passion . . .'. The incident was never entirely forgotten, and it has been considered to be the single most important incitement to the coming war of independence. Yet other Americans at the time were not so stirred, and deplored the passions of the Bostonian crowd; the *New York Gazette* declared that 'it's high time a stop was put to mobbing'.

So the drift of events was unclear and uncertain even to those closest to it. Some on both sides believed that a show of force would make the other party back down. Some Americans cried 'Tyranny!' while some English cried 'Treason!' Each side had a false impression of the other, and such mutual misunderstanding could be a source of conflict.

Three small incidents are suggestive. In 1770 a customs collector was beaten up in New Jersey. In June 1772 a vessel being used by the British revenue ran aground off the coast of Rhode Island; it was promptly burned by the inhabitants. In March 1773 the assembly of Virginia suggested that all the colonial assemblies engage in correspondence, to which Benjamin Franklin responded that 'a congress may grow out of that correspondence'. A congress would represent common concerns and ambitions that would greatly alarm the ministers at Westminister. The force of events could now silently do its work.

22

The magical machines

Two brothers, John and Thomas Lombe, erected a manufactory in 1719 on an island in the River Derwent. It housed a silk engine which became the subject of popular curiosity and amazement, 'a new invention' combining, according to the original patent, 'three sorts of engines never before made or used in Great Britain, one to wind the finest raw silk, another to spin, and the other to twist . . .'. An application for the renewal of the patent, fourteen years later, referred to '97,746 wheels, movements and individual parts (which work day and night)'. Malachy Postlethwayt, in his *The Universal Dictionary of Trade and Commerce*, reported 'this little being, not above five or six feet in height, with two arms, will dispatch as much work as a giant'.

The genteel came in coaches from all over the county to witness the marvel. The manufactory, a stone edifice of five storeys, was powered by a large water-wheel; within the building tall cylindrical machines whirred and rotated. One man was responsible for sixty threads. It was the principal sight of Derby and, with its machinery, its continuous operation and its specialized workforce, can be considered as the prototype for the silk mills and cotton mills of the later eighteenth and nineteenth centuries. It was said that the Lombes had stolen the idea from Italy, and that as a result John Lombe was poisoned in 1722, but this was no doubt part of the romance of the new age. By the early nineteenth century it sat on the landscape with all the authority of an ancient monument.

Other wonders abounded. Daniel Defoe, writing in the year after the silk mill was constructed, remarked upon the 'new undertakings in trade, inventions, engines, manufactures, in a nation pushing and improving as we are'. There was yet no concept of the factory as a powerhouse; it was generally used to describe a building inhabited by foreign merchants. But these solid, grim edifices began to enter social and economic calculations. Matthew Boulton completed his Soho manufactory, on Handsworth Heath in northeast Birmingham, in 1769; it was used for the manufacture of various 'toys' or small goods such as buckles and buttons. The main warehouse was nineteen bays wide, and three storeys high, with a Palladian front. But it looked more like a prison than a country house. This was the site where in 1776 James Watt began the manufacture of steam engines. Seven years before, Watt's separate condenser and Richard Arkwright's water-frame had been granted patents; new engines powered by steam could now be developed, and the water-frame could create miles of inexpensive cotton for cheaper and cheaper clothing.

Again in 1769, at a time when the political world was exercised by 'Wilkes and Liberty!', Josiah Wedgwood opened his vast pottery works of some 350 acres beside the Trent and Mersey Canal in Staffordshire and named it Etruria in homage to its classical predecessors; thus the factory could be given the illusion of a picturesque past, even if its principles were thoroughly modern. Wedgwood effectively inaugurated the age of beautiful china in England. It was he who introduced neo-classicism to the English consumer and customer. This was one of the more aesthetic consequences of industrial change, but one which had taken place without any great technological innovation.

Two years after the establishment of Etruria Richard Arkwright built a factory at Cromford in Derbyshire to accommodate his newly invented machinery, and then constructed a village to house his hundreds of workers, men, women and children. The water-frame itself, built in units of 1,000 spindles, created the first pure English cotton cloth. As a result cotton became the paramount product of the textile industry. By the early nineteenth century cotton was king.

An anonymous poem, *The Temple of Nature*, published in 1803, celebrated the mighty change:

> So Arkwright taught from cotton-pods to cull,
> And stretch in lines the vegetable wool;
> With teeth of steel, its fibre knots unfurl'd
> And with the silver tissue cloth'd the world.

If the Dutch could erect a statue to the man who taught their nation how to cure herring, it was asked, surely a statue might be raised for the creator of a great national manufacture and manufacturing system?

Some observers, however, tilted at the first factories in the manner of Don Quixote riding at windmills. They were compared to workhouses, which indeed in certain respects they resembled; workhouses themselves were known as 'houses of industry', and the first factory for the production of steam engines was known in 1702 as a 'workhouse'. There was a connection perceptible to contemporaries between the forced regulation of the poor and the treatment of industrial workers. The manufactories were also compared to army barracks, with the same emphasis on strict timing, order and efficiency.

The new industrial system, still in its very early stages of growth, came out of a practice that has become known as 'proto-industry' or 'primitive capitalism'. It centred upon domestic labour, whereby agricultural workers and their families spun and wove as well as worked the land. Daniel Defoe described it well in the course of his tour of Britain when he crossed the Pennines. He visited the premises of a large clothier and found 'a house full of lusty fellows, some at the dye-vat, some dressing the cloth, some in the loom'. In the immediate area were innumerable cottages 'in which dwell the workmen who are employed, the women and children of whom are always busy carding, spinning etcetera'. Any child over four years old was gainfully employed.

It was in a literal sense a cottage industry with a small merchant, or small capitalist, putting out the raw material for spinning or weaving to the families of agricultural workers before collecting the finished yarn or cloth at a stated time. The farmer's wife, and the farmer himself, would work the loom at all hours; the carding, spinning and weaving took place at the same time as the harvesting of wheat, peas and beans. The independent cottagers might sell socks and cheese, hogs and cloth. In Lincolnshire cow dung could be used to make fuel, while hog dung was used as a bleaching agent for cloth; hence the saying about Lincolnshire, 'where the hogs shit soap and the cows shit fire'.

Cloth-making was ill-paid labour, dependent upon seasonal change, and generally took place in cramped and filthy conditions. The cottagers worked through the night, and in darkness, because they were too poor to own a light. They worked through the frost and cold, when the fields yielded nothing. The weavers and tailors called the summer 'cucumber time', because that was all they could afford to eat. Industrialism did not seem at the time to be the greater evil.

The origins of industrialism are hard to find precisely because they are ubiquitous. Some say that the small merchants who became 'putters out' to the agricultural workers in time became master manufacturers by bringing twenty or thirty looms within one building. Others say that the pressure of an ever-growing population led ineluctably to cities and to mass employment in the industry of cities. Between the years 1760 and 1830 the population grew from 6.1 million to 13.1 million; it had in other words more than doubled in size. The land did not need the people. So they gathered in urban conurbations where employers were happy to use cheap labour on a larger and larger scale. Other consequences inevitably followed; more houses had to be built, and transport improved.

Some say that technical change and innovation were the spark of industrialism, an incremental process sometimes interrupted by giant leaps forward like the introduction of the steam engine or of complex and efficient textile machinery. It was often claimed, in this context, that the British were in any case a thoroughly empirical and practical people, free of the French and German predilection for theory; that is one generalization which has in fact been accepted over time. Louis Pasteur once remarked that 'chance favours only the mind that is prepared'. It was said that every factory had its own inventor.

Others say that industrialism was fuelled by cheap credit and that its rapid growth was prompted by the abundance of capital combined with an interest rate of approximately 3 per cent. England was a rich country, made evident in the subscriptions to the Bank of England and the myriad 'bubbles' on the Stock Exchange. An opportunity had now come to invest in industries that had an illimitable future. The remarkable increase of foreign trade in the last six decades of the eighteenth century has also been invoked as the motive for further industrialization.

Another incentive came from the absence of government intervention; it cleared the ground a little, with low interest rates, but it did not attempt to direct industrial policy. There was no active opposition to technological change or improvement, and what obstruction there was came from irate workers who found their livelihoods being taken away by machines. The government did nothing.

Other causes for the speed of industrialism have been adduced. There were no wars on home soil; the political system remained infinitely adaptable, and there was no revolution like that within France. Politics is only part. The factories encouraged economies of scale but, more importantly, they increased specialization of labour.

The power of science, and rational calculation, mightily impressed the commercial classes; watches, clocks and precision instruments, like lathes and planing machines, were the appurtenances of the age. It was not unusual to see microscopes and telescopes in the grander homes; the barometer became a conversation piece. From 1675 to 1725, the proportion of richer London homes with clocks on display rose from 56 per cent to 88 per cent. By 1800, 8,000 men worked on watches in Clerkenwell, each with his own particular speciality. John Harrison, the man who solved the problem of longitude in 1759, fashioned the chronometer that Captain Cook took with him on his voyages around the world.

One other, perhaps more spiritual, cause may be mentioned for radical industrial change. The ubiquity of dissent among experimentalists and innovators, and the role of the dissenting academies in training young men in practical skills, has led many to conclude that the Protestant spirit of independent thought and practice had been a contributing fact to the rise of industrialism. The Catholics were believed, quite unfairly, to be incapable of facing new frontiers. It would be unwise to pick out any one of these putative causes or themes, however, as the most significant. If we may steal from

Romans 8:28, all things worked together for good, at least for those who considered it good.

The nature of the change has also been interpreted in a hundred different ways. It is now described as 'the Industrial Revolution', but the phrase was never used at the time. It was coined by a French socialist, Auguste Blanqui, in 1837 and was then taken up seven years later by Friedrich Engels in an essay entitled 'The Condition of England'. It was then widely publicized by Arnold Toynbee in his *Lectures on the Industrial Revolution of the Eighteenth Century in England*, published posthumously in 1884. If this indeed were a revolution there was nothing sudden or shattering about it. It can best be seen as part of a cycle that lasted for approximately a hundred years. The increase in national growth seems to have started in the 1740s, and then made rapid advances in the 1780s and 1790s, with a further increase in the 1830s and beyond.

If the term did not exist, how was the reality to be interpreted by contemporaries? Were they even aware that something surprising or unfamiliar was happening all around them? Arthur Young in his *Political Arithmetic*, published in 1774, asked his readers to 'consider the progress of everything in Britain during the last twenty years'; the sentiments were repeated two years later in Adam Smith's *The Wealth of Nations* where he contemplated 'the natural progress of England towards wealth and improvement'. The *Encyclopaedia Britannica* of the same period noted that 'the discoveries and improvements' of the age 'diffuse a glory over this country unattainable by conquest or dominion'. The solid foundations of the change were also understood. In 1784 it was reported that 'Britain is the only country hitherto known in which seams of coal . . . iron ore and limestone . . . are frequently found in the same fields and in the neighborhood of the sea'. So the observers of the time were aware of a decisive change in the state of the nation.

What became clear was the sheer continuity of change, bolstered by one innovation following another in an almost evolutionary form. Periods of social or technical change had at some stage, in preceding centuries, reached an equilibrium; but in the latter part of the eighteenth century there seemed no end to the process of innovation. E. J. Hobsbawm in *Industry and Empire*, published as late as 1968, remarked that 'no change in human life since the invention of agriculture, metallurgy and towns in the New Stone Age has been so profound as the coming of industrialization'.

The most profound, and most elusive, manifestations of change can really only be seen in retrospect. Perhaps it did not occur to inventors, engineers, or scientists that they were seeking power over nature. It might have seemed blasphemous. Yet that power was indeed the result. The substitution of coal for wood provided what seemed at the time to be an inexhaustible source of supply. The soil that had previously been devoted to growing timber could now be harnessed for the supply of food. When the forests and woods had been cleared for fuel, there was a biological limit to the period of their renewal; with the source of power under the ground, the problem no longer arose. As a result of the country's natural resources, the scale of energy available to Britain was for a crucial period greater than that of any other European economy. This is one of the keys to industrialism.

It has been estimated by the celebrated historian of the Industrial Revolution, E. A. Wrigley, that the output of 10 million tons from the coal industry in 1800 provided energy equivalent to that produced by 10 million acres of land. The escape from the limits of an organic economy meant in turn the escape from the constraints upon growth. No more time and tide, no more wind and water. The coal was to all intents and purposes limitless, incalculable, mineral 'gold' packed to blackness within caverns measureless to man. England had once been known as a land of woods and forests; now it had become a realm of coal.

The improvement, however, was slow and imbalanced. While some parts of the economy, such as iron-smelting, textiles and mining, experienced rapid change, much of Britain's work and workforce remained in the traditional economy for a further hundred years. Bakers, millers, blacksmiths and tanners stayed essentially in the mid-eighteenth century well into the reign of Victoria. Many workshops were still in the seventeenth century. Different levels of time, and experience, existed simultaneously.

The increase in the production of coal was gradual but inexorable; in the course of the eighteenth century the output rose from

3 million tons to 10 million tons before rising fivefold between 1800 and 1850. As a result the landscape was changed for ever. The *Birmingham Mail* recorded that 'blue skies change to a reeking canopy of black and grey smoke. The earth is one vast unsightly heap of dead ashes and dingy refuse. Canals of diluted coal dust teach how filthy water may be and yet retain fluidity. Tumbledown houses, tumbledown works, tottering black chimneys, fire-belching furnaces, squalid and blackened people.' The same Sisyphean vision of sublimity or horror is recorded by Charles Dickens in his study of the midlands in *The Old Curiosity Shop* (1841).

When Little Nell and her grandfather pass through the region they see 'paths of coal ash and huts of staring brick . . . trembling with the working of engines, and dimly resounding with their shrieks and throbbings; the tall chimneys vomiting forth a black vapour which hung in a dense ill favoured cloud above the housetops and filled the air with gloom'. The two pilgrims are taken into an iron-works 'echoing to the roof with the beating of hammers and roar of furnaces, mingling with the hissing of red-hot metal plunged in water, and a hundred strange unearthly noises never heard before'. The wild imagination of the novelist is as powerful as his observation, but he was right in at least one respect; such noises had never been heard on earth before, except, perhaps, during a volcanic eruption.

Dickens describes the iron workers as 'moving like demons among the flame and smoke, dimly and fitfully seen, flushed and tormented by the burning fires'. Some slept among the ashes and cinders while others drew out the glowing sheets of metal 'emitting an insupportable heat, and a dull deep light like that which reddens in the eyes of savage beasts'.

Yet heat and light represented more, much more, than the conditions of a working life. It was the manifestation of a great change. Coal could not simply be used to fashion metal. It could create iron. The centre of that alteration was the vale of Coalbrookdale, in Shropshire. Nowhere could look less like a vale of pastoral verse.

A Quaker iron-master, Abraham Darby (the first of three), settled in Coalbrookdale where in 1708 he leased an old blast furnace with some attendant forges. Within a year of his arrival in this vale of unhealth he became the first man to produce pig iron of quality smelted with coke. The area had numerous advantages, among them the fact that it harboured coal with fewer sulphuric impurities than elsewhere, thus improving the quality of the iron manufactured by its means. Darby fed his furnaces with coal, and with the coke produced the iron for casting pots. Coke out of coal took the place of charcoal out of wood. The making of iron was no longer dependent upon the life and death of organic things. These were the procedures that would lead in time to the bridges, the railway engines, the pipes, the cylinders, the cannon, the shot, and the machine parts that would create the life of the nineteenth century.

The first iron rails were cast at Coalbrookdale in 1767. The technology of the time was now entering an expansive and self-sustaining phase that would never pause or rest. In the course of this history we will come to remark upon the stunning interdependence of techniques and inventions; all things seem to come together, so that one cannot exist without the other.

The significance of the change was not immediately realized; Abraham Darby himself was of a modest and quiet nature, and his Quaker brethren seem happy to have kept the new technique within the religious family. But to their credit the Darby family never took out a patent, unlike most of their colleagues, on the grounds that it would be wrong 'to deprive the public of such an acquisition'.

The possibilities of the human sublime are nowhere more evident than in Philip Loutherbourg's painting *Coalbrookdale by Night* (1801), where sulphuric flames belch into the night sky only faintly illuminated by a pale moon. It is a landscape of fire in which the only source of light is the inferno; it is apposite that one of the names for this manufactory was 'Bedlam'. Yet the spiritual connotations of the flame and fire do not impede the recognition that this is also a place of industry and production; in the foreground horses are pulling away a filled wagon while a dog trots beside them.

Turner's *Limekiln at Coalbrookdale* (*c*.1797) is also ravished by light, with a white, blue and orange glare drawing the attention to the left side of the painting; a small line of light travels down the hillside, illuminating two workers with horses, while an arch into the kiln itself reveals fire and shadow as if it were some enchanted cavern. This was the significance of the beginnings of what became known as the Industrial Revolution. It was a time of vast possibility, not unlike that suggested by the alchemical magic of the sixteenth century, whereby the womb of the earth might bring forth new life. In *The Old Curiosity Shop* one old worker, tending the furnace, remarks to Little Nell that 'it's my memory, that fire, and shows me all my life'. The fire would never go out.

The steady progress of industrialism was itself bound by the unwritten laws of mutual interdependence. Examples of simultaneous invention and change are suggestive. It so happened, for example, that in the summer and autumn of 1815 George Stephenson in Newcastle upon Tyne and Humphry Davy in London both hit upon the construction of the safety-lamp for miners; one of Stephenson's collaborators conceded that the two men 'were original and separate discoverers of the principle'. Clusters of inventions with similar purposes occurred within a matter of years or even months. The 'puddling' of iron, allowing bar iron to be made without charcoal, was developed within months both in South Wales and in Fontley near Plymouth; neither inventor knew of the other. Was this more than a happy accident?

The elements of reciprocity are everywhere apparent. The technique of boring cannon, for example, was used for the making of steam-engine cylinders; the invention of a coke-blast furnace led to cast iron; cast iron led to Newcomen's first steam engine; the steam engine then permitted the large-scale production of iron. When it was discovered that a steam engine was too powerful for wooden machinery, iron machinery was for the first time employed in its place; this allowed for the construction of heavier machinery which in turn demanded a more powerful engine. Everything worked together, pushing on the rate and nature of technological change. Machines were employed to make larger and better machines. We may be reminded of the development of robots.

The growing demand for steam, at the forge and the factory, helped to create more efficient steam engines. The use of iron rails for the wagons carrying coal, to the furnaces at Coalbrookdale, had a direct influence upon the first railway lines. The mass manufacture of pottery pipes played an important part in the sanitary provisions of the nineteenth century; more importantly, perhaps, it allowed the proper drainage of fields, which in turn increased the yield of the land. The increase in agricultural production in turn supported a larger and larger industrial population. The massive increase in the manufacture of cloth made it vital to devise a new form of rapid bleaching; so the chemists turned their attention to oil of vitriol, or sulphuric acid, rather than the chimerical *elixir vitae*.

Machine production ensured large-scale manufacturing which in turn encouraged wider and wider markets; so does mass production lead to popular consumption, or consumption encourage production? It is a familiar dichotomy. Other questions arise. How was it possible, for example, that two entirely different industries, cotton manufacture and iron-making, could advance simultaneously? It resembles some of the problems of natural evolution, as if machinery itself had the characteristics of a biological entity. We may even begin to parrot Darwin's theories of organic evolution to account for the slow, gradual and inexorable process of the 'Industrial Revolution'.

None of these developments would have been possible without the diffusion of what might be called the scientific attitude, descended directly from the example of Isaac Newton who in the previous century had been an instrument-maker as well as a theoretician; at the age of twenty-six he constructed his own telescope, and made its parabolic mirror from an alloy of tin and copper that he himself had devised. As president of the Royal Society he emphasized the central roles of reason and experiment that would become crucial in the industrial world of the next century. By the early eighteenth century scientific lectures, under the aegis of the Royal Society, were being heard in London and elsewhere complete with 'barometers, thermometers and such other instruments as are necessary for a course of experiments'. A disciple of Newton, the Reverend John Harris, delivered lectures on mathematics at the Marine Coffee-House in Birchin Lane 'for the public good'. John Theophilus Desaguliers, a British natural philosopher, lectured on experimental philosophy but included a disquisition on an early steam engine that 'was of the greatest use for draining mines, supplying towns with water, and gentlemen's houses'. By the 1730s the magical properties of electricity were being thoroughly examined.

One group of scientists and industrialists formed a club in which to converse and to share their experimental learning. The Lunar

Society of Birmingham had first been established in the late 1760s by a group of innovators, radical in politics and religion as well as in science. Among them were botanists, manufacturers, philosophers, industrialists, natural scientists and geologists eager to harness the unrivalled curiosity and experimentation of the period. The members included Matthew Boulton, Josiah Wedgwood, James Watt and Joseph Priestley; industrialists, iron-masters and men of science exchanged information on matters of practical technology as well as more intellectual concerns. It was a forcing house for change, a collective endeavour in the application of science. Most of the members owned laboratories for their enterprises and Wedgwood, for example, was intent upon mineral analysis and the chemistry of colour.

Matthew Boulton at the age of eighteen created a technique for inlaying steel buckles with enamel, but he also cultivated what he called the 'philosophic spirit'; in his notebook he jotted down entries on the human pulse and the movement of the planets. This was the spirit of enterprise which drove the scientific culture of the eighteenth century. No human knowledge was alien to the inventors. Joseph Priestley has been awarded the palm for identifying 'phlogiston' or oxygen and for discovering photosynthesis; Boulton prompted and assisted Watt in the construction of the steam engine.

The Society for the Encouragement of Arts, Manufactures and Commerce had been established in 1754 as a sure token of the advance in national understanding. It was designed, in the words of its charter, 'to embolden enterprise, to enlarge science, to refine art, to improve manufacture and to extend our commerce'. It established premiums as an award for mechanical invention, as well as artistic enterprise, confirming the general movement of innovation; art and science were not considered to be necessarily separate activities, and in the notebooks of the society are minute investigations into blue cobalt and red madder. Those constituents could also be used in industrial dyeing. So once again everything came together.

It has been described as an aspect of the 'Enlightenment', although that essentially European movement of thought did no more than touch English shores. It was clear, however, that in Walpole's words 'natural history is in fashion'. The figure of the virtuoso, and assemblies of virtuosi discussing such matters as human anatomy, were noted in the *Spectator* not without mild irony. Jonathan Swift satirized the tendency in 'A Voyage to Laputa, Balnibarbi, Luggnagg, Glubbdubdrib, and Japan', the third part of *Gulliver's Travels* written between 1706 and 1709, when he describes 'the grand academy of Lagado' where its experimenters are engaged in such pursuits as extracting sunbeams from cucumber, transforming ice into gunpowder, and reducing 'human excrement to its original food'.

Yet the new spirit of scientific change could not be denied in areas such as mechanics, metallurgy and industrial chemistry. An experimental coal-gas system for public lighting was ready by 1782. The emphasis was always upon industry and commerce, and Adam Smith believed that those engaged in industry were 'the great inventing class'; we may include among them the chemists and the new professions of electricians and engineers. Samuel Smiles wrote at a later date that 'our engineers may be regarded in some measure as the makers of modern civilisation'.

The level of inventiveness may also be gauged by the rise in the number of patents applied for and granted. Before the middle of the century approximately a dozen patents were issued each year; the number reached 36 in 1769 and 64 in 1783. In 1792 it reached 85. The inventions ranged from newly designed pumps to the process whereby alkalis might be derived from salt; shaving materials, false teeth, fire alarms and washing machines, burglar alarms and water closets were among the items proposed for patenting. The saving of labour and, more importantly, the saving of time were the results intended. Greater efficiency, accuracy and uniformity were also the goals of the patentees; in that sense they reflect the spirit of industrial change itself.

It may be termed the age of improvement but the word of the day was innovation. 'The age is running mad after innovation', Samuel Johnson said, 'and all the business of the world is to be done in a new way . . .' Incremental change of a practical kind was the soul of eighteenth-century endeavour. 'Almost every master and manufacturer', Dean Tucker wrote of Birmingham operatives in 1757, 'hath a new invention of his own, and is daily improving on those of others.'

The awareness of progress was nowhere more apparent, perhaps, than in the changes in transport. The state of the old roads was considered to be a national disgrace. Daniel Defoe reported that in Lewes a lady went to church in a coach drawn by six oxen, since no horses could manage the stiff and deep mud. Many of the roads had not been repaired for fourteen centuries, ever since the Romans first built them. The main road of a parish was often a mere horse-track, but the mud was so soft that the horses sank to their bellies. Even the road from Kensington Palace to the centre of London was a treacherous gulf of mud, with ruts and potholes and loose stones. It took a week to travel from York to London, and one Yorkshireman made his will before venturing on the journey. Arthur Young, in his *Northern Tour* of 1771, said of the roads to the north of Newcastle upon Tyne that 'I would advise all travellers to consider this country as sea, and as soon think of driving into the ocean as venturing into such detestable roads.'

The remedy lay in private improvements on a local scale, with the profit motive well in evidence. A series of 'turnpike trusts' was established, by which the members were charged with the duty to construct and to maintain a certain stretch of road; to recuperate their costs, and any loans they raised, they were permitted to collect tolls at either end of their route. Some said that there was no discernible change and others complained that the tolls were extortionate but, slowly and haphazardly, the roads improved. They were of course helped enormously by engineers such as Telford and McAdam who rivalled the Romans in their genius for road-making.

In Richard Graves's *Columella*, a novel of 1779, a character asks, 'Who would have said that coaches would go daily between London and Bath in about twelve hours, which, twenty years ago, was reckoned three good days' journey?' In 1763 six stagecoaches made the journey from London to Exeter; ten years later, there were four times that number. An advertisement promised that 'however incredible it may appear, this coach will actually (barring accidents) arrive in four days and a half after leaving Manchester!!' Some passengers grew sick with the speed; it was called 'being coached'. As a result the mail posts became quicker and more frequent, shaping the ambience of Samuel Richardson's epistolary fiction. Everything went faster, from the carriage of grain or coals to the improvements in agriculture.

Other advances in transportation occurred at the same time. In the early decades of the eighteenth century there was a concerted effort to improve the rivers of the country by widening and deepening their channels and by strengthening their banks. They were joined from the mid-eighteenth century by the network of canals that created one great transport system; between 1755 and 1820 3,000 miles of canal were constructed. In 1755 the first industrial canal, the Sankey, was carved from the River Mersey to St Helens; three years later the duke of Bridgewater created a canal between his coal mines at Worsley to Manchester, a distance of 7 miles; the fact that the price of coal in Manchester was halved as a result concentrated the industrial mind wonderfully. Between 1761 and 1766 another canal was completed from Manchester to the Mersey above Liverpool. By the last decade of the eighteenth century London, Birmingham, Bristol, Hull and Liverpool were all joined together with innumerable smaller destinations. The artificial rivers carried coal, iron, wood, bricks and slate; they transported cotton, cheese, grain and butter.

The economic activity of the country was transformed, and Adam Smith noted that 'good roads, canals and navigable rivers, by diminishing the expense of carriage, put the remote parts of the country more nearly upon a level with those in the neighbourhood of the town'. Local and regional centres came together to create a national market, which in turn helped participation in international markets. Another consequence followed. The fact that various regions of the country were now brought in closer communion, one with another, helped to sustain the burgeoning national consciousness of the people in times of war and foreign revolution.

23

Having a tea party

In the spring of 1773 the administration of Lord North was moved to pass a Tea Act which allowed tea to be sold directly to the Americans by the East India Company, but with a duty of three-pence per pound that had first been introduced six years before. Tea was still much cheaper in America than in England but for the colonists this was tantamount to a direct tax imposed by parliament, arousing all the old fears of imperial dictation. It was considered by some to be a scheme to erode American liberties. The *Boston Gazette* of 11 October, serving the port to which most of the tea was shipped, urged that the commodity be sent back as a mark of 'the yoke of slavery'. The first of the tea ships, the *Dartmouth*, arrived at Boston Harbor on 27 November, and two days later a mass meeting of Bostonians resolved to take charge of any others that docked. The activists became known as 'the Body'.

On 16 December a group of Bostonians, disguised as Mohock Indians, approached the door of the local assembly and gave a 'war whoop' which was answered by some in the building itself. They then made their way to the wharf where three tea ships now lay and began the systematic destruction of their cargo, with 342 chests of tea thrown overboard.

The question was now one of power, and the challenge to parliament could not be ignored or evaded. Lord North laid the matter before the House of Commons on 7 March 1774, and demanded that the port of Boston be closed. A number of other measures were passed by parliament, principally to teach the rebellious Americans a lesson. They came to be known as the 'coercive' or 'intolerable' Acts. The Boston Port Act closed the port and customs house; the Massachusetts Charter Act was designed to curb the elected legislature; the Justice and Quartering Acts were introduced to impose order upon the populace. Lord North declared that 'convince your colonies that you are able, and not afraid to control them, and, depend upon it, obedience will be the result of your deliberations'. It seems that the majority of the population was behind him, and Edmund Burke reported that 'the popular current, both within doors and without, at present sets strong against America'.

Burke himself will reappear in this history as the exponent of conservatism and tradition in the face of innumerable challenges; he was an Irishman with the gifts of a supreme advocate for the preservation of the principles of the past which emerge from 'the nature of things by time, custom, succession, accumulation, permutation and improvement of property'. Institutions and customs were rendered sacred by longevity and continual use. It was a uniquely reasssuring doctrine for those opposed to change or frightened of chance.

The response of the Americans to the 'intolerable' Acts was perhaps inevitable. In early September 1774 a congress of the old colonies was held in Philadelphia, and became known as the First Continental Congress; in the following month it proposed a bill or declaration of rights to the effect that American assemblies had the right and duty to determine legislation in all domestic matters without the intervention of the English parliament. The delegates declared that Americans 'were entitled to their life, liberty and property'. George Washington wrote that 'the crisis is arrived when we must assert our rights or submit to every imposition that can be heaped upon us'. By the end of the year local associations or revolutionary committees were piling up supplies of arms and gunpowder while at the same time enforcing what were now called 'the laws of congress'. Imports from Britain and its colonies were prohibited. The prospect of outright war, and of a trade embargo, seemed to paralyse the English merchant class who wavered between the desire for uninterrupted trade and the instinct of national loyalty.

The call to arms gathered strength, and bodies of volunteers became known as 'minute men' for the speed with which they could muster with their rifles. Meanwhile 10,000 fresh British troops disembarked on American soil. If they had struck at once they might have done considerable damage; instead under the command of General Gage they rested. It was the Americans who acted first. This was the moment that heralded serious conflict.

In America local committees and hastily called provincial congresses began to plan for military action, and groups of citizens took matters into their own hands. At the beginning of April 1775, the commander of the English forces in Boston received orders from London to suppress what were called the rebels. The main supply of American weaponry was stored in Concord, 16 miles from Boston, and the English advanced upon it. They were stopped by militiamen at Lexington Green, where eight Americans were killed. The English kept on moving towards Concord but the fire of the militiamen, hiding in houses or concealed behind trees and hedges, scattered them. They retreated in haste to Boston but by the time they had reached the relative safety of that city 273 of their number were dead. The god of war had risen once again, calling for more blood.

Some colonists, as they were still called, were alarmed by the violent turn of events, and urged restraint while others distrusted the calls for independence. It might be a step too far. But the more committed and the more passionate of the members of the Second Continental Congress, called at Philadelphia in the summer of 1775, overwhelmed the more moderate voices. It was resolved that an army, representing the 'united' and 'confederated' colonies, should be established; a Virginian gentleman, George Washington, was granted the command. He was reticent and not a good public speaker but he was resourceful and methodical; he had an innate dignity which, combined with moderation and self-control, could make him a master of men. He took the command itself with extreme reluctance, but a sense of duty and of his own honour persuaded him. Even at this stage he was not at all convinced that he could win the war against the English redcoats or, as they were known, 'lobsters'.

On the night of 16 June – the night following the first day of the congress – a contingent of Americans silently and stealthily took occupation of Breed's Hill, a prominence beside Bunker Hill overlooking Boston on a peninsula north of the River Charles. On discovering their presence a battery of six guns opened on the insurgents from an English vessel, and a detachment of redcoats was ferried across the River Charles to reach them. As the English forces climbed Breed's Hill, they were met with prolonged and accurate firing from the entrenchments; many of them fled back to their boats. At this juncture Gage and a group of other officers crossed the river and rallied or forced them to climb the hill again. The soldiers were confronted by the same onslaught of bullets but bravado or good fortune forced them forward. The Americans then fled towards Bunker Hill, but not before inflicting severe casualties; more than 1,000 soldiers and officers lay dead or wounded, while the American losses were in the low hundreds.

The news of the defeat alarmed and shocked the English who had believed fondly that the colonials would never meet the English army on open ground. It was considered to be a calamity, a national humiliation and a military disgrace. A force of volunteers had overcome a trained and disciplined army. Some now speculated that this battle was an omen of eventual American triumph. General Gage was replaced by General Howe, a transfer which turned out to be that of a blockhead succeeding a dunderhead.

The two sides now confronted one another, with no chance of conciliation. The king declared that 'the die is now cast, the colonies must either submit or triumph'. At the beginning of 1776 a pamphlet was being passed among the colonials. The effect of Thomas Paine's 'Common Sense' was immediate and profound; in his history of the American revolution, George Trevelyan remarked that 'it would be difficult to name any human composition which had an effect so instant, so extended and so lasting'. It was in essence a clarion call for America to declare its independence from a brutal foreign power, with the sentiment that 'the cause of America is in a great measure the cause of all mankind'. How could a tiny island arrogate to itself the control of a great country? America had become a haven for all nations, and should no longer be shackled to England which merely dealt with the colonists for its own benefit and its own interests. To call itself the 'mother country' was a gross scandal, for what mother would treat her children so brutally? The king 'hath shewn himself such an inveterate enemy to liberty and discovered such a thirst for arbitrary power' that he must be resisted. Paine added that 'we have it in our power to begin the world over again'. His tone and language were sharp and to the point, thus undermining decades of rational or inconsequential political discourse.

His appeal was irresistible to the general populace, and at a later date John Adams wrote to Thomas Jefferson that 'history is to ascribe the American Revolution to Thomas Paine'. History does not perhaps deal in coincidences but, seven months after the publication of 'Common Sense', the continental congress declared its independence with twelve affirmative votes and one abstention from New York. The congress had come to its decision after much hesitation and opposition from delegates who feared that the Declaration was premature and that they needed foreign allies before coming to open confrontation. Yet the final text was passed on 4 July 1776, ever afterwards known to Americans as Independence Day. The Americans absolved themselves from fealty to the Crown, and declared themselves to be free states that had no connection to England, with a ringing endorsement of 'life, liberty and the pursuit of happiness'. Burke said that he had anticipated that the Americans might disturb authority but 'we never dreamt that they could of themselves supply it'.

It became known as 'the king's war' with the obvious presumption that those who opposed it were disloyal subjects; the people were asked to rally to the cause of Church and Crown against rebels and revolutionaries. George III was in fact the driving force of the war against Americans, believing that his crown and country would not be secure if the colonists were able to secede from English rule. Yet there were some in England who supported the American cause. The principle of 'no taxation without representation' found an echo among the disenfranchised of a nation where half the towns had no voice in parliament. In the later riots at Peterloo and Manchester, this was the slogan inscribed upon many banners.

It was believed by many radicals that the attempt to crush the movement for liberty in the thirteen colonies was an experiment that, if successful, could be repeated in England itself. The king and his ministers were supposed to be intent upon invading the rights of the individual, curtailing the liberty of the press, misusing the public funds and engaging in open and widespread corruption of members of parliament. There was even talk of the imposition of military government. Even if these charges were ill-founded they found an audience ready and willing to believe in a conspiracy by the ruling class against the people of England. These were the men and women who supported the Americans.

Those who supported the king's war, however, were aware of the historical parallel in the fight against king and Church by the Puritan enthusiasts of an earlier age. They believed the Americans to be traitors and seditionaries, ungrateful for the benefits that had accrued to them and unwilling to pay a fair contribution to the expenses of empire. There were still others who just wanted peace, peace at almost any price to maintain trade and good relations.

While Washington began to equip and train a voluntary militia, the administration in London found it hard to make up the numbers of soldiers and sailors. A savage 'press' for sailors took place in the streets of London and the port cities in 1776; 800 men were seized in the capital alone. A third part of the army to be employed against the rebels were Hessian soldiers, recruited through George III's German allies; the others were English recruits or loyalist Americans, but a large number of convicted criminals had been released from prison in order to serve their country.

Despite this show of strength it is not clear that the English administration knew how formidable its difficulties were. The supply lines from England to America were 3,000 miles in length; weapons, ammunition, horses, men and provisions had to be shipped across the Atlantic in a journey that often took two or three months of misery. The men were then faced with an ocean coast many hundreds of miles in length, where the population was distinctly hostile to their presence. The terrain of the interior was also inhospitable both to professional soldiers and to raw recruits. John Hayes, an English combatant, described 'a country full of marshes and small rivers, woods and insects, and a sun so powerful in heat' that many men fell sick of a putrescent fever.

In the summer of 1776 General Howe captured New York, New Jersey and Rhode Island. The failure of the Americans thoroughly demoralized Washington, whose letters are filled with complaints about the unruliness and indiscipline of his troops. It would seem that on paper the English held the advantage, and there were real fears among the Americans that their revolution was close to being lost. But Howe did nothing to build on his success, and during the winter months the English remained in their entrenchments. Paine described it as 'the gloomy campaign of 1776', and at the end of the year Washington confessed that without a new army 'the game is pretty near up'. Yet eight days later he organized a swift descent upon the Hessian troops guarding Trenton, New Jersey, and seized the town; it was only a temporary victory but it restored the morale of his soldiers and officers.

The air on the other side of the Atlantic was also filled with gloomy prognostications. General Howe had demanded 20,000 men for the next year's campaign, but he received only 2,500. Parliament had little money, and the king himself was badly in debt. The difficulties of organizing a war at such a distance were becoming more and more obvious. A quick victory had become necessary, but how was it to be achieved?

The English command sought to regain the initiative by isolating the rebellious New England colonies. An English army under General Burgoyne would sweep downwards from Canada, and an army under Howe would march upward from New York; when they met the colonies would be encircled. But it did not quite go according to plan. By a mixture of bad communications and incompetence the two armies missed each other. Howe had decided to capture Philadelphia instead. Burgoyne and his army, isolated from any possible help, were surrounded by the American forces at Saratoga in what is now New York State. He had no choice but to surrender, in the autumn of 1777, and at the same time gave up any hope of an eventual British victory. It was simply a matter of time.

The defeat of the English forces brought joy to Versailles and in early February 1778, the French, finding the convenient moment, officially joined the United States in its war against Britain. This of course brought a different complexion to the conflict that now assumed a global aspect. It was the outcome that the British had most feared. The ministry was bankrupt of ideas, and one army was still imprisoned in the United States. The British now had to defend their possessions in India and the West Indies against the French while at the same time pursuing a war in the inhospitable territory of North America. The Spanish joined the new alliance in the following year, with the express intention of reclaiming Gibraltar and Minorca. The English had no allies left, and were hard stretched to cover all the possible theatres of war.

They offered concessions, including the repeal of the controversial Tea Act and the promise not to levy more taxes on the colonists. The announcement astonished and alarmed the faithful followers of the ministry, who now saw that they had been fighting for nothing but an illusion. But the Americans, having tasted victory, demanded complete independence. Almost at once they appreciated the value of the French alliance, because the British had to divert troops and ships for the defence of the West Indies; the Americans then advanced into Philadelphia and Rhode Island. It was less than likely that the British would eventually prevail.

Lord North had had enough. His management of the war had been a dead failure. He had made demands only to abandon them under pressure. He had lost an army and a continent. He was forty-six years of age, but he felt tired and much older. In March 1778, at the time France sealed its treaty with the Americans, North wrote to the king that 'capital punishment itself is, in Lord North's position, preferable to that constant anguish of mind which he feels from the consideration that his continuance in office is ruining his majesty's affairs'. Two months later he wrote once more to the king that 'every hour convinces me more of the necessity your majesty is under of putting some other person than myself at the head of your affairs'. Yet the king did not agree. He needed North. He distrusted and despised most of his political opponents, but knew that he could still rely upon the loyalty of his principal minister; North was, as it were, a bulwark against chaos at Westminster.

It was at Westminster in this period that Pitt the elder, the earl of Chatham, rose to speak for the last time. There was a sentiment abroad that the time had come for Britain to withdraw all its forces from America. To this the earl was implacably opposed. He came into the chamber on crutches, wrapped in flannel to protect his skin, and supported by friends; to some he looked as if he were already dead. His voice was feeble at first but rose in eloquence.

'My lords, I rejoice that the grave has not closed over me; that I am still alive to lift up my voice against the dismemberment of this ancient and most noble monarchy!' The mouth of the grave closed a month later.

The course of the war in 1779 was neither warm nor cold for either party. The attention of the British was in any case turned to their adjacent seas rather than to the Americas, since the combined forces of the French and Spanish promised some form of invasion. But the ships and the men were needed across the Atlantic. Sir Charles Hardy, commander-in-chief of the Channel fleet, could muster thirty-seven ships against the combined enemy force of sixty-six; the English fleet was in any case poorly maintained and in bad condition. Many guns were without powder. The situation was so grave that the French and Spanish practically controlled the Channel and one MP, Sir William Meredith, wrote of a 'fatal torpor which hangs like the night-mare over all the powers of this country'. Yet Hardy was saved by chance or good fortune; the season was one of storms, and the conditions aboard the French and Spanish ships were dominated by sickness. He waited them out, remaining for much of the time in the safe haven of Spithead, until they sailed away. And so the summer passed. Hardy died of a seizure in the following spring. The first speech of Sheridan's *The Critic* suggests the atmosphere of the time. Mr Dangle is reading from a newspaper: "It is now confidently asserted that SIR CHARLES HARDY" – Pshaw – Nothing but about the fleet, and the nation! – and I hate all politics but theatrical politics.'

North was once more deep in depression, and he wrote that 'nothing can be more miserable than I am . . . all is confusion and each department blaming another'. A colleague, William Eden, perhaps exasperated by his continual self-lacerating complaints, wrote to him that 'if you cannot rouse the powers of your mind you ought to quit as immediately as is consistent with the urgent circumstances in which we find ourselves'. Yet the king was immovable. North had to stay. The chief minister said that he was kept to his task 'by force'.

The possibility of a long war without peace or resolution provoked dismay and disquiet among the merchants, the shopkeepers and the taxpayers. Only the iron-masters had some reason to be happy, with the constant demand for ships and munitions. To make matters infinitely worse, Ireland seemed to be going the way of America in the demand for independence. It had occurred to the Irish that the English were in no position to defend them from enemy fleets; so they established Volunteer Associations to protect their shores. Both Catholics and Protestant dissenters joined the cause of national self-defence, and thus created a national army that had more authority than the parliament in Dublin.

The Volunteers now demanded freedom of trade with England and the ministers, in no position to face riot and insurgency on a neighbouring island, promptly gave way. The Irish did not stop here but, in imitation of their cousins across the Atlantic, also demanded legislative independence. In April 1780, Henry Grattan moved a resolution that 'no power on earth but the kings, lords and commons of Ireland was competent to make laws for Ireland'. The controversy was of course long and vociferous but the independence of the Irish parliament was formally agreed. At the beginning of 1783 the English ministry accepted 'the right claimed by the people of Ireland to be bound only by laws enacted by his Majesty and the Parliament of that kingdom'. Grattan rose to his feet in the Parliament House in Dublin and declared that 'Ireland is now a nation'.

The controversies in Ireland had in turn an effect upon the English. A movement for the cause of 'National Revival' emerged in this period, instigated by the prevailing fear that parliament was becoming subservient to the bribes and corruptions of the government. At the end of 1779, from a county meeting in Yorkshire, emerged the Yorkshire Association which had as its aims shorter parliaments, more equal representation of the people, and a reduction in taxes. It was led by Christopher Wyvill, a cleric and landowner, who soon proved himself to be an expert organizer and propagandist. He drew up a petition and persuaded other counties and county committees to participate in it. He represented the landed interests of the country, not the London crowd that had followed Wilkes with slogans and cat-calls, and thus had to be taken more seriously by the masters of the country. The *London Courant* carried a letter from 'The Whig' in November who observed that 'the people of original right, as a free people, will vindicate their country, correct their parliament, and reform their throne . . . *In*

England every man is a politician.' In a similar spirit, in the spring of 1780, the Society for Constitutional Information was established with the express purpose of restoring the 'lost rights' of 'our ancient constitution' by distributing texts and pamphlets.

This is the appropriate context for a parliamentary debate of 6 April on the motion that 'the influence of the Crown has increased, is increasing, and ought to be diminished'. It was carried by 233 to 215 votes, but it was what a military observer might call a forlorn hope. The very fact that the motion had passed suggested that the Crown was not as omnipotent as it was proclaimed to be. Nothing came of it, in any case, and in the following month Lord Camden wrote that 'our popular exertions are dying away and the country returning to its old state of lukewarm indifference'. The radical societies themselves slipped out of view until they were once again aroused by the spectacle of the revolution across the Channel.

Any movement of popular or urban radicalism was in any case fatally tainted in June 1780, with the worst mob riots of the eighteenth century. Lord George Gordon was a born incendiary of extreme, and almost insane, views. Like the salamander he was born to live in fire. He called himself the 'people's pilot', and no more so than in his denunciation of the Roman Catholic menace in the wake of a parliamentary measure known as the Catholic Relief Act. He was part revolutionary, part radical and, if the anachronism may be allowed, part Romantic. He attempted to adopt the status and attributes of all those who had fought through history against tyranny, and became known to his followers as the 'English Brutus'.

He established an 'association', in the style of the time, and the Protestant Association soon came to include men of property, artisans, London apprentices and all those elements of the city that were known as the *mobile vulgus* or more colloquially 'the mob'. On 2 June they accompanied Gordon's petition to parliament with the burning desire to repeal all the late concessions to the Catholics; only six members of the Commons concurred with them, setting off among the petitioners a lightning bolt that came close to blasting London. About midnight, as the cry of 'No Popery' rang through the streets of the city, the irate crowds invaded Broad Street and Golden Square; the chapel of the house of the Bavarian ambassador was put to the torch among what William Blake, a willing or unwilling participant in the riots, described as 'Howlings & hissings, shrieks & groans, & voices of despair'.

Five days later Blake was caught up in the rush of an over-powering mob which was careering down Holborn and towards the Old Bailey with the sole intent of destroying Newgate beside it. The huge gates of the prison, sometimes known as the gates of Hell, were attacked with swords, pickaxes and sledge-hammers while the building was itself enveloped in fire begun by arsonists. The prisoners shrieked in terror of being burned alive but the rebels swarmed over the walls and the roof to tear off the very stones and slates. The prisoners were dragged away from the fires, or crawled out by their own volition, the fetters still clinking about their legs. The mob made a path for them shouting 'A clear way!', 'A clear way!' before leading them to any blacksmith they could find. On the same day houses of wealthy Catholics or Catholic supporters were sacked and burned to the ground.

On Wednesday, 7 June, long to be known as 'black Wednesday', the fears of the populace reached fever pitch. The mob sent warning that it would storm the Bank of England and distribute its contents, that the lions of the Tower's zoo would be set free, that no prison or Catholic chapel would be safe and that they would tear down Bedlam and release its inmates into the streets. One priest, the Reverend O'Donoghue, watched the inmates of Bedlam dancing and shrieking 'in the glare of writhing flames . . . in the glass of the hospital window'. This provoked especial fears. A contemporary Londoner, Richard Burke, wrote that 'the metropolis is possessed by an enraged, furious and numerous enemy . . . What this night will produce is known only to the Great Dispenser.' He watched as a boy, no more than fifteen, mounted a house in Queen Street and began to demolish it, throwing down the bricks and wood to two young accomplices. Yet some semblance of order was retained. While a huge fire burned in the churchyard of St Andrew's in Holborn, where many were later killed by drinking burning spirits, a watchman went by calling the hour with a lantern in his hand.

Eventually the military restored order with some judicious threats and violence. Many of the ringleaders were hanged on the spot where they had committed their crimes. Lord George Gordon was taken into custody, and eventually converted to Judaism. No one believed that such frantic and fanatic violence could still erupt in the streets of the eighteenth century; the scenes of destruction and violence were from a different world. London had become a different city.

But it was not a case of the mob attacking the poor Catholics and their priests; it was an attack of the poor against the rich. The London poor did not attack their own. The Catholics who were pursued were wealthy gentlemen, lawyers and merchants. It came as an unwelcome surprise to those who placed their hopes in popular resistance to a corrupt administration, and confirmed the beliefs of those who believed that savage anger lay just below the surface of the century. Edward Gibbon, the chronicler of the decline of the Roman Empire, noted that he had witnessed 'a dark and diabolical fanaticism which I had supposed to be extinct'. He referred here to the religious extremism that was supposed to have been rendered obsolete a hundred years before. Many now sought the safety of the established order in the supposedly reassuring shape of Lord North who was even then writhing in his shackles of government.

Despite the victory at Saratoga, the advance into Providence and Rhode Island, and the alliance with the French, George Washington was downcast. He wrote at the beginning of 1781 that 'I see nothing before us but accumulating distress . . . we have lived upon expedients till we can live no longer'. There was no food, no money and few reinforcements. The Americans had come to rely almost entirely upon the support of their new allies, but many in the French government were alarmed at the mounting expense. In turn the war weariness of the English was compounded by the fears of radicals that the prospect of American rebels and the Gordon mob would lead ineluctably to an absolute monarchy. The more practical realized that the war against the erstwhile colony was a pointless waste of money.

Such was the mood on both sides before Yorktown. In the late summer and autumn of 1781 an English army under the command of General Charles Cornwallis had been out-marched and out-manoeuvred by Washington, until it was isolated at Yorktown in Virginia. With a French fleet at his back, surrounded by 8,000

French troops and 5,000 Americans, Cornwallis had no choice but to surrender. The English troops marched away from their broken and abandoned positions to the tune of 'The World Turned Upside Down'. With American victory assured, independence could not be far away.

Just before the news of Yorktown had reached London the king had written to Lord North that 'the dye is now cast whether this shall be a great empire or the least dignified of European states'. The defeat seemed definitively to have answered the question. The surrender of the English army caused outrage and sorrow. The report reached London on 25 November 1781, just days before the opening of parliament. Lord North is reported to have cried out, 'Oh God, it is all over!' He knew that the end of his political days was coming.

Yet the king, the architect of the American policy, seemed prepared to fight on. In his speech from the throne at the opening of the session he reaffirmed his belief in the justice of the cause and refused to surrender the rights and interests of the country in the search for a febrile peace. There then rose up Charles James Fox, a leader of the Whig interest and a firm supporter of the American cause. He upheld the supposed fiction that George III's speech had been composed by a cabinet council only to attack the king more vehemently as 'an arbitrary and unfeeling monarch, who, having involved the slaves, his subjects, in a ruinous and unnatural war, to glut his enmity or satiate his revenge, was determined to persevere, in spite of calamity and even of fate'.

These were hard words, but they bear the spirit of Fox. He has only made a passing appearance in this history as yet, having been part of a larger chorus of disapproval against the Crown and its ministers. He has been described as a born oppositionist, an aristocrat who moved in the highest Whig circles without being in the least impressed by considerations of rectitude. He was drunken and profligate, paying as much attention to gambling as to politics; but this was not unusual in eighteenth-century politicians. His charm lay in his happy and buoyant personality, often compared to that of a child. Burke confessed that he was 'of the most artless, candid, open and benevolent disposition'. The duchess of Devonshire, a Whig grandee and devotee, described 'his amazing quickness in seizing any subject' and added that 'his conversation is like a brilliant player at billiards: the strokes follow one another, piff! paff!'

But he was not born to rule a party or lead a faction. He was careless and ill-organized; his speeches in the Commons were impetuous and impromptu, and he was utterly impervious to public opinion. He made no attempt to marshal the ranks of his followers. Politics was for him, as for so many of his contemporaries, a game of Hazard. He was, according to a German observer, Karl Philipp Moritz, 'dark, small, thickset, generally ill-groomed', his plump face overset by thick, shaggy eyebrows. His nickname was 'the Eyebrow' and his fat, dishevelled appearance became the object of a thousand caricatures. He would come to the chamber from a night of dissipation, perhaps still the worse for wear from drink, and deliver an oration of two hours that enchanted all who heard it. He was one of the greatest politicians of the age.

The war with America, to which Fox had always been opposed, was 'put down' rather than concluded. On 27 February 1782, three months after the news of Yorktown had reached London, the House of Commons voted against the pursuit of military actions across the Atlantic. That was the equivalent of surrender. A month later the Commons prepared a vote of no confidence in Lord North and his ministers, a humiliation that North escaped by precipitate resignation. He wrote to the king that 'the torrent is too strong to be resisted'. He had been first minister for twelve years, but he could no longer bear the perpetual anxious strain of administration at the time of the American war. The king was not impressed. He was of the opinion that North had somehow deserted him at a time of peril. 'At last,' he wrote, 'the fatal day is come.'

He was faced with competing factions and personalities who were avid for the benefits of office. In one period he even entertained the possibility of abdication, and drafted a speech declaring his imminent departure for Hanover. But it was never delivered. With the collapse of the Tory war faction, he was obliged to turn to sundry Whigs who were united only in their desire for peace with America. Even as they took over the administration they were divided, and four ministries emerged in the next two years. One of those who bobbed to the top was William Petty, 2nd earl of Shelburne. He was considered 'slippery' and an 'arch-deceiver' as well as being excessively ambitious, but that was practically the definition of any politician in the period. He is remembered principally, if at all, for his conduct of the negotiations for peace with the Americans.

The negotiations did not concern the Americans alone; settlements with France, Spain and Holland, who had all taken the offensive against Britain in its time of crisis, involved intricate diplomatic niceties. The preliminary articles of peace with America were signed in Paris in January 1783, with the most important clause that Britain acknowledged the thirteen united states to be free, sovereign and independent. The Americans made no concessions to the loyalists among them who had fought for the British; they were left to the mercy of Congress, a decision that infuriated many at Westminster. What kind of treaty was it that abandoned the allies? Further treaties with France and Spain were signed at Versailles. France surrendered Grenada, St Vincent and other islands in exchange for Senegal in Africa, Pondicherry in India, and several islands. Spain gave up the Bahamas but obtained Minorca and the two Floridas. A cartoon of 1783 was entitled 'The General Piss of Peace' in which all the protagonists, including a Native American, urinate into a common pot:

> A little time past, sirs, who would have thought this
> That they'd so soon come to a general piss?

So ended the American war that had created the first newly independent nation in the world that had full control of its common destiny. In the process of the fighting George Washington had in the face of extreme need managed to create a national army; his was the model followed by revolutionary France that inspired a new form of warfare. Another consequence followed. For the first time a group of people had advanced the cause of a nation without a king, without an aristocracy and without a national Church.

The British truly believed that their empire was now in decline but in fact their commercial and maritime links remained intact and would lead to ever greater prosperity in future years. The French had emerged from the conflict with mixed fortunes, but the truth was that their subvention of the American colonists led to a grave financial crisis that found its culmination in the revolution of 1789.

The foreign trade and domestic production of the United States were enlarged by the successful outcome of the war. In England, too, the cessation of hostilities encouraged the development of industry and commerce on a scale not seen for twenty years. The army and navy were cut back, to the great relief of the taxpayers, but the popularity of George III himself increased. He represented the still point in a turning world.

That popularity did not attach itself to his ministers. A resolution concerning the treaty devised by Shelburne was put before the Commons by Lord John Cavendish; it stated that 'the concessions made to the adversaries of Great Britain . . . were greater than they were entitled to, either from the actual situation of their respective possessions, or from their comparative strength'. The atmosphere was perhaps not conducive to strenuous debate. Karl Philipp Moritz noted that 'it is not at all uncommon to see a member lying stretched out on one of the benches, while others are debating. Some crack nuts; others eat oranges.'

The condemnation was passed by seventeen votes, and Shelburne resigned. It is unlikely that any other politician would have negotiated a more favourable peace, but he fell victim to a general mood of dissatisfaction and weariness. At a later date Benjamin Disraeli would acclaim Shelburne as the greatest statesman of the eighteenth century, but in his lifetime the earl was never thanked by a grateful nation for an unpopular but indispensable peace.

The departure of Shelburne left the king in the unenviable position of being surrounded by men whom he either distrusted or hated. One parliamentarian, James Grenville, later recalled that George III exhibited all the signs of his anxiety; he remarked that 'the feelings which then agitated his mind were strongly pictured in his countenance and gestures'; Grenville observed 'the quick step and disordered motion of his body, his rapid utterance, his eager and uninterrupted speech, admitting neither of pause nor answer, and shifting perpetually in unconnected digressions' which were perhaps a harbinger of his later nervous collapse. Yet he had some reason to be angry and alarmed.

To popular amazement, and much disgust, Lord North and Charles James Fox had entered an arrangement; the dissolute Whig and the fatigued lord had in the past traded insults with abandon.

Fox, for example, had accused North of 'unexampled treachery and falsehood' as well as 'public perfidy'. But now they found themselves to be the very best of friends, staunch allies ready to form a ministry. James Gillray portrayed the two men on a roundabout, or the 'new state whirligig', while robbers plunder the house behind them; the inscription read: 'Poor John Bull's house plundered at noon day'. But they had the numbers, Fox with 90 votes and North with 120 against a combined ministerial alliance of 140. They had in the phrase of the time 'stormed the [royal] closet'. The king had a particular hatred of Fox, whom he despised as a wanton reprobate, and was disgusted by what he considered to be the treachery of Lord North who had deserted him. He could not stop their alliance but he was clear that he would make it very difficult for them to continue; he barred them from using any sources of patronage, which was the lifeblood of a successful government. But even to the end he struggled to find an alternative.

In his extremity the king approached William Pitt, son of the 'great commoner', who at the age of twenty-four was already chancellor of the exchequer. He bore a famous name, but in the course of his career he made it more illustrious still. 'He is not a chip off the old block', Burke said. 'He is the old block itself.' He had been brought up in the purple of the political aristocracy and had been marked out early for high office; it was said that he had never been a boy and knew nothing of men or manners except through the distorting mirror of Westminster. He was characterized by his pale face and his stiff, formal bow; tall and thin, he had all the hauteur of one who knows his destiny. He could be stern, supercilious and supremely uninterested; he had what Lord Holland called 'an eye in the air'. He entered the chamber of the Commons without looking either to the right or to the left, and he sat in his place without nod or greeting to those around him.

That was the public man. In private, after a few glasses of port, he was good-natured and even humorous. One of his colleagues, Sir William Napier, recalled an occasion when Pitt was playing with some children of his acquaintance; his face had been blackened with cork, and he was throwing cushions with abandon. It was suddenly announced that two great ministers wished to see him on an urgent matter. He called for a basin, washed his face, and hid the cushions under a sofa. Napier recalled the change that came over him. 'His tall, ungainly, bony figure seemed to grow to the ceiling, his head was thrown back, his eyes were fixed immovably.' He listened to them, answered with a few curt sentences, 'and finally, with an abrupt stiff inclination of the body, but without casting his eyes down, dismissed them. Then, turning to us with a laugh, caught up his cushions and renewed our fight.' His temperament was in that sense unstable. It was said that he was 'always in the cellar or in the garret'.

When the king approached the young man with the offer of being first minister, Pitt rejected it out of hand. He could not command a majority, and he could not work either with Fox or with North. So he waited. He realized that the new ministry was so unstable, so riven by internal weakness, that it could not hold. He could bide his time. Richard Porson summed up the characters of Fox and Pitt with an observation. 'Mr Pitt conceives his sentences before he utters them. Mr Fox throws himself into the middle of his, and leaves it to God Almighty to get him out again.'

Balloons were the rage of the early 1780s. For the first time in human history it seemed that men could fly. Excited crowds in Paris and London watched the ascents, and for a moment seemed to be exhilarated by a sense of liberation from the woes of the world. This was freedom, or at least the promise of freedom, for future generations. At the time of the French Revolution a political writer, Etienne Dumont, remarked that 'the people of Paris were filled with inflammable gas like a balloon'. In the spring of 1785 Horace Walpole wrote, less dramatically, that 'Mr Windham, the member for Norwich, has made a voyage into the clouds, and was in danger of falling to earth and being shipwrecked. Three more balloons sail today; in short we shall have a prodigious navy in the air, and then what signifies having lost the empire of the ocean?'

24

The schoolboy

The first British Empire, largely consisting of the thirteen American colonies, had gone. Yet many were glad to be rid of it. Its surcease had become inevitable. It was better to trade with the Americans than attempt to rule them, and this salutary lesson became the single most important principle of the second British Empire which was even then being created. It was not in England's interests to have colonies scattered over the globe; it was more important to have a line of trading posts that could create a worldwide commercial empire along the routes of the oceans. These markets and factories would then be guarded by the navy in the world's first maritime empire.

Trading posts were set up in Borneo and the Philippines, while Lord Macartney led a commercial mission to the imperial court at Peking [Beijing]. The forts and factories of Britain stretched out to Penang and Malaya, to Trinomali [Tiruvannamalai] and Kandu, to Cape Town and central Africa. And of course the Indian sub-continent beckoned with its riches. It was said that the Tudor spirit of ocean-going adventure had revived, and indeed the idea of the British Empire was first raised in the Elizabethan period. John Dee had prophesied an empire that would unite all the peoples of Britain in its acquisition, a remarkably accurate vision of the future. Where could the ships and sailors not go? To Greece? To Araby? To the dark continent of Africa or to the realms of the Orient?

The memories of the old empire had not entirely faded; Britain held on to Quebec and to Canada. It also established New South Wales as colony and prison compound. But the Pacific and Indian oceans were to become the bearers of merchants with commodities to buy and to sell. In the process the nature of empire changed. The first empire had been essentially an English enterprise with the reminders of the old home in names such as New York and New England. The second empire was truly British in scope with areas such as Bengal, and eventually the whole of the Indian sub-continent, patrolled by native troops strengthened by Scots, Irish and Welsh regulars.

It was in many respects a ramshackle empire, made up of sep-arate constitutions and agreements. One territory was supervised by informal pacts, while another might be guarded by troops or circum-scribed by treaties. Different types of colony had different types of constitution. Indian provinces were situated beside the older trading posts. There was really no guiding plan or intention in the acqui-sition of a second empire. There may have been some general feeling that English authority was 'good' for the native peoples, but there was also a great deal of hypocrisy and greed in the arrangements. This was not intended to be a political invasion but a mercantile policy in which British governors would work with the local elites to preserve good administration and flourishing trade.

This sounded to many like the old empire in all but name. The pursuit of trade in India, for example, led ineluctably to a policy of conquest and dominion by the East India Company. Trade could not be separated from power. And power fed upon itself. Ceylon was therefore annexed to protect the trade routes to India. By 1816 Britain possessed forty-three colonies, compared to twenty-six in 1792; the territories comprised 2 million square miles and contained some 25 million people, the majority of them non-white and non-Christian. This was a unique phenomenon that the ministers in London found it hard to grasp or to control. How could the power implicit in empire be reconciled with traditional British liberties? They approached the problem with extreme caution and an innate conservatism.

As early as 1782, when peace negotiations were being pursued between England and America, the king informed the Commons that 'the regulation of a vast territory in Asia opens a large field for your wisdom, prudence and foresight'. Asia was in fact the major problem for the administration at Westminster. Since wisdom and prudence were too feeble a match for cupidity and cunning, there seemed to be no way to supervise or to control the workings of the East India Company.

Its administrators had grown too rich and too powerful. They needed to preserve their trade by imposing political stability upon the territories with which they negotiated; they required alliances with local princes or rulers, and they needed to master the complex procedures of both Koran and Hindu law; they needed an army, preferably of friendly natives. The government in Westminster was uneasy at this abrogation of its powers, and distressed by the news of exploitation and even of violence that reached it.

The ministers were no doubt also eager to get their hands on the surplus revenues that the company was accruing from its flourishing trade. The 'nabobs', the Englishmen who returned rich from Indian service, were treated with considerable disquiet; the combination of 'new money' with greed and exploitation was not considered suitable. They had become so familiar, and so despised, that Samuel Foote's *The Nabob* (1772) became a great success at the Haymarket Theatre. 'With the wealth of the East,' one character laments, 'we have, too, imported the worst of its vices. What a horrid crew!' The nabob has 'grown great from robbing the heathens'. This was also the perceived problem of the East India Company itself.

With his usual mixture of self-assurance and optimism Charles James Fox believed that he could resolve the problems of India. He proposed that the existing Court of Directors that administered the company should be replaced by seven commissioners. It soon became clear that the chosen commissioners were all supporters of the administration, and of Fox in particular; it was widely believed that Fox wished to transfer the patronage and wealth of the East India Company into his own political service. A cartoon was published at the end of 1783 showing him, wearing a turban and riding an elephant, trampling upon India House and its directors with the caption 'Carlo Khan's Triumphal Entry into Leadenhall Street'.

It was a moment of peril for Fox, who could be accused of purloining the king's bounty, and his opponents were ready to fall upon him. The supporters of Fox and North were able to press the measure through the Commons but, at this juncture, on 11 December, the king let it be known through an intermediary 'that whoever voted for the India Bill were not only not his friends, but he should consider them as his enemies'. It seems more than likely that William Pitt had a certain responsibility for this intervention since, if the bill fell, it effectively signalled the demise of the coalition. And so it proved. As the debate moved on, Thomas Orde, a Tory member, reported that Fox's 'countenance, gesture and expression were in the highest degree ludicrous from the extremity of dejection and rage, going off with an exclamation of despair'. As soon as the Lords objected to Fox's measure, and voted it down on 17 December, the king asked for the resignation of his two principal ministers. They were gone by the next day. Pitt came forward almost at once. He was still only twenty-four.

The shambles of the coalition, the effrontery of Fox's proposal to appoint the commissioners, the growing unpopularity of the government, gave Pitt his opportunity to strike where he had not struck before. He gambled that he could survive a combined opposition just long enough to be ready to go to the country. Fox, on the contrary, believed that 'we shall destroy them almost as soon as they are formed'. It was nicknamed 'the mince-pie administration' fit only to last for the festive season. A verse was circulated:

> A sight to make surrounding nations stare;
> A kingdom trusted to a school-boy's care.

Parliament reassembled on 12 January 1784, and Pitt would remain in office for the next eighteen years.

From the beginning he was cool, precise and determined; his aims and methods were clear, his calculations cogent and his command of the Commons exemplary. He had from the beginning the support and loyalty of the king, who opened for him the gates of patronage; some of his supporters were immediately made peers. But he was not above the convenient lie. When Fox charged that his India bill had been rejected by the Lords as a result of 'secret influence', Pitt replied that 'he knew of no secret influence, and his own integrity would be his guardian against that danger'. It would not be the last time that he invoked his 'integrity'.

He chose to be the only member of his cabinet in the Commons, and soon demonstrated his mastery of that assembly; he believed that innate loyalty to the king, his own new powers of patronage, and his steadiness in the face of fire, would allow him to survive until the next election. Slowly he whittled down the number of his opponents while keeping a grave and composed face.

His principal purposes, apart from the obvious necessity of staying in power, were to reform the national finances and to extend national commerce. These were the two props for safety and peace. In matters of money he was a master, and knew that the first priority must be to pay off or pay down the national debt incurred after years of warfare. It was also vital, as far as he was concerned, to cut expenditure by a process of careful and lengthy clearance of superfluous offices and sinecures. Of what, then, might Fox and his Whig colleagues complain? They had in any case given every sign that they would be profligate with the nation's revenues. Pitt's oratory was precise, cogent and irrefutable. As one of his opponents, Dr Parr, put it, 'the dog talks grammar'; or, as Samuel Taylor Coleridge said, Pitt manifested 'a premature and unnatural dexterity in the combination of words'.

The long-anticipated elections took place in the spring of 1784, with a campaign that lasted for five weeks; it soon became clear that the advantage lay with Pitt and the king over Fox and his adherents. 'We are cut up root and branch,' one MP, William Eden, confessed, 'the country is utterly mad for prerogative.' It was not a battle between Crown and parliament; it was a struggle for or against a parliament sanctioned by the throne. Pitt had on his side the landowners and the manufacturers, the merchants and the clergy. All wanted efficiency, security and, if possible, honesty in the administration. More than a hundred Whig members lost their seats; they became known as 'Fox's martyrs' after *Foxe's Book of Martyrs* published 200 years before. Pitt regained office as first minister, more powerful than any of his predecessors. Thomas Paine wrote, at a later date, that 'Mr Pitt had merited nothing, but he promised much.'

He was not given to visionary plans or solutions; he did not press too far into matters of principle and was loath to question the status quo. He dealt principally with practical, administrative and factual details. It was hard to know whether he was a Whig or a Tory, but the distinction made very little difference. He had been brought up as a Whig but the party he commanded was now essentially Tory in nature. In any case, he was not a 'party man'. He relished his independence, and confided in very few of his colleagues. On the question of India, he was pragmatic. He set up a Board of Control, composed of six members of the privy council, to oversee the affairs of the East India Company; the new governor general of India, the Earl Cornwallis, was sent out two years later. The idea of imperial trusteeship was in the air. Pitt's proposals did not differ markedly from those of Fox, but they were regarded as more honest and more open than any projected cabal of Fox's friends.

In matters of finance Pitt was in his element. His private secretary, the Reverend George Pretyman, gave a sermon before the House of Commons in St Margaret's, Westminster, where he expatiated on the perils of the national debt and the critical state of the country 'especially with regard to its revenue'. So the raising of taxes became a national endeavour. Pitt did not invent the window tax, but he made sure that it yielded much greater sums. He taxed horses and carriages; he taxed bricks, hats and perfumes; he increased the cost of postage and the taxes on newspapers; he invented probate and legacy duties. What could be squeezed was hard pressed. For the national debt itself, Pitt had a novel solution; the cutting of expenditure, together with the raising of taxes and customs duties, had led to a surplus in the public funds. Instead of spending that surplus, Pitt decreed that it would become part of a sinking fund to pay off the national debt. The fund could not be used for any other purpose.

For these measures Pitt relied upon tranquillity at home and abroad. He could not afford war, and wished to avoid public protest. He had decided upon a new tax on the cotton industry but a procession of 2,000 marched through Manchester with banners proclaiming 'Let commerce flourish for ever!', 'Freedom restored', 'May Industry never be cramped'. To all these sentiments, Pitt was in fact thoroughly sympathetic and after much agitation and parliamentary protest, he gave way. From the mid-1780s there was indeed a recovery in the building trade and elsewhere, and consequently something of a 'boom'.

Defeats in parliament did not seem to injure him in the least. He had in a sense already risen above party. In matters of Europe he was also a conciliator and negotiator by nature. It was said that he had no interest in, or knowledge of, foreign affairs, but his study in Downing Street was decorated with four sets of maps and his library was stocked with gazetteers and atlases.

He did believe in pursuing diplomacy through commerce, however, and in the autumn of 1786 he concluded a trade treaty with France that allowed the products of both countries to pass with the minimum of interference. Given the scale of English manufacture, the balance of trade would be inevitably favourable to Britain. Over the next few years Pitt also attempted to devise trade treaties with seven other countries. As the *Public Advertiser* put it, 'it is no less than a general arrangement of the commerce of the greatest commercial power that ever existed with all the great commercial powers of the world'. As with many grand schemes, however, it came to nothing.

The problems of empire were never far removed and the trial of Warren Hastings, formerly governor general of Bengal, illustrated the deep uncertainty and confusion which still surrounded Britain's imperial status. Fox had already stated in the Commons that India should be governed 'by those principles of equity and humanity implanted in our hearts'. If this was the dream of empire, the reality was sometimes very different.

On his return to Britain, having spent most of his life in India, Hastings was charged by Edmund Burke and others with high crimes and misdemeanours: he was accused of accepting, and giving, bribes; he was accused of selling the aid of his troops to a local despot; he was accused of extortion against the begums of Oudh and the nabob of Benares who had been forced to flee his territory. The names were not familiar to the English, and suggested an alien sub-continent of which they understood very little, but all of Hastings's supposed crimes could be seen to represent the East India Company itself.

Richard Brinsley Sheridan, a politician as well as a playwright close to Burke, rose in the Commons in February 1787, to appeal to his colleagues 'to wipe off the disgrace affixed to the British name in India, and to rescue the national character from lasting infamy'. Many were not happy with the country's imperial role, especially when it was no longer seen as guardian of a white Protestant empire. The accusations could also be used to diminish the standing of George III and Pitt who might be accused of seeking to use the company's revenue for themselves. Sheridan spoke for five and a half hours and, at the conclusion of his speech, he was greeted by a 'universal shout' of approbation.

The impeachment of Hastings had become inevitable and, for a few months, it afforded the spectacle of an empire questioning, and deciding upon, its destiny. Everybody flocked to Westminster Hall for the proceedings which began on 13 February 1788. No one could then have guessed that the process would last for a further seven years. It became the sensation of the season, with the leading orators of the day – Sheridan, Burke, Fox – launching tirades against an old man in a blue French coat. Macaulay wrote that 'the grey old walls were hung with scarlet. The long galleries were crowded by an audience such as has rarely excited the fears or gratified the emulation of an orator.' The queen and the court were there; the leaders of fashion and art were there; the ambassadors were there; 'society', in all its manifestations, was there. A ticket might be sold for 50 guineas.

The speeches of denunciation would have given credit to the Haymarket or Covent Garden. Burke opened the proceedings with a speech that lasted four days; in the excitement he created, several ladies fainted in the galleries. Sheridan went one further; at the end of his final speech he fell, fainting, into the arms of Edmund Burke. The noted actress, Sarah Siddons, fainted simultaneously. It was a festival of fainting. Gibbon visited Sheridan on the following day. 'I called this morning, he is perfectly well. A good actor!' Burke himself seems to have fainted five times in the course of his orations. 'Your lordships will spare my weakness,' he said, 'I have not spared myself . . . I cannot command strength to proceed further at present.' It was all very stirring, but nothing came of it in the end.

Hastings was after seven years acquitted on all counts, but national attention had already turned elsewhere. The impeachment can best be construed as a momentary spasm of conscience in a country still ambiguous over its imperial role. It would take the greater self-belief of a later generation to quell all doubt.

Another source of doubt and disquiet, in the face of empire, was the continuing survival and prosperity of the slave trade. Not many people cared about it. It was believed that if the English gave up the selling or bartering of slaves, then the French would take over. The country needed the gold, the elephants' tusks and the slaves. The merchants of London, Bristol and Liverpool sent out gaily coloured clothes, hats, rum, powder and flint. In return they were given men, women and children often taken in tribal wars. By 1750 the numbers of slaves had reached over 270,000 per decade. By 1793 Liverpool handled three-sevenths of the slave trade of all Europe. Who would willingly let them go? From their slave labour in the West Indies came tobacco, cotton and sugar. They were vital tributes to the great god of commerce that ruled the nation.

Yet a small band of persistent opponents of slavery was active in its efforts and, during the course of the reign of George III, several petitions had been presented to parliament on the total abolition of the trade or on the more humane treatment of slaves in the West Indies. William Wilberforce, one of the founders of the Society for the Abolition of the Slave Trade, stated to the Commons that no more than half of the transported slaves lived to see their destination; some plunged into the sea and were said to hold out their arms in joy for the brief sensation of liberty before they sank beneath the waves.

Conversations and committees ensued but nothing was achieved until 21 May 1788, when Sir William Dolben proposed a bill to monitor the transportation of the captives who were forced to endure irons, putrid fever and scant space to move or breathe. It was the first measure against slavery to be tabled at Westminster and the ensuing legislation – one slave to be carried for each ton of the ship's burthen – was passed by a considerable majority in both houses. The victory pleased the supporters of the bill, and in particular William Wilberforce. Pitt made brave speeches against the trade, admitting that 'the perversion of British commerce carried misery instead of happiness to one whole quarter of the globe', but was cautious with legislative action. As first minister he relied upon the immense popularity of a national cause before he committed himself to it.

This was not the case for slavery. Its abolition was not given legislative force for another forty-five years. The slaves were part of the engine of trade.

And were there not, some people argued, enough and more than enough slaves at home?

25

The steam machines

In the spring and summer of 1788 George III visited a pin
manufactory in Gloucestershire as well as a carpet works and
china factory in Worcestershire; he also took in the new Thames–
Severn canal south-east of Stroud. In the following year he visited
the carpet manufactory at Axminster and, according to its owner,
'attended to the workers and asked many questions concerning
the principles and processes of the manufacture'. It was the first
time, perhaps, that the king had given his consideration to the
industry and manufactures of the country which in his reign were
growing at an accelerated rate. By this date the steam engine and
the power loom were in full operation, with the astonishing
revelation that a mechanical hammer could strike 150 blows per
minute. It seemed to summarize or represent the remarkable
change.

Everyone dreamed and spoke of steam. Erasmus Darwin, the
grandfather of Charles Darwin, eulogized it in his long poem, *The
Economy of Vegetation* (1791):

> Soon shall thy arm, UNCONQUER'D STEAM! Afar
> Drag the slow barge, or drive the rapid car;
> Or on wide-waving wings expanded bear
> The flying chariot through the fields of air.

Matthew Boulton had written in 1781 to his partner, James Watt, the great pioneer of the steam engine, that 'the people in London, Manchester and Birmingham are *steam mill mad*'. Charles Babbage, one of the first proponents of the computer, declared at a later date that 'I wish to God these calculations had been executed by steam'. Its uses seemed to be infinite. It blew the furnaces and punched the metal; it drove the lathe and rolled the iron; it raised the water and drained the mines. It lent the power for spinning and weaving. It was used in flour mills, in malt mills and in flint mills. It was of course also used to make more steam engines. The first steam engine for a textile mill was installed in 1792; eight years later, eighty engines were being employed for the same purpose.

In 1803 a steam carriage made its way through the streets of London. A year later the first railway locomotive in history made its maiden journey of 10 miles from the Penydarren Ironworks by Merthyr Tydfil to the Glamorgan Canal. Lord Jeffrey wrote of the steam engine that 'it can engrave a seal, and crush obdurate masses of metal before it; draw out, without breaking, a thread as fine as gossamer, and lift a ship of war like a bauble into the air'. What was once done by wind and water, by human effort and animal strength, could now be accomplished by heat alone.

The Albion Mill had been constructed in 1786, on the south side of the Thames near Blackfriars Bridge, with the intention of expediting the manufacture of flour by means of steam; it was the great mechanical spectacle of the age, a wonder of modern life, sporting the most powerful machines in the world, and was described by Erasmus Darwin as 'a grand and successful effort of human life'. It led directly, however, to William Blake's condemnation of 'these dark Satanic Mills' in 'Jerusalem' (1804–10). It burned down three years later in what may have been suspicious circumstances. The millers danced and sang on Blackfriars Bridge. Not everyone was enamoured of the age's mechanical marvels.

All this activity was propagated by a delicate and melancholy mechanic, James Watt, who was described by the historian, William Lecky, as 'a slow, shy, plodding, self-concentrated boy, with weak health and low spirits, entirely without brilliancy and fire but with an evident natural turn for mechanics'. Watt once said that 'of all things in life there is nothing more foolish than inventing'. He added, on another occasion, that 'I find myself out of my sphere when I have anything to do with mankind'. It was this somewhat lugubrious individual who changed the shape of the age, since his sudden intuition that the two stages of the engine's life, the heating and the cooling, could be disconnected provided the breakthrough. With a separate condenser, the engine was more efficient and more stable. The idea came to him in a flash while walking on College Green in Glasgow, but it is doubtful whether the fully conceived scheme would have come to fruition without the active and energetic assistance of Matthew Boulton; Watt himself extolled the 'active and sanguine disposition' of the manufacturer and industrialist who drove him forward.

It was Boulton who had told James Boswell, on a tour of his manufactory, 'I sell here, sir, what all the world desires to have – Power.' Power was the source and origin of what would soon become the full-blown factory system that spread across the midland and northern counties so that the whole aggregation was considered to be one vast factory. Lancashire, Derbyshire, Yorkshire, Nottinghamshire, Denbighshire and Cheshire became the home of the machine. At a later date Andrew Ure, author of *The Philosophy of Manufactures* (1835), compared the factories to 'the boasted monuments of Asiatic, Egyptian and Roman despotism'. There was therefore a hint of the sublime about their construction, with suggestions of darkness, terror and despair.

They were constructed from solid brick or stone while some of them contained an iron frame; the same care and ingenuity went into their making as that of the great cathedrals, with which they were sometimes compared. Previous industrial buildings had been almost always domestic in scale which lent them a human dimension; the factories with their several storeys, their iron pillars, their windows grouped vertically rather than horizontally, were a new presence in the landscape. They looked as if they were trying to free themselves from the shackles of the land, like the great single-span iron bridges. Early in the new century the factories were some of the first public buildings to be illuminated by gaslight, so that the brilliancy of their achievement could be seen from far off. An historian of Stockport, Henry Heginbotham, wrote that 'the drivers of London coaches when passing the mill slackened their speed in order to tell of the miraculous operations performed therein'. Others were not impressed. A contemporary diarist, John Byng, after visiting the silk mills in Derby wrote that the mills 'quite bewildered me; such rattlings and twistings. Such heat, and stinks!'

The change was slow, and not fully completed until the middle of the next century, but gradually in the last decades of the eighteenth century great spreads of industry and manufacture were established that had their centre in the mills and in the factories. Many of them were constructed at a distance from the old cities and guilds, so the industrialist was able to create new communities that could service his creations; rows of cottages, chapels, churches, schools, kitchen gardens and even public houses were built on-site. Benefit schemes and rudimentary health insurance were also established; organized sports were encouraged as well as annual outings to some local beauty spot or another. When some industrial rioters threatened Arkwright's factory at Cromford, he armed his employees with guns and spears.

The purpose of the new factories was of course readily apparent. By congregating all the workers under one roof it was easier to control and to supervise them; it also led to more efficiency so that a series of 'shops' or work-rooms could concentrate on one part of the industrial process. Only the factories could house and maintain the great engines that were now being introduced. One external source of power, such as a river, could create the energy for a thousand machines. The forbidding walls could also protect the industrialist from the theft of his trade secrets. But the large number of workers – men, women and children – meant that there was room for experimentation with time and divisions of labour; it was possible now for the working life of factories to be maintained throughout the night as well as the day.

The great advantage was that of speed. Everything was running faster. The workers were obliged to quicken their pace in order to keep up with one another, while the wheels and belts ran faster. The old guild legislation and medieval ordinances disappeared under the onslaught of this new form of production; the relationships between workers and employers, together with the customary rhythms of life, were changed for ever. It is not surprising, therefore, that this revolution provoked enormous hostility among those whose lives and livelihoods were threatened by it. The building of the first steam mill in Bradford, Holme Mill, was plagued by protests and riots. Staverton Mill, near Totnes in Devon, was sabotaged by its own operatives.

The machines were meant to save labour, but the flood of cheaper goods meant that the market grew faster than the available labour force. In turn the relative shortage of labour led to more and more persistent attempts at efficiency and innovation. Robert Owen, the great mill-owner and philanthropist, declared in 1816 that 'in my establishment at New Lanark . . . mechanical powers and operations superintended by about two thousand young persons and adults . . . now completed as much work as sixty years ago would have required the entire working population of Scotland'.

The key lay in the successful division of labour, a concept that Adam Smith had extolled in the first chapter of his *Wealth of Nations* (1776). He contemplates the nature of pin-making under the industrial system.

> One man draws out the wire; another straights it; a third cuts it; a fourth points it; a fifth grinds it at the top for receiving the head; to make the head requires two or three distinct operations; to put it on is a peculiar business; to whiten the pins is another; it is even a trade by itself to put them into the paper; and the important business of making a pin is, in this manner, divided into about eighteen distinct operations . . .

Eighteen men could perform in a few seconds a task that would absorb the energy of one man for a whole day. This in turn required the presence of specialized workmen who were all the time seeking more and more technical efficiency; their goal was greater accuracy and precision. But this division of labour also needed the efforts of many hundreds of women and children who were put to the most routine and repetitive tasks. So the changes in national industry created new divisions among the working population.

The other great shibboleth of industrial change was the need for standardization. This was the context for mass production, and was part of the drive for accuracy, regularity, efficiency and speed. The elimination of variability was indispensable for the creation of a national market. And for this, of course, mechanization was essential. As the Scottish engineer and inventor James Nasmyth put it:

> the irregularity and carelessness of the workmen . . . gave an increased stimulus to the demand for self-acting machine tools . . . The machines never got drunk; their hands never shook from excess; they were never absent from work; they did not strike for wages; they were unfailing in their accuracy and regularity, while producing the most delicate or ponderous portions of mechanical structures.

So by default the men and women themselves had to be trained to behave and work in the same way as machines. The *Edinburgh Review* noted that 'the human operative, in imitation and by the aid of the machine, acquires a perfection little less than marvellous'. But what of these men and women and even children? The last word had been said more than 2,000 years before by Xenophon, the Greek historian, who in *Oeconomicus* condemned the arts of manufacture that 'utterly ruin the bodies of workers and managers alike, compelling men as they do to lead sedentary lives and huddle indoors, or in some cases to spend the day before a fire. Then as men's bodies become enervated, so their souls grow sicklier.'

It is clear enough that many of those who entered the doors of the factory were being introduced to a more intense or at least more visible form of servitude. Social historians have argued for many years over the relative privation involved in agricultural labour or domestic service, but the factory represented coercion and discipline on a much larger and more organized scale. The personal tie had been broken, and the illusion of independence had disappeared. To enter the new sphere of unfreedom, to be introduced to a world of strict routine and discipline, to work for set hours in a set pattern, marked a profound change in status. The wage labourers were believed by many to have lost their rights as free-born Englishmen. In 1765 Adam Ferguson wrote that 'we make a nation of helots, and have no free citizens'. The men and women had become 'hands' or instruments totally at the disposal of the master industrialist who considered them to be part of his great machine. Once such workers had been known as 'souls', and the change in discourse is notable. It was reported to parliament that the operatives expressed 'the

21. Joseph Wright's *The Iron Forge, circa* 1773.

22. The Ball from 'Scenes at Bath'. It looks very respectable.

23. From the sublime to the domestic. A teapot, *circa* 1775.

24. The Boston Tea Party, 16 December 1773. Do you want tea with your water?

25. George Washington, from
slave owner to liberator.

26. William Pitt the Younger.
Not a chip off the old block,
but the old block itself.

27. A disconsolate and melancholy Edmund Burke at the loss of America.

28. Samuel Taylor Coleridge, 1804.
He had a glow-worm in his head.

29. Wordsworth, in characteristically
reflective mind.

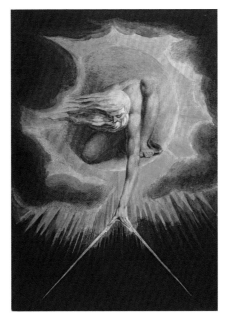

30. A mythological depiction of *The Ancient of Days* by William Blake.

31. Taking the waters at the pump room in Bath.

32. Ladies in coffee-houses: It was a city of coffee-houses.
They had begun life in the 1660s, and before long they were considered to be
the most essential component of city life. It was important to be noticed.

33. A modern Belle creeping around
Bath like a caterpillar in a chrysalis.

34. The Duchess of Richmond organized a ball for the Duke of Wellington and other famous participants two days before the Battle of Waterloo.

35. The great Battle of Trafalgar.

36. Napoleon in excelsis.

37. The Duke of
Wellington at Waterloo.
To the victors go
the spoils.

utmost distaste' for regular hours and regular habits. It was against nature.

William Hutton was placed in the Derby silk mill at the age of seven where, as he reported, 'I had now to rise at five every morning during seven years, submit to the cane whenever convenient to the master . . .' The factory system was known on the continent as the 'English system', and a contemporary commented that 'while the engine runs, the people must work – men, women and children are yoked together with iron and steam. The animal machine – breakable in the best case, subject to a thousand sources of suffering – is chained fast to the iron machine which knows no suffering and no weariness.'

Their work was continually supervised by overseers, and a strict code of discipline was generally introduced. Anyone found straying from his or her own 'alley', or talking to another employee, was fined. Any worker who struck or abused an overseer immediately lost his job. Anyone found smuggling liquor into the factory was fined 2 shillings. A list of misdemeanours, from the mills owned by Jedediah Strutt at Belper in Derbyshire, included 'Idleness and looking thro' window . . . calling thro' window to some soldiers . . . riotous behaviour in room . . . riding on each other's back . . . telling lies . . . throwing bobbins at people . . . using ill language . . . quarrelling . . . rubbing their faces with blood and going about the town to frighten people'. The ebullition of high spirits was not permitted. Other crimes were 'running away . . . being off drinking . . . going to Derby fair . . . sending word she was ill when in fact she was not'.

It was not difficult to understand the motives of those who ran away. The factories were generally stinking and filthy, filled with the constant clamour of harsh machinery; the workshops on the premises were often dark and narrow, suffocating in summer and too frosty in winter. One report, of a later date, stated that 'altogether I never saw a [work]shop in more filthy or wretched condition . . . Mr Wallis objected to my examining the children in his counting house because he stated "it would make the place stink so, that his customers could not stay in it"'.

The precision and regularity of their working hours had all the characteristics of a military drill. At Tyldesley Mill, not far from

Wigan and Manchester, the operatives worked fourteen hours a day, including a nominal hour for 'dinner'; the doors were locked in working hours, except for half an hour at teatime, and the workers were not allowed to ask for water despite the heat of the factory. It was reported that in some instances the managers cheated, and stretched the hours as far as they could go; as a consequence, no workman was allowed to wear a watch on the premises. Working hours gradually improved from thirteen and a half to twelve hours in the course of the century based on a six-day working week. There was no more talk of 'St Monday', the day when in an earlier period the operatives were allowed the leisure of the tavern or the green. When at the end of the century coal gas became a source of light, many workers were obliged to work through the night hours. This had become a world of bells, clappers, hooters, horns and clocks.

It seems that a relative rise in wages differentiated this work from the labour of the farmers or the casual slavery of the domestic system, but this was not appreciated by some observers. In 1771 Arthur Young, a writer and traveller, remarked that 'every body but an idiot knows that the lower classes must be kept poor or they will never be industrious'. Surplus cash encouraged only idleness and drunkenness. Sir Willam Temple made a similar point fifteen years later when he observed that the only way to make labourers sober and industrious 'is to lay them under the necessity of labouring all the time they can spare from meals and sleep, in order to procure the necessities of life'. The usefulness of poverty was widely accepted; since wealth and power depended upon the combined labour of the vast mass of the population, then those masses must be set to work at the lowest possible cost. It was, as some thought, the law of God as much as the law of man.

For some observers the condition of the mills and factories became a metaphor for society itself, where social relations were bound by laws of obedience and discipline. Was this the way the world was about to go? In many respects it was. It has been observed that in the eighteenth century there emerged a greater interest in punctuality and the constant demand for more rapid and expeditious methods. The wheels of machines and carriages revolved faster. Sir John Barnard, successful London merchant and lord mayor, advised in *A Present for an Apprentice* in 1740 that 'above all things learn to put a due value on *Time*, and husband every moment as if it were to be your last; in Time is comprehended all we possess, enjoy, or wish for; and in losing that we lose them all'.

It was observed that in London and in the larger industrial cities greater hurry was noticeable in the crowds, and Londoners became well known for their punctuality. By the 1730s one third of the inhabitants of Bristol owned a watch, and it is perhaps no exaggeration to state that every respectable citizen of London had a timepiece in his waistcoat pocket. The public buildings of the cities more often than not supported a large clock which broadcast the hours to the teeming thousands who passed beneath them. Benjamin Franklin once more caught the spirit of the age when in 1748 he coined the phrase 'time is money'.

Of course it must also be true that some of the woes and hardships were exaggerated by those who were opposed to the industrial system, but the direct testimony of the workers themselves suggests that there was more than a modicum of truth to even the harshest allegations. The workers did not rise up, however, because they were being paid more, fed better and clothed better. The theorists invoked the laws of God and man, but the laws of the market were in the end more powerful.

The growth of manufactures and the extension of the transportation system required an increase in labour that could not simply be satisfied with a expansion in population; so general complaints were made about workers leaving the land, and domestic servants abandoning their former employment, to make up the deficiency. Corbyn Morris, a customs administrator and economist, noted in 1750 that farmers throughout the kingdom were complaining 'of the excessive increasing prices of workmen, and of the impossibility of procuring a sufficient number at any price'.

The increase in wages implied a rise in living standards. The roughest estimates, the only ones possible, suggest that in the 1760s and 1770s, home consumption increased at a faster rate than exports and that between 1784 and 1800 the increase in demand for mass commodities, such as soap and printed fabrics, tobacco and beer, was twice the rate of population growth. It has been calculated that as a result of these changes, by the beginning of the nineteenth century, industrial output was almost twice that of 1770.

Many workers enjoyed the benefit of tied cottages, schools and hospitals provided by the management. But of course conditions were attached to this apparent beneficence. Henry and Edward Ashworth, two mill-owners of Turton in Lancashire, told a government enquiry that 'we exercise a control or superintendence over them, for their moral and social improvement . . . at frequent and irregular intervals visits are paid to every workman'. The rooms should be clean; the beds and children lice-free; their joint incomes, and their general habits of life, were recorded in special accounting books.

Josiah Wedgwood described the state of the Potteries after he had, as it were, colonized the neighbourhood. In a small pamphlet, 'An Address to the Young Inhabitants of the Pottery', he celebrated the new conditions with 'the workmen earning nearly double their former wages – their houses mostly new and comfortable, and the lands, roads and every other circumstance bearing the most evident marks of the most pleasing and rapid improvements . . . Industry has been the parent of this happy change.' William Radcliffe, the author of the *Origin of the New System of Manufacture* (1828), described in glowing terms the weavers under the patronage and control of Samuel Oldknow, cotton manufacturer, with 'their dwellings and small gardens clean and neat – all the family well clad – the men with each a watch in his pocket . . .'.

We may of course turn to conflicting testimony. A surgeon, asked to recruit working men into the marines, noted that 'the mechanics are shorter, more puny, and altogether inferior in their physical powers. Many of the men presented for examination are distorted in the spine and chest, which witness attributes to the confined position in which they work.' The risks of disease and illness were infinite. The supposedly happy potters of Staffordshire, men and boys, often worked continually for twelve hours in temperatures of 100 degrees Fahrenheit. The fork-grinders of Sheffield worked in an atmosphere of stone and metal particles, where lung disease was endemic; the plumbers, who used lead, were slowly poisoned; the hatters, who employed mercury, suffered from nervous debility; the cotton workers contracted byssinosis. Leather workers died of anthrax and lung disease struck down those who worked with wool. Grinder's rot and bricklayer's elbow, potter's rot and miner's phthisis were some of the occupational hazards. Tailors and seamstresses often lost their sight. Even as late as 1842 a Manchester labourer had a life expectancy of seventeen years, and a Leeds operative of nineteen.

Industry could not exist without misery. One traveller, William George Maton, observed in the copper manufactories that 'some of the poor wretches who were ladling the liquid metal from the furnaces to the moulds looked more like walking corpses than living beings'.

Industrial victims of another kind were also evident. The hand-loom weavers of Lancashire and elsewhere lost their occupations, as new weaving technologies made their skills redundant; a report on the textile settlements by Angus Reach concluded that they 'are a wretched and hopeless set'. They were joined in their suffering by southern agricultural labourers who had been used to increase their incomes with industrial labour in the wintry seasons, until the factories had left the south. They were also threatened by agricultural change that encouraged more enclosures and more scientific land use.

The infants were not far behind. The children at work in the mills were reported as suffering from extreme debility, fatigue and deformations of the body. One famous observer, Friedrich Engels, described various children as manifesting 'pain in the back, hips and legs, swollen joints, varicose veins and large persistent ulcers in the thighs and calves'. If Engels might be considered a less than reliable witness his testimony is confirmed by a Manchester doctor who wrote that:

> I stood in Oxford Road, Manchester, and observed the stream of operatives as they left the mills at twelve o'clock. The children were almost universally ill-looking, small, sickly, barefoot and ill-clad. Many appeared to be no older than seven. The men, generally from sixteen to twenty-four, and none aged, were almost as pallid and thin as the children . . . it was a mournful spectacle.

The children, then, may become a true test of the industrial system. The life of what became known as 'the factory child' was a symbol of the age. One operative, Charles Aberdeen, who had begun work as a boy, told a committee: 'I have seen the race become diminutive and small: I have myself had seven children, not one of which survived six weeks; my wife is an emaciated person, like myself, a little woman, and she worked during her childhood, younger than myself, in a factory.'

The benefits of child labour, however, were deemed to be considerable. Children had, after all, worked from a very early age in the fields, in the shops and in domestic dwellings. They were no strangers to hard labour. It was considered to be good for them. It inculcated obedience and discipline. It added to the family purse. It was of value to the nation and of infinite advantage to the poor themselves. Defoe had commented, in his travels around the country, that in Norwich 'hardly any thing above four years old but its hands are sufficient to itself'. The unspoken proverb here is that the devil makes work for idle hands. In Norwich, too, he commented that 'the very children after four or five years of age, could every one earn their own bread'. As late as 1796 Pitt informed the Commons that 'experience had already shown how much can be done by the industry of children'. So there was no outcry against the employment of very young children in the mills and factories; there was no outrage. They helped to keep wages down. They supported their families. What was wrong with that?

It was customary in the more populous parishes of London to send their children on poor relief to the proprietors of the cotton mills in Lancashire and Yorkshire; they were sent by the wagon-load as a welcome deduction from the poor rate. Many of the pauper children were collected from the workhouses of London and Westminster and transported north in large groups. One London parish negotiated a bargain with a Lancashire mill-owner that it could send one idiot child with twenty sound children. It is not at all clear who was paying whom. In the beginning the authorities paid a nominal sum to the mill-owners for taking their children off the rates, but there were also many reports of the factory-owners paying the parish for what was essentially slave labour.

The parents had no voice in the matter since they, too, customarily relied upon parish relief. And so the children were dispatched with as little care as if they were being shipped to the West Indies. When one slave-owner from that region heard that the children were worked at the cotton mills from five in the morning to seven at night, he observed that 'we never in the West Indies thought it possible for any human being to be so cruel'. Children were also engaged in night work when the pressure of demand required it.

The conditions in which they worked were uniformly deplorable. They were unprotected from the grind of machinery, and there are many reports of fingers being cut off or limbs crushed in the wheels. One boy who worked in a cotton manufactory for twenty years remarked that 'I got deformed there; my knees began to bend in when I was fifteen; you see how they are.' He was part of what Engels called 'a crowd of cripples'. The ceilings were low, the windows narrow and generally closed. In this unventilated state epidemic disease was rife, with 'factory fever' first coming out in 1784. The food was often rancid, with porridge and black bread as staples. Some of the children had to raid dust heaps or fight with the pigs to get into their troughs. Discipline was considered to be essential in such conditions. It was normal for a sleepy or slow child to be hit with a whip, cane, or clenched fist; if any tried to escape they were put in irons. For serious offences the child might be suspended in a 'cage' or basket from the ceiling. There is no doubt that some of the overseers were brutish, with a predilection for giving pain to infants. One factory in Manchester was known as 'Hell's Gate'.

Nevertheless the children were very useful. They were generally docile and uncomplaining. To whom, in any case, could they complain? They were quick and nimble, small enough to insert themselves into the machinery where required. Some machinery was constructed with child operatives in mind; the spinning jenny had a horizontal wheel best handled by children aged from nine to twelve. One observer, Samuel Schroeder, noted that 'a small boy makes the blanks red-hot in a small furnace. Another boy puts them under the punch, one by one. The third picks them out of the punch and greases the upper mould between each punching with a greased brush. All this goes quite quickly.'

The children were also very cheap, some of them earning nothing more than their food and lodgings. The age of their labours began at four or five. Pin-makers, for example, began at five, and it was said that going into their workshop was like entering an infants' school. Jedediah Strutt of Belper explained to a Commons committee that he would take children at the age of seven but preferred those between eleven and twelve. There can be no doubt that these factory children were the least favoured, and least protected, group in eighteenth-century society.

There were occasions when an adult male was given work only if he also sent his children to the mill. Thus there grew up 'families' of operatives. Secure work for husbands, wives and children could thereby be gained. The adults were better able to look after their children, at least in theory, and their joint earnings were larger than the average.

Natural exaggeration cannot be discounted in the more appalling accounts, and of course the horrors of the workhouse were not visited upon all the children. The dire conditions afflicted the majority, but some escaped them. The more enlightened employers, such as the Arkwrights and Oldknows, for example, tried to mitigate the hardships of the children's condition; schools were established, and special 'apprentice houses' were built; the boys and girls (specially segregated) were sometimes allowed to play in the fields. But this only put a gloss upon their misery. Robert Owen explained in *A New View of Society* (1813) that David Dale of the New Lanark mills paid particular attention to the health, cleanliness and diet of the children in his employ; it was reported that 'the rooms provided for them were spacious, always clean and well ventilated; the food was abundant'. Nevertheless they were employed from six in the morning to seven in the evening, winter and summer; it was observed that 'many of them became dwarfs in body and mind, and some of them were deformed'. It was concluded that the kind intentions of David Dale were 'in their ultimate effect almost nugatory'.

Women as well as children provided the human energy of the Industrial Revolution. They too were considered to be docile, nimble and cheap. They also had to be resourceful in a world where they could be employed among the machinery as well as earning their livings as gun-makers, blacksmiths, pin-makers, armourers, or chimney sweeps. William Hutton travelling through the north country in 1741 noticed, with an attempt at irony, that in some of the factories 'I observed one, or more females, stripped of their upper garment, and not overcharged with their lower, wielding the hammer with all the grace of their sex. The beauties of their face were rather eclipsed by the smut of the anvil . . .'

There is a suggestion of sexual licence here that other observers had already taken up as one of the evils of industrialism. One factory reformer, Michael Sadler, observed: 'I never did hear it denied that many of the mills, at least those in which night work is pursued, are . . . little better than brothels.' A Children's Employment Commission, established a few years later in 1842, reported that the factories were characterized 'by the practice of gross immorality, which is prevalent to a great extent, in both sexes, at very early ages'. Some of the female workers complained that their male colleagues often resorted to drink and other stimulants to counter their fatigue, and in a general atmosphere of heat and monotony the results were inevitable. So the industrial age promoted promiscuity.

The women were particularly sought out, however, for delicate repetitive tasks such as painting on pottery or polishing in the japanning trades. It was thought that they would not 'combine' in the manner of their male colleagues, and would be more tractable in matters of hours and subsistence wages. In the mills and factories, young women in fact comprised the majority of the employees. Women made up the bulk of the textile trade and were most heavily employed in those industries which favoured technical innovation. This relatively new workforce could be exploited more easily, and could be used to bypass traditional rules and work regulations.

One recognizable group of people has been left out of this survey of early industrialism, and they are the industrialists themselves. In these first years they had to be at the same time adventurers, entrepreneurs, salesmen, managers and, if possible, inventors. Some of them had been drapers or shopkeepers, part of that 'middling' class which was even then struggling to find its voice. Others had been apprentices ready to exploit their training. Yet not all of them had to rise entirely by their own efforts; some of the most successful industrialists were of the second generation, with fathers or even grandfathers ahead of them in the trade, But they might also be the sons of farmers, yeomen, gentlemen and physicians. They might acquire their education in dissenting academies, in technical schools, in private schools that specialized in mathematics and geometry, or in the lectures arranged by the learned societies of their neighbourhood. There was also a plethora of technical literature from pamphlets and manuals to encyclopaedias.

Some had been mill-wrights who had constructed and designed machinery. One of the most famous of them, Sir William Fairbairn, recalled that 'a good mill-wright was a man of large resources; he was generally well educated, and could draw out his own designs and work at the lathe; he had a knowledge of mill machinery, pumps and cranes, and could turn his hand to the bench or the forge with equal adroitness and facility'. Such a man could quite easily turn industrialist.

Others had been merchant-manufacturers who saw the value of expanding their trade. Others were by training scientists or engineers eager to put their expertise to practical account; there were few factory managers who were not interested in scientific and technical change. That was the key to their enterprise. Josiah Wedgwood established an 'experimental company' while Matthew Boulton set up a 'research assay office'.

The history of successful industrialists is instructive. William Radcliffe wrote that

> availing myself of the improvements that came out while I was in my teens, by the time I was married [in 1784 at the age of twenty-four] with my little savings and a practical knowledge of every process, from the cotton bag to the piece of cloth, such as carding by hand or by the engine, spinning by the hand-wheel or Jenny, winding, warping, sizing, looming the web, and weaving either by hand or fly-shuttle, I was ready to commence business for myself; and by the year 1789 I was well established and employed many hands both in spinning and weaving, as a master manufacturer.

So a beginner, with the help of a little capital, could progress by degrees to become a master manufacturer. This is the human face of industrial change.

Peter Stubs of Warrington, a master file-maker, was also an innkeeper and brewer when he began his business. There were times when he had difficulty in recruiting youth to his workshops; the mother of Edward Lancelot of Liverpool wrote that 'I hope you will excuse mee for not sending my son. The reason is I ad no shoes.' Yet he prospered, and in various stages of his business career he was selling cast-iron bookcases and glass cylinders as well as potatoes and coconuts. His company still survives and remained in private hands until the 1960s.

Jedediah Strutt of Belper invented a stitching machine known as the 'Derby rib machine' that manufactured ribbed stockings, with which he gathered fame and prosperity. Part of the epitaph he wrote for himself affords a good if idealized description of the eighteenth-century industrialist who 'without having wit had a good share of plain common sense – without much genius enjoyed the more substantial blessing of a sound understanding – with but little personal pride despised a mean or base action . . .'.

Samuel Oldknow of Stockport was the first to manufacture muslin in England. He established an industrial centre, with a steam-powered manufactory, a bleaching plant, finishing factories and warehouses; he also had a zeal for organization, and decided to develop a community of workers on the site. A thousand weavers were employed in the immediate area of the manufactory, while another 1,000 worked in related factories in the same neighbourhood. Another aspect of industrial change can be seen in Oldknow's enterprise; six of his employees eventually set up in industrial business on their own account.

There was almost a religious zeal in this propensity for progress. One merchant, Samuel Salte, told Oldknow, that 'you must both have the perseverance of saints and the resolution of martyrs'. Charity, too, could also be found. One mechanic, Laurence Earnshaw, devised a machine that could spin and reel cotton in one operation; but then he destroyed it for fear that it would take bread from the mouths of the poor.

It is a nice question, however, to determine the actual religion of the industrialists or even of those touched by industry. They were in large part dissenters; very few Anglicans, except for some of the nobles and the great landowners, participated in business. It needed the industry, the self-reliance and the determination of the large body of dissenters to promote industrial change. Since they were forbidden to hold civil or military posts, and were excluded from the English universities, their ambitions were concentrated in other areas. The dissenting academies were in any case fertile ground for young inventors and engineers.

Many of the great iron-masters were Quakers, sturdy, self-reliant and highly conscious of kith and kin; they did not care to marry 'out of the Society' and as a result Quaker dynasties like that of the Darbys were established; the first Abraham Darby came from a family of Quaker locksmiths near Dudley in the west midlands. Thrift and austerity encouraged the accumulation of capital, while prudence and industry directed that capital back into the business. The Quaker network no doubt also led to price-fixing or what might more respectably be called trading agreements.

Methodism was perhaps a more significant force. In all its forms that faith was an intrinsic aspect of industrial change through its missionary activities among the northern working class; they sought through their hymns and sermons to encourage aspiration rather than despair among those who laboured in factories; the pursuit of success was seen as a Christian obligation, while the quest for innovation and self-improvement was the most honest of causes.

Drunkenness, time-wasting, laziness and all the other pre-industrial vices were to be exorcized; as alternatives to misery and its various opiates, the Methodists set up their own communal activities, which afforded a sense of belonging, and of participation, in an industrial world that still seemed alien to most of its workers. That is why hand-loom weavers, in particular, became indoctrinated with Methodism as a way of life rather than of devotion. In the summer of 1784 John Wesley 'found a lovely congregation at Stockport much alive to God'. It was stated as a general rule that 'where there is little trade, there is seldom much increase in religion'. It has been said, therefore, that Methodism was the religious arm of the Industrial Revolution. In the words of one of Charles Wesley's hymns:

> Help us to help each other, Lord,
> Each other's cross to bear,
> Let each his friendly aid afford
> And feel his brother's care.

As a caveat it might be added that a significant number of weary workers, of both sexes, might profess no religion at all. God could not have made the mills.

The iron-masters tended to be assertive and aggressive. They were the first identifiable group of industrialists, some of them coming from agriculture and some from the metal trades. Many of them had names taken from the Old Testament – Shadrach Fox, Nehemiah Lloyd, Job Rawlinson, Joab Parsons, Zephaniah Parker – and they seemed to possess the same primal force. 'The orders I have made', Ambrose Crowley told his managers, 'are built upon such a rock that while I have my understanding it shall be out of the power of Satan and all his disciples to destroy them.' Iron was in their blood. They could be callous and even ruthless but they seemed to take a proprietary interest in what they called 'our men'.

Their employees were obliged to work in conditions that were compared to those of Hades. The furnace, the flames, the smoke, the heat, the white-hot ingots, the whole intricate network of chains and pulleys, are worthy of the graver of Piranesi or Gustave Doré. The glare of the furnaces and the lights of the hearths lit up the nights of the Black Country just as surely as if they had been raked by searchlights. It is perhaps no wonder that Ambrose Crowley invoked the name of Satan.

The case of iron is instructive in another sense. One great innovation changed the nature of the product. By means of 'puddling', a process of melting and stirring invented by Henry Cort in 1783, coke was used to refine pig iron into wrought iron or bar iron. The furnaces became ever larger and the uses of the iron multiplied; it was mined, smelted, refined, rolled into plates and rods. The demand grew for iron chains, iron pipes, iron wheels, iron stoves, iron grates, iron rails, iron mortars, iron nails, iron pots, iron fences, iron pillars, iron buildings, iron ships and iron paving. It was the age of iron. It could be manufactured in apparently unlimited quantities and before long England became the largest iron producer in Europe, providing half of that continent's supply. The iron bridge that spans the Severn in Shropshire was considered to be one of the wonders of the world and the dramatist Charles Dibdin predicted that 'it will apparently be uninjured for ages'. Indeed it still stands.

From the development of the steel industry emerges a similar story of innovation and growth. A clock-maker from Doncaster, Benjamin Huntsman, was the pioneer; in testing the methods for producing finer clock-springs he hit upon a method by which he could maintain the steel at an intense heat in a crucible of clay while its impurities were burned away. It became known as 'Huntsman's crucible' by means of which cast steel was produced in greater and greater quantities. He took out no patent but was determined to keep his secret until he was foiled by a rival manufacturer, Samuel Walker, who on a wintry night disguised himself as a homeless beggar and pleaded to be close to the warmth of the furnace where he could spy with more ease.

In textiles, the glory of England, growth was apparent on all fronts, from silk to wool, from cotton to linen. The clue to improvement was of course the plethora of machines for carding, for combing, for winding, for warping, for weaving, for lapping, for slubbing, and a score of other operations. One improvement led to another, one technical idea promoted another idea. The new inventions were at first only readily applicable to cotton but they soon spread to wool and to linen.

It was a process of what might be called incremental change which was not necessarily written down but worked out in practice by the operatives who passed on their skills by demonstration and word of mouth. Men and women, and even children, learned by doing. This is one of the great engines of the industrial change of the late eighteenth century. The knowledge of skilled workers was of indispensable benefit in the spread of inventiveness, with a pool of young mechanics and apprentices who were eager to learn. It was the practical side of the Industrial Revolution which was perhaps most important. Goethe observed that 'we [Germans] regard discovery and invention as a splendid personally gained possession . . . but the clever Englishman transforms it by patent into real possession'. This may be less than fair on men such as Arkwright and Darby, but it does contain an important truth. The English artisan was well known for his discipline, concentration and urge for practical perfection.

Thus in the manufacture of cotton there were innumerable minor adjustments, and a stream of suggestions, for the better employment of the operatives. At the accession of George III in 1760 3 million pounds of raw cotton were imported; twenty-nine years later the figure had risen to 32.5 million. Cotton goods became cheaper and much more plentiful; as a result some of the problems of human well-being were reduced. Francis Place, the social reformer, noted that the new cottons worked 'all but wonders in the health and cleanliness of women'. It took an Indian hand-spinner approximately 50,000 hours to prepare 100 pounds of cotton, whereas the process on Arkwright's rollers and 'the mule' took 300 hours. The production of cotton moved from the East to the West. The plight of the hand-spinners in India and the hand-loom weavers in England was left out of account, leading ineluctably to their suffering in the nineteenth century.

Two other elements of manufacturing, at this time of change and innovation, deserve notice. A manager at Whitbread's brewery wrote in the spring of 1786 that 'last summer we set up a steam engine for the purposes of grinding our malt and we also raise our liquor [water] with it'; the improvements 'are very great indeed'. The London breweries were soon wholly mechanized, among them the Black Eagle Brewery in Brick Lane, Courage's Brewery by Butler's Wharf, the Anchor Brewery at Southwark and Whitbread's Brewery in Finsbury. The brewers themselves became rich and influential citizens. Some became members of parliament, while others became mayors, justices of the peace and aldermen. They were the aristocrats among London businessmen.

The brewers also invented a new refreshment that helped the wheels of industrial change turn with better grace. In 1722 a brewery in Shoreditch prepared the first mug of 'porter', a black and bitter beer, with more hops than malt, that pleased the palate of Londoners accustomed to strong and sharp flavours. It was cheaper than pale ale, and was the first beer to be suitable for mass production; by the 1760s, the sale of porter accounted for almost a half of the market in beer. London tastes were also gratified by another marvel of mechanics. Canned soup and canned meat were on sale by 1814.

Yet the textile industry was central. The mechanization of wool processing lagged behind that of cotton, but eventually it displaced

the conditions of work at home where women and children managed the sorting, cleaning and spinning while the men concentrated
upon the combing and weaving. The flying shuttle and, eventually,
the spinning jenny and the combing machine took their place.
New urban districts devoted to wool clustered around Leeds, Hud-
dersfield, Bradford and Halifax while the old wool towns of the
south-west dwindled away. These changes were not of course without
consequences of their own, among them the series of events that
became known as the 'Wiltshire Outrages'. Was it just or proper
that a whole way of work, or way of life, should be eliminated? The
new wool factories were seen as themselves great machines bent
upon destroying custom and ancient practice, employing men and
women who did not possess any of the traditional skills or, more
importantly, traditional values. One Norwich wool-comber told his
employers, in the middle of a working dispute: 'We are social creatures and cannot live without each other; and why should you destroy
community?' There was no satisfactory answer.

It was therefore inevitable that 'combinations' of workers should
be established to agitate for better terms and conditions in their
respective trades. The destruction of custom, and the attempt to
repeal apprenticeship, added to the general unrest. The Leicester
Sisterhood of Female Handspinners was established by 18,500
women in 1788, but most of the workers who joined in the first
'trade unions' were skilled male workers in the metal trades anxious
to fight employers who wished to cut their wages or change their
working hours. They were also intent upon forming a 'closed shop'
against the incursion of women, children and other forms of cheap
labour. When the makers of muslin in Glasgow tried to cut down
piece-rates, they were confronted by boycotts and organized resistance. As early as 1726 a parliamentary committee was informed
that the serge weavers had their own club houses 'where none but
weavers are admitted, and that they have their ensigns and flags
hung out at the door of their meetings'.

In 1758 a warrant was issued at the Lancaster Assizes for the
arrest of nineteen senior weavers who were believed to act as
stewards for a combination of several thousand weavers. They had
agreed to collect money 'for supporting such weavers as should by
their committee be ordered to leave their masters and made other

dangerous and illegal regulations: that they had insulted and abused several weavers who had refused to join in their schemes and continued to work, and had dropped an incendiary letter with threats to masters that had opposed their design'. This activity did not only anticipate the machine-breaking of 1802 and the Luddite riots of 1811, but it also can be seen as a harbinger of the professional and organized trade unionism of the nineteenth century. Even in the last decades of the eighteenth century there were attempts at discipline, organization and cohesion among the ranks of the workers.

Their example prevailed in other trades. The journeyman hatters formed what Francis Place called a 'perpetual combination'. Weavers combined in Gloucestershire and Wiltshire, while wool-combers were organized in Leicestershire and Yorkshire. Plumbers, carpenters, shoemakers and house-painters had joined them by the end of the century. The factory system was no doubt the true parent of protest and unrest; it seemed to be large and growing ever larger, creating a new world of penury and exploitation.

The workers were perhaps following the example of their employers since, by the middle of the eighteenth century, the steel manufacturers of Birmingham, the nail-smiths of Gloucester and pin-makers of Nottingham were among the many manufacturers who formed what might be called self-help organizations or, less kindly, price- and wage-fixing rings.

Outbreaks of riot and machine-breaking were common in the eighteenth century. As early as 1719 the striking keelmen of Newcastle upon Tyne were met by a regiment of soldiers and a man-of-war. In 1726 riots and loom-breaking broke out in the West Country, and in 1749 the silk, cotton and iron trades were disrupted by demonstrators. In 1768 Hargreaves's spinning jennies were destroyed by irate workers and, a decade later, Arkwright's machines met a similar fate. The first law to prevent the growth of trade unions, the Combination Act of 1721, banned journeymen tailors from entering into 'combinations to advance their wages to unreasonable prices and lessen their usual hours of work'. The law and the employers got their way, and created the context for more severe Combination Acts at the end of the century. In *The Condition of the Working Class in England in 1844*, Friedrich Engels made the observation that 'the history of the proletariat in England begins with the invention of the steam engine and of machinery for working cotton'.

Engels may have misinterpreted the signs of social change in England, and was clearly mistaken in basing them upon continental models; the British form of industrial protest had none of the proto-socialist shrillness of the agitators in France and Germany. It was more formal, more measured and more pragmatic; it relied to a certain extent upon humour and sarcasm, and was maintained by a deep deference for national institutions.

Yet no doubt something was happening. There was something in the air of the industrial towns and villages that had not been sensed before. An observer, Richard Ayton, going among 'the people of the lower orders in Lancashire', noted in *Voyage round Great Britain* (1813) that they are 'fully aware of the importance of their labour'. He noted also that they were 'rude, coarse and insolent . . . Much vice and profligacy necessarily prevail among them; but while their morals are corrupted the powers of their minds are called forth; they become lawless and unprincipled, but quick, cunning and intelligent.' Was this the new kind of labour that the factory system, and industrial change itself, had elicited?

26

On a darkling plain

The industrial geography of the later eighteenth century was dominated by 'the drift'. It was in large part fuelled by the movement from the rural hinterlands to the industrial areas of the north and the midlands where the demand for labour was most intense. Who would work in the fields for a pittance when they could work in the factories for a living wage? The looms called them. There was no sudden or general migration, from the south-west and the south-east to the north; it was a process that was gradual and incremental. It is true, however, that the readily available labour drifted from neighbouring rural areas to the nearest industrial centre. It was essentially an aggregate of small movements over a restricted area. That is why, over the eighteenth century, furnaces and forges quickly came to a halt when the harvest had to be brought in.

Yet there was slow but significant change. Charles Dibdin in his *Musical Tour* of 1788, noted that 'manufactories that begin about the centre of the kingdom push on to the north – having taken up their residence in Yorkshire – they expand to the east and west; but particularly the west, in a most astonishing way. Thus, from Leeds to Liverpool – through Bradford, Halifax, Rochdale, Manchester, Warrington and Preston – the population is wonderful'.

The metal industries had found their home in the midlands, rivalled by the growing cotton manufactures of Lancashire or

Cheshire and the woollen manufacture in the West Riding of Yorkshire. That was the geography of trade in the broadest possible terms. Lancashire, the West Riding, Staffordshire and Warwickshire (together with Middlesex) were by 1800 the most populous counties in England. The consequence was that the rural areas of Essex, Suffolk, Kent, Surrey, Berkshire and Hampshire became ever more agricultural as all traces of industry vanished.

Special trades flourished in separate small areas. Prescot specialized in watch-parts, Chowbent and Leigh made nails, while Ashton-in-Makerfield manufactured locks and hinges. Staple materials could be found in different regions. Tin and copper were mined in Cornwall; lead was everywhere in the Mendips, but there were large supplies of the same metal in Cumberland and Derbyshire. Salt was the preserve of Cheshire, while slate found its natural home in Cumberland and North Wales. Portland was of course famous for its stone. In the eighteenth century England was a capacious storehouse of natural resources that could be easily exploited, and this in turn promoted industrial progress.

The result was that each region and each town was fundamentally different from its neighbours; some employed more female than male labour, while others were more dependent upon the 'boom or bust' cycle of certain industries. Prices rose and fell according to different variables. Craft industries were shaped by artisan production in manufactories or by the 'putting out' system of domestic labour. When a banker, Mr Oakes of Bury St Edmunds, made a journey to Lancashire on business in 1803, he believed that the county was 'like a different country'. Nothing was familiar or recognizable; even the people seemed different. The simple peasant of Cromford, according to a diarist and traveller, John Byng, had turned into 'an impudent mechanic'. Joseph Healy, a poet who later celebrated the resistance at Peterloo, observed the 'half-burnt cadaverous looking animals' to be found at the Stourbridge glass-works in 1777. This was a new nation.

Why had this social revolution happened in England rather than in France or Austria? It may be related to Defoe's dictum that England had by the early eighteenth century become 'the most flourishing and opulent country in the world'. In France, for example, raw materials were scarce and the possibilities of investment few;

the traditions of the country also favoured small-scale enterprise in a manner which the larger farmers of England soon abandoned. In England, too, there was virtually no state or bureaucratic control to guide the process of change; instead, by a series of statutes, the administration actively assisted those who were willing to break up the customary traditions of industry and manufacture. The decay of 'custom', as it was known, really meant the end of the old order. Popular traditions were denounced as immoral and popular beliefs were derided as superstition; the familiar perks of the daily job, such as the odd piece of cloth or metal, were now considered to be theft.

The history of patents, as we have seen, exemplifies a prolonged period of inventiveness and ingenuity in the later part of the eighteenth century which may be related to the natural pragmatism and practicality of the English. Science and manufacture were closely aligned in the period, with institutions such as the Lunar Society bringing together manufacturers and experimentalists. From their collaboration came much of the machinery of change. The individual entrepreneur was also free to assert himself, with the spirit of competition and acquisitiveness all around him. Contemporaries noted in fact that the English, of all people, were possessed by the spirit of gain and were characterized by aggression and ruthlessness in its pursuit. All things worked together.

The industrial towns represented some of the most evident signs of the new order. Some of them, Wigan, Bolton and Preston among them, were known as mill towns. They were anomalies. They had no corporate structure for the most part, and were singularly free of churches and hospitals. They were just planted when industrial conditions were suitable and to a certain extent resembled the towns of the 'gold rush' of 1849 in California. The lead mills of Sheffield provoked one visitor to note that the houses were 'dark and black, occasioned by the continual smoke of the forges'. It was written of Barnsley, known as 'Black Barnsley', that 'the very town looks as black and smoky as they were all smiths that lived in it'. From Rochdale to Wigan, from Bury to Preston, the dark stain grew and grew. In 1753 Bolton was little more than a village with one street of thatched houses and gardens; twenty years later its population had risen to 5,000; within a further sixteen years it had risen to 12,000 and by the beginning of the nineteenth century to 17,000.

The dwellings of the manufacturing towns were largely back-to-backs with one room on each floor; it was common for the houses to be occupied by more than one family, and many residents dwelled in the cellar which consisted of two rooms under the ground with a small window in the ceiling. Since there was no administrative control of the building trades, the houses were generally narrow, dark and unhealthy. Even the once-affluent dwellings had degenerated into slums, and workshops were built over the gardens. This was a world of small courts, alleys and tenements, generally with one outside privy for four families. The new streets, so quickly knocked up, were without drains, pavements, or public lighting. Everything seemed temporary, makeshift, haphazard, testifying to the distress and uncertainty of this new world of work.

A medical report, compiled in 1793 by Doctor Ferriar for a police committee in Manchester, states that 'in some parts of the town the cellars are so damp that they are unfit for habitation . . . Fever is the usual effect.' Large masses of people were streaming towards specific areas of cheap and dangerous housing. In Lancashire many thousands of cottages were built, between the late eighteenth and early nineteenth centuries, to accommodate a labour force of some 170,000 people. This was a measure of the change from what had once been a predominantly agricultural region. Ferriar also reports that 'a lodger fresh from the country often lies down in a bed filled with infection by its last tenant, or from which the corpse of a victim to fever has only been removed a few hours before'.

Harsh conditions, however, may serve to bring people together. Over time the residents of what were once little more than shanty towns developed a strong sense of community, in some sense equivalent to the 'combinations' of the industrial workers and others. People sought out their kin, and also others who had originally come from the same rural neighbourhoods. Neighbours themselves were the first line of defence against sickness and unemployment; there was no benevolent state to assist them.

In 1807 the poet Robert Southey visited Birmingham:

A heavy cloud of smoke hung over the city . . . the contagions spread far and wide. Everywhere around us . . . the tower of some manufactory was seen at a distance, vomiting up flames

and smoke, and blasting every thing around with its metallic
vapours. The vicinity was as thickly peopled as that of London
. . . Such swarms of children I never beheld in any other place,
nor such wretched ones.

The city expanded at an enormous rate, year by year, and an observer
wrote that 'the traveller who visits her [Birmingham] once in six
months supposes himself well acquainted with her; but he may
chance to find a street of houses in the autumn, where he saw his
horse eat grass in the spring'.

Mr Pickwick in the course of his perambulations took in this
'great working town' with all 'the sights and sounds of earnest
occupation', where 'the streets were thronged with working people.
The hum of labour resounded from every house, lights gleamed
from the long casement windows in the attick storeys; and the whirl
of wheels and noise of machinery shook the trembling walls.' This
was not the harsh music of London with which Dickens was familiar;
this was more intense, and more concentrated. These were streets
filled with 'working people', not with the motley London citizenry
in all its variety. You would not find here the dandies or the actors
or the 'shabby-genteel' or the madwomen who appear in Dickens's
novels; these had all been elbowed aside in the rush for work and
trade.

Birmingham had become the toy shop of the world, when a
'toy-maker' was a manufacturer of buckles, trinkets, small arms,
locks, buttons, tweezers, snuffboxes and a multitude of other small
metal goods. Hundreds of workshops were locked in a cycle of
manufacture whereby various small parts of each device were cast
eventually to form a whole, a sprocket-wheel here and a strap there.
The guns were passed from shop to shop in the course of their
construction, and were handled by specialized operatives at every
stage of the procedure. This was what was generally perceived to
be the real Industrial Revolution. Matthew Boulton's Soho works
were 2 miles from the centre of the town, with his thousand workers
providing the fuel that fed the flame of commerce. By 1775
Birmingham was the largest industrial centre outside the capital.
The rolling mill and the rotary steam engine were the future.

The people of Birmingham had dirty faces and no names,

according to one contemporary, but some of them at least were fired by an enthusiasm for making. William Hutton, the first proper historian of the city, wrote in 1741 that 'I was surprised at the place but more so at the people. They possessed a vivacity I had never beheld. I had been among dreamers, but now I saw men awake. Their very step along the streets showed alacrity. Every man seemed to know and prosecute his own affairs.' So the disparate reports conjure up images of energy, determination, eagerness, industry. It may have been the air of Birmingham, therefore, that created the conditions for the emergence of dissent and radicalism as the two significant elements of city life. Dissenters played a large part in the corporate life of the town and the Lunar Society, with its fair share of free-thinkers and dissenters, was established in Birmingham. They represented the richer citizens who funded a town hall, a corn exchange, a theatre and a new market hall as well as the 'improvements' of New Street. Of course it was unwise to ignore the sheer determination and contrariness of what was known as 'the bunting, beggarly, brass-making, brazen-faced, brazen-hearted, blackguard, bustling, booby Birmingham mob'. Soon enough they would take their revenge upon some of the dissenting elite in the town.

Manchester also arose in the time of industrial change. Robert Southey again deplored the conditions of the people who were fed into the machine, whose 'health physical and moral alike is destroyed; they die of diseases induced by unremitting task work, by confinement in the impure atmosphere of crowded rooms'. A foreign contemporary observed that there was no sun in Manchester; only a dense cloud of smoke that covered the bright orb. The only light came from Vulcan, the god of fire and of metal-working, and from his monstrous furnaces.

Its major trade was in cloth, and, in particular, cotton, but it contained twelve iron foundries as well as numerous tin-plate workers, braziers and lock-makers. It was, in other words, a prodigious industrial town. A rapid increase in new housing occurred in the 1770s, and within ten years more than a third of all new dwellings had been erected. Such was the demand that many of the houses were occupied even before they were finished.

The new streets were narrow and badly lit, if they were lit at all; the land was so valuable that courts and lanes and alleys were crowded together at the expense of light and air. In a city of almost 100,000 people, at the beginning of the nineteenth century, there was not a single public garden. This is what was meant by the truism that England had changed from a rural to an urban civilization. Joseph Kay, a barrister, was at a slightly later date delivering a speech to the Manchester Statistical Society in the course of which he stated that 'in no former era and under no former phase of national life has anything at all similar been witnessed'. This was true enough. The impact of Manchester upon political and economic life would be immense.

Other cities had other histories. Newcastle upon Tyne was of course dominated by its coal trade, and the deliveries of its ships kept the hearths of London burning with what was known as 'sea coal'; the cheap fuel encouraged the growth of brewing, dyeing, glass-making and soap-making. It was the fourth largest town in England and as such dominated the economic and social life of the north-east. It was also a centre of printing, and in the eighteenth century published more books than any other city except London. It supported three newspapers, three circulating libraries and seven subscription libraries. The men of business took a keen interest in public affairs, and it has been estimated that there were more than fifty clubs of Whig or radical tendency. This is the other face of the industrial change, when the men of wealth and influence no longer necessarily took the side of established power and authority.

An American businessman, Louis Simond, approached Leeds at night, and saw a quintessential industrial nightscape where 'from a height, north of the town, we saw a multitude of fires issuing, no doubt, from furnaces, and constellations of illuminated windows (manufactories) spread over the dark plain'. In more placid style John Dyer, in 'The Fleece' (1757), noted the growth of 'busy Leeds' where:

> Some, with even line,
> New streets are marking in the neighb'ring fields.

The most evocative literary description of an industrial town comes later in Charles Dickens's *Hard Times*, where his love of darkness and decay, of stunning contrasts and of reality touched by stage fire, found its true subject. 'It was a town of red brick, or of brick that would have been red if the smoke and ashes had allowed it; but, as matters stood, it was a town of unnatural red and black like the painted face of a savage.' The horrid vista is presumably based upon Preston, which Dickens had just visited, but it could be an emblem of any mill town of the period.

Amid this gloom and blackness and soot and grime, however theatrically elaborated by Dickens into a vision of hell, there was much industrial misery. The factory system often represented a sentence of death. In addition the industrial towns had many paupers, debarred from work by sickness and injury, who huddled together in the poorest districts. Even the labourers still in employ were often in some way deformed with swollen limbs or unsteady legs.

Yet this picture of unrelieved misery, so much emphasized by social historians of the twentieth century, is incomplete. Could a country be racked by manifold suffering on such a scale without visible revolt? Other developments must be cast in the opposite scale. By the early years of the nineteenth century industrial wages were keeping pace with the cost of living, and industrial change itself was providing the necessities of the labouring classes. Cottons and woollens, food and drink, were now more amply distributed, and it was believed that the diet of the workers had greatly improved. Wheat replaced rye, and meat became a staple dish. Cheaper and better-distributed coal provided heat for the hearth. The rise in family earnings and the greater regularity of pay in the industrial districts were also not insignificant benefits. In 1830 Macaulay observed that 'the laboring classes of this island . . . are on the whole better off as to physical comforts than the inhabitants of any equally extensive district of the old world . . . The serving man, the artisan and the husbandman, have a more copious and palatable supply of food, better clothing and better furniture.' But of course, as a result, examples of comparative suffering and real poverty were 'more acutely felt and more loudly bewailed here than elsewhere'.

The industrial system itself led to manifest improvements. The employment of female workers gradually helped to establish the social and economic independence of women, while the scandal of child labour provoked such outrage that it promoted attempts at some form of primary education by charitable institutions; the 'ragged schools' began their long life in 1818, while the charity schools of Andrew Bell and Joseph Lancaster had already created 'the steam engine of the moral world'. The combinations of the workers led in turn to friendly societies, savings banks, mechanics' institutes and of course trade unions. The ills of life were to be remedied rather than endured.

Long and complex arguments have been made ever since about the relative rise or fall of the 'standard of living'. Since the measure or index of such an impalpable entity seems to vary with each debate, it becomes a nice question. It is not practicable, for example, to compare a modest rise in wage rates with the manifestly unhealthy and even mortal conditions of the new cities. Does the spread of cholera balance the lower cost of bread? Cheaper clothing cannot compensate for overcrowding. Yet one statistical measurement may be granted without much objection. The average height of the population deteriorated in the second half of the eighteenth century, and continued to decline through the first half of the next century. This was most obvious of course in the vast difference between the poor and the rest of the population; agricultural distress and industrial decline in certain areas led to a class of people living in what Charles Booth later called 'chronic want'.

The worst cases of economic failure must be set against evidence of falling mortality. The absence of epidemic plague and the increased attention to sanitation and hygiene may help to explain the improvement, and one influential London physician, Doctor Lettsom, remarked that the people 'have learnt that most diseases are mitigated by a free admission of air, by cleanliness, and by promoting instead of restraining the indulgence and care of the sick'. Not everyone cared for the new methods. In 1768 a hospital for inoculation was burnt down by a mob in Peterborough.

The number of infants who died shortly after birth in the British Lying-in Hospital, in Holborn, fell from 1 in 15 in the 1750s to 1 in 118 by the turn of the century. In the course of his travels in the 1770s John Wesley observed the crowds of young children that seemed to populate the towns and villages. In 1726 life expectancy was put at a meagre twenty-five years; by the 1820s it had risen to forty-one years. The length of life, however, remained very low in the newly industrialized cities.

It is perhaps impossible, therefore, to gauge the general effects of industrial change in the eighteenth century. It represents a complex of so many particular forces and events that it might best be treated as a natural phenomenon with all the random and inexplicable details that surround such an event. Yet some tentative conclusions may be advanced. The people, according to Thomas Hardy, now served smoke and fire rather than frost and sun. They became accustomed to the machine and to the clock; they worked for a wage rather than for subsistence, and they had no essential stake in the objects they produced. The nature of the family and household was wholly changed.

England was no longer predominantly an agricultural society, a state in which it had remained for approximately 10,000 years. It was no longer plausible to propound a natural hierarchy of power based upon land; the twin imperatives of custom and deference began to disappear. The powers of patronage began subtly to change as the 'middling classes' aspired to more political and economic power. The abolition of the laws of apprenticeship, and of the assize of bread where that commodity was granted a 'fair' price, marked the onset of an economy that was based upon competition and self-interest.

That was why the labouring masses, the working people, soon became a class apart. It was considered as impossible to mix the higher and lower classes as to mingle oil and water. One employer, quoted by Arnold Toynbee in his lectures on the Industrial Revolution, stated that 'there can be no union between employer and employed, because it is in the interest of the employer to get as much work as he can, done for the smallest sum possible'.

The professional artisan, too, began to separate himself from manual labour and from too close an involvement with the working men; in the previous dispensation a metal manufacturer might spend the day with his employees, superintending and assisting them, but that collaboration was now coming to an end. Samuel Courtauld was considering a career in engraving at his family's silk mill but his father told him that 'you seem to forget that mere manual labour – though of the higher class – is very rarely indeed so valuable as a business – as those modes of trade or manufacture which allow us a profit from the labour of many persons'.

The practitioners of 'mere manual labour' were now moving

towards the more backward parts of the town where they were segregated from their 'betters'. The business of trade, which had always been conducted as close as possible to the street – the gloves that Shakespeare's father made were on show at the front window – were now relegated to a back room while the front quarters were for sleeping and eating.

The same changes were taking place in the world of agriculture. Small farms disappeared, and large enclosed farms became the standard for excellence. The small farmer gave way to the great agriculturalist who was the rural equivalent of the master manufacturer; he was already accruing vast profits from the easy availability of food. The labourer had once been part of the farmer's household, eating at the same table, but that contiguity had ended. One labourer complained, according to Arnold Toynbee, that 'the farmers take no more notice of us than if we were dumb beasts; they let us eat our crust by the ditch side'. The farm labourers themselves were now housed in a species of barracks.

This division between the ranks of society might have perilous consequences. By dint of schooling, even of the most elementary kind, the younger workers were becoming more literate and therefore less ignorant of the wider ways of the world. They were less abject and less easily led or cowed. New men might have new ideas. From the period of the 'combinations', for example, we may date the early organization of workers in a common cause, a movement that led to the emergence of Chartism in the late 1830s. The ties between the ranks or classes of society had been broken, provoking ambition, restlessness, or confusion.

It has been suggested that in the late eighteenth and early nineteenth centuries crime rose at an unanticipated rate, particularly in the newly urbanized and manufacturing regions. It had become necessary to supervise the people in a stricter and more organized fashion. In 1792 the creation of the London Police Magistrates initiated a trend for stipendiary magistrates in other urban regions. For most of the eighteenth century prisons were simply large and verminous dungeons where a variety of criminals was promiscuously held, so that by 1789 the prison reformer, John Howard, was suggesting the innovative model of 'regular steady discipline in a penitentiary house'; he was advocating the modern form of prison, in other words, which can also be seen as one of the fruits of the Industrial Revolution.

The laments came in many forms. Some decried the changes in the landscape, where the mills had risen in the valleys and the great rocks were cut for limestone. The earth, in the striking phrase of John Britton, 'is covered and loaded with its own entrails'. William Blake saw into the heart of the new dispensation and correctly estimated its consequences.

All the arts of life they chang'd into the arts of death . . .
And in their stead, intricate wheels invented, wheel without wheel,
To perplex youth in their outgoings, & to bind to labours
Of day & night the myriads of Eternity, that they might file
And polish brass & iron hour after hour, laborious workmanship,
Kept ignorant of the use: that they might spend the days of wisdom
In sorrowful drudgery, to obtain a scanty pittance of bread.

The literary complains were taken up by popular songs and street ballads, as in one poem composed by Joseph Mather against master cutler Watkinson who counted thirteen knives as a dozen when he paid his men:

That monster oppression behold how he stalks
Keeps picking the bones of the poor as he walks . . .

In an anonymous and powerful ballad, 'The Complaint of a Kidderminster Weaver's Wife to her Infant', the master manufacturers are called 'murderers', 'tyrants' and 'oppressors':

Hush thee, my babe! thy feeble cry
Tells me that thou ere long wilt die:
I'm glad thou hast not liv'd to curse
Our cruel masters. That were worse.

The movement of Romanticism might itself be interpreted in one of its aspects as an assault upon, or retreat from, the new industrial age. In the eighth book of 'The Excursion' William Wordsworth is astonished by the fact of a 'huge town' emerging 'where not a habitation stood before'. One of his editors cites the case of Middlesbrough, which in 1830 was no more than a farmhouse by the bank of the Tees and which fifty years later was a town of more than 50,000 inhabitants:

> O'er which the smoke of unremitting fires
> Hangs permanent, and plentiful as wreaths
> Of vapour glittering in the morning sun.

As so often in his work Wordsworth is equivocal, refusing to give judgement. In a subliminal way he seems to enjoy the experience of industrialism even as he denounces it.

The 1760s and 1770s became known as 'the age of sentiment' guided by 'the sentimental muse'; it was a time of high feeling and moral sensibility which can be seen as an alternative to the harsh and unremitting world of industry and manufacture. What was natural; what was free; what was spontaneous and governed by the heart. Such were the themes of Robert Blair's *The Grave* of 1743 and Edward Young's *Night Thoughts* of 1745. These were the precepts of a movement that excluded from view the mills and the chimneys. Since *The Grave* and *Night Thoughts* were established upon artifice and false nostalgia, they could not endure as the poems of the 'Romantic age' managed to do.

There was as much or more to be said for the art, rather than the poetry, of the Industrial Revolution. If you could surpass nature, as some of the industrialists had done, it should be possible to reach the sublime in another sphere. The industrial landscapes of John Martin are filled with fulminating life as if the energies of the earth had finally been manifested in flame, smoke and fiery blaze. He was in particular inspired by the spectacle of the Black Country than which, as Martin's son said, 'he could not imagine anything more terrible, even in the regions of everlasting punishment. All he had done, or attempted in ideal painting, fell far short, fell very far short of the fearful sublimity of effect when the Furnace could be seen in full blaze in the depth of night.' This was the painting of magnificence and chiaroscuro. His canvases seem to roar, whether in rage or in defiance. He drew upon Egyptian, Oriental and Greek imagery to conjure up visions of sublimity and terror, where the unfamiliar landscape of caves, ruins and pyramids whispered of ancient powers now once more unleashed upon the earth. Another Cyclops might walk among the mills and manufactories. In mezzotint he scraped away blackness to create form.

A more gentle sensibility had also come to life. When a professional architect, John Wood, listed the pleasures of industrial change he mentioned deal floors covered with carpets, marble rather than stone hearths, mirrors and trinkets in the 'Chinese' or 'Oriental' manner, walnut and mahogany furniture. He was concerned in other words with the material stuff of life that had been improved by the age of the machine. 'I went to see the beautiful manufacture of silk, carried on by Mr Fulton and Son', William Cobbett, no avid champion of industrialism, wrote. 'I never like to see the machines, lest I should be tempted to endeavour to understand them . . . as in the case of the sun and the moon and the stars, I am quite satisfied with witnessing the effects.' He wrote these words as late as 1833, at a time when it would have been hard to believe that England was indebted for her success and prosperity to Arkwright and Watt rather than to Nelson and Wellington.

27

Fire and moonlight

Science and industry were the twin horses of the eighteenth-century apocalypse. Even as parts of the landscape were altered by iron-works and manufactories, so itinerant 'experimentalists' or 'natural philosophers' would tour the larger towns and houses with their compendia of wonders. In taverns, in coffee-shops and in the houses of the wealthy, they would bring out their alembics, their orreries, their lunaria and their electrical machines in order to elucidate the workings of the universe to a largely uninstructed audience. They were the conjurors of the eighteenth century. It was the first public phase of the scientific revolution.

It needed, perhaps, the genius of an artist to see it clearly. Joseph Wright was born in Derby, in 1734, just thirteen years after the first fully mechanized factory was erected in the vicinity. Lombe's Mill has already entered these pages as one of the wonders of the new age, and it soon became an object of pilgrimage for those who wished to view the new engines of power. Since much of Wright's subsequent work is devoted to the manifestations of industry, we may fairly guess that he was one of its admirers.

This is the context in which to set one of Wright's most cele-brated paintings, *An Experiment on a Bird in an Air Pump* (1768). A travelling experimenter, with a magus-like flourish, has set up an air pump for the delectation of the members of a wealthy family (perhaps of merchant stock from the midlands); in the glass dome of its receiver a white cockatoo is clearly struggling for life and breath as the air is drawn off. Two small girls can barely look while their father reassures them; another well-dressed man is timing the action with a watch while in the background a young couple are looking into each other's eyes rather than at the experiment on the beleaguered bird. An older man, sitting in the foreground, contemplates a glass vessel containing what seems to be a pair of human lungs.

The magus or scientist stares out of the painting with a wild look and an expansive gesture of his arms as if to welcome the spectator to a new world. It is not at all clear whether the bird is to live or die, and this dramatic tableau does nothing to resolve the matter. It is a moment of maximum intensity, conveyed by the chiaroscuro that models the human figures. Joseph Priestley, a member of the Lunar Society and well known to Wright, argued in a public lecture at Warrington that 'real history resembles experiments by the air pump, condensing engine and electrical machine which exhibit the operation of nature and the God of nature himself'. It is not clear, however, whether this is a study in the inevitability of death or, if the stopcock is released, in the blessings of God's air. Wright himself suffered from severe asthma, perhaps as a result of nervous melancholia, and his condition lends significance to the pair of human lungs under glass. The despair of his desire for air, and the rapture of relief, give the painting its air of intensity and foreboding.

The air pump of the painting is, however, a curious anomaly. Its design is taken from Sir Robert Boyle's early 'pneumatic engines' first used by him in the late 1650s. By the time of the painting's composition the glass receiver had been replaced by a leather 'plate' on which a bell-jar rested. But Wright retained the then anachronistic glass globe. It was for him an emblem more important than the claims of scientific accuracy. The empty globe, the bubble, was in his period a profound symbol of transitoriness and deceit. Glass balls, empty globes and soap bubbles were the familiar language of *vanitas* painting. That is why Wright felt moved to create a hybrid machine, with the double-barrelled pumping mechanism of the eighteenth century and the glass globe in use a century before. Pictorial, scientific and religious connotations reinforce one another.

We may put as its companion piece another painting, completed two years before, *A Philosopher Giving that Lecture on the Orrery, in which a Lamp Is Put in the Place of the Sun*, where another travelling lecturer is demonstrating the mechanical contrivance used to mark the movements of the sun and the planets. A concealed light casts illumination on the faces of the principal spectators while leaving the room in darkness; the spherical bands of the scientific instrument are viewed in all their internal geometry, while the intent faces gazing at the experiment are like planets caught in the radiance of a fleeting sun. It is one of the most arresting depictions of the light of knowledge, and the fire of invention, that came from the mid-eighteenth century.

A subsequent series of five paintings from the early 1770s, including *A Blacksmith's Shop* and *An Iron Forge Viewed from Without*, have been classified as 'night pieces' largely as a consequence of Wright's continued employment of chiaroscuro to celebrate the quality of light. But they might easily qualify as industrial pieces because of the intensity of their focus on industrial labour and industriousness itself. Servitude to work is now celebrated as a spark of the divine.

In *An Iron Forge Viewed from Without* Wright paints the new machinery of the ironworks in the light of the eighteenth-century sublime. The iron worker may be seen as a modern Vulcan, the god of fire who was often portrayed with a smith's hammer; the white-hot ingot, created in a shed or manger-like structure, can be seen as an image of the Christ Child or Robert Southwell's 'The Burning Babe' in the paintings of the Nativity. The light is holy. We may take as its text some words from William Beckford's *Fragments of an English Tour*, published in 1779. 'The hollow wind in the woods mixing with the rushing of waters, whilst the forges thundered in my ear. To the left, a black quaking bridge leading to other wilds. Within, a glowing furnace, machines hammering huge bars of red-hot iron, which at intervals cast a bright light and innumerable sparks through the gloom.' The tone and sentiment of early nineteenth-century Romanticism are beginning to emerge. It had an early apotheosis in France.

28

The red bonnet

In the summer of 1788 the political order seemed secure. The first
minister, William Pitt, had the full confidence of George III, and
their congenial partnership promised a long period of stability. In
the phrase of the time Pitt was 'the king's friend'. He had cause to
be. He had helped to mend the finances of the administration by
producing budget surpluses and cutting the national debt; he reduced
smuggling, and managed to raise the revenues. He repaired the fleet
and, by means of a triple alliance with Holland and Prussia, he
restored the country's standing in Europe and elsewhere. When
Spain attempted to seize British trading vessels off the western coast
of Canada, she was forced to yield and return the ships; her ally,
France, had been in no position to help her. So England was known
for her domination of the sea.

Yet in the autumn of the year all was changed. There was
something wrong with the king. Pitt received a note from the king's
physician that his patient was in a state 'nearly bordering on delirium'.
He had always spoken rapidly and with decision, but now he became
chattering and incoherent. It is widely accepted that his were the
symptoms of porphyria, which is not a sign of madness or mental
disorder but rather a physical condition that affects the toxins of
the nervous system and thus the brain. It is believed that he had
inherited the condition by indirect means from the Stuart line. It

might be called the royal disease. None of this was known at the time, of course, and the king had all the appearance of a howling lunatic.

The dilemma was for Pitt acute. It was not a situation any first minister had ever been forced to confront. The king was completely incapacitated, and his future sanity in doubt; the prince of Wales would be his successor, but the prince was on very bad terms both with the king and with the king's ministers. The prince was, in addition, close to Fox and to the Whig cause. He was Pitt's worst enemy. It was in Pitt's interests therefore, to postpone any regency for as long as he could. He believed that the security and peace of the country would otherwise be jeopardized.

He presented his proposals to Prince George on 30 December. The regent would be granted no powers to create peers or to bestow places for life; the regent would have no share in managing the king's estate; the queen would be responsible for all household matters. The prince was not impressed. He had in effect been deprived of any powers of patronage, which was the lifeblood of rule.

He was too eager for his own good; he insulted his father and quarrelled with his mother, all the time anticipating with infinite satisfaction his acquisition of the throne. His supporters were no less indiscreet. Fox in particular declared that the prince had an inherent right to become monarch, thus contradicting or disowning his Whig preference for parliamentary privilege. Pitt was heard to say that he would 'unwhig' Fox for life. Fox then peremptorily removed himself to Bath, where he was treated for dysentery. His fellow Whig, Edmund Burke, was no more subtle or restrained; he dilated on the problems of insanity, and the possibility of a relapse. When he stated that he 'had visited the dreadful mansions where the insane are confined', even some of his party were horrified at his presumption and lack of tact.

Prince George was not himself a model of royal deportment. His life had been guided by pleasure rather than by principle and his politics were fashioned on the basis of convivial companions rather than settled convictions. He was accused, justifiably, of greed and drunkenness, compounded by gambling and sexual profligacy. It was also widely believed that he had contracted a forbidden marriage with Maria Fitzherbert, a Roman Catholic; she was a woman of some charm and authority so that, in the phrase of the time, she was a 'whapper'. But as a Catholic she was not eligible to be the prince's wife, and so she became the cause of lies and prevarications and ambiguities that did nothing to recommend the prince to the public. Prince George himself seemed to forget about the clandestine marriage and soon attached himself to Caroline of Brunswick, this time his wife by legal marriage, but with equally disastrous consequences.

Pitt put himself forward as the champion of George III and of constitutional monarchy, a position all the more satisfying as it became evident that the king was beginning slowly to recover his mental powers. Pitt's decision to delay any sudden intervention by the prince or his supporters now proved eminently successful; by the time a Regency Bill was about to pass, the king's recovery was declared by his doctors to be complete. The vessel, as contemporaries said, had righted itself. On 23 February 1789 the king, in full possession of his wits, wrote: 'I am anxious to see Mr Pitt any hour that may suit him tomorrow morning, as his constant attachment to my interest and that of the public, which are inseparable, must ever place him in the most advantageous light.' The illuminations and bonfires, on the news of the king's return to health, stretched from Hampstead to Kensington. Pitt himself was also the hero of the hour. The king's son, however, was now lampooned for his heartlessness and ambition. The opposition Whigs were believed, at the very least, to have wanted judgement. The reign of Prince George was postponed for thirty-one years.

The king's disorder was prognostic of a great convulsion in the European order. In the early summer of 1789 a commotion troubled France. The country was almost bankrupt as a result of its support for the American insurgents, and a series of bad harvests and freezing weather brought low its population. The English already had the upper hand in commerce as a result of their naval supremacy. There seemed to be no other place for the French to turn, except to some general reformation.

At a meeting of the States General at Versailles the commons, or third estate, prevailed over the nobility and the clergy; in the middle of June the deputies declared themselves to be the National

Assembly. Louis XVI announced that their meetings were suspended, whereupon they assembled at an indoor tennis court nearby where they swore a solemn oath that they would remain in permanent session 'until the constitution of the kingdom is established'. 'We are here by the power of the people', the comte de Mirabeau stated, 'and nothing but the power of bayonets shall drive us away.' This was the defiance that inspired many of those who would become revolutionaries in the months that followed; the National Assembly represented the people, and the people were supreme. Patriotic societies and revolutionary clubs flourished in Paris and elsewhere.

On 14 July the citizens, with the help of the French guards, stormed and captured the Bastille; the head of its governor was carried in celebration through the streets. The crowd had triumphed, and the old regime could not survive the combined will of a populace intent upon change. Another lamentable harvest created the conditions of famine in the capital, and the people were lean and hungry; they were dangerous. It was said that a fourth of the population had been driven to sell everything they owned in order to buy bread, and so a desperate people sought for revenge as well as sustenance. The tax collectors of the state and the seigneurial courts were the villains of the day who were subject to very rough justice. The conditions in the rest of the country were no better. There were continual outbreaks of violence and insurrection. Several French cities followed the example of Paris, and in the surrounding countryside the peasants armed themselves against their former masters.

The king had sensed the overwhelming necessity of change and, in an attempt to placate his subjects, put on the tricoloured cockade and pledged to help in the formation of a new government. Yet it was rumoured that his protestations were not sincere; it was suspected that all the while he was plotting to overthrow the new order and its 'liberty'. Liberty was the keyword; it could be uttered in support of violence and of murder. It was born in flames. Yet it also had a more benign aspect. In August the newly composed National Assembly issued a 'declaration of the rights of man', the first three provisions of which determined that men 'are born and remain free and equal in rights' and that these rights included 'liberty, property, security and resistance to oppression'; the third article confirmed that 'the principle of all sovereignty resides essentially in the nation', and not in any single person.

On 5 October many thousands of men and women armed themselves and assembled with the cry 'To Versailles!' The citizen militia joined them in attacking the royal palace, at the conclusion of which Louis and the royal family were taken in triumph to Paris. The heads of many of the king's supporters, impaled on pikes, decorated the path to the city where the king was once more obliged to accede to a new constitution. The ties of history and tradition had been cut through; the sanctions of custom and time were abandoned. This was an ideology based upon rational principle, the reification of 'the people' and a fervent devotion to '*la patrie*' or the fatherland. The clergy were now aliens, and the nobles beyond help; any aristocrats who wished to survive became leaders of the citizens or the citizen militia. It was a new order governed by a commitment to ideals, no less potent for being wholly vague; a vision of reality became more important than the reality itself, and the twin shibboleths of liberty and equality left power in the hands of those who were most ruthless and most determined. Only the perceived will of the nation now mattered.

The news of the events in France astonished the English, who had not anticipated the virtual collapse of the monarchy and the insurgency of the people. Some viewed the events with suspicion and alarm, but many welcomed the apparent defeat of despotism and the restoration of liberty. It was thought to resemble the 'Glorious Revolution' of 1688 when the Stuart king, James II, was deposed. It was also widely believed that the French would be too distracted by inner turmoil to pose any threat to English interests and English commerce.

William Pitt remained cautious and maintained a policy of cool neutrality; he wanted peace at all costs in order to sustain prosperity and to curb government expenditure. Bishop Porteous recorded in his diary for July 1789 that 'This day Mr Pitt dined with me in Fulham. He had just received news of the French Revolution and spoke of it as an event highly favourable to us and indicates a long peace with France. It was a very pleasant day.' Pitt himself remarked that 'our neighbours in France seem coming to actual extremes', a situation which rendered 'that country an object of compassion even to a rival'. So there was an element of self-satisfaction in the face of the tumult across the Channel.

Charles James Fox, ever the libertarian and for the time being bearer of the Whig standard, reacted very differently. He declared: 'How much the greatest event it is that ever happened in the world, and how much the best!' He confirmed his joy when he stated in the Commons that the new constitution of France was 'the most stupendous and glorious edifice of liberty'. Nothing was to be feared from this newly free country; it would do no more than spread liberty. His enthusiasm was largely shared by the dissenters and nonconformists of England who believed that the king, courtiers and clergy of France were little better than limbs of the devil.

In the *New Annual Register* for 1789 William Godwin wrote that 'from hence we are to date a long series of years, in which France and the whole human race are to enter into possession of their liberties'. William Blake composed 'A Song of Liberty' to conclude *The Marriage of Heaven and Hell* (1790–3): 'Look up! look up! O citizen of London, enlarge thy countenance! . . . Spurning the clouds written with curses, stamps the stony law to dust, loosing the eternal horses from the dens of night, crying: *Empire is no more! and now the lion & wolf shall cease.*' In those days, as Lord Cockburn recalled, 'everything, not this thing or that thing, but literally everything, was soaked in this one event'. The consequences for England itself could not be anticipated in anything but the most general and over-optimistic terms. It was not clear even to the far-sighted, for example, that the revolution would engage the nation in a war that would last a generation, and would fundamentally change the state of domestic politics. France itself passed from monarchy to represent-ative democracy, from arbitrary dictatorship in the name of the people to the basic components of a military state.

The exhilaration survived for a few months yet. On 9 November 1789, a number of politicians met at the London Tavern under the name of 'The Revolution Society' where they drew up a congratu-latory address to the National Assembly in Paris with the hope that the late events might 'encourage other nations to assert the inalien-able rights of mankind, and thereby introduce a general reformation in the governments of Europe'. There were of course many who did not share these sentiments, and considered them to be pernicious talk of reform for reform's sake; such sceptics believed that the ancient constitution of England, albeit unwritten, was a greater stay against the dark.

This was the intuitive reaction of Edmund Burke, the Whig statesman who had become more and more alarmed by the revolutionary sentiments of such colleagues as Fox and Sheridan who outbid each other in their fervour for the new order in France. Burke had at first been uncertain. In a letter of 9 August 1789, he described 'England gazing with astonishment at a French struggle for Liberty and not knowing whether to blame or applaud!' But in February 1790, he disparaged in the chamber of the Commons 'the spirit of innovation' as one 'well calculated to overturn states, but perfectly unfit to amend them'. This was followed in the same year by a treatise, *Reflections on the Revolution in France*, that was taken up by all those who feared and distrusted the event.

It was a majestic polemic in which Burke excoriated 'those children of their country who are prompt rashly to hack that aged parent to pieces and put him into the kettle of magicians in hopes that by their poisonous weeds and wild incantations they may regenerate the paternal constitution'. His animus was directed not only against the Jacobins and the radicals, but also some of the members of his own party. He declared that no nation or movement can rely upon the private stock of reason of any one individual, but must trust the 'general bank and capital of nations and of ages'. He despised the 'men of theory', the intellectuals who thought to lead a revolution with their first principles and rational calculations. He put his faith in historical experience, practical utility and the fund of common knowledge transmitted from generation to generation. He put no faith in a 'sick man's dream of government'. He remarked that:

> because half a dozen grasshoppers under a fern make the field ring with their importunate chink, whilst thousands of great cattle, reposed beneath the shadow of the British oak, chew the cud and are silent, pray do not imagine that those who make the noise are the only inhabitants of the field; that, of course, they are many in number, or that, after all, they are other than the little shrivelled, meagre, hopping, though loud and troublesome insects of the hour.

George III came up to Burke at a reception and told him that 'you have been of *use to us all*, it is a general opinion'.

Thomas Paine, who had already made his mark on behalf of the Americans with *Common Sense* was now moved to compose a rejoinder to Burke in which he would celebrate the virtues of the revolution. The first part of *The Rights of Man* was published in pamphlet form in February 1791 with great popular success; it was hailed by the reform societies as an enduring testament to their convictions. Paine himself wrote at a later date that 'it had the greatest run of any work ever published in the English language. The number of copies circulated in England, Scotland and Ireland, besides translations into foreign languages, was between four and five hundred thousand.'

It had arrived at the opportune time. It provided an explanation and a defence for the great movement of the age. The revolution produced the harsh and strange music, while Paine composed the libretto. He loathed aristocrats and traditional aristocratical government; he characterized Burke's appeal to custom and history as no more than 'contending for the authority of the dead over the rights and freedom of the living'; Burke had commiserated with the sufferings of the quondam rulers of France, and in so doing 'he pities the plumage but forgets the dying bird'. Had he no notion of the millions of starving workers and peasants for whom there was no room in the world? Government should be conducted for 'the common interest of society, and the common rights of man'. In England, that boasted land of liberty, it had become clear that 'taxes were not raised to carry on wars, but that wars were raised to carry on taxes'. This was a fundamental hit against William Pitt's financial and military regime; Paine was asserting that war was part of the system of government. This opened men's eyes, in a phrase of the period, and immeasurably helped in the popularity of the treatise. At a later date President Andrew Jackson declared that *The Rights of Man* 'would be more enduring than all the piles of marble and granite man can erect'.

It soon became clear that most parliamentarians, including the largest number of Whigs, were supporting the arguments of Burke rather than those of Charles James Fox and Thomas Paine. There was a singular confrontation between the two parliamentary protagonists in May 1792; both Burke and Fox were debating the constitutional rights of Canada in the Commons when they began to stray into the dangerous territory of France. Fox was still an ardent supporter of the revolution but Burke now stood up. 'Fly from the French constitution', he said.

Fox whispered to him that 'there is no loss of friends'.

'Yes,' Burke replied, 'there is a loss of friends. I know the price of my conduct. I have done my duty at the price of my friend. Our friendship is at an end.' At this point, according to those in the chamber, Fox broke down and wept. It was a private example of the divisions within the country itself.

The people of England were now taking sides; the dissenters and reformers in favour of the French revolutionaries were largely opposed by those who supported 'Church and King'. If we may use Burke's analogy the grasshoppers were largely outnumbered by the cows, but that was not at all clear at the time. A Catholic Relief Bill was passed in 1791, removing certain legal restrictions from those who practised that faith; it was believed that Catholics, after the anti-clerical terror of the revolution, were now firmly on the government side. Panics about popular insurrection were still commonplace, however, and were in large part responses to the growth and development of 'reform societies' who took their inspiration from the revolution in France, from the war for independence in America and from the recent popular agitation associated with 'Wilkes and Liberty!' These men could be shopkeepers or artisans, merchants or schoolteachers, dissenting ministers or dissenting businessmen, booksellers or attorneys. Among these 'middling classes' there was a vast desire for change.

Their grievances included a demand for parliamentary reform, at a time when only 17 per cent of constituencies were contested and more than 60 per cent were controlled by the patronage of a neighbouring grandee. As Paine stated in *The Rights of Man*:

> The county of Yorkshire, which contains near a million of souls, sends two country members; and so does the county of Rutland, which contains not a hundredth part of that number. The town of old Sarum, which contains not three houses, sends two members; and the town of Manchester, which contains upwards

of sixty thousand souls, is not admitted to send any. Is there any principle in these things? Is there anything by which you can trace the marks of freedom, or discover those of wisdom?

He was also directly attacking Edmund Burke's deference to the traditional order. For many that order was nothing but old corruption writ large.

The first popular reform society, the Sheffield Society for Constitutional Information, was established in 1791; with a predominant membership of cutlers and metal craftsmen it emphasized the connection between the new industrialism and radical discontent. That is why the Sheffield society reprinted 1,600 copies of *The Rights of Man*. The London Society for Constitutional Information was instituted at the end of the year.

There had already been a sharp and salutary warning, however, for those who believed that reform was inevitable. On 14 July 1791, a 'Bastille dinner' was held in Birmingham, at a hotel in Temple Row, in order to celebrate the achievements of the revolution. A hostile crowd, largely made up of labourers and artisans from Birmingham, gathered outside the tavern in threatening numbers; after the diners had precipitately left, the crowd ransacked the premises. They then moved on to the houses and workshops of the most prominent dissenters in the town, notably the library and laboratory of Joseph Priestley. Priestley was one of the eminent members of the Lunar Society who included among their number nonconformists and free-thinkers whose doctrines were beyond the comprehension of the loyalist supporters of 'Church and King'. Priestley was forced to flee Birmingham and eventually to take refuge in America; the king himself observed that 'Priestley is the sufferer for the doctrines he and his party have instilled'.

So in the early months of 1792 the country was in an unsettled state, pursued by vague fears and unknown horrors precipitated by the French Revolution. In February the second part of Thomas Paine's *The Rights of Man* was published, with its radical notions of social welfare; he suggested that £4 a year be granted to every child under the age of fourteen for the purposes of schooling, and that a remission of taxes should be given to the poor. He also proposed a scheme of old age pensions 'not of the nature of a charity but of a right'. This was too much for the authorities, who could never conceive such a state of affairs, and three months later a royal proclamation against seditious publications was issued with particular attention paid to Paine.

This was no impediment to the growth of popular reform movements that were committed to promoting their aims by peaceful and constitutional means. The London Society for Constitutional Information, animated by the examples of Sheffield, Manchester, Norwich and Middlesex, proposed a motion denouncing Burke and celebrating the doctrines of Paine. These nascent bodies were organized by John Horne Tooke, an early disciple of John Wilkes as well as a philologist and perpetual activist, to give the impression of a nationwide movement; their membership probably ran into thousands rather than tens of thousands. But they were by no means revolutionaries; their members, who were obliged to pay a subscription, were composed of country gentlemen, peers, MPs and merchants who were intent upon constitutional liberty and an extension of the franchise.

In January 1792 a Piccadilly shoemaker, Thomas Hardy, called a meeting of radical colleagues at the Bell Tavern in Exeter Street, off the Strand, where he proposed a society with a wider provenance and a subscription of a penny a week. It was resolved by the members of this London Corresponding Society that their number and composition be 'unlimited'. It was soon composed of what Hardy called 'tradesmen, mechanicks and shopkeepers'; these were butchers and bakers, bricklayers and cordwainers, who had played no previous part in any political movement. At the same time it expressed 'its *abhorrence* of tumult and violence' with its emphasis on reform rather than revolution or anarchy. Its members campaigned for manhood suffrage, annual parliaments and cheaper legal costs.

The politicians at Westminster were not about to let this singular method of association go unchallenged and, in March 1792, a group of young Whig members of parliament established an Association of the Friends of the People which would be concerned with the possibilities of parliamentary reform. They in fact provoked embarrassment among their Whig colleagues who believed that the growing agitation for parliamentary reform was misdirected and even dangerous; yet at the same time the young men alienated the more radical reformers by refusing to subscribe to universal male suffrage and annual parliaments. They were marooned in the middle and, having provoked the suspicions and antipathies of both sides, were devoid of influence.

It was a hot spring – the temperature had reached 82 degrees Fahrenheit by the middle of March – and in that unseasonable warmth there was a kind of fever or madness in the air. The wheat crop was not successful, and the torrential rains of August and September spelled more trouble for the farmers. The state of the land always had a direct effect upon the state of the nation; in a sense it was the nation in living and visible form. The general prosperity of the previous few years now seemed in jeopardy, and there was fear of economic collapse.

This was exacerbated by news of European turmoil. It was reported in July that the forces of Prussia and Austria were advancing on Paris under the command of the duke of Brunswick; this was meant to be the counter-revolution of the older European aristocracies. The men and youths of France were called out, many of them streaming into the capital, and on 10 August the National Assembly determined on the deposition of the king on the grounds that he had been collaborating with the enemy. When important fortresses on the French frontier were surrendered to the invading armies, the panic and suspicion were redoubled. No one was safe. In the events known as the 'September massacres', the priests and aristocrats – many already herded into prisons – were murdered. The Jacobins now ruled Paris and, under the command of rulers such as Robespierre and Marat, thousands of other citizens were thrown into prison before being judicially murdered. The guillotine was the new king.

The invasion of the duke of Brunswick and his forces was not necessarily welcomed by William Pitt and his colleagues. A revolutionary France, albeit one not under immediate control, would be preferable to a country in the grip of Austria and of Prussia. The French were in any case provoked to fury, and the violent republicans of a newly established National Convention now pressed for immediate war.

It was considered that the well-trained forces of the duke of Brunswick would make short work of the ill-disciplined and badly armed citizens of the revolution. But with all the fury of their revolutionary zeal the *citoyens* resisted; they would not surrender to the enemies of their goddess liberty and, with new-found inspiration, the national defences were prepared and organized. At Valmy in north-eastern France, on 20 September, the armies of the Austrians and Prussians were thwarted. There had been no set battle. In truth the duke of Brunswick had lost his nerve; he was faced with thousands of French soldiers, albeit in not very prosperous condition, chanting the 'Marseillaise' and screaming *'Vive le nation!'* It was not an army he had ever faced before, and he ordered his troops to retire. Valmy was not a very significant encounter in the history of warfare but, in the history of the world, it was one of the most notable. The well-trained and well-equipped forces of the old wars had given way to – what? A rabble? A group of amateur soldiers? Goethe was at the time in the Prussian camp and predicted that 'from this day forth begins a new era in the history of the world'. A Prussian colonel offered similar sentiments. 'We have lost more than a battle. Our credibility is gone. The 20th of September has given the world a new shape. It is the most important day of the century.' On the following day the first French republic was proclaimed, and Valmy itself was the harbinger of a war that lasted for a generation.

The enthusiasm and joy of victory were palpable throughout France. Now was the time to press forward in pursuit of the dream of a universal republic in which all the people of Europe would be free. The French said that they had come to remove tyrants and pull down palaces, to extirpate the power of the clergy, to confiscate the property of Church and State in order to reduce the taxes on the poor. By the beginning of November the French army had entered Mons and Brussels; Savoy and Nice had been annexed, Italy and Spain threatened. 'We must break with all the cabinets of Europe', said the revolutionary Brissot. 'We must set fire to the four corners of Europe.' A new order of things was being born.

Pitt and his colleagues were now thoroughly alarmed by the miraculous resurgence of France. If the French should incorporate the Austrian Netherlands [Belgium] and should stir the United Provinces [the Netherlands] against the house of Orange, they would at once become a mighty sea power threatening the very frontiers of England.

The resurgent calls for liberty after the duke of Brunswick's retreat excited the political reformers in England to the extent that *The Times* in October wrote that 'the police should look to those Revolution mongers who are pasting up bills with a view to incite a mob to rise'. Yet Pitt's ministry seemed strangely enervated and cautious. It was considered that the military did not have the strength to quell any uprising in the towns and cities. The government seemed also unwilling to declare war against France itself, for fear that the people would not tolerate such a conflict against the new republic. By November warnings were reaching the Home Office from all parts of the country; it was reported that the 'lower orders' were in active cabal and that weapons were being furnished and concealed in certain quarters. When the ministry did determine to call out the militia in certain parts of the country, Fox and his colleagues were furious. 'I fairly own', Fox wrote, 'that if they have done this I shall grow savage and not think a French Lanterne too bad for them.' The lamp-post was used to string up the victims of the Terror. In December Thomas Paine was convicted in his absence of seditious libel for the publication of the second part of *The Rights of Man*.

Fox had said that the ministry was helping to revive the memories of civil war, and indeed the country ran the risk of serious division. Where there were reformers there were also loyalists, who could be subtly encouraged by magistrates and police to assert themselves. In November 1792, for example, a meeting at the Crown & Anchor Tavern in London established an 'Association for Preserving Liberty and Property against Republicans and Levellers'. The most arresting incidents were those of 'Paine burning' where an effigy of the author was consumed in flames. In November a crowd of loyalists burned his image in Chelmsford, Essex, where a local newspaper reported:

[T]he effigy of that infamous incendiary, Tom Paine, was exhibited in this town, seated in a chair, and borne on four men's shoulders – in one hand he had 'The Rights of Man' and under the other arm he bore a pair of stays [in recognition of his former employment as a corset-maker]; upon his head a mock

resemblance of the Cap of Liberty, and a halter round his neck.
On a banner carried before him, was written: 'Behold a Traitor!
Who, for the base purposes of Envy, Interest and Ambition,
would have deluged this Happy Country in BLOOD!'

It is reported that there were over 400 such conflagrations in all
parts of the country.

The temperature was raised in the same month when the
National Convention in Paris declared that the French government and people pledged 'fraternity' to all 'subject peoples' with the
declaration that 'all governments are our enemies, all people our
friends'. This was an open invitation to reformers or democrats to
rise in all of the European countries, most notably in England and
her allies. Pitt began to make cautious preparations. The militia
were moved closer to London, and the Tower was more safely
secured. Radical clubs were more closely watched, and foreigners
supervised under the aegis of an 'Aliens Office' staffed by graduates
from Christ Church, Oxford. The secret service of Francis Wal-
singham, in the reign of Elizabeth, and of John Thurloe, under the
rule of Cromwell, was becoming more professional.

The harshest news came with the execution of Louis XVI on
21 January 1793; when his head came off, 80,000 armed men
erupted in cheers, and curious bystanders closer to the event dipped
their fingers or handkerchiefs in his blood. 'It is well salted!' one
called out. Gouverneur Morris, the American minister in Paris,
predicted to Thomas Jefferson that 'the English will be wound up
to a pitch of enthusiastic horror against France which their cool
and steady temper seems to be scarcely susceptible of'. The London
theatres were closed, and all who could afford black went into
mourning. Even Fox, the born Francophile, declared it to be a
'revolting act of cruelty and injustice'. The escalating accounts of
murders and outrages were shouted out on every street corner;
when the English king drove out, he was surrounded by cries of
'War with France!' It was reported that Paris was ruled by tigers.

The wish was father to the deed. On 1 February 1793 the
National Convention declared war on England; war was also to be
waged against Holland, and an immediate invasion of that country
was ordered. Pitt entered the conflict with strictly limited aims, and

he believed that any struggle would be a short one. His purpose was to finance his allies in the European theatre while his own navy could concentrate on stripping France of its colonial possessions; it was widely believed that Pitt's purpose was to annex the French West Indies. By the summer of 1793 the first minister was sending funds to Russia, Austria, Prussia, Sardinia and other interested parties. It was important that no one country should dominate the continent, so he ringed northern France with a circle of arms and men. This might be called 'the balance of power'. Hessian mercenaries were recruited into the English forces, but the national dislike of a standing army limited their deployment. Yet the question of national purpose remained. Was Pitt intent upon subjugating France in Europe, or upon stripping that country of its overseas wealth? Nobody seemed to be sure.

The costs of the war, including the subvention of allies, were already provoking consternation, and in the early months of 1793 a sudden collapse of credit was the consequence. There was a run on the banks by those who wished to put their money in safer keeping, and the number of bankruptcies doubled in a year. One industrialist, Stephen Barber of Walsall, asked for a bill to be speedily paid in ready money 'as we are so circumstanced in this country [county] we have not cash to go on with'. Coincidentally, perhaps, Pitt was believed to be drinking more heavily than usual.

Yet his political situation was now more than ever assured. The more moderate, or less radical, Whigs felt obliged to part company with Charles James Fox and his particularly vociferous support of the French cause. It was deemed to be unpatriotic at time of war. At the beginning of 1793 one of the Whig grandees, William Windham, announced the formation of a 'third party' that might find a middle path between Pitt and Fox while supporting the war against France. It was no coincidence that the rise of a 'political middle' comprising what the *Cambridge Intelligencer* called 'the middle ranks of men cooperating with the declared and active advocates of moderate reform' should be accompanied by praise of a new 'middle class' or 'middle rank'.

The war seemed to be going well. The Austrian Netherlands were released from threat of French invasion, largely by the strength of the Hessian mercenaries, and the English navy retained its control of the seas and was even then planning to move against the French colonies. In the summer of 1793 a group of counter-revolutionaries based in Toulon captured the port and handed it over to the English. But the sheer stamina and ferocity of the French had been under-estimated. Toulon was back in their hands by the end of the year, while Holland and Belgium were still under threat. Even the naval expedition to the French West Indies was crippled by dysentery and epidemic disease. The French technique of *levée en masse*, when the whole population might be thrown at the enemy, signalled a new form of warfare. The French hurled their men forward, however terrible the casualties, and lived off the land rather than maintaining supply lines; they were more flexible and far more fierce. The English and their allies seemed close to victory on many occasions but then in the face of the enemy began a protracted and sometimes wearying retreat. That could have been their catchphrase: not defeat, but retreat. At the battle of Hondschoote in September 1793 the duke of York attempted the siege of Dunkirk; but he was heavily out-numbered and his men were constantly assailed by a reviving enemy. He was eventually forced to withdraw, but the French were in no position to strike at his demoralized army. It might be an emblem of the continental war itself.

Parliament reassembled on 21 January 1794 and the ministers accentuated the positive. Dunkirk had not been taken by the duke of York but the Austrian Netherlands were still free. The West Indies had not been occupied but Tobago had been captured. Sardinia and Spain were co-operating. The British navy was still in control of the seas, and French trading vessels were constantly under attack. Austria and Prussia were not providing all the military resources expected of them and they were, in any case, in a constant state of mutual suspicion. Still, this was for the future.

The members turned their attention to domestic affairs. On 12 May Thomas Hardy, John Horne Tooke and twelve others were arrested and tried for high treason; Hardy had first organized the London Corresponding Society in the Bell Tavern, while Tooke had helped to organize the radical societies in a national movement. Hardy was taken at his shoemaker's shop in Piccadilly, while all the papers of the various London reform societies were seized. A report by a new Committee for Secrecy, established by parliament, concluded on 16 May that all such parties 'must be considered as a Traitorous Conspiracy for the Subversion of the established Laws and Constitution, and the Introduction of that System of Anarchy and Confusion which has fatally prevailed in France'. Two days later the Habeas Corpus Act was suspended so that political prisoners could be held without trial. The measure was excused on the grounds that it would prevent outrages similar to those of Paris.

The trial of Hardy and others for high treason began on 25 September at the Old Bailey, with much technical discussion on the nature of the charge. Hardy was the first to be acquitted for absence of evidence, and was carried in triumph by a cheering throng from the court. The proceedings were followed by great crowds outside in the street, and by excited spectators within. Tooke was the next in the dock, and was acquitted after eight minutes. John Thelwall, one of the most radical orators and lecturers, was the third to be found not guilty. The government then dropped the other cases, to the joy of the multitude who still filled the London streets; the accused had been found innocent of treason simply because there was not enough evidence to support a high crime that merited hanging.

Despite the failure of the prosecution, some of the spirit left the supporters of reform. The war with France, now of course deemed to be the enemy, and the sanguinary events in Paris helped to diminish the enthusiasm for the cause. The threat of treason, although lifted, was still potent. The Society for Constitutional Information no longer met in London, for example, and Horne Tooke withdrew from political activity.

The period has been described as the beginning of Pitt's 'reign of terror', culminating four years later with many more arrests of reformers, and has sometimes been compared with that unleashed on Paris by Marat and Robespierre; yet, if it were so, it was singularly weak in inspiration and execution. It is true that the prolonged series of assaults upon the members of the societies had effectively silenced some of them. But it has been estimated that there were only 200 prosecutions over ten years and some, like those of Tooke and Thelwall, ended in acquittal. This does not sound like a revolutionary situation.

The temper of the nation was better expressed on the occasion of the defeat of the French fleet in the Atlantic by Admiral Howe

in the early summer of 1794, which became known as the 'Glorious
First of June'. When news of the victory reached London the
performance at the Opera House was suspended, while the auditorium rang with 'Rule Britannia' and the national anthem. The city
was illuminated and the king travelled to Portsmouth with his
consort to greet the returning ships.

In the following month the more conservative and loyalist
Whigs, having already abandoned the leadership of Fox and Sheridan, agreed to join the administration of 'Pitt the patriot' as he
was sometimes known. He never called himself a Tory but always
an 'independent Whig'; nevertheless here were the makings of the
nineteenth-century Tory Party. At this stage, however, it might be
described as a powerful administration for national unity, its cohesion materially increased by a *coup d'état* in Paris on 27 July when
Robespierre and the instigators of the Jacobin 'terror' were summarily
dispatched by 'Madame Guillotine' or 'The National Razor'. This
by no means implied that the military threat from France was
arrested. Brigadier-General Buonaparte was already considered to
be indispensable for the disposition of the war.

That conflict had already entered a stage of frustration and
indecision when it became clear that England and its allies on land
were not so capable as England on the high seas. The English forces
were themselves overstretched, and their supposed allies had begun
to plot one against another. The Prussians mistrusted the Austrians
while the English berated the Dutch even as the French army
approached the borders of Holland. While the allies had the habit
of dispersing their armies to confront various contingencies, the
French forces just grew bigger; it could be said that they were
winning through size of numbers rather than revolutionary fervour.

In England itself dearth was causing unprecedented misery.
This was the largest cause of unrest. Thomas Fuller had already published his *Gnomologia* in which he recorded contemporary proverbs.
'Where bad's the best, bad must be the choice.' 'All's good in
a famine.' 'Hunger finds no fault with the cookery.' 'Hungry dogs
will eat dirty puddings.' Hungry men, women and children will of
course eat almost anything. By the end of 1795 prices had risen
some 30 per cent from 1790.

An attempt to ameliorate the harshest conditions, and also to divert the rage of the people, was attempted by the magistrates of Speenhamland at a meeting held in the Pelican Inn near Newbury in Berkshire. It was concluded that, if the price of bread rose above a certain level, the poor would receive a special subsidy from the parish funds. It seemed a remarkably efficient system of benefit and was adopted by other counties where it became known as the 'Speenhamland system'. It was soon, to all intents and purposes, a national system from Dorset to Yorkshire. Yet it had its critics, who believed that it kept wages artificially low; the farmers felt no need to pay their workers more if the parish was about to supplement their incomes. It was deemed by some to be demoralizing, and there were complaints that some labourers threatened the parish overseers for insufficient aid. So began the argument over 'welfare dependency' that continues to this day.

Even the most liberal provisions were not enough to stay the rising tide of anger from reform societies that had weathered the storm of Pitt's 'terror'. In late June a crowd of many thousand, organized by the London Corresponding Society, met in St George's Fields south of the Thames where they demanded the end of war and a reduction in the price of food; the old demands of manhood suffrage and annual parliaments were made, but the principal cry was for 'Bread! Bread!' Baskets of biscuits were distributed stamped with the legend 'freedom and plenty, or slavery and want'. This was not the Jacobin activism of the previous year but a more potent domestic combination of rage, frustration and hunger. Bread riots also erupted in Birmingham and Coventry, Nottingham and Sussex. In July some demonstrators broke a window of Pitt's residence in Downing Street; he described it ironically to his mother as 'a single pebble'. In the following month the Sheffield Constitutional Society held an open-air meeting on Crooke's Moor where it was pleaded, in imitation of Luke's gospel, that 'when we ask for bread, let not the father of his people give us a stone'.

When the new session of parliament opened on 29 October 1795, the price of bread had reached its highest level. Pitt's carriage was surrounded by a jeering crowd shouting 'No Pitt! No War! Bread! Bread! Peace! Peace!' The king's own carriage was mobbed by ill-wishers and at one point a stone, or bullet, pierced its window. A ballad-seller, hawking Paine's *The Rights of Man* for a penny, was arrested; he was promptly rescued by the crowd and chaired in triumph. Pitt took advantage of the situation by bringing forward a bill for 'better securing the king's person'. This was accompanied by the 'Two Acts' or 'Gagging Acts' that were designed to curtail the right of assembly and to widen the scope of high treason. All public meetings comprising more than fifty people were to be supervised and controlled by local magistrates; prior notice of, and specific details about, any meeting or public lecture had to be given in writing. As for the bill against treason, the death penalty could be applied to people who advised the death or imprisonment of the king and, more significantly, who attempted to change his counsels or opinions. Pitt also summoned more militia to London, and told William Wilberforce that 'my head would be off in six months were I to resign'. Wilberforce commented, with a hint of understatement, 'I see that he expects a civil broil.' A physician whom Pitt consulted, Walter Farquhar, also reported that the functions of 'his stomach are greatly impaired and the bowels very irregular' which he attributed to 'the excess of public business and the unremitting attention upon subjects of anxiety and interest'. So Pitt was in deadly earnest; he feared revolution.

It is an open question whether he was right in his judgement. Despite the apparent severity of the 'Two Acts' they were rarely enforced with rigour, and the usual process of muddling through seems to have been paramount. When in November a further protest meeting was held at Copenhagen Fields a contemporary noted that

> You may have seen in the papers of prodigious numbers being at the meeting. This is not true in the sense such accounts would be understood. In the course of the day many thousands were doubtless in the field, but never at one time. I was there between two and three and I don't believe there were five hundred in the field, and I saw it at the fullest time so far as I can understand.

This was nothing like the march on Versailles.

There was undoubtedly a revolutionary fringe hoping to take advantage of the general misery; some of them were from Ireland, some from France, and some of them home-grown revolutionaries. Reports reached the Home Office of secret meetings and plottings, but nothing ever came of them. This poses the larger question of England's apparent immunity from the revolutionary disorders that had swept France. A number of explanations present themselves, all with a modicum of truth. The fact that England was at war with France did of course much to dampen any enthusiasm for republican ideals; it would have been like sleeping with the enemy. The sceptical attitude hardened what can essentially be viewed as the conservative cast of the English people, accustomed to an established order and to the traditions of historical existence. Edmund Burke himself, as we have observed, appealed in his speeches and pamphlets to the significance of precedent and continuity in the life of the nation, a contract between the dead, the living, and those yet to be born.

The role of the Churches should not be underestimated. There was a broad and wide church polity that softened religious unrest and division. It was an advantage, of course, that the major religions all took for granted the nature of human inequality; Anglicans and Methodists were united in their assertion of the virtues of loyalty and obedience. It has often been suggested that in England the 'lower orders' have never risen without an impulse from above to rouse them; the circumstances of the Peasants' Revolt in 1381 and the Luddite machine-breaking of 1811 may be exceptions to this argument but certainly, in the 1790s, there was no disaffected aristocracy to lead the charge as there was in Paris.

More subtle explanations for the absence of revolutionary enthusiasm may be adduced. The English had always been known as a practical and pragmatic race. That is why they had taken the lead in the progress of the Industrial Revolution. The French, on the other hand were known to be speculative and enthusiastic; they followed their theories and ideas like ignes fatui wherever they might lead them. This was, at least, the caricature. Whether a stubborn *paysan* would concur is another matter.

Nevertheless it was believed by many English contemporaries that the revolution had simply got out of hand, that it had been so driven by first principles that it had strayed from its proper path. The more ardent French revolutionaries saw the events that surrounded them as a miracle play in which they took on the most important roles. They identified themselves with the people; they identified themselves with the national will; they identified themselves with *la patrie*. William Pitt observed that it was 'a species of tyranny which adds insult to the wretchedness of its subjects, by styling its own arbitrary decrees the voice of the people, and sanctioning its acts of oppression and cruelty under the pretence of the national will'.

One other national myth was at work on the other side of the Channel. Ever since the time of the Glorious Revolution, and perhaps earlier, the English were accustomed to believe themselves to live in a land of liberty. There are traces of this conviction in the thirteenth century, and in the sixteenth century; perhaps it has always been an aspect of national consciousness. The fact that this had never really been the case did not deter its exponents, many of whom would declare the danger to 'English liberties' at any opportunity. Such was the profound sense of many of the English people. They were not likely to follow Danton or Robespierre or even Buonaparte. They were still predominantly in support of George III and William Pitt, king and nation in harmony, even though the king was mad and the nation in distress.

29

The mad kings

David Garrick first played the part of King Lear at the Goodman's Field Theatre in Whitechapel, in the spring of 1742; he was twenty-five years old, a relatively youthful age that suggests both precocity and ambition. Two friends watched his performance from the pit, and suggested alterations. He listened carefully and took notes. He came back in the same part six weeks later and caused a sensation. This was Lear as raw nature, full of fear and trembling, moving from pathos to anger, from despair to grief, keeping 'the audiences in a tumult of continuous passion . . . his performance was interrupted by open sobs and weeping'. Tears were an important element of the social world. Thomas Gray was told that readers had wept over every line of his 'Elegy Written in a Country Churchyard' (1750). The members of parliament often broke down and had to be led out of the chamber, weeping after a quarrel. It was reported that one parliamentarian, George Tierney, 'sobbed so, he was unable to talk; I never saw a more affecting scene'.

Horace Walpole recorded how two executioners fought over the rope used to hang a notorious highwayman, 'and the one who lost it cried'. Anna Seward, a celebrated poet of the period known as 'the Swan of Lichfield', returned to her childhood haunts and 'could not restrain the gushing tears, through almost the whole of the five hours I passed in that dear village'. She was a champion weeper.

The words of a contemporary, observing the role of Garrick as Lear, emphasize the new sensibilities of the eighteenth century. The members of the audience 'seemed to shrink away and cower' when he cursed his daughters' ingratitude. When they erupted in vehement applause, as Garrick hit upon a brilliant stroke of art, he whispered to one of the other actors onstage, Tom King, 'Damn me, Tom, it'll do.'

It was said that Garrick 'speaks tragedy truly and natural'. That was the key response: this was nature rather than art. This was the language of real feeling. It was the wholly new art of whisper, and gesture, and unstudied enunciation. It does not matter that it would now seem absurdly stylized. All versions of what is natural or realistic change and decay. When Garrick played Macbeth he turned to the first murderer and said, 'There's blood upon thy face.' The line was not in the play. The actor started back, and put a hand to his cheek. 'Is there, by God?' He had heard a fellow actor speak as a human being, and he was surprised to the point of consternation. The neo-classical stage had been established upon decorum, declamation and dignity. Its successor, which may perhaps be called Romantic, relied upon expressiveness, activity and more realistic detail.

Garrick did not really play Lear as conceived by William Shakespeare. The original was deemed, in the eighteenth century, to be too crude and wayward. It did not preserve the unities. It was, in many respects, tasteless. Its ending was unsatisfactory. The play Garrick performed was that rewritten by Nahum Tate in 1681. It was considered to be the proper *Lear*, the acceptable *Lear*, purged of all its absurdities and obscenities. Tate himself regarded the scenes of Shakespeare's 'old honest play' to be 'heaps of jewels unstrung and unpolished'.

In Tate's play the Fool is removed altogether, since tragedy and farce were not deemed to be compatible. In this version, too, Cordelia falls in love with Edgar to provide a more gentle diversion. There is a less strenuous ending in which Lear, Edgar and Cordelia are reunited to live happily ever after. As one critic of the time suggested, *Lear* as amended by Tate 'will always be more agreeable to an audience'. The love affair itself 'can never fail to produce those gushing tears, which are swelled and ennobled by a virtuous joy'. The prevailing sentiments

of the day are here revealed. One critic, Thomas Cooke, preferred
Tate 'because almost every character . . . is an instance of virtue being
rewarded and vice punished'. He added: 'I have read many sermons,
but remember none that contains so fine a lesson of morality as this
play.' This was all that needed to be said. Ethics, and not aesthetics,
was the test of true art.

The audience of the time could not have endured the tragedy
and horror of Shakespeare's play. If it was reduced to storms of tears
by Garrick's performance, how could it have coped with Lear's
death? Gloucester's blinding takes place discreetly offstage. Even
Shakespeare's stern editor, Samuel Johnson, could not bring himself
to reread the last scenes of the play until it became his duty to do
so. It seems almost as if he and his contemporaries were afraid
of madness and deep feeling. In many respects it was not an age of
confidence or of stability at all. It was one that needed comforting.
It needed consolation.

Garrick played the part of the mad king for the rest of his career.
He cut and modified the text for his various performances, sometimes reintroducing more of the Shakespearian original. People stood
for hours outside the theatre where he was playing, waiting for
tickets. When again he took on the part in 1774 the writer, Hannah
More, said: 'I thought I should have been suffocated with grief:
it was not like the superficial sorrow one feels at a well-acted play,
but the deep, substantial grief of real trouble.' Garrick's *Lear*
concluded with a performance in June 1776 thirty-four years after
his first entry in the theatre at Whitechapel and one month before
his retirement from the stage. He had begun a farewell tour,
screwing up the emotions of the audience to an unprecedented
pitch. Sir Joshua Reynolds, after seeing him, was prostrate for three
days. Garrick furnished new scenery for this last year of *Lear*, and
provided more resplendent historical costumes. It was agreed that
the applause was 'beyond description'. Whenever he came upon, or
retired from, the stage he was wildly applauded.

The centre of all feeling lay in the 'mad scene' when the insane
old king rages on the heath. It was painted by Benjamin Wilson,
a friend of the actor, in 1762 as a study of the magical or the sacred.
Garrick stands at full length wearing a shirt, breeches and a robe
of scarlet trimmed with ermine. This was the costume of royalty,

however dimmed. He raises his right arm towards the storm-tossed sky, from which a shaft of light drenches him in radiance. The gesticulation became part of a repertoire of theatrical images; it was reproduced in prints and on porcelain. It became the token of madness, and was re-employed in many other works.

A more accomplished artist, Benjamin West, painted the same storm scene sixteen years later as a Gothic nightmare in the style of Henry Fuseli or even William Blake. It is in certain aspects close to Wilson's vision of the king, but the dramatic figures and expressive style suggest a sea-change in sensibility; this is no longer the world of neo-classical restraint but of Romantic wildness. In Wilson's study Lear is very much an eighteenth-century figure addicted to sentiment; in West's version, the king is beside himself with sorrow. He points up at the storm as if claiming a place there, and his expression is one of longing as well as of fear. The painting was approximately 12 feet by 9 feet, so that it positively towered above its spectators; it was part of the 'Shakespeare Gallery' established in the spring of 1789 by Alderman John Boydell in Pall Mall as a tribute to the national genius and as an example of a new taste for the passionate sublime. It was also naturally related to the passionate intensity with which, a generation before, the Methodist preachers dominated their congregations. Garrick himself was described as introducing 'a new religion'. The age of reason and satire was also the age of rapture.

We may note the strange coincidence that in the year of West's composition, 1788, the real king became mad. George III began to talk rapidly and continuously, passing in and out of delirium. Benjamin West, by this time, knew him well. King George had in 1772 appointed him to be historical painter to the court, and West completed two portraits of his royal patron. He had observed him closely for some years, and it is not hard to believe that some elements of George appear in the frenzied figure of King Lear. In the autumn of 1788 West had shown his sovereign his new landscape of Windsor Castle in which a lion, for some reason, had been placed. The king insisted that it looked more like a dog and immediately scored marks over the image before drawing his own. He did it with tremendous energy accompanied by a great flurry of words. All was not well.

It was in any case an age much possessed by madness. Insanity was known as 'the English disease' together with its companion, melancholy. It was attributed to the natural sensitivity and imaginative nature of the English confined to an island of ghosts and spirits. Garrick himself is said to have visited Bedlam in order to study the words and postures of the insane. He wished to introduce a touch of nature to the requirements of art. One critic, on seeing his performance, noted that 'as madness is defined to be right reasoning on wrong principles there is consistency in the words and actions of a madman'. Garrick provided this. Yet also, according to a different observer, 'Garrick had displayed all the force of quick transition from one passion to another: he had, from the most violent rage, descended to sedate calmness'. On studying West's painting the critic George Cumberland suggested that the king's 'loss of reason has arisen from the tender rather than the inflammatory passions; or there is a majestic sensibility mixed with the wildness of his distraction'.

Controversies arose over the origin of Lear's madness. Was it the shock of losing his throne? Or was it anger at his daughters' ingratitude? The polite classes of the eighteenth century were aficionados of insanity.

Henry Fuseli stated that one medical man who visited Bedlam believed that the larger part of its inmates were women unhappy in love, while the second category in terms of numbers were 'hackney and stage coachmen', whose constant shaking in their vehicles disturbed the pineal gland. But Garrick did not visit Bedlam only. He had a case study closer to home. A certain gentleman and friend of the actor lived in a house in Leman Street, Goodman's Fields, where he had been playing with his two-year-old daughter near an open window. Accidentally he dropped her onto the paved area below, whereupon the young girl was instantly killed. The man lost his senses and 'remained at the window, screaming in agonies of grief'. For the rest of his life he would go over to the window and play with an invisible girl, drop her, and fill the house 'with shrieks of grief and bitter anguish'. Then he would fall into silent melancholy, and slowly look round at the fateful scene, 'his eyes fixed on one object, at times looking slowly round him as if to implore compassion'. Garrick stated that it was there 'I learned to imitate madness'. According to one who watched his performance, 'he had no sudden starts, no violent gesticulation; his movements were slow and feeble; misery was depicted in his countenance; he moved his head in the most deliberate manner; his eyes were fixed or, if they turned to any one near him he made a pause, and fixed his look on the person after much delay . . .'.

Since madness was considered to be curable, many treatments were prescribed. George III was given what was called 'mad physic' which caused inflammation, eruptions and violent disorders. The famous Dr Jenner treated his mad patients by 'keeping them sick with tartar emetic' and camphor water. Some spas were considered to be healthful. A madwoman, Mrs Jessop, was cured by the waters at Buxton; the 1st earl of Egmont reported that 'she is now very orderly behaved and has got a lover'.

George III had a naturally hurried and impulsive manner which the pressing affairs of state could only intensify. He also spoke of 'the anxiety I have for the success of my endeavours to fit my children for the various stations they may fill, and that they may be useful and a credit to their family'. He had broken down completely in the autumn of 1788 and it was reported that 'his case must be hopeless'.

The king seized his eldest son by the throat and threw him against a wall, demanding who it was that had forbidden him to whisper. Captain Jack Payne, comptroller of the prince of Wales's household, let it be known that the monarch awoke in his bed 'with all the gestures and ravings of the most confirmed maniac'; he howled like a dog and spoke distractedly about matters of religion. Fanny Burney met him by chance in Kew Gardens in February 1789; he had been taken for the air, and she reported that he lost control of his speech repeating the word 'No!' a hundred times. He talked about Handel and tried to sing the composer's oratorios 'in a voice so dreadfully hoarse that the sound was terrible'. Eventually he was locked in his room and tied to his bed at night. By the end of the year he had become so violent that he was confined to a straitjacket. He was also on occasions beaten with sticks, no doubt according to the much earlier belief that the 'devils' within him could be expelled by rods and violence. Yet after this treatment of enforced restraint, he seemed to make a full recovery. He relapsed at the beginning of 1801 but was soon considered to be fit for rule again even though he was on many occasions irritable and agitated.

For George III, as for Lear, much attention was paid to the concept of the king's 'two bodies'. One was the 'body natural' as opposed to the 'body politic'. The natural body was susceptible to all the infirmities of the human condition, but the body politic was free from all defects or weakness and could not be affected by the natural body. It was the sovereign will of the nation incarnate. That is why Garrick felt able to project royal dignity into the role even while enacting all the symptoms of mental distress.

Charity asylums were established in the eighteenth century with the purpose of healing the deranged. The rich in particular were happy to consign their mad relations to private care so that those out of mind could also be kept out of sight. The inmates were essentially trapped in a prison where chains, manacles, leg-locks and handcuffs could be employed with impunity. It was believed that the untamed maniac was not susceptible to bodily disease so that Thomas Willis, in his *Two Discourses Concerning the Soul of Brutes*, could recommend 'severe government and discipline' without considering the physical consequences.

This could of course be the stuff of entertainment, and until 1770 Bedlam, the most famous of all asylums, was open to casual visitors. In the following year the hero of that quintessentially eighteenth-century text, Henry MacKenzie's *The Man of Feeling*, observed: 'I think it an inhuman practice to expose the greatest misery with which our nature is afflicted to every idle visitant who can afford a trifling perquisite to the keeper.'

The madness of King George of course brought back a reign of tears. When the lord chancellor, Thurlow, visited the mad monarch 'the tears rolled down his cheeks, and his feet had difficulty to support him'. The queen was drowned in tears, and the members of the royal household 'all cried, even bitterly, as they looked on'. It was no better when he recovered. Fanny Burney, on hearing the good news, confided to a friend that 'I assure you, I cried twenty times in the day'.

In the autumn of 1810, after the death of a favourite daughter, the king once more slid into mania and his condition became irreparable. He had now become at times 'so violent that correction had been necessary and he is confined'. One of his doctors, Sir Henry Halford, concluded that George III was 'totally lost as to mind, conversing with imaginary personages'. One member of the court reported that the king 'was no longer treated as a human being. His body was immediately encased in a machine which left no liberty of motion. He was sometimes chained to a stake. He was frequently beaten and starved, and at best he was kept in subjection by menacing and violent language.' Wasn't that a dainty dish to set before a king? He had been the great English monarch of the latter part of the eighteenth century. An engraving of him, with long beard and long hair, bears an uncanny resemblance to the images of King Lear by Benjamin Wilson and Benjamin West.

30

The beast and the whore

William Pitt the younger was the minister most concerned with, and identified by, the war against newly revolutionary France. He did not believe in boards and committees; he was the sole agent. One bureaucrat of the Admiralty noted that 'Mr Pitt does all the material business at his own house, signs the papers, and then two other Lords sign them of course'. Pitt himself claimed that 'there can be no rivalry or division of power. That power must rest in the person generally called the First Minister'; he added that the first minister ought to be in charge of finances as well as strategy. This management worked well in practice and the tremulous king found few instances of what he called 'anything unpleasant' between himself and the administration.

The war of 1795 consisted of stalemate followed by disappointment. The situation on land was muddled and confused by the claims and counter-claims of England and its allies; the Austrians, the Dutch, the Prussians and the others failed to press their advantage home. The Prussians were the first to sign a peace treaty with the French. The Dutch were the first to surrender to the French, ceding the left bank of the Rhine to their erstwhile enemy; Holland followed a month later. In the following year, Spain also changed sides. It was imperative, therefore, that Austria remained in the war on the British side; Russia hardly counted. The prospect before Pitt was of a lonely landlocked war with the maritime power of England unable to sway the balance of Europe. In any case France now had three navies, its own as well as those of Holland and of Spain. The world was turned upside down.

In 1796 Napoleon, perhaps best known at this time for the capture of Toulon from British forces, surprised the world still further with his lightning Italian campaign, urging his troops ever further north and closer to the principal enemy of Austria. 'Soldiers!' he told his troops at Nice near the frontier with Piedmont. 'You are almost naked, half starved; the government owes you much and can give you nothing. Your patience and courage in the midst of these rocks are admirable; but they reflect no splendour on your arms. I am about to conduct you into the most fertile plains on earth; fertile provinces, opulent cities, will soon be in your power; there you will find rich harvests, honour, and glory . . . Will you fail in courage?' This is the language of Buonaparte, at once curt and magniloquent.

He conquered Piedmont, setting up the municipal republic of Alba in the process, before crossing the Adda, a tributary of the River Po, and scattering the Austrian army at Lodi in Lombardy. This victory was a singular event in Napoleon's career and he said it was the moment when he first dreamed of world glory; it came as an annunciation.

Dangers pressed upon England from every direction. At the end of 1796 the French had launched an invasion force upon Bantry Bay in support of the United Irishmen. These were the men who hoped and believed that they could bring under one banner the Irish dissenters and the Catholics, equally oppressed by the members of the Protestant Ascendancy, who might then become a revolutionary force under French leadership. The invaders had even brought French military uniforms for their Irish allies to wear on their anticipated march to Dublin. Great storms and treacherous seas dispelled any hope of success. Yet the fact that the French had sailed so far, and had in the process broken through an English naval blockade, had alerted Pitt and his colleagues to further French adventures. On 25 February 1797, news reached London that some French troops had landed at Fishguard Bay in Pembrokeshire; it was in truth a forlorn hope, the soldiers having surrendered to the local militia.

The incursions bred rumour, and rumour created fear, and fear easily degenerated into panic. Napoleon was on his way! A run on the banks proved fatal, since they did not hold enough bullion to meet their commitments; the Bank of England was obliged to suspend cash payments and issue notes of £1 and £2 as legal tender. A rhyme passed through the streets:

> So of Pitt and of England
> Men say without vapour
> How he found it of gold
> And left it of paper.

The possibility of French intervention once more ignited the hopes of the United Irishmen, who began to arm and to drill the peasantry. But there were dangers of insurrection even closer to home. A naval mutiny began at Spithead in the middle of April; the sailors' grievances included low pay and prolonged periods at sea. Within a week their undoubtedly legitimate demands were met, and the admiral of the fleet was rowed from ship to ship with the king's free pardon in his hand. In the following month the sailors of the north fleet, no doubt emboldened by the actions of their colleagues, mutinied at the Nore. A fighting address was read to the delegates from the different ships, in which it was stated that 'the Age of Reason has at length revolved. Long have we been endeavouring to find ourselves men. We now find ourselves so. We will be treated as such.'

They were perhaps more determined and more dangerous than the sailors of Spithead, and at one stage managed to blockade the Thames; but their revolt was suppressed and their leader, Richard Parker, hanged on board his ship. Parker blamed his own men for their fickleness and divided opinions, calling them 'cowardly, selfish and ungrateful'. Reports circulated that they had in fact been instigated by members of the United Irishmen and of other revolutionary groups, but no solid evidence has ever been offered.

Meanwhile Napoleon Buonaparte had advanced onto the soil of Austria. At the beginning of April 1797, he marched his army north until they reached the town of Leoben, just 90 miles from Vienna, where an armistice was quickly followed by a preliminary peace treaty between France and the Holy Roman Empire (now dominated by Austria and Prussia) in which each side agreed not to interfere in the domestic affairs of the other. Certain secret clauses surrendered Austrian possessions in the Mediterranean and the Adriatic, as well as the Austrian Netherlands, while Buonaparte magnanimously gave Venice to the Austrian emperor, thus blotting out the watery city's thousand years of independent existence. 'La Serenissima' never recovered from the blow.

It was the peace that the French people had craved. Unfortunately it left England alone on the stage of the world. There were attempts by Pitt and his ministers to reach some form of treaty with Paris, but their efforts were rebuffed. The first coalition against Napoleon had failed.

The personal success of Buonaparte, from his first days as a corporal, had by no means been guaranteed. Yet the combination of skill, luck and fortitude led him forward. He was in particular an inspired strategist and tactician. It is well known that he relied upon artillery rather than infantry and muskets; a massive and deafening bombardment would be followed by rapid sorties, which were in turn succeeded by the assaults of cavalry and infantry. It was not simply the manpower that won the victories, it was the spirit of the French army that under the leadership of Buonaparte became a highly flexible and responsive machine for warfare. The Austrians and Prussians, under different styles of leadership, seemed to be woefully old fashioned.

Buonaparte had a few simple rules. The lines of supply and communication must always be clear. Always attack. Never remain on the defensive. Timing was all important. He had a master plan in his head for each battle that he conceived in precise detail. He tried to leave nothing to chance, but he was able to improvise at dangerous moments. He was a bold man, none bolder, but he was also an opportunist who acted decisively when circumstances were favourable. 'Accident, hazard, chance, call it what you may,' he once said, 'a mystery to ordinary minds, becomes a reality to superior men.' He knew himself to be one of those 'superior men' who can bend the world to their will; he worked tirelessly, and his decisiveness was combined with determination. One conquest or one battle was only a preliminary to the next; he was always advancing in order to extend his dominion. He told his soldiers that 'our task is not to defend our frontiers, but to invade the territory of our foes'. It was to be war forever.

His large grey eyes were almost expressionless but an old French general confessed: 'I tremble like a child when I approach him.' Most significantly he had the ferocious desire to win which he was able to impart to his soldiers. 'You must speak to the soul', he said. Hegel glimpsed Napoleon riding through the streets of the city of Jena just before the battle of that region and observed that he had seen 'the world-soul . . . astride a horse'.

Away from Buonaparte's campaigns on land, Britain made gains at sea. In February 1797 the French and Spanish fleets were defeated off Cape St Vincent by Sir John Jervis while nine months later Admiral Duncan defeated the Dutch at the battle of Camperdown. After two peace missions under the leadership of Lord Malmesbury were rejected by the French, serious proposals were made to abandon the land campaign and to extend the mastery of the sea by picking up colonial treasure and colonial possessions wherever they offered themselves. But that smacked of defeatism. There was still a widespread desire to continue the struggle, and when Pitt sat down after a spirited speech to rouse the nation the Commons rose and sang 'Britons, strike home!' Pitt also declared, in words that would have cheered Edmund Burke, that neither truces nor treaties could curb France's 'unrelenting spirit' in 'the subversion of every state into which, either by force or fraud, their arms could penetrate'.

So unabated war continued. This aggressive and uncompromising spirit dismayed those liberal Whigs who still saw some good in the revolution and the revolutionary spirit. They decided simply to secede or, more accurately, to walk away. They got up from their benches and left, with the simple understanding that nothing they could say or do would change the course of the administration. Now that Pitt had acquired the support of the 'moderate' Whigs, in return, he was for all practical purposes unassailable. So why should the 'liberals' go to the trouble of travelling to Westminster where their voices would not be heard? It was perhaps a sensible solution but it did not endear Fox and his friends to the political world; they were accused of lacking political courage, let alone loyalty, and putting their own interests above the proper working of government.

Some of them did not stay away indefinitely and Fox himself spoke three or four times in the next couple of years, but their absence was a great blow to the national cause of reform.

War required money, of course, and all Pitt's efforts were bent on providing revenue. He had already taxed bricks and sugar, spirits and tea, but now he hit upon the bold solution of dividing all taxpayers into three categories in accordance with their ability to pay; the measure became known as the Triple Assessment, and was based upon what was called 'consumed property' such as watches, carriages and windows (an earlier window tax had been introduced in 1696). This was a tax on expenditure but there was another prospect which intrigued him with its possibilities. He hinted at it in the Triple Assessment where it was agreed that a person might choose instead to pay a tax on his income. In the following year he introduced a graduated tax on incomes of over £60 per year and, despite the expected storm of outrage over the threatened liberties of the people, it was accepted. Yet it endured only as long as the war, after which all the records of the tax office were destroyed. Such was the depth of feeling about the action of 'spying' into the financial affairs of the people.

The shadow of Buonaparte was never very far away. He was the reason why the taxes were being imposed. In the winter of 1797 his forces took up position along the French coastline with the clear purpose of invasion. In response the administration called upon local officials to question every eligible male about his ability and willingness to take up arms. In the spring of 1798, in what had now become a predictable response, certain members of the English radical societies were taken up and detained. Five men were arrested at Margate just as they were about to embark for France. William Blake wrote in the margin of a book, 'To defend the Bible in this year 1798 would cost a man his life. The Beast and the Whore rule without control.' The fear of invasion lasted throughout the spring and summer of the year, until at last it became clear that Buonaparte had another destination in mind.

The atmosphere of extreme peril encouraged the United Irishmen to attempt rebellion once again in the spring of 1798. It acquired the name of 'the great rebellion' but in truth it was a badly organized and somewhat incoherent affair that was quickly put down. But the revolutionary inclinations of certain Irishmen, and the deep dissatisfaction of many others, led the English administration to believe that the best solution to the continuing problem was a union between the two countries. Fraught with difficulties though it was, and regarded with deep suspicion both by the king and by the Dublin parliament, it was pushed and pulled through the legislatures of Westminster and Dublin for two years with much argument, threats, rhetoric and money. The act of union with Scotland in 1707 had been purchased by bribes to the Scots, now the union with Ireland was expedited by bribes to the Irish; it could be said that the United Kingdom had been conceived in a pot of gold. The new union was not welcomed by all participants. Henry Grattan, the great Irish moderate, said of his nation: 'I see her in a swoon, but she is not dead – though in her tomb she lies helpless and motionless, still there is on her lips a spirit of life, and on her cheek a glow of beauty.'

Buonaparte had meanwhile sailed into another sea of troubles. By the early spring of 1798 he had abandoned his apparent attempt at invasion and sailed towards Egypt. It turned out to be a rash decision but, on the face of it, that province of the Ottoman Empire was tempting; it might provide a land route to India, the reputed home of treasure, and immeasurably increase the amount of French trade. 'Soldiers!' Napoleon told his army as it sailed from Toulon. 'The eyes of Europe are upon you! You have great destinies to fulfil.'

Admiral Nelson, who now enters this history for the first time with a predictable flourish, chased after him. He had a sense of destiny, and a flair for self-projection, equal to that of Napoleon; he crossed and recrossed parts of the Mediterranean looking for his quarry. Buonaparte had taken Malta, but had then gone eastward. Nelson sailed to Alexandria but found no sign of him; he scoured the Levant and then sailed west to Sicily. There was still no sign. Finally, after weeks, of searching, he found Napoleon's ships at Aboukir Bay beside Alexandria to which the French had secretly returned. The signal was given for battle. 'Before this time tomorrow,' Nelson said in his usual vain and magnificent manner, 'I shall have gained a peerage or Westminster Abbey.'

In the subsequent battle of the Nile, at the beginning of August, the French fleet was overwhelmed; only four ships escaped Nelson's onslaught. Three and a half thousand French sailors were taken prisoner, and 2,000 were killed. No British ships were destroyed. Napoleon himself was now stranded in Egypt without a fleet, without reinforcements and without supplies. The British navy was once more in charge of the Mediterranean, and the victory at Aboukir prompted Turkey to enter the war against France. The news was greeted in England with predictable jubilation. A British official, George Pretyman, wrote to his wife: 'Mr Pitt is confident that Buonaparte *must be destroyed*. Oh my Love, what joy!'

An uneasy peace held for eighteen months until the forces against Buonaparte entered what was called a second coalition, a band of armies that included those of Russia and Austria as well as England. The British under the grand old duke of York arrived in Holland in the late summer of 1799, marched about a bit, and then returned home in November. Their allies did not fare any better. The Austrians and the Russians were embroiled in internal conflicts, and the tsar left the coalition in October. The Austrians were defeated decisively in the following year. Much of the French success may be credited to Napoleon who, abandoning his army in Egypt, made his way back to Paris and named himself First Consul. To the stranded army in Egypt it seemed like an act of betrayal. One of his generals, Jean-Baptiste Kléber, told his colleagues: 'That bastard has left us with his breeches full of shit. We will go back to Europe and rub them in his face.' But for Buonaparte matters of private honour and fidelity were of no consequence in his relentless pursuit of victory and glory.

If war was to be sustained by England against him, it required the maintenance of discipline at home. In the summer of 1799 William Pitt introduced the Workmen's Combination Bill which forbade any working men to come together for the purpose of seeking higher wages or shorter hours, with a minimum penalty of three months' imprisonment or two months of hard labour. 'Combination' was already illegal, but it was believed necessary to suppress anything that resembled political agitation. It might compromise the war effort.

It is significant that these prohibitions were maintained against workmen in general and not against any particular craft or trade; this added to the sense of injustice and oppression experienced primarily in the manufacturing areas. 'Secret' unions sprang up, however, among workers in cotton and wool which played some part in the outbreak of the Luddite protests of the next century. As early as 1799 the shearmen of Wiltshire sent threatening letters to those who were intent upon harnessing new machinery. 'We shall keep some people to watch you about with loaded blunderbuss or pistol.' Yet as always the practical implementation of the Combination Act was muddled and uncertain, with magistrates of the different regions varying greatly in their response. Like much legislation from Westminster, it probably made very little difference in the end.

The spirit of unrest was stirred further by another season of dearth. In the spring of 1800 an official wrote to the Home Office from Birmingham that 'many thousands, especially children, are all but starved'. It was recognized that conditions near to famine would gravely destabilize the nation already at war. Pitt wrote in the autumn that 'the question of peace or war is not in itself half so formidable as the scarcity with which it is necessarily combined, and for the evils and growing dangers of which I see no adequate remedy'. He wrote at a time of riot. In September 1800, the corn exchange in Mark Lane, London, was stormed after some handbills were posted on the Monument, proclaiming that 'Bread will be sixpence the quarter if the people will assemble at the corn market on Monday.' On the following day some bakers' shops in Whitechapel were attacked by a mob; on the day after that, a handbill was addressed to 'starved fellow creatures' asking them to meet on St George's Fields 'to defend your rights. Never mind the blood-thirsty soldiers. We shall put them to flight . . .' Riots erupted in all parts of the country, and Matthew Boulton said that there were so many soldiers in Birmingham that it resembled an armed camp.

The policy of the administration itself was in disarray. The coalition against Napoleon was not holding; Prussia and Russia, Russia and Austria, Austria and Prussia, were all quarrelling over control of various parts of the continent. England itself could not be attacked, but neither could it strike. Some members of the cabinet preferred a return of the Bourbon dynasty in Paris, a policy which seemed to hold out little chance of success; others believed that there was no point in negotiating with Buonaparte, while certain colleagues argued that negotiation was the only way forward. Disagreements arose also about the role of the allies in any peace talks; should they be allowed to participate or should Britain stand on its own?

The general sentiment, however, was in favour of peace. This seems to have been the overwhelming desire of the people who were thoroughly weary of a war that had already endured for more than seven years. This desire was further intensified by the resurgence of the enemy. It was Buonaparte who took his armies over the Alps, in the spring of 1800, and defeated the Austrians at Marengo. At the subsequent treaty of Lunéville on 9 February 1801, he gained the German districts on the left bank of the Rhine, Belgium and Luxemburg as well as large swathes of Italy. Buonaparte had not conquered the enemy, one strategist wrote, but rendered it harmless. Britain was once more on its own.

This was the moment when William Pitt decided to resign his office, just five days before the signing of the treaty. His departure came as a surprise to the political world, however, and was for a while considered as suspicious – as a 'juggle' somehow to further Pitt's interest. It was said that he did not want to be the legislator who would be forced to broker a peace with Napoleon. It was surmised that he was exhausted; he was in bad health; he was unnerved by the scale of famine and of riot; he was tired of holding the balance between opposing interests. But in truth it had nothing to do with the war or famine. It had to do with Ireland.

In his negotiations over the Act of Union – during which Henry Grattan had lamented the sleeping beauty of his country – Pitt suggested, or intimated, or let it be known, that the emancipation of the majority Catholic population would duly follow and that they would be able to hold legal and political office. But he had not reckoned with the king, who regarded any such concession to be against the spirit and letter of his coronation oath in which he had pledged to defend the Church of England. He could not countenance a country in which there was more than one established religion. George III could be stubborn as well as principled, and on this matter he was adamant. He went over to one of Pitt's allies, Henry Dundas, at a royal levee and questioned him in a voice loud enough to be overheard by many of those present. 'What is the question you are all about to force on me? What is this Catholic emancipation . . . I will tell you that I shall look on every man as my personal enemy who proposes that question to me. I hope all my friends will not desert me.'

Pitt was aware of the exchange within a matter of minutes. He, who treasured his reputation more than anything else, then felt obliged to resign. The king, knowing that he had an alternative administration in waiting, accepted the first minister's wish. Pitt left office and gave way for Henry Addington, who was what might be called a 'solid' choice, dependable, hard-working and honest. He also had the advantage, for the king, of being opposed to Catholic emancipation. Unfortunately none of these qualities was enough in itself to guarantee pre-eminence and in a cruel rhyme spread by a young minister, George Canning, it was said that 'Pitt is to Addington what London is to Paddington'. The new prime minister was also known as 'the Doctor', since he had practised for some years as a physician for the wealthier and unhealthier portion of society. His father had also been an eminent physician who in fact had numbered Pitt's father, the earl of Chatham, among his patients. The Doctor was no great orator and found it difficult to exert his authority over the Commons, let alone the nation.

The king, in a state of excitement close to hysteria, now began to suffer once more from his old malady – or, as some put it, his old madness. He himself blamed Pitt and the Catholic question for his relapse, and Pitt had felt obliged to promise him that he would never raise the matter again. Within a month the king recovered. Pitt had fallen, but no party had gone with him. He was but one man, and many of his ministers agreed to serve under Addington. A few chairs had been arranged in a different fashion, but nothing further. Yet there was one significant change that would affect the political world in succeeding years. Without Pitt's personal hegemony the various parties that had comprised his administration now began to fall apart. Pitt sat on the treasury benches but at a distance from the members of the new administration; he did nothing, however, to oppose it. He felt it his duty, in fact to support it as the visible representative of the king's wishes.

It became clear enough that Addington desired peace at almost any price. The nation desired it. The finances of the country required it. It no longer seemed to be a symbolic clash of ideologies but, rather, a more familiar contest over the balance of power on the continent. By the beginning of October the government announced the preliminary terms of a treaty. The depth of public approval became evident when a London crowd dragged the coach of the French envoy through the streets crying out 'Long live Buonaparte!'

But the governing class was not so happy. It was believed that Addington, weak as he was, had purchased peace at too high a price. All Britain's wartime conquests in the Mediterranean and outside Europe were to be returned; the acquisitions in the East Indies, the West Indies and South America (with the exception of Ceylon and Trinidad) would all be relinquished. The French would retain control of the Netherlands, Switzerland and parts of northern Italy. The treaty, when it was eventually signed at Amiens in the spring of 1802, confirmed that France had been allowed to expand to what it termed its 'natural frontiers' without making any parallel concessions of its own. Addington declared that 'this is no ordinary peace but a genuine reconciliation between the two first nations of the world'. Others were not so sure. Food was still dear; commerce was in disarray; the dreadful income tax was not abolished.

Some considered it to be the best of bad alternatives. The *Morning Chronicle*, which spoke for Fox and his liberal Whig allies, stated that 'the country has been degraded by the peace, though it is necessary'. Some of Pitt's old ministers, who had left office with him, were less ambiguous. William Windham said that 'the country has received its death blow'; George Grenville stated that 'all confidence in the present government is completely and irretrievably destroyed'. Henry Dundas was more circumspect, telling Pitt that 'the only wise and friendly thing I can do is to impose upon myself silence'. Pitt himself, despite private reservations, continued publicly to support the government. The treaty of Amiens was widely regarded as a truce, a time to recuperate so that the two countries might be able to resume the fight at a later date. Buonaparte was himself already busy with the plans for new wars, eager to gain mastery over the entire continent. In the autumn of 1802 he marched his armies into Switzerland, to which blatant abrogation of the treaty Addington made only the mildest of protests. The era known as that of the 'Napoleonic wars' had truly begun.

31

A Romantic tale

On 5 June 1797, Samuel Taylor Coleridge 'did not keep to the high road, but leapt over a gate and bounded down the pathless field, by which he cut off an angle'. So William Wordsworth recalled one of the first meetings between himself and the fellow poet who together with him would help to change the language of expression and inaugurate what would become known as the 'Romantic movement' in poetry. They already had much in common. They were both engaged in blank verse tragedies, but Coleridge's *Osorio* and Wordsworth's *The Borderers* did not find favour with theatrical managers. Each man had written two slim volumes of poetry – Wordsworth's *An Evening Walk* and *Descriptive Sketches* were published in 1793, while Coleridge's *Poems on Various Subjects* and *Poems* were presented to the world in 1796 and 1797. But they had already encountered one another at the house of a sugar merchant in Bristol. Coleridge had been impressed by what he called Wordsworth's 'novel imagery' and 'vivid colouring', and in turn Wordsworth remarked that Coleridge's 'talent appears to me very great'. Wordsworth was twenty-seven, and Coleridge three years his junior.

Eight years before, at a most impressionable age, they had woken up in Year One of the French Revolution. They had celebrated the death of tyranny, the breaking of the idols of Church and King, of tradition and authority. Anything was possible. Everything was possible. Coleridge, still at school, composed a celebratory poem called 'The Destruction of the Bastille'. Wordsworth had gone to France, tasted some of the excitement, and then retreated, leaving an illegitimate daughter behind. He still mingled with what were known as 'the friends of liberty', however, and in the early months of 1793 wrote an open or public letter, never published, in which he refers to himself as 'a republican'; in the following year he wrote to a friend that 'I am of that odious class of men called democrats'.

Yet the Terror in the late months of 1793 and the French invasion of Switzerland in 1798 had a chastening effect upon the erstwhile enthusiasts of revolution. Coleridge had vowed to put down 'my squeaking baby-trumpet of sedition', and gone back to the springs of Unitarian theology where 'Truth is Christ'. Wordsworth went on a walking tour before settling with his sister in Dorset. The flame of the revolution was now only flickering as he was vouchsafed glimpses of the pantheistic vision that would support his later poetry.

They already shared an enthusiasm, even reverence, for a poet of Bristol. William Wordsworth had been introduced to Thomas Chatterton's *Miscellanies* by his schoolmaster; in 1802, in 'Resolution and Independence' he referred to Chatterton as the 'marvellous Boy'. Coleridge wrote and rewrote a 'Monody on the Death of Chatterton' from the age of thirteen to the time of his own death. Thomas Chatterton was the Romantic avatar in an age of false taste, a status which his early demise had only confirmed. It was believed that at the age of seventeen he had committed suicide by arsenic poison in his little garret on Brooke Street in Holborn; it was widely surmised that he had died of poverty and starvation in the unequal stuggle to find an audience for his fervid poetry which had conjured up the spirit of an antique age. His verses were supposed to be the work of a medieval monk, Thomas Rowley, who had chronicled the heroic and martial world of the Middle Ages. The verses opened up a world of wonder and delight. They stirred the two young men like a trumpet. Here was a genuine entry into a lost world of imagination, of supernatural event and superhuman courage. The fact that they were fakes mattered not at all; they were still authentic.

Chatterton's apparent suicide was then considered to be the sublime death of a genius cast aside by the world; in the words of Keats, another avid devotee, a 'dear child of sorrow – son of misery!' In due course his life, and his death as depicted in a painting by Henry Wallis, became the paradigm of the Romantic sensibility. Chattterton's 'solemn agony', in the phrase of Shelley, was the first intimation of Romantic suffering which in the early decades of the nineteenth century became the sensibility of Europe. Chatterton was the solitary genius *in excelsis*.

But solitariness and genius were not then vital principles for Wordsworth and Coleridge. By 1797 they were unsettled and undecided about their futures, in need of money or of patrons. What is more, they seemed to need one another. They engaged in long walks through the countryside of Somerset in which they had both eventually settled, Coleridge with his wife and son and Wordsworth with his sister. Wordsworth walked in a straight line, while Coleridge was divagatory. They considered an epic poem entitled 'The Wanderings of Cain', but it came to nothing. Two weeks after that failure, on a walking tour along the Bristol Channel in November, they devised the plan of 'The Ancient Mariner'. But even as they started work upon the joint project Wordsworth realized that their writing was incompatible and that he could only be a 'clog' on Coleridge's vividly realized narrative. As he said, 'we pulled different ways'. Dorothy Wordsworth was the catalyst between them. Her watchful interest in, and enthusiasm for, the workings of the natural world helped to recreate the landscape in which they walked together; the intimate simplicity of her journals, begun on 20 January 1798, was a token of the world of feeling in which the young poets flourished.

Coleridge's fluency and vivacity had in any case an inspiring effect upon his colleague. Wordsworth wrote much between November 1797 and June 1798, with the peak of his powers manifest between March and May. The poems he composed concerned the plight of the poor and the progress of the poet's mind. In April 1798, he wrote to a prospective publisher that 'I have gone on very rapidly adding to my stock of poetry.' This was to include many of the poems that eventually found their place in *Lyrical Ballads* (1798). At a later date in *Biographia Literaria* (1817) Coleridge explained that in their conversation on the proposed new volume they determined upon poetry of two sorts. In the first 'the incidents and agents were to be, in part at least, supernatural'. Thus the inclusion of 'The Ancient Mariner'. But for the second sort 'subjects were to be chosen from ordinary life; the characters and incidents were to be such, as will be found in every village and its vicinity'. The egalitarian fury of the revolution had subsided but their feelings for equality and democracy, for shared human experience and shared human values, had found a safer haven.

They had found it, in part, in language. If the intention was to choose incidents and situations 'from common life', the instinctive medium had to be 'a selection of language really used by men'. The tone could be discursive and colloquial but, equally, it could partake of the street ballads and Scottish ballads that were popular; on no account, however, could it seem to be artificial. Poetic diction and periphrasis were the ornaments of sheer habit and custom. They were the 'mind-forg'd manacles' that Blake condemned.

With the chastened language came new meanings. The 'Advertisement' of the book promised 'a natural delineation of human passions, human characters, and human incidents'. This was not necessarily a new experiment or daring innovation; the poetry of the 1790s had sought a ballad-like simplicity in tales of mad mothers or idiot boys. What was new (and understood by some as such) was the vividness of tone and feeling. The key was simplicity, not of a naïve or unconsidered kind but well pondered and conceived so that it became more powerfully evocative of the belief in 'a motion and a spirit' which 'rolls through all things'. There is even a tone of inward uncertainty that deepens the language, rendering it a vehicle for associations and preocccupations that are more powerful than the ostensible subject. The two poets were relocating dignity in the commonplace, restoring grace and simplicity to ordinary lives where saints and sinners walked unannounced and unknown. This was real liberty, equality and fraternity. That is why Francis Jeffrey, in an acerbic notice in the *Edinburgh Review*, compared *Lyrical Ballads* with Tom Paine's *The Rights of Man*.

So in the autumn of 1798 appeared a volume of 210 pages at the price of 5 shillings. Of the twenty-four poems, nineteen were composed by Wordsworth. But his fellow poet had opened the collection with 'The Ancient Mariner', a decision which Wordsworth later deemed to be a mistake. Yet Coleridge considered the poems to be '*one work, in kind, tho' not in degree*'. 'The Ancient Mariner' itself could in fact be conceived of as an example of the Wordsworthian sublime, for example, concerned with the intrinsic power of human sympathy in an uncaring world; the old mariner himself was obliged to live for ever as an outcast, the solitary wanderer of the Romantic vision, but the aspiration of the poem is towards benevolence and human community.

Lyrical Ballads concluded with 'Lines Written Above Tintern Abbey', a powerful meditation in blank verse that opened the way to the great poems of Wordsworth's maturity such as *The Prelude* and *The Excursion*. 'Tintern Abbey' in particular helped to change the understanding of landscape and of nature which, for many, took on the sacred vesture of natural religion. They had once been considered picturesque but now they conveyed a spiritual or supernatural force. By means of Wordsworth's poetry nature was granted religious significance as the nurse of piety and wisdom. It was a moral agent, an agent for good and benevolent change in the human heart. Coleridge and Wordsworth were described as representing 'the modern school of poets' and when Wordsworth eventually moved to the Lake District in 1799 they were known as 'the Lake school'. Pilgrims began to travel to that neighbourhood and Wordsworth wrote a guidebook for these new spiritual travellers.

So even if the little book was not a popular success on its first appearance, it had an abiding significance. Over the course of years it became the source and fountain of what became known as the Romantic sensibility of the early nineteenth century in England, part of a movement of taste which stretched across France and Germany, Russia and Italy and Spain.

Yet a strange light appeared on the fringes of the distant clouds. By the late nineteenth century the imperatives of the Romantic movement had been transformed into an appeal for state 'benevolence' and 'human community' to oppose the tyranny of laissez-faire. That is material for another volume.

32

Pleasures of peace

In the summer of 1802 Napoleon had been appointed as 'first consul for life' after a national referendum that apparently gave him 99 per cent of the vote. The ideals of the revolution were now effectively dead; the tree of liberty had been torn from its roots, and equality was now honoured only in name. Jacobin republicanism of the English variety had lost its purpose. 'Jacobinism is killed and gone,' Sheridan said, 'and by whom? By him who can no longer be called the child and champion of Jacobinism – by Buonaparte . . . he gave it a true fraternal hug and strangled it.' The days of the champions of liberty and democracy were over, and in 1801 William Godwin, the author of *An Enquiry Concerning Political Justice* and himself once a fervent Jacobin, noted that 'even the starving labourer in the alehouse is become a champion of aristocracy'.

The parlous state of Jacobinism was revealed in an inept conspiracy of certain so-called revolutionaries led by Colonel Despard. He and his associates had formed a secret society which migrated from tavern to tavern in London, from The Two Bells in Whitechapel to The Bleeding Heart in Holborn, with the express purpose of 'an equalization of civic, political and religious rights'; the authorities, alerted by informers and police spies, arrested Despard. Forty of his followers were seized at The Oakley Arms in Lambeth. At the subsequent trial it was alleged that they had conspired in a *coup d'état* in which the Bank of England and the Tower would be captured, the prisons thrown open, and the king killed or taken prisoner. Despard was found guilty and hanged at Tyburn.

The drift to war continued at an ever-accelerating speed, as soon as it became clear that Napoleon had no intention of abiding by the principles of the treaty of Amiens. Yet Britain was also at fault; it had not evacuated Malta and returned it to the Knights of St John, as it had agreed to do in the treaty. At a reception in the Tuileries on 13 March 1803, Buonaparte admonished the English ambassador, Lord Whitworth, in front of other diplomats. 'It is you who are determined to make war against us; you want to drive me to it.' Buonaparte was not the one to shirk any challenge and told Whitworth that 'you will be the first to draw the sword; I shall be the last to sheathe it. Woe to those who show no respect for treaties!' The last sword was not put back in its scabbard for thirteen more years.

The first consul had already made preparations for conflict. French ships in the Mediterranean had embarked men, and French troops in Belgium had been moved towards Dunkirk and Le Havre. A message from George III to parliament urged the need for action; more men were to be enlisted in the fleet by means of bounties and, if further persuasion were needed, a 'hot press' was to be instituted in the streets and taverns of London.

It soon became clear that Henry Addington was not equal to the task of first minister imposed upon him. His acceptance of what was considered to be an ignominious and ill-considered treaty did not help his reputation, but he was in any case believed to be too weak and indecisive; his preferred policy in the face of Napoleonic threat was inaction. The man about to become home secretary, Charles Yorke, told his brother that Addington 'is not equal to the crisis in which we stand. In truth I think there is but one man among us who is; I mean Pitt.' Yet Pitt was not ready to replace his successor; he believed Addington to be 'a stupider fellow than he had thought him' but he was not ready to defy the king's wishes.

The current administration's position was rendered more precarious by its ill-considered and ill-managed attempt to call up volunteers for the army to confront Napoleon. The response was very encouraging but it soon became clear that there were no instructors to train them and no arms to furnish them; the local officials were obliged to give orders to discourage further recruitment and then to abandon it altogether. Any central authority was thrown into doubt. Where Buonaparte had the will and genius to create a *force armée*, the English equivalent was in disarray.

On 16 May 1803 George III ordered the seizure of all French shipping and, on 18 May, war between France and England was formally declared. The British fleet under the command of Cornwallis sailed towards Brest, and a force was dispatched against the French in San Domingo. Buonaparte in turn was now making active preparations for the invasion of England. An armed camp was set up at Boulogne, as close to the coast of England as possible, and it had been calculated that a flotilla of small ships would be able to cross the Channel in a single night. An atmosphere close to panic now descended upon England; despite the early discouragement in organizing volunteers, it was estimated that approximately half a million men were now under arms. The south coast was fortified with beacons and the new Martello towers. Yet in fact the French fleet did nothing at all. Its flotilla of boats would not be able to master the English navy and, for the time being, Buonaparte lost all interest in an invasion.

On the day that war was formally declared, Pitt finally took over office from Addington. But he was weaker now, in body and in spirit, and he was forced to patch together an administration from several different elements. He had become more erratic and less business-like, refusing to write letters or to deal with affairs after dinner; he also had a greater tendency to weep in public, which did not endear him to his less tender colleagues who were already cultivating a mid-nineteenth-century *gravitas* and sobriety.

At the end of 1804 Buonaparte was graciously pleased to allow himself to be crowned emperor of the French as Napoleon I. As emperor, rather than king, he was outflanking the Bourbon dynasty and claiming for himself the mantle of Charlemagne as absolute ruler of Europe in the west. Pope Pius VII had been invited to Paris in order to preside over the official coronation, but Napoleon took the crown from the pontiff's hands and placed it on his own head. The Prussians, the Russians and the Austrians looked on with disquiet.

On 2 January 1805, the new emperor addressed an apparently fraternal letter to George III in which he outlined the pleasures of peace. Was there no way of coming to an agreement after seven years of war? 'Should this moment be lost, what limits can be set to a war that all my efforts could not bring to an end?' The letter was such a breach of protocol that it could not be answered – George considered it to be 'much below my attention' – but the message itself was received with some interest. The perfidy and self-interest of Buonaparte, who believed all treaties and concordats to be so many pieces of paper, may have dictated its content; but it was perhaps also an intimation that the French did not fully believe that they could stand against any future 'confederacy' of Europe or the financial and naval power of the British. To the Commons Pitt quoted a speech by Cicero to the Roman senate in condemnation of Mark Antony. 'Why therefore do I refuse peace? Because it is ignoble, because it is dangerous and because it cannot be.' He might have added, however, Cicero's caution that 'the sinews of war are infinite money'.

The task for Pitt was therefore to confront the emperor on as broad a basis as ever, and he set about constructing a new coalition of allies who were united in their fear of Napoleon rather than upon any overall continental policy. In April 1805, Austria and Russia joined forces; when in the following month Napoleon was crowned king of Italy, with Genoa and Savoy as the immediate spoils, they formed a new alliance with England. The third coalition comprised England, Austria, Russia, Sweden and, finally, Prussia; but like its predecessors it was not destined to endure. Within a year it had been broken apart by the emperor of the French.

While creating the alliance Pitt decided to engage in sudden strikes that would deter Buonaparte from his threatened invasion of England and, in the autumn of the year, the English commander seized the bullion carried by a Spanish convoy and sank the ships. It was an open provocation to Spain to declare war, but Pitt already knew that the Spaniards had taken the side of France; he was only helping himself to a little of their gold.

In the course of these preparations the two great protagonists of sea and land, Admiral Nelson and Major-General Sir Arthur Wellesley, soon to become Viscount Wellington and, later, duke, met accidentally in an ante-room at the Colonial Office in White-hall. Wellington later recalled that 'he entered at once into conversation with me, if I can call it conversation, for it was almost all on his side, and all about himself, and in, really, a style so vain and silly as to surprise and almost disgust me. I suppose something that I happened to say may have made him guess that I was *some-body*.' Nelson left the room for a moment, to ascertain the identity of his unwilling companion. When he returned 'all that I thought a charlatan style had vanished and he talked . . . with a good sense and a knowledge of subjects both at home and abroad that surprised me equally and more agreeably than the first part of our interview had done; he talked like an officer and a statesman'.

Here we have a convincing portrait of the mercurial admiral, often vain and silly, but also informed and persuasive. He was ambitious but he was also determined. Wellington shared his deter-mination and decisiveness but he was less flamboyant; he had been trained in the hard school of India, and was reserved to the point of reticence. Yet both of them knew how to outwit Napoleon.

The central purpose of the third coalition was to drive Buona-parte behind the frontiers of France as they had existed in 1791; this meant that its members had to expel France from Hanover, Holland, northern Germany, Switzerland, Naples and northern Italy. This mighty undertaking was not helped by the different purposes and sensibilities of the participants. England was simply opposed to Buonaparte's aspirations, while Austria deemed him and his 'empire' to be a shocking affront to its imperial presence. Tsar Alexander seems to have been motivated by simple jealousy of his rival, but of course private feelings can change in different circumstances.

The war on land did not go well for those opposing the French. Napoleon had decided to destroy the Austrian army before its Russian allies had time to reach it; so he made a rapid advance with almost 200,000 troops from the Rhine to the Danube, where they surrounded the Austrian forces who surrendered at Ulm on 20 October 1805. The speed and efficiency of the *grande armée* were confirmed when Napoleon led them up the valley of the Danube before capturing Vienna. Its 'great turn', when it wheeled right from the Rhine to the Danube, was one of the outstanding military movements of the war.

This French victory was, at least in English eyes, overshadowed by the news at sea. Nelson in the *Victory* had joined his fleet outside Cadiz at the end of September, where his excitement and enthusiasm reduced some of his officers to tears. He wished to achieve 'not victory, but annihilation'. He planned to lure the French out of Cadiz towards Gibraltar, with the steep cliffs of Cape Trafalgar to the east. On 21 October, he relayed his final orders with the famous phrase 'England expects that every man will do his duty.' He gave one other order just as the firing began. 'Engage more closely!' The French were in a loose crescent line while the English came up in two columns, Nelson to the left in the *Victory* and Collingwood to the right in the *Royal Sovereign*. Thick clouds of smoke drifted across the scene of war, but the English ships sailed straight against the French and broke their line apart.

One by one the French vessels surrendered, but the losses were not all one side. Nelson himself was struck by a stray bullet and fell mortally wounded onto the deck. He is supposed to have said 'They have done for me at last.' He lingered for more than two hours, until three in the afternoon, and by five the battle was concluded with the blowing-up of a French ship of the line, the *Achille*. The superior skills of the British crews, and the superior acumen of the British commanders, had prevailed.

Seventeen of the French and Spanish vessels, out of a total of thirty-three, were captured or destroyed. No British ship had been lost. The victory confirmed the naval supremacy of the British, and from this time forward there was no talk of a French invasion across the Channel. At the Lord Mayor's banquet in the following month, Pitt was toasted as the 'saviour of Europe'. He replied, modestly enough, that 'I return you many thanks for the honour you have done me, but Europe is not to be saved by any single man. England has saved herself by her exertions, and will, as I trust, save Europe by her example.'

The victory of Trafalgar was soon glorified in national memory and naval legend. Napoleon, deep in Europe, did not learn of the outcome for some days; on hearing the result he is said to have leaped up from the table exclaiming, 'I cannot be everywhere!' He was in any case about to launch a final and mortal attack upon the Russian and Austrian armies. On 13 November he entered Vienna, where he began to reorganize the affairs of the archduchy, but by the end of the month he was advancing against the combined forces of the enemy. He moved swiftly and at nine in the morning on 2 December confronted them between the towns of Brno and Austerlitz, where in a series of manoeuvres he succeeded in cutting the allied armies in two. 'One sharp blow,' he said, 'and the war is over.' He had feigned indecision to lure them forwards and, when they counter-attacked, he sent forward reinforcements concealed in fog. Several cavalry charges, in which 10,000 horse were involved, guaranteed French victory.

It has been called 'The Battle of the Three Emperors' and on this occasion Tsar Alexander I of Russia and the last Holy Roman emperor, Francis II, left the field in confusion and dismay. Their forces fled. One observer declared that 'there were no longer regiments or army corps, there were only disorderly bands of marauders'. The Austrians and Russians lost approximately 26,000 men, while the French army forfeited 7,000. Alexander agreed to withdraw his forces behind his frontier, while Francis was obliged to accept humiliating terms of peace. Napoleon was finally the master of Europe.

It was said that the news of Austerlitz effectively killed Pitt. For days and weeks after he wore what was called an 'Austerlitz face' of deep sorrow. One Whig peer, Lord Auckland, said that the event involved 'not only the well-being but the very existence of the British Empire'. The joy over Trafalgar now seemed premature.

Napoleon returned in triumph to Paris after Austerlitz. He made one of his brothers, Joseph, king of Naples; another brother, Louis, was announced as king of Holland. His old adversary, William Pitt, was now facing death. Pitt's private secretary, Dacre Adams, wrote later that his eyes were 'almost lifeless' and his voice was 'hollow'; he could not eat without vomiting, and survived on raw egg mixed with brandy. He told his doctor, Sir Walter Farquhar, that 'when in conversation with persons upon important business, I felt suddenly as if I had been cut in two'. It might have been his liver, his kidneys, or his stomach.

When he lay on his deathbed in the first month of 1806 he sometimes muttered 'Hear! Hear!', as if he were listening to a debate in the Commons; then on the night of 22 January he called out, according to different reports, 'How I love my country' or 'How I leave my country'. He died early on the following morning at the age of forty-six. For twenty-five years he had been the guiding star of Westminster. Now the star had faded and there was, according to Fox, 'something missing in the world'.

The group of politicians, known as 'Mr Pitt's friends', had been in a state of some confusion; all were competent but none was pre-eminent, and when the king asked the surviving ministers if they could continue under a new leader they declined the opportunity. They could not agree to raise any one man above the others. When the king realized that they would not be able to form an administration he had turned to William Grenville as a possible successor; Grenville's father had been first minister, and he himself had been foreign secretary as well as a first cousin of Pitt's. He was a pillar of the political world but he was by no means, in the jargon of the day, a 'Pittite' or anything close to Pitt himself.

He in turn reached out towards Charles James Fox and his Whig supporters. The eventual administration was known, perhaps sarcastically, as 'The Ministry of All the Talents', and it included Fox as foreign secretary. What were then known as Grenvillites, Foxites, Windhamites, Lansdownites, Sidmouthites and Addingtonians had also joined the ministry, an indication that Whig policies had largely given way to personalities in the great Westminster game. Grenville himself had decided to adopt the role of chairman of the board, exhorting and guiding various independent managers. It was not the most stable of positions, and the government itself lasted for little more than a year. One ardent Whig, John Cam Hobhouse, wrote that 'the odium affixed to that coalition survived their short-lived power'. They were accused of nepotism and corruption which came under the all-encompassing description of 'jobbing'. It was not a good year for the Whigs.

Fox himself had now to expedite negotiations with Buonaparte and his agents. It had been Fox who had celebrated the revolution with fervour and had embraced the French cause long after other devotees had abandoned it. But he was now in the uncomfortable position of realizing that his erstwhile hero, Napoleon Buonaparte, was as perfidious and as dangerous as any ordinary politician. His abortive negotiations with the French minister, Talleyrand, convinced him that peace was not to be achieved at any reasonable cost. The French were still bent upon aggression and territorial conquest. Fox noted to his nephew, Lord Holland, 'the shuffling, insincere way in which they act, that shows me they are playing a false game'. Yet some believed that Fox, once the ardent francophile, would conclude a peace on whatever terms; the young Palmerston wrote that 'I cannot see how at present peace can bring us anything but dishonour and defeat'. Fox did not have to bear his own dismay and disillusion for very long, as he died in the autumn of the year.

Napoleon's recalcitrance had been well founded. At the beginning of August 1806, several principalities and kingdoms of south Germany formally seceded from the Holy Roman Empire, which now came to its long-awaited end, and accepted Buonaparte's protection as head of their new confederation. In the month after Fox's death, October 1806, the French army met the Prussian forces at Jena and inflicted a resounding defeat. The Prussian army had once been feared for its military skills and redoubtable leadership but its chain of command had become arthritic and its mobility therefore weakened. The legacy of Frederick the Great had been broken. Hegel considered the battle to mark 'the end of history', by which he meant that he foresaw the end of nation-states in the wake of Napoleon's imperial ambitions.

As if on cue the French armies invaded Prussia, taking Berlin in their path, and the king Frederick William III fled east with his family to enjoy the protection of the tsar. Mirabeau, one of the early revolutionaries, had said that 'the Prussian monarchy is so constituted that it could not bear up under any calamity'. And so it proved. Napoleon's thoughts, too, were turning east with territorial longings greater than ever before. The victory over Prussia provoked jubilation in France where one French minister of state, Pasquier, remarked that 'nothing could have appeared so incredible'. Yet the joy of the French was tempered by the desire for the palpable fruits of victory, the greatest of which was peace.

But Napoleon was not in a peaceful mood. Ensconced in the newly captured city of Berlin, according to Pasquier, he 'affected the language and attitude of a sovereign who commands his subjects'. The Prussians were no longer the enemy but a band of rebels, and the nobles of that country were no more than petty courtiers to be dismissed with a wave of the hand. His preoccupation now was with Russia, and he began to march further east into Poland which might once have sufficed as a barrier state between France and Russia; he occupied Warsaw and then rested, having driven the Russians 50 miles east of that city. He came in the apparent role of liberator, since that country had been partitioned over the years by Russia, Prussia and Austria. He said that 'it is a dead body to which life must be restored before anything can be made of it'. So some Poles welcomed him as a deliverer. He even created an independent state, to be known as the duchy of Warsaw, but it did not survive.

While in Berlin his thoughts had turned again to his old enemy. If he could not assault Britain by sea or land, he could attack her by means of commerce. Trade was the key to Britain's success; if that could be cut off or curtailed then the country would greatly suffer. If she were reduced to commercial isolation, then she might be induced to surrender. That at least was his intention.

The Berlin Decrees, issued from that city in November 1806, declared that the British Isles were subject to total blockade; no country should trade with Britain, and no foreign ports should be open to her. All her foreign markets were forthwith to be closed. It sounds like a draconian decree but in truth the Continental System, as it became known, had no permanent effect. Britain was too rich, and too productive, to be permanently cowed; the continent of Europe could not command enough resources to survive. Even Napoleon's soldiers were clothed with textiles made in northern England. There was a crisis in trade in 1808, and then again in 1811, and there was for a time the phantom of famine, but the economic order soon stabilized. The regulations were either ignored or thwarted across vast swathes of Napoleon's empire, and a black market in prohibited goods was established. It became clear that Napoleon had to fight more battles, and plan more campaigns, to ensure that the Continental System was being obeyed.

In retaliation the British issued Orders in Council at the beginning of 1807 which were designed to mount a blockade against

France; no neutral ships were permitted to enter French ports, and the greater efficiency of the British navy ensured that this barrier was not one to be crossed with impunity. Coffee, tobacco and other commodities became rare in the French capital.

In the winter of 1806 Napoleon was still on the march. The weather was terrible, the winds sharp and the snow treacherous, but 'impossible' was not a word to utter to the emperor. With the hostile forces of Russia, Prussia and Sweden about him, and Austria threatening in the rear, his army moved eastward; it was checked at Eylau, in a particularly bloody and inconclusive battle, but then advanced still further until it crushed the Russian army at the battle of Friedland. By the summer of 1807 the tsar was forced to come to terms with the emperor on a raft in the middle of the River Neman at Tilsit. A separate treaty with Prussia was signed two days later, by the terms of which that country was effectively dismembered. It had now been confirmed to all the protagonists that Napoleon was the undisputed master of Europe and, with Russia by his side, he might hope eventually to destroy an isolated Britain. The Russian commander noted that 'the two emperors have shaken hands. Europe has cause to tremble.' George III himself was convinced that some kind of accommodation would have to be made with Napoleon.

What was everyone really talking about in the autumn of 1807? Lady Bessborough, lover of Sheridan and mother to Lady Caroline Lamb, wrote to the British envoy in St Petersburg about the news of the day. 'War with Russia? Nothing like it. America? Still less. What can occasion such a ferment in every house, in every street, in every shop, in every garret about London? It is the Light and Heat company . . . That strong light that has lit up Pall Mall for this year past has all at once blaz'd up like a comet.' The streets of London were now illuminated by gas, and seemed to any stranger to be paved with gold.

The unfortunate Ministry of All the Talents had already resigned, in the spring of the year. William Grenville had fallen not so much as a result of Napoleon's victories but from the continuing struggle between the king and his ministers over Ireland; the government wished to make concessions to the majority Catholic population, but the king demurred. When George insisted that all the members of the cabinet should sign a pledge to renounce any further attempt at Catholic emancipation, they resigned in protest. Gillray published a cartoon entitled 'The Pigs Possessed or the Broad bottom'd Litter running headlong into ye Sea of Perdition'. George, portrayed as a farmer, denounces the pigs as they jump over the cliff: 'Oh you cursed ungrateful brutes!' 'Broad bottom' was the name given to a cross-party administration.

The Ministry of All the Talents had achieved one notable feat, however, in the abolition of the slave trade. Its moment had come. In the spring of 1807 the Act for the Abolition of the Slave Trade passed the Commons by a majority of 283 votes to 16 votes, a victory that surprised even William Wilberforce who ascribed it to Providence. Slavery itself, as opposed to the trade, was not abolished until twenty-six years later.

Another pig popped up, in the shape of the duke of Portland, as all the talents sank beneath the waves. When Grenville was obliged to resign, therefore, he was replaced by a sixty-nine-year-old man who was crippled with bad health and with an addiction to laudanum; the duke of Portland could not have controlled a crèche let alone a cabinet. He was soon incapable of political business, unable either to read long dispatches or engage in lengthy conversations. The stone consigned him to long periods of continual pain, and it was said that he was generally asleep or silent. This left him essentially as a figurehead, supposedly controlling a cabinet that contained rival personalities and principles. The conglomeration of them, plotting and planning against each other, became known as 'The Ins and Outs'.

This was not perhaps the best administration to continue the fight against Napoleon. At the opening of parliament, on 28 January 1808, George III readied the people for the struggle yet to come. In an official 'Note' published in the *Moniteur* twelve days later Buonaparte pledged that peace would come only after England had been stripped of her overseas possessions which were 'the principal source of her wealth'.

The war had in any case assumed a different aspect when Napoleon was obliged to look to his southern flank. The Iberian peninsula had become dangerous. In the spring of 1808 the emperor had decreed that his older brother, Joseph, should assume the monarchy of Spain as part of the French imperium; the Spanish were not willing to have a foreign ruler imposed upon them and fomented a nationalist rebellion. Six delegates from Asturias sailed to England and, having arrived at Falmouth, beseeched aid from the British government. The response could not have been more enthusiastic. Here was the opportunity to open another front against the French, with a line of command and communication that relied upon the sea. Nothing could have been more promising. Ten thousand men were dispatched to the peninsula under the command of Sir Arthur Wellesley.

Portugal was also in rebellion against the French who had occupied Lisbon the year before. Napoleon had decided that his blockade of Britain would have a better chance of success if all the Portuguese ports were closed, a decision in which the Portuguese themselves did not concur. The emperor believed that it would be relatively easy to dominate the Iberian peninsula with an army, but he mistook the nature of the terrain and the spirit of the inhabitants. The people, most notably the peasants and the clergy, rose up against the foreign oppressors and created havoc with guerrilla attacks, shooting and banditry which could be neither anticipated nor controlled. Local forces, in this and other contests, were more than a match for a foreign army.

Wellesley landed in the early summer of 1808 at Oporto, where his army was enlarged by reinforcements and by Portuguese troops. At the battle of Vimeiro, in the middle of August, the French forces were heavily defeated. But the British negotiators, under the command of Sir Hew Dalrymple, conceded too much; the French were obliged to leave the country but they were permitted to take with them all their arms and equipment. When news of the treaty reached London there was disgust and dismay at such an inadequate response. George III was said to be 'extremely angry', and a special *Gazette* reported that 'the public indignation this day is at its height . . . the people seem quite wild'. The British had bungled a great opportunity. It was widely believed and asserted that the expedition to Portugal had turned from triumph into disaster. A court of inquiry was held later in the year. Wellesley was exonerated, but Dalrymple never held another command.

The French, however, were no more successful in Spain than in Portugal; after a particularly galling defeat at Bailen, where 20,000 French soldiers were obliged to surrender to a Spanish army, Buonaparte decided that his presence was necessary on the ground. The British had sent Sir John Moore to parry the imperial thrust, and by the winter of 1808 Moore was close to Salamanca, but at this point the emperor burst through Spanish defences and occupied Madrid; Moore could not complete his mission but he was able to divert the attention of Buonaparte by marching north-west through the mountains of Galicia towards the port at Corunna where, with heroic and indeed fatal rearguard action, he managed to embark the majority of his men. He had significantly delayed Napoleon, who lost the opportunity of recapturing Portugal or finally of subduing Spain, and this interruption helped eventually to determine the struggle for the Iberian peninsula. It was to prove a costly adventure, both in men and money, for the emperor who found himself distracted by this second front which he had no realistic possibility of overcoming. It had become an open pit, swallowing up arms and armies. The day after the battle of Corunna – 17 January 1809 – Napoleon left Spain, never to return.

Yet the British came back; if for Napoleon the Iberian peninsula was at first a peripheral issue, in comparison with his great plans for European dominion, it was for his enemy a vital component of the armed struggle which provided a direct link to the European continent through the ports of Lisbon and Oporto. Its dominance in the region also gave Britain a more powerful voice in later negotiations. Wellesley returned to the peninsula in the spring of 1809 and, as commander of the allied forces, defeated the French in two significant battles. As the victor in the battle of Talavera, south-west of Madrid, he was created Viscount Wellington.

Napoleon had finally committed 350,000 troops to Spain, but they were not enough. They were diverted and dispersed by the guerrillas, and slowly worn down by Wellington in his methodical and practical logistics. He would often conceal his troops in suitable terrain before unleashing them on the unsuspecting enemy in a 'long red wall'. Buonaparte always underestimated him, calling him merely a 'sepoy general' as a consequence of his service in India, but Wellington, more than any other general, brought down the French army.

The war news further north was not so good. At the beginning of 1809 a 'fifth coalition', that between England and Austria, had been made ready to engage Buonaparte. A victory by Archduke Charles of Austria in the battle of Aspern delivered a fatal blow to the myth of Buonaparte's invincibility, but the subsequent defeat of the Austrians at Wagram tempered any false optimism.

On 28 July, three weeks after the battle of Wagram, the British sent an expedition to destroy the French naval base at Antwerp. This was the port where Napoleon was assembling a new fleet. It was a welcome opportunity for the British navy to crush an incipient maritime threat. A fleet was assembled off the coast of the South Downs and sailed to Walcheren, an island in the mouth of the Scheldt estuary within reach of the port of Antwerp. Yet here they met an enemy as deadly as it was unexpected. The island was full of malaria, and the English very quickly succumbed; 4,000 died, and 12,000 were unable to fight. By the end of the year 'Walcheren fever' had incapacitated half the British troops, and on 23 December the remnant sailed home. The campaign had become a disaster, to a universal chorus of indignation at home. It had resulted in a wanton loss of men and a vast waste of money.

The failure further unsettled an already weak administration. The betrayal at Sintra in the previous summer, when the French were allowed to leave Portugal with their arms intact, had begun the process of breaking an administration where quarrels and dissensions in the cabinet were already wounding its effectiveness. By the spring of 1809 Portland's health had deteriorated so badly that the chance for a successor looked promising. George Canning, the foreign secretary, aspired to the office but he saw a rival in Lord Castlereagh, the secretary of state for war and the colonies. Canning pressed for his dismissal, citing his supposed incompetence in the management of the war, and reached a secret pact with Portland that Castlereagh would be removed from his post as soon as practicable. Castlereagh, however, became aware of these negotiations, and rightly sensed betrayal. In the autumn of the year he challenged Canning to a duel on Putney Heath. Castlereagh was a good shot, but Canning had never used a pistol before in his life; when Canning was wounded in the thigh, both men felt obliged to resign from the high posts which their juvenile or old-fashioned behaviour had damaged. Lord Portland, with a broken cabinet, left office soon after.

The surviving ministers looked at one another with a wild surmise, and soon proceeded with what Canning called 'constant meetings and co-jobberations'. Canning himself still held ambitions for the highest office, even though his recent conduct had effectively disqualified him; he wrote that he was 'still not wholly *out*, yet not altogether *in* office'. The other members of the cabinet in any case considered it bad form on his part to enter into a secret pact with Portland against a colleague.

The king chose as the safest option the chancellor of the exchequer, Spencer Perceval; Perceval was a devout evangelical who had gathered an informal network of friends and families advocating moral and social reform. A man of the old stamp, Perceval was solid, reliable and principled. Henry Grattan, the Irish campaigner and parliamentarian, surmised that 'he is not a ship of the line, but he carries many guns, is tight built, and is out in all weathers'. He was small, spare and energetic. He took office just three weeks before the death of Portland himself.

It was not at first considered to be a viable administration. We may continue with the naval metaphors that were so popular in this era. When the Honourable Frederick Robinson turned down the relative minor post of an under-secretary he wrote that 'by embarking in a crazy vessel, I may chance to go to the bottom with the rest'. Yet it defied the odds, and sailed on.

There were, however, storm conditions ahead. The British people seem to have become weary of a war against Napoleon that had lasted, with infrequent intervals, for seven years. The discontent was exacerbated by the economic conditions of 1808 and 1809 when wartime privations led to a deterioration in export trade and, eventually, a general 'slump'. By 1811 many county banks were forced to close, tightening even more the lines of credit that sustained the country. The cotton spinners of Manchester, and the hand-loom weavers of Lancashire, were among the groups who demanded a return to peace and prosperity.

The measure of discontent may be seen in the sporadic but intense rioting that unbalanced the capital. When in 1810 Sir Francis Burdett wrote to his constituents of Westminster – in a letter published by William Cobbett's radical *Political Register* – against an alleged breach of privilege by the House of Commons, his letter was deemed to be libellous and worthy of imprisonment in the Tower. When the warrant for his arrest had been issued the crowds of London arose and virtually took control of the city. Burdett refused to leave his house in Piccadilly and the centre of London became a cockpit for the mobs and the militia. Burdett was finally confined, but Wellington wrote that 'the government and country are going to the Devil as far as possible; and I expect every day to hear that the mob of London are masters of the country'. Burdett himself was celebrated as a national hero standing up against the 'rats of the nation'.

Such was the hot temper of the capital that another riot had already taken place over the relatively innocuous question of the price of tickets to the Covent Garden Theatre. When in the autumn of 1809 the theatre reopened after a fire, the managers had increased the price of tickets and constructed more private boxes. This was considered as an affront to the ordinary citizens, and a dedicated group of protests disrupted performances nightly and managed to close the theatre for ten days at the end of September.

This was the inflamed atmosphere when in the autumn of 1810 the king succumbed once more to the babbling condition, akin to madness, induced by porphyria. On this occasion there would be no recovery. He held imaginary conversations with dead friends, and reviewed imaginary troops.

At the beginning of the following year the prince of Wales was declared to be prince regent whose powers would be curtailed for one year in case his father suddenly grew well again. But George III was for long periods strapped in a straitjacket and confined to a darkened room. The regent was king in all but name. It had been confidently believed that he would turn to his old Whig friends to form an administration but, as he had grown older, he had grown more conservative. He liked Spencer Perceval, perhaps because the strict sabbatarian was of so opposite a character; we admire those whom we cannot hope to emulate. Perceval was opposed to Catholic emancipation, as was the regent, and he was bold and resolute in matters of war. When confirmed in office, he would have to be equally resolute in matters domestic.

The great comet that streaked across the night sky in 1811 might have been considered to be a harbinger of more woe; the bad winters of 1811 and 1812 contributed to Napoleon's blockade and resulted in acute shortages of food. Over 45,000 inhabitants of Spitalfields petitioned to be allowed into the workhouses for want of bread. This was the prelude to protest on a much larger scale against what was known as 'The Thing' or 'Old Corruption', a movement encouraged by radical periodicals such as *Pig's Meat*, *Black Dwarf* and *Axe to the Root*. The cotton weavers of Bolton declared in February 1811: 'Oh misery and wretchedness when will ye cease to torment the industrious artisan?' A petition for help came from 40,000 Mancunians.

The most serious and sustained threat came from those who became known as 'Luddites'. In the spring of 1811 the framework knitters of Nottinghamshire were in dispute with their employers over low wages and the use of unskilled workers. The breaking of frames then became part of their industrial tactics, and their example was followed in parts of Derbyshire and Leicestershire. Over a period of eleven months 1,000 frames were destroyed as a result of approximately a hundred incidents. An army captain, Francis Raynes, explained that 'the Luddites attained a military style of operation, and held their meetings upon commons and moors for the purpose of drilling etcetera'.

When the disturbances spread to Yorkshire with arson and attempted assassination as part of their operation, the militia was called out and the assizes began their work. Seventeen of the operatives were hanged. The employers also fought back, opening fire on any protesters who threatened their factories. Two hundred protesters marched through Bolton with 'a man of straw' at their head – the name of Jack Straw, the rebel leader of the late fourteenth century, may not have been forgotten – representing as the Leeds *Mercury* said 'the renowned General Ludd'. What had started as industrial action, therefore, had burgeoned into social and political protest. In 1813, 30,000 people in Lancashire and Yorkshire signed a petition for parliamentary reform. Industrial and political unrest could not in this period be cleanly divided.

There never was a 'Ned Ludd' or 'Captain Ludd' or 'General

Ludd'. The protesters did not need any titular hero. They were led by solid grievances over the price of provisions, over the conditions of employment, over the breaking-up of traditional practices and over the unpopularity of war. The movement could only be countered with state force. A mass trial was held at York in which sixty defendants were sentenced to hanging or to penal transportation, and when a parliamentary bill was passed to render frame-breaking a capital crime, Lord Byron, in his maiden speech, was moved to declare that 'when a proposal is made to emancipate or relieve you hesitate, you deliberate for years, you temporize and tamper with the minds of men; but a death-bill must be passed off hand, without a thought of the consequences'.

At the height of the disturbances, in May 1812, Spencer Perceval was shot in the lobby of the House of Commons by a deranged merchant called Bellingham. His death was seen by the Luddites and strikers as a great victory of liberty against an oppressive administration. A local newspaper reported that in the Potteries 'a man came running down the street, leaping into the air, waving his hat around his head, and shouting with frantic joy: "Perceval is shot, hurrah! Perceval is shot, hurrah!"'

Whatever the jubilation outside Westminister, anxiety and consternation reigned within. Once more the question of suitable leadership arose. It was thought that Wellington's brother, Henry Wellesley, might be the candidate for first minister; but several ministers refused to serve under him. Eventually the chalice, golden or poisoned according to taste, was passed to Lord Liverpool. He was a practical leader, cautiously moving forward when opportunity allowed, and his administration was to last until his death fifteen years later. The final victory over Napoleon, and the success of the European allies, sealed his ascendancy.

The French emperor was now actively and seriously considering the invasion of Russia. The tsar, Alexander I, had withdrawn from Napoleon's blockade of Britain; Buonaparte's purpose seems to have been to engage the Russian army in one climactic battle and force the Russians to accede to his demands. He had also hoped for a short campaign, perhaps just within the borders of the invaded country. He probably never imagined a deep penetration of the icy and wintry realm, but the grand duchy of Muscovy led him ineluctably forward. It was his date with doom.

With an army of approximately 600,000 men he crossed the River Neman in the early summer of 1812; it was reported to be the largest army ever assembled but, in the words of the emperor himself, 'a man like me troubles himself little about the lives of a million men'. All seemed to be going well as the huge force made its way through western Russia, but its supply lines were growing steadily weaker. Buonaparte's troops were thwarted on their advance to St Petersburg and all their power was now directed upon Moscow. At the battle of Borodino, on 7 September, the two sides fought themselves into deadlock; the French took the battlefield, but the Russian army had not been defeated. The Russians could always muster fresh recruits, but the French were on their own. A week later Napoleon entered Moscow, to find scorched earth and forced evacuation. There was nowhere to go, a hazard enhanced by the possibility of epidemic sickness. The winter was closing in, with the threat of blizzards and swollen rivers impossible to cross. Frost, and ice, and falling snow, became the enemy.

Napoleon ordered his army to retreat to Smolensk on 17 October before crossing the River Berezina towards the end of November. One observer reported that 'it looked like a caravan, a wandering nation'. The food had all gone. The cold was intense, disease rampant, the horses slipped and died on the ice; the Russian peasantry took their own vengeance on the departing enemy, burning or burying them alive, or beating out their brains with hoes and shovels. Typhus and dysentery helped to complete their work. An army that had numbered many hundreds of thousands was now reduced to less than 30,000. At Smorgoni, on 5 December, the emperor left his army with the plea that he had to be in Paris to fight his other enemies there. He left in disguise with only a small escort. It had been a total, humiliating disaster. When he returned to Paris, he ordered a round of balls and masquerades but everybody knew that his adventure was coming to an end.

Jubilation among the British at the humiliating conclusion of the emperor's Russian expedition was heightened by the fact that Viscount Wellington had successfully entered Madrid in the summer of 1812 and had ousted the emperor's brother from the imperial throne. At the subsequent battle of Vittoria, in the summer of the following year, he chased the French out of Spain altogether. It was a signal moment in European history, when the balance of power finally shifted against the French. A *Te Deum* was sung in the cathedral of St Petersburg, and Beethoven composed *Wellington's Victory* in honour of the event.

A temporary truce in the summer of 1813 lasted only from June to August, and it seemed inevitable that there would be one last battle between France and its multiple enemies, including Prussia, Russia, England, Sweden and Austria. That is why it became known as 'the battle of the nations' or, perhaps more accurately, the battle of Leipzig. Over the course of four days Napoleon was roundly defeated, and emerged from the mayhem with only 80,000 troops. He had lost the military war. Lord Aberdeen wrote to Castlereagh, the foreign secretary, that 'the deliverance of Europe appears to be at hand'. It seemed that 'the ogre' had finally been smashed and the defeat inflicted infinite damage upon Napoleon's military reputation; he was no longer invincible on the battlefield. The news of Leipzig had thoroughly alarmed the French and the prefect of police in Paris, Étienne-Denis Pasquier, wrote that 'there was no longer any hope in anything: every illusion had been destroyed'.

In the early days of 1814 Napoleon was on the defensive but once again his audacity, cunning and strategic skills renewed his confidence. In February he launched what became known as the 'six day campaign' in which he brilliantly out-manoeuvred the opposing forces and with an army of only 30,000 men achieved a number of small victories. They were not enough, in the face of the overwhelming numbers of his enemies. In a treaty signed at the beginning of March the allies strengthened their purpose by agreeing to a formal alliance. Austria, Russia, Prussia and Great Britain were now recognized to be the four 'great powers' of Europe, a political and geographical fact that changed the face of the continent.

Napoleon, in the face of rebellion at home and defeat abroad, saw the end of days coming. At the close of March the armies of Russia and Prussia reached the outskirts of Paris, and on 31 March the French surrendered. No foreign army had entered the capital for 400 years. Napoleon, struggling to reach the beleaguered city, was two days too late. He had no wish to sign a treaty of surrender, but his marshals forced the issue. 'The army will obey me', he told them. To which came the answer that 'the army will obey its chiefs'. The game was up.

On 6 April 1814 the emperor signed the document of abdication in which he stated that 'the emperor Napoleon, faithful to his oath, declares that he renounces for himself and his heirs, the thrones of France and Italy'. Three weeks later he went on board HMS *Undaunted* and sailed to Elba under escort. A few days later Louis XVIII entered Paris, to no very warm reception. Yet peace was infectious and the capital had become, in the words of Metternich, the Austrian foreign minister, 'a great, vast, beautiful madhouse'. Every sovereign and politician in Europe seemed to be participating in an endless round of balls, assemblies and receptions. It was here, at the end of May, that a further treaty reduced the territory of France to its borders of November 1792, before the newly revolutionized citizen army had poured over Europe.

All was then detailed, finely divided and eventually drawn up, at a congress held in Vienna in September 1814. The globe was carved up by the participants in a series of negotiations that continued from that early autumn to June 1815; it was one of the most significant conferences in modern history, mapping out the nation-states that were to survive for a century while all the time recognizing the authority of the 'four great powers'. Mistrust, fear, intrigue and suspicion were of course the dominant motifs, as each 'power' tried to ensure that it was not being out-manoeuvred by the others. Castlereagh sought what he called a 'just equilibrium' between the various parties which, by subtly negotiating the demands of the participants, he eventually achieved. Austria and Prussia agreed to a loose confederation of German states, while the territorial ambitions of Tsar Alexander were reined back. The nations pledged to maintain a general peace and make no attempt, as Buonaparte had done, to dominate the continent. France remained a strong nation, but it had lost its commanding position for ever.

But then all seemed in peril. A telegraph reached Louis XVIII on 4 March 1815; he opened the envelope, read the message and sat with his head in his hands. 'Do you know what this telegraph contains?' he asked a minister.

'No, sir, I do not.'

'Well, I will tell you. It is revolution once more. Buonaparte has landed on the coast of Provence.'

Napoleon had escaped from the island of Elba to which he had been consigned by the victors. The ogre was back, and at once assumed an air of natural command. He told his small retinue: 'I will arrive in Paris without firing a shot.' And so it proved. On his slow trek to the capital by way of the Alpes Basses, any sign of opposition disappeared with cries of '*Vive l'empereur!*' Louis XVIII fled to the Belgian border and, on 20 March, Napoleon entered Paris to wild acclamation. The great powers at once denounced him as an outlaw and prepared for a necessary and inevitable war to extirpate him. Napoleon was not for a moment daunted.

Yet all was not as it seemed. This was not the same man who had dominated Europe only a short time before. One of his supporters, Paul Thiébault, noted that his visage 'had lost all expression and all its forcible character . . . everything about him seemed to have lost its nature and to be broken up; the ordinary pallor of his skin was replaced by a strongly pronounced greenish tinge'. He had not been defeated by any army; he had brought his misfortunes upon himself. He had ceased to be the leader of the forces of liberty, dispatched by the revolution, but another conqueror of independent peoples. His energy and almost manic certainty had begun to desert him; he now craved sleep and often seemed curiously tardy even in the hours before battle.

But his will was indomitable. He started north to Belgium with the intention of confronting the two armies now raised against him; the army under Wellington consisting of British, Dutch and Germans, and the Prussian army under Field Marshal Blücher, must not be allowed to combine into a single fighting force. He must get between them and destroy each one in turn. A series of errors by Napoleon and his commanders, however, permitted the British and Prussian armies to retreat towards Brussels along two parallel roads that led to Waterloo and Wavre. At a distance of one mile from Waterloo, Wellington, sensing the strength of the terrain, turned to confront the enemy. A prominent ridge known as the Mont-Saint-Jean escarpment gave cover, while the large farmhouse or château of Hougoumont as well as a hamlet in the area could be fortified and garrisoned.

Napoleon drew up his forces along the Brussels road but he

could not see the extent of Wellington's army concealed by the prominent ridge. The French army attacked Hougoumont without making great advances, and then the cavalry of both sides engaged in charge and counter-charge in a series of attacks which became, for the survivors, the most prominent aspect of the battle. By the evening Blücher's troops had arrived from Wavre, and began to attack the French troops. Buonaparte thought that he saw a weakness in Wellington's centre and sent forward his imperial guard to take advantage of the opening; but the guards, repulsed with artillery and with bayonets, wavered, collapsed and began to retreat. The cry went up that '*La garde recule. Sauve qui peut.*' Wellington then took off his hat and waved it into the air, signalling a general attack upon the French whose lines were now disintegrating. The battle had been won. It was, as Wellington wrote to his brother, 'a damned nice [finely balanced] thing – the nearest run thing you ever saw in your life'. The Prussians always believed that they, not Wellington and the British, had won the battle of Waterloo.

Wellington and Blücher now regrouped and began the final march upon Paris. On 22 June Napoleon abdicated for the second time, and on 15 July he surrendered to the British at Rochefort by going aboard HMS *Bellerophon*. He had thought, before his surrender, that he might make his new home in the United States; but no such haven was permitted to him. He was taken instead to the island of St Helena, and spent the rest of his life on the volcanic rock in the South Atlantic. It had been the most expensive war in English history, and the most protracted since the 'Hundred Years War' of the fourteenth and fifteenth centuries.

Every word was now of peace, a peace guaranteed by the quadruple alliance of the great powers. And indeed there was to be no more serious strife on the continent until the time of Crimea in 1853. 'It is impossible not to perceive', Castlereagh wrote, 'a great moral change coming on in Europe, and that the principles of freedom are in full operation.' He might have added that Britain now considered itself to be the great moral leader in the struggle for freedom and against tyranny. It was clearly now the foremost power in terms of territory, and its empire included Canada, New Zealand, South Africa, India, Australia and the Caribbean. It ruled, therefore, a large proportion of the earth's surface.

Yet there was no triumphalism and little sense of success. After the long war, weariness and hardship were as ever part of daily life. The problems of Ireland, the difficulties of empire itself, the clamour for parliamentary reform, the decay in trade, and the rise in industrial violence, were the shadows that victory cast. It was not at all clear, in 1815, that such problems could be resolved.

Further reading

This is by no means an exhaustive list, but it represents a selection of those books the author found most useful in the preparation of this fourth volume.

GENERAL HISTORIES

Ashley, M.: *England in the Seventeenth Century* (London, 1952)

Aubrey, W. H. S.: *The National and Domestic History of England* (London, 1878)

Baxter, S. B.: *England's Rise to Greatness, 1660–1763* (London, 1983)

Black, J.: *Britain in the Age of Walpole* (Basingstoke, 1984)

—— *British Politics and Society from Walpole to Pitt 1742–1789* (Basingstoke, 1990)

Christie, I. R.: *Crisis of Empire: Great Britain and the American Colonies, 1754–1783* (London, 1966)

—— *Wars and Revolutions: Britain 1760–1815* (London, 1982)

Clark, J. C. D.: *English Society 1688–1832: Ideology, Social Structure and Political Practice during the Ancien Regime* (Cambridge, 1985)

Coward, B.: *A Companion to Stuart Britain* (Oxford, 2003)

Dickinson, H. T.: *A Companion to Eighteenth-Century Britain* (Oxford, 2002)

Harlow, V. T.: *The Founding of the Second British Empire, 1763–1793* (London, 1952–64)

Harris, B.: *Politics and the Nation: Britain in the Mid-Eighteenth Century* (Oxford, 2002)

Harris, R. W.: *England in the Eighteenth Century, 1689–1793: A Balanced Constitution and New Horizons* (London, 1963)

Harvey, A. D.: *Britain in the Early Nineteenth Century* (London, 1978)

Hill, C.: *1530–1780: Reformation to Industrial Revolution* (Harmondsworth, 1969)

Holmes, Geoffrey S.: *The Making of a Great Power: Late Stuart and Early Georgian Britain 1660–1722* (London, 1993)

Holmes, Geoffrey S. (ed.), *Britain after the Glorious Revolution, 1689–1714* (London, 1969)

Holmes, Geoffrey S. and Szechi, D.: *The Age of Oligarchy: Pre-industrial Britain 1722–1783* (London, 1993)

Hoppit, J.: *A Land of Liberty? England, 1689–1727* (Oxford, 2000)

Jensen, M.: *The Founding of a Nation: A History of the American Revolution, 1763–1776* (New York & Oxford, 1968)

Jones, J. R.: *Country and Court: England, 1658–1714* (London, 1978)

Lecky, W. E. H.: *A History of England in the Eighteenth Century* (London, 1892)

Levack, B. P.: *The Formation of the British State: England, Scotland and the Union, 1603–1707* (Oxford, 1987)

Lingard, J. and Belloc, H.: *The History of England* (London, 1915)

Macaulay, T. B.: *History of England from the Accession of James II* (London, 1906)

Marshall, D.: *Eighteenth-Century England* (London, 1974)

McLynn, F.: *The Jacobites* (London, 1985)

Michael, W., MacGregor, A. and MacGregor, G. E.: *England under George I* (London, 1936–39)

Namier, L. B.: *England in the Age of the American Revolution* (London, 1963)

O'Gorman, F.: *The Long Eighteenth Century: British Political and Social History 1688–1832* (London, 1997)

Owen, J. B.: *The Eighteenth Century, 1714–1815* (London, 1974)

Plumb, J. H.: *England in the Eighteenth Century* (London, 1953)
———— *The Growth of Political Stability in England, 1675–1725* (London, 1968)

Pocock, J. G. A.: *Three British Revolutions, 1641, 1688, 1776* (Princeton, 1980)

Prest, W. R.: *Albion Ascendant: English History, 1660–1815* (Oxford, 1998)

Ranke, L. von: *A History of England, Principally in the Seventeenth Century* (Oxford, 1875)

Schama, S.: *Citizens: A Chronicle of the French Revolution* (London, 1989)

Smollett, T.: *The History of England: From Revolution in 1688, to the Death of George II* (London, 1822)

Speck, W. A.: *Stability and Strife: England, 1714–1760* (London, 1977)

Stone, L. (ed.), *An Imperial State at War: Britain from 1689 to 1815* (London, 1994)

Szechi, D.: *The Jacobites: Britain and Europe, 1688–1788* (Manchester, 1994)

Trevelyan, G. M.: *England under Queen Anne* (London, 1965)
—— *England under the Stuarts* (New York, 1938)

Watson, J. S.: *The Reign of George III, 1760–1815* (Oxford, 1960)

Williams, B.: *The Whig Supremacy, 1714–1760* (Oxford, 1952)

CULTURE, SOCIETY & RELIGION

Allen, R. C.: *Enclosure and the Yeoman* (Oxford, 1992)

Archer, J. E.: *Social Unrest and Popular Protest in England, 1780–1840* (Cambridge, 2000)

Ashton, J.: *Social Life in the Reign of Queen Anne* (London, 1882)

Beckett, J. V.: *The Aristocracy in England 1660–1914* (Oxford, 1986)

Beljame, A.: *Men of Letters and the English Public in the Eighteenth Century, 1660–1744* (London, 1897)

Bennett, G. V.: *The Tory Crisis in Church and State 1688–1730: The Career of Francis Atterbury, Bishop of Rochester* (Oxford, 1975)

Borsay, P.: *The English Urban Renaissance: Culture and Society in the Provincial Town 1660–1770* (Oxford, 1989)

Brewer, J.: *The Pleasures of the Imagination: English Culture in the Eighteenth Century* (London, 1997)

Cannon, J.: *Aristocratic Century: The Peerage of Eighteenth-Century England* (Cambridge, 1984)

Carter, P.: *Men and the Emergence of Polite Society: Britain 1660–1800* (Harlow, 2001)

Chadwick, W. *The Life and Times of Daniel Defoe* (London, 1859)

Chalklin, C. W.: *The Provincial Towns of Georgian England: A Study of the Building Process, 1740–1820* (London, 1974)

Christie, I. R.: *Stress and Stability in Late Eighteenth-Century Britain: Reflections on the British Avoidance of Revolution* (Oxford, 1984)

Clark, J. C. D.: *Revolution and Rebellion: State and Society in England in the Seventeenth and Eighteenth Centuries* (Cambridge, 1986)

Cockayne, E.: *Hubbub: Filth, Noise, and Stench in England, 1600–1770* (New Haven & London, 2007)

Corfield, P. J.: *The Impact of English Towns, 1700–1800* (Oxford, 1982)

Defoe, D.: *A Tour thro' the Whole Island of Great Britain, By a Gentleman* (London, 1742)

Earle, P.: *The Making of the English Middle Class: Business, Society and Family Life in London, 1660–1730* (London, 1989)

Elioseff, L. A.: *The Cultural Milieu of Addison's Literary Criticism* (Austin, 1963)

Ford, B. (ed.), *The Cambridge Cultural History of Britain, Vol. 5, Eighteenth-Century Britain* (Cambridge, 1992)

Foss, M.: *The Age of Patronage: The Arts in Society, 1660–1750* (London, 1971)

Gatrell, V.: *City of Laughter: Sex and Satire in Eighteenth-Century London* (London, 2006)

George, M. D.: *England in Transition: Life and Work in the Eighteenth Century* (London, 1931)

George, M. D.: *London Life in the Eighteenth Century* (London, 1925)

Guillery, P., Donald, A. and Kendall, D.: *The Small House in Eighteenth-Century London* (New Haven, 2004)

Hay, D. and Rogers, N.: *Eighteenth-Century English Society: Shuttles and Swords* (Oxford, 1997)

Hill, B.: *Women, Work and Sexual Politics in Eighteenth-Century England* (Oxford, 1989)

Hilton, B.: *A Mad, Bad, and Dangerous People? England 1783–1846* (Oxford, 2006)

Holmes, Geoffrey S.: *Augustan England: Professions, State and Society, 1680–1730* (London, 1982)

Jenkins, P.: *The Making of a Ruling Class: The Glamorgan Gentry 1640–1790* (Cambridge, 1983)

Kirby, P.: *Child Labour in Britain, 1750–1870* (London, 2003)

Langford, P.: *A Polite and Commercial People: England, 1727–1783* (Oxford, 1989)

——— *Public Life and the Propertied Englishman 1689–1798: The Ford Lectures Delivered in the University of Oxford 1990* (Oxford, 1991)

Lees, L. H.: *The Solidarities of Strangers: The English Poor Laws and the People, 1700–1948* (Cambridge, 1998)

Linebaugh, P.: *The London Hanged: Crime and Civil Society in the Eighteenth Century* (London, 1991)

Mackay, C.: *Memoirs of Extraordinary Popular Delusions and the Madness of Crowds* (London, 1852)

Malcolmson, R. W.: *Life and Labour in England, 1700–1780* (London, 1981)

O'Toole, F.: *A Traitor's Kiss: The Life of Richard Brinsley Sheridan* (London, 1997)

Palliser, D. M., Clark, P. and Daunton, M. J.: *The Cambridge Urban History of Britain*, Vol. 2 (Cambridge, 2000)

Porter, R.: *English Society in the Eighteenth Century* (London, 1991)

Rivers, I.: *Books and their Readers in Eighteenth-Century England* (Leicester, 1982)

Rogers, P.: *The Augustan Vision* (London, 1974)

Rule, J.: *Albion's People: English Society, 1714–1815* (London, 1992)

Rupp, E.: *Religion in England 1688–1791* (Oxford, 1986)

Sambrook, J.: *The Eighteenth Century: The Intellectual and Cultural Context of English Literature 1700–1789* (London, 1986)

Scull, A.: *The Most Solitary of Afflictions: Madness and Society in Britain, 1700–1900* (New Haven & London, 1993)

Seed, J.: *Dissenting Histories: Religious Division and the Politics of Memory in Eighteenth-Century England* (Edinburgh, 2008)

Sharpe, P.: *Women's Work: The English Experience, 1650–1914* (London, 1998)

Simmons, J. R. (ed.), *Factory Lives: Four Nineteenth-Century Working Class Autobiographies* (Peterborough, Ont. & Plymouth, 2007)

Snell, K. D. M.: *Annals of the Labouring Poor: Social Change and Agrarian England, 1660–1900* (Cambridge, 1985)

Sykes, N.: *From Sheldon to Secker: Aspects of English Church History, 1660–1768* (Cambridge, 1959)

Uglow, J. S.: *Hogarth: A Life and a World* (London, 1997)

——— *The Lunar Men: The Friends who made the Future, 1730–1810* (London, 2002)

Vicinus, M.: *The Industrial Muse: A Study of Nineteenth-Century British Working-Class Literature* (London, 1974)

Vickery, A.: *Behind Closed Doors: At Home in Georgian England* (New Haven and London, 2009)

Warburg, J.: *The Industrial Muse: The Industrial Revolution in English Poetry* (London & New York, 1958)

White, T. H.: *The Age of Scandal: An Excursion through a Minor Period* (London, 1950)

Williams, D.: *The Triumph of Culture: 18th Century Perspectives* (Toronto, 1972)

Wilson, K.: *The Sense of the People: Politics, Culture and Imperialism in England, 1715–1785* (Cambridge, 1995)

MILITARY HISTORY

Black, J.: *War for America: The Fight for Independence, 1775–1783* (Stroud, 1991)

Blanning, T. C. W.: *The French Revolutionary Wars 1787–1802* (London, 1996)

Brewer, J.: *The Sinews of Power: War, Money and the English State, 1688–1783* (London, 1989)

Chandler, D. G.: *The Campaigns of Napoleon* (London, 2002)

Conway, S.: *The War of American Independence, 1775–1783* (London, 1995)

Esdaile, C. J.: *Napoleon's Wars: An International History, 1803–1815* (London, 2007)

Gash, N. (ed.), *Wellington: Studies in the Military and Political Career of the first Duke of Wellington* (Manchester, 1990)

Gates, D.: *The Napoleonic Wars, 1803–1815* (London, 2003)

McLynn, F.: *1759: The Year Britain became Master of the World* (London, 2004)

——— *Napoleon: A Biography* (London, 1997)

Muir, R. *Britain and the Defeat of Napoleon, 1807–1815* (New Haven and London, 1996)

Schneid, F. C.: *Napoleonic Wars* (Washington, 2010)

Southey, R.: *The Life of Nelson* (London, 1941)

Zamoyski, A. *Rites of Peace: The Fall of Napoleon and the Congress of Vienna* (London, 2007)

MONARCHS AND COURTS

Beattie, J. M.: *The English Court in the Reign of George I* (London, 1967)

Black, J.: *George II: Puppet of the Politicians?* (Exeter, 2007)
────── *George III: America's Last King* (New Haven, 2006)

Bucholz, R. O.: *The Augustan Court: Queen Anne and the Decline of Court Culture* (Stanford, 1993)

Clark, G. N.: *The Later Stuarts, 1660–1714* (Oxford, 1949)

Field, O.: *The Favourite: Sarah, Duchess of Marlborough* (London, 2002)

Gregg, E.: *Queen Anne* (London, 1984)

Hatton, R. M.: *George I* (New Haven, 2001)

Kenyon, J. P.: *The Stuarts: A Study in English Kingship* (London, 1977)

Miller, J.: *The Stuarts* (London, 2004)

Pares, R.: *King George III and the Politicians* (Oxford, 1967)

Smith, H.: *Georgian Monarchy: Politics and Culture, 1714–1760* (Cambridge, 2006)

Somerset, A.: *Queen Anne: The Politics of Passion* (London, 2012)

Thompson, A. C.: *George II: King and Elector* (New Haven and London, 2011)

ECONOMIC HISTORY AND THE INDUSTRIAL REVOLUTION

Alexander, D.: *Retailing in England during the Industrial Revolution* (London, 1970)

Ashton, T. S.: *An Eighteenth-Century Industrialist: Peter Stubs of Warrington, 1756–1806* (Manchester, 1939)

——— *An Economic History of England: The 18th Century* (London, 1955)

——— *Iron and Steel in the Industrial Revolution* (Aldershot, 1993)

Berg, M.: *The Age of Manufactures, 1700–1820: Industry, Innovation, and Work in Britain* (London, 1994)

Broadberry, S. N. and O'Rourke, K. H.: *The Cambridge Economic History of Modern Europe*, Vol. 1 (Cambridge, 2012)

Brown, R.: *Society and Economy in Modern Britain, 1700–1850* (London, 1991)

Chapman, S. J.: *The Cotton Industry and Trade* (London, 1905)

Cipolla, C. M.: *Before the Industrial Revolution: European Society and Economy, 1000–1700* (London, 1976)

Coleman, D. C.: *Myth, History, and the Industrial Revolution* (London, 1992)

Court, W. H. B.: *The Rise of the Midland Industries, 1600–1838* (Oxford, 1953)

Crafts, N. F. R.: *British Economic Growth during the Industrial Revolution* (Oxford, 1985)

Daunton, M. J.: *Progress and Poverty: An Economic and Social History of Britain, 1700–1850* (Oxford, 1995)

Dickinson, H. W.: *James Watt: Craftsman and Engineer* (Cambridge, 1935)

Dickson, P. G. M.: *The Financial Revolution in England: A Study in the Development of Public Credit, 1688–1756* (London, 1967)

Fitton, R. S. and Wadsworth, A. P.: *The Strutts and the Arkwrights 1758–1830* (Matlock, 2012)

Flinn, M. W.: *Men of Iron: The Crowleys in the Early Iron Industry* (Edinburgh, 1962)

——— *The Origins of the Industrial Revolution* (London, 1966)

——— *The Industrial Revolution, The History of the British Coal Industry, Vol. 2* (Oxford, 1984)

Floud, R.: *The Cambridge Economic History of Modern Britain*, Vol. 1 (Cambridge, 2014)

Floud, R. and McCloskey, D. N.: *The Economic History of Britain Since 1700* (Cambridge, 1981)

Hammond, J. L. and Hammond, B. B.: *The Rise of Modern Industry* (London, 1937)

Harris, J. R.: *The British Iron Industry, 1700–1850* (Basingstoke, 1988)

Hartwell, R. M.: *The Industrial Revolution in England* (London, 1965)
———— *The Causes of the Industrial Revolution in England* (London, 1967)
———— *The Industrial Revolution and Economic Growth* (London, 1971)
Hartwell, R. M. (ed.): *The Industrial Revolution* (Oxford, 1970)
Holderness, B. A.: *Pre-industrial England: Economy and Society, 1500–1750* (London, 1976)
Hopkins, E.: *The Rise of the Manufacturing Town: Birmingham and the Industrial Revolution* (Stroud, 1998)
King, S. and Timmins, G.: *Making Sense of the Industrial Revolution* (Manchester, 2001)
Kussmaul, A.: *A General View of the Rural Economy of England 1538–1840* (Cambridge, 1990)
MacLeod, C.: *Inventing the Industrial Revolution: The English Patent System, 1660–1800* (Cambridge, 1988)
Mantoux, P.: *The Industrial Revolution in the Eighteenth Century: An Outline of the Beginnings of the Modern Factory System in England* (Chicago, 1983)
Mathias, P.: *The First Industrial Nation: An Economic History of Britain, 1700–1914* (London, 1969)
———— *The Transformation of England: Essays in the Economic and Social History of England in the Eighteenth Century* (London, 2011)
McKendrick, N. and Plumb, J. H.: *The Birth of a Consumer Society: The Commercialization of Eighteenth-Century England* (London, 1983)
Minchinton, W. E.: *The Growth of English Overseas Trade in the Seventeenth and Eighteenth Centuries* (London, 1969)
Moffit, L. W.: *England on the Eve of the Industrial Revolution: A Study of Economic and Social Conditions from 1740–1760, with Special Reference to Lancashire* (London, 1925)
Mokyr, J.: *The Lever of Riches: Technological Creativity and Economic Progress* (New York, 1990)
———— *The Enlightened Economy: Britain and the Industrial Revolution 1700–1850* (London, 2011)
Mui, Hoh-Cheung and Mui, L. H.: *Shops and Shopkeeping in Eighteenth-Century England* (Kingston, Ont., 1989)

O'Brien, P. and Quinault, R. E.: *The Industrial Revolution and British Society* (Cambridge, 1993)

Osborne, J. W.: *The Silent Revolution: The Industrial Revolution in England as a Source of Cultural Change* (New York, 1970)

Plumb, J. H.: *The Commercialisation of Leisure in Eighteenth-Century England* (Reading, 1973)

Quickenden, K., Baggott, S. and Dick, M.: *Matthew Boulton: Enterprising Industrialist of the Enlightenment* (Farnham, 2013)

Radcliffe, W.: *Origin of the New System of Manufacture Commonly Called Power-Loom Weaving* (Clifton, 1974)

Randall, A.: *Before the Luddites: Custom, Community and Machinery in the English Woollen Industry, 1776–1809* (Cambridge, 1991)

Reilly, R.: *Josiah Wedgwood, 1730–1795* (London, 1992)

Richards, J. M. and De Maré, E. S.: *The Functional Tradition in Early Industrial Buildings* (London, 1958)

Rule, J.: *The Vital Century: England's Developing Economy 1714–1815* (London, 1992)

Toynbee, A.: *The Industrial Revolution* (Boston, 1956)

Unwin, G. and Hulme, A.: *Samuel Oldknow and the Arkwrights: The Industrial Revolution at Stockport and Marple* (Manchester, 1924)

Weatherill, L.: *Consumer Behaviour and Material Culture in Britain, 1660–1760* (London and New Haven, 1996)

Wilson, R. G.: *Gentlemen Merchants: The Merchant Community in Leeds, 1700–1830* (Manchester, 1971)

Wrigley, E. A.: *Continuity, Chance and Change: The Character of the Industrial Revolution in England* (Cambridge, 1988)

—— *Energy and the English Industrial Revolution* (Cambridge, 2010)

POLITICAL HISTORY

Black, J.: *Pitt the Elder* (Cambridge, 1992)

—— *The Politics of Britain, 1688–1800* (Manchester, 1993)

Brewer, J.: *Party Ideology and Popular Politics at the Accession of George III* (Cambridge, 1976)

Browning, R.: *The Duke of Newcastle* (New Haven, 1975)

Butterfield, H.: *George III, Lord North, and the People, 1779–80* (London, 1949)

Cannon, J.: *The Fox–North Coalition: Crisis of the Constitution, 1782–4* (Cambridge, 1969)

———— *The Whig Ascendancy: Colloquies on Hanoverian England* (London, 1981)

Colley, L.: *In Defiance of Oligarchy: The Tory Party, 1714–1760* (Cambridge, 1982)

Derry, J. W.: *Politics in the Age of Fox, Pitt and Liverpool: Continuity and Transformation* (Basingstoke, 1990)

Dickinson, H. T.: *The Politics of the People in Eighteenth-Century Britain* (Basingstoke, 1994)

Dickinson, H. T.: *Walpole and the Whig Supremacy* (London, 1973)

Ehrman, J.: *The Younger Pitt* (London, 1969–1996)

Field, O.: *The Kit-Cat Club* (London, 2009)

Goodwin, A.: *The Friends of Liberty: The English Democratic Movement in the Age of the French Revolution* (London, 1979)

Gray, D.: *Spencer Perceval, the Evangelical Prime Minister, 1762–1812* (Manchester, 1963)

Harris, T.: *Politics Under the Later Stuarts: Party Conflict in a Divided Society, 1660–1715* (London, 1993)

Hill, B. W.: *British Parliamentary Parties, 1742–1832: From the Fall of Walpole to the First Reform Act* (London, 1985)

———— *The Growth of Parliamentary Parties, 1689–1742* (London, 1976)

Holmes, Geoffrey S.: *British Politics in the Age of Anne* (London, 1967)

Jones, C.: *Britain in the First Age of Party, 1680–1750: Essays Presented to Geoffrey Holmes* (London, 1987)

Kenyon, J. P.: *Revolution Principles: The Politics of Party, 1689–1720* (Cambridge, 1977)

Lawson, P.: *George Grenville: A Political Life* (Oxford, 1984)

Linklater, A.: *Why Spencer Perceval had to Die: The Assassination of a British Prime Minister* (London, 2012)

Marshall, A.: *The Age of Faction: Court Politics, 1660–1702* (Manchester, 1999)

Middleton, R.: *The Bells of Victory: The Pitt-Newcastle Ministry and the Conduct of the Seven Years' War 1757-1762* (Cambridge, 1985)

Namier, L. B.: *The Structure of Politics at the Accession of George III* (London, 1957)

O'Gorman, F.: *The Whig Party and the French Revolution* (London, 1967)

—— *Edmund Burke: His Political Philosophy* (London, 1973)

—— *The Rise of Party in England: The Rockingham Whigs, 1760–82* (London, 1975)

—— *Voters, Patrons, and Parties: The Unreformed Electoral System of Hanoverian England 1734–1832* (Oxford, 1989)

Owen, J. B.: *The Rise of the Pelhams* (London, 1957)

Pearce, E.: *The Great Man: Scoundrel, Genius and Britain's First Prime Minister* (London, 2007)

Perry, K.: *British Politics and the American Revolution* (Basingstoke, 1990)

Peters, M.: *Pitt and Popularity: The Patriot Minister and London Opinion during the Seven Years' War* (Oxford, 1980)

Pincus, S. C. A.: *1688: The First Modern Revolution* (New Haven, 2009)

Plumb, J. H.: *Sir Robert Walpole: The Making of a Statesman* (London, 1956)

Reilly, R.: *William Pitt the Younger* (New York, 1979)

Rogers, N.: *Whigs and Cities: Popular Politics in the Age of Walpole and Pitt* (Oxford, 1989)

Rudé, G. F. E.: *Wilkes and Liberty: A Social Study* (London, 1983)

Tomkins, S.: *William Wilberforce: A Biography* (Oxford, 2007)

Western, J. R.: *Monarchy and Revolution: The English State in the 1680s* (London, 1985)

Williams, E. N. (ed.): *The Eighteenth-Century Constitution, 1688–1815: Documents and Commentary* (Cambridge, 1960)

Index

extracts reading groups
competitions books new
discounts extracts
competitions
books
new
events extracts
new titles reading groups
interviews
events extracts
discounts
new books events
events new
events
books
discounts extracts discounts

www.panmacmillan.com

books

extracts events reading groups
competitions books extracts new